A Companion to the Nibelungenlied

Studies in German Literature, Linguistics, and Culture

Edited by James Hardin
(*South Carolina*)

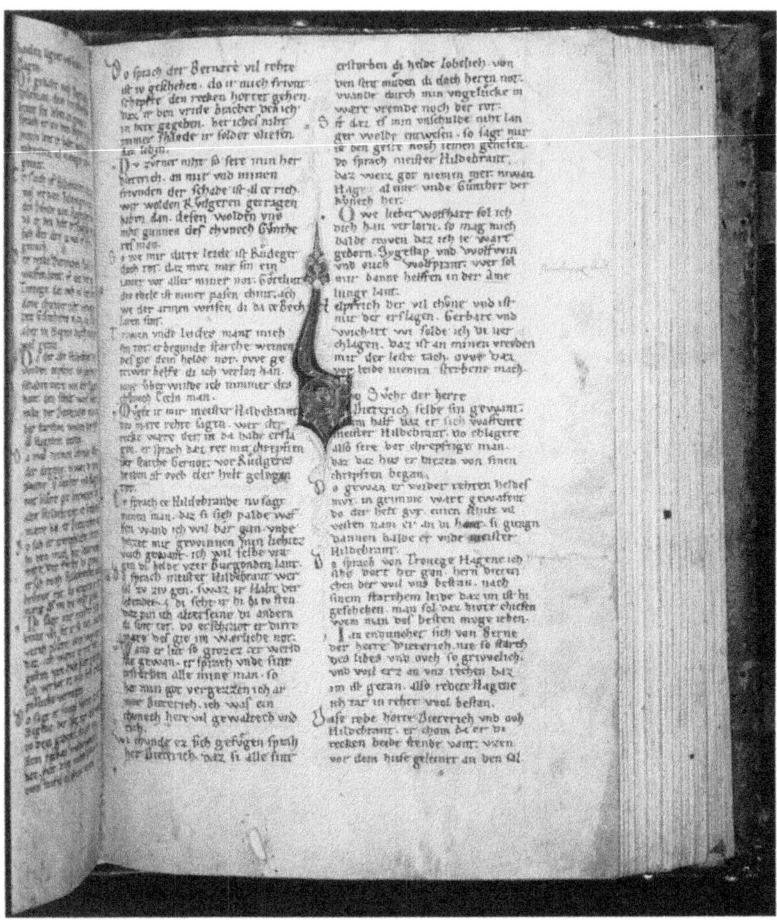

A leaf from manuscript B,
Stiftsbibliothek St. Gallen, Cod. Sang 857, p. 411

A Companion to the Nibelungenlied

Edited by
Winder McConnell

CAMDEN HOUSE

First published 1998 by Camden House
Reprinted in paperback and transferred to digital printing 2010

Camden House is an imprint of Boydell & Brewer Inc.
668 Mt. Hope Avenue, Rochester, NY 14620, USA
www.camden-house.com
and of Boydell & Brewer Limited
PO Box 9, Woodbridge, Suffolk IP12 3DF, UK
www.boydellandbrewer.com

Paperback ISBN-13: 978-1-57113-459-2
Paperback ISBN-10: 1-57113-459-X
Hardback ISBN-13: 978-1-57113-151-5
Hardback ISBN-10: 1-57113-151-5

Library of Congress Cataloging-in-Publication Data

A companion to the Nibelungenlied / edited by Winder McConnell.
p. cm. — (Studies in German literature, linguistics, and culture)
Includes bibliographical references and index.
ISBN 1-57113-151-5 (hardcover: alk. paper)
1. Nibelungenlied. 2. I. McConnell, Winder. II. Series: Studies in German literature, linguistics, and culture (Unnumbered)

PT1589.C66 1998
831'.21—dc21

98-2818
CIP

A catalogue record for this title is available from the British Library.

This publication is printed on acid-free paper.

Cover illustration: Kriemhild's last confrontation with Hagen
Staatsbibliothek zu Berlin — Preußischer Kulturbesitz, Ms. germ. fol. 855, illustration no. 37, fol. 158 verso.

Contents

Acknowledgments

Dr. Cornel Dora of the Stiftsbibliothek, St. Gall, Switzerland, provided the facsimile of manuscript B of the *Nibelungenlied* which has been used as the frontispiece. Thanks are also due to the Staatsbibliothek zu Berlin — Preußischer Kulturbesitz for permission to publish Bild Nr. 37, fol. 158 verso, of Ms. germ. fol. 855, the Hundeshagen Codex, on the dustcover of this volume. I also thank Dean JoAnn Cannon of the College of Letters and Science and Kevin M. Smith, Vice Chancellor for Research, University of California, Davis, for a grant to defray the costs of obtaining the illustrations contained in this volume. Various individuals within my department provided support and encouragement throughout the production process, foremost among them Peter Hays, my current Chairman, who generously granted me with funds for a computer accessory that produced an indispensable (and portable) backup copy of the entire manuscript. I am grateful as well to Carolyn Jamison and Katherine Perrone for their assistance with various administrative matters. I owe a debt of gratitude to Professor James Hardin of the University of South Carolina who initially asked me to serve as editor for the *Companion to the Nibelungenlied* and who, together with Jim Walker, was always available with invaluable technical advice and assistance throughout the various stages of the book's production. I fully intend to make good one day on my promise to invite Marion Gibbs (London) to lunch for a last-minute bit of bibliographical information that allowed me to stay on schedule. Without the expertise of Jeremy Smith, who patiently and effectively responded to each of my naive queries regarding the world of computers and who provided me in the last stage of production with a printer capable of meeting the publisher's resolution expectations, this manuscript would have been many more weeks, if not months, in the making. My wife, Kathleen, took the time to proofread the entire book and her eagle eye found numerous items I had overlooked.

Finally, I thank my colleagues and co-contributors to this collection. One could not have wished for a more conscientious, erudite, and pleasant group of individuals as collaborators.

W.M.
April 1998

Contributors

Otfrid Ehrismann is Professor of German Language and Medieval Literature at the Justus-Liebig-Universität Gießen. He is the editor and author of numerous books and articles on medieval literature, including *Nibelungenlied. Epoche — Werk — Wirkung* (1987) and *Ehre und Mut, Aventiure und Minne. Höfische Wortgeschichten aus dem Mittelalter* (1995). His research is currently concentrated on medievalism in Germany from the eighteenth century to the present.

John L. Flood is Professor of German and Deputy Director of the University of London Institute of Germanic Studies. He has published extensively on the Middle Ages and the Early Modern period. Recent works include *The German Book 1450–1750*, edited with W. A. Kelly (1995) and (with D. J. Shaw) *Johannes Sinapius (1505–1560), Hellenist and Physician in Germany and Italy* (1997).

Francis G. Gentry is Professor of German and Co-Director of the Max Kade German-American Research Institute at the Pennsylvania State University. He has written and edited numerous books and articles on medieval works, authors, and concepts. In addition, he has lectured and published extensively on the phenomenon of medievalism in Germany and in the United States.

Will Hasty is Associate Professor of German at the University of Florida. He is the author of *Adventure as Social Performance: A Study of the German Court Epic* (1990) and *Adventures in Interpretation: The Works of Hartmann von Aue and their Critical Reception* (1995) as well as numerous articles on medieval German court literature. He has also edited two volumes of the *Dictionary of Literary Biography* on medieval German writers and works.

Edward R. Haymes is Professor of German and Comparative Literature and Director of the Program in Classical and Medieval Studies at Cleveland State University. He has published on Middle High German and Old Norse literature and on oral epic poetry. In 1977 he edited a Festschrift for Helmut Kreuzer (*Kreuzungen/Crossings*) which was published by Camden House.

Joachim Heinzle is Professor of German and Germanic Philology at the Philipps-Universität Marburg. He is President of the Wolfram von Eschenbach Society and Editor-in-Chief of the *Zeitschrift für Deutsches Altertum und Deutsche Literatur*. He has published numerous books and articles on German literature of the High and Late Middle Ages.

Werner Hoffmann was Professor of Medieval German Literature at the University of Mannheim until his retirement on October 1, 1997. He is the author of numerous books and articles on medieval and modern German Literature, including Middle High German heroic poetry, above all the *Nibelungenlied.*

Joyce Tally Lionarons is Professor of English at Ursinus College. She has published articles on Old and Middle English and Old Norse literature, and is the author of *The Medieval Dragon: the Nature of the Beast in Germanic Literature*, forthcoming from Hisarlik Press.

Winder McConnell is Professor of German and Director of the Medieval Studies Program at the University of California, Davis. He has published numerous books and articles on German heroic epic, including the *Nibelungenlied.* His translations of *Kudrun* (1992) and the *Klage* (1994) have also appeared in Camden House.

James M. McGlathery, Professor of German and of Comparative Literature at the University of Illinois at Urbana-Champaign, is the author of monographs on E. T. A. Hoffmann, Heinrich von Kleist, Grimms's Fairy tales, and Richard Wagner's operas. His history of criticism on Grimms' Fairy Tales (1993) and an edited volume of essays on Music and German Literature (1992) were published by Camden House.

Brian Murdoch is Professor of German at the University of Stirling in Scotland, and has been Visiting Fellow of Trinity Hall, Cambridge and Magdalen College, Oxford, where he gave the Waynflete lectures in 1994. He is currently the Hulse Visiting Lecturer in Divinity at Cambridge, and has published widely on medieval German and comparative literature, especially on religious poetry and on the heroic epic.

Werner Wunderlich is Professor of German and teaches Media Culture at the University of St. Gall (HSG) in Switzerland. He is a critic for German and Swiss newspapers and journals and the co-editor of several academic series (Kulturwissenschaftliche Skizzen; Facetten; Medieval Myths). He has published numerous books, articles, and anthologies on German Medieval

Literature, Medievalism, St. Gall's Media Culture, Symbolic Archetypes, Authorship, and Mozart.

Introduction

On May 8, 1945, in the area of Landshut, the capital of Lower Bavaria, a German military unit surrendered to American troops, mirroring several thousand similar events throughout Europe on that day. In the preceding weeks, they had been engaged in combat throughout the Danube basin around Vohburg, Neustadt, and Kehlheim. The fighting was a fruitless last-ditch stand against overwhelming odds, the outcome evident from the moment they went into battle. Unlike members of the German *Wehrmacht*, whose belt buckles bore the traditional "Gott mit uns," the caption on the buckles worn by these men was more worldly in nature: "Meine Ehre heißt Treue." Their *Hoheitszeichen* was not to be found on the right breast of their tunics, but rather on the upper left arm. Had the war continued and not ended in May, they would eventually have boasted a cuffband on the lower left sleeve bearing the designation "Nibelungen." They were members of the 38th SS-Grenadier-Division, the formation of which had begun on Hitler's orders on March 4, 1945 from officer candidates of the *SS-Junkerschule* Bad Tölz, augmented by recruits from the *Wehrmacht* and various miscellaneous units. In the approximately two months of its existence, the "division" never exceeded much more than regimental strength.[1] Fascinating, from a

[1] All thirty-eight *Waffen-SS* (Combat-SS) divisions, regardless of ultimate strength, were named, several of them, such as the 9th SS-Panzer-Division "Hohenstaufen," the 17th SS-Panzer-Grenadier-Division "Götz von Berlichingen," and the 33rd Waffen-Grenadier-Division der SS "Charlemagne," after prominent figures or, in the case of the 9th, a dynasty, in earlier German(ic) history. The "Nibelungen" division, formed so late in the war, was never issued the cuffband in question, despite the occasional (postwar) "replica" that one may come across. Veterans referred to the unit, in fact, as the "Niegelungene Division." See Georg Tessin, *Verbände und Truppen der deutschen Wehrmacht und Waffen SS im Zweiten Weltkrieg 1939–1945*, ed. Bundesarchiv-Militärchiv with the assistance of the Arbeitskreis für Wehrforschung (Frankfurt a. M.: Verlag E. S. Mittler & Sohn, [n.d.]) 5: *Die Landstreitkräfte 31–70*, 77; also Kurt Mehner, *Die Waffen-SS und Polizei 1939–1945*, Schriftenreihe Führung und Truppe (Norderstedt: Militair-Verlag Klaus D. Patzwall, 1995) 263–264, and K.-G. Klietmann, *Die Waffen-SS, eine Dokumentation* (Osnabrück: Verlag "Der Freiwillige," 1965) 305–306. Seventeen years after World War II, the "Nibelungen" division would be "resurrected" by the German author Hans Hellmut Kirst in his novel, *Die Nacht der Generale* (1962), subsequently translated into English by J. Maxwell Brownjohn (1963), and released as a British-made film in 1967. The portrayal of the unit in both the novel and the film is completely fictitious and on the screen is inclined to appear somewhat ludicrous: "Nibelungen" first appears as a *Wehrmacht* formation in Poland, assigned the task of

psychological viewpoint, is the decision taken in the closing months of the Second World War to accord this last division of the élite Waffen-SS a designation taken from what was, at the time, considered to be the national epic. The chief impetus for such a choice undoubtedly lay with the association of the name with the concept of *Nibelungentreue*, although for those familiar with the medieval *Nibelungenlied*, the designation may also have conveyed as well the aura of annihilation, of the "fight to the end against insurmountable odds" without any hope of victory. A subconscious "knowledge" of the ultimate outcome of the war, reflected here in the selection of this designation for the last élite military unit formed within the German armed forces, represented a stark contrast to public proclamations by party leaders and members of the Propaganda Ministry that the war would still culminate in German victory. As Härd has stated, "[d]ie Wirklichkeit wird ein Teil des Mythos, sie bestätigt ihn."[2] We thus find manifested in history the continuity of certain archetypal images in the *Nibelungenlied* that have bridged the centuries and found expression in a reality that bears some uncanny parallels to the Armageddon-like conclusion of the epic. Myth, fiction, and history merge in the final weeks of the Third Reich, particularly in the fall of Berlin in May, 1945, with the Berlin Philharmonic's broadcast of Wagner's *Götterdämmerung* providing a continual musical backdrop to the slaughter of attacking Russian, and defending German troops, along with contingents of Scandinavian and French volunteers who, paradoxically, were among the last defenders of the besieged and battered *Reichskanzlei*.

Almost eight and a half centuries separate the Berlin of May, 1945 from the first appearance of the *Nibelungenlied*, the epic which has exemplified, in the minds of many over the centuries, the ideal comportment of warriors on the brink of extinction. The stories — whether rooted in history or in myth — on which the *Nibelungenlied* is based are old, dating back perhaps as far as the period of the Great Migrations in the fifth century (the Burgundians under Gundahari were decimated in 436–437 by the Huns), although it cannot be definitively stated when the various tales that make up the Nibelungen complex had their genesis. It is not until the turn of the thirteenth century that the two major strands of the tradition, the (mythical) death of Siegfried and the (historical) demise of the Burgundians, are

carrying out "difficult" missions, only to be transferred in 1944 to France and, simultaneously, "transformed" *en masse*, and without the slightest commentary, into a fully armored *Waffen-SS* division. The idea of *Nibelungentreue* is, however, intimately associated with the spirit inherent to the formation.

[2] John Evert Härd, *Das Nibelungenepos. Wertung und Wirkung von der Romantik bis zur Gegenwart*, trans. from the Swedish by Christine Palm (Tübingen and Basel: Francke, 1996) 19.

brought together in the epic form that has been passed down to us. Homer had written his *Iliad* and the *Odyssey* approximately two millennia earlier, the Indian *Mahabharata* was composed sometime between 200 B.C. and 200 A.D., the Old English *Beowulf, may* have originated about the beginning of the eighth century, the Welsh *Mabinogion* prior to 1000 A.D., after which it was carried to the continent and served as a basis for some of the Arthurian romances. With its initial appearance dating from ca. 1200, the *Nibelungenlied* is thus relatively "young" in terms of its ultimate composition, although the ethos which drives the work does appear to be much older. While it may share with the romances of the late twelfth and early thirteenth centuries an appreciation of the virtues of honor and loyalty, it provides no forum for the major ideal of the time, the concept of moderation, of *mâze.* The anonymous poet has furnished his characters with the trappings of courtly society, but the accent is less on the *relatively* refined atmosphere prevailing among thirteenth-century western European aristocracy than on the more primitive, and absolute, ethos of loyalty to the clan. Unlike the Arthurian romances, where the movement of knights revolves around the great courts of the nobles or in the space between them (with occasional forays into such Otherworlds as Munsalvaesche and Schastel Marveile), "epic" landscape predominates in the *Nibelungenlied.* The action ranges from Iceland to Hungary; it culminates in the movement, not simply of a court, but of masses of people, and ultimately in their destruction far beyond the borders of their homelands.

To what extent the poet of the *Nibelungenlied* was familiar with the Scandinavian analogues that reached back to the period of the Great Migrations and culminated in the thirteenth century in the *Poetic Edda*, the *Vǫlsunga saga*, and the *Þiðreks saga*, we shall probably never know. Sigurd's slaying of Fafnir was not something that he dwelt upon, but the event, as well as the continued intimate association with the Otherworld in general, were elements so integral to the character of Siegfried that they could not simply be ignored. Nor are we dealing with only one Otherworld, as Joyce Tally Lionarons demonstrates in "The Otherworld and its Inhabitants in the *Nibelungenlied.*" In a time when people believed in a literal Hell, references to dragons, giants, dwarfs, and fabulous treasures are endowed with a significance that is, perhaps, virtually incomprehensible in the post-Enlightenment era. In particular, Siegfried, Hagen, Brünhild, and eventually Kriemhild (in that order) embody an "otherness" or "strangeness" which must have fascinated a medieval audience and which continues to inspire new attempts at interpretation by contemporary scholars.

Courtly romances such as those by Hartmann and Wolfram focus on the quest and the ability of the knight(s) errant to restore *ordo* to a society in which harmony has been temporarily suspended. Inasmuch as we can speak, in Jungian terms, of a process of individuation for medieval fictional characters, it is most certainly in evidence with Erec, Iwein, or Parzival. (The notable exception within romance is, of course, Tristan, whose own brand of individuality has the potential for creating almost as much chaos at court as does Siegfried's. Society is preserved, however, and it is the individuals who perish.) In the *Nibelungenlied*, any such "individuation" process is entirely lacking, at least in terms of a positive "development" on the part of an individual with resulting benefits for society as a whole. Siegfried remains quite static throughout the first half of the epic: he is arrogant, naive, overconfident, given to a spontaneity and imprudence in his words and actions that cannot help but delineate him as a danger to society. One might suggest that his sojourn in the Otherworld and his bathing in the blood of the dragon have transformed him into a demi-god, but it must be remembered that Siegfried would have had to have been already endowed with incredible strength to perform the feats attributed to him prior to his encounter with and defeat of the dragon. Seven and a quarter centuries after the composition of the *Nibelungenlied*, the film maker Fritz Lang, drawing more extensively on the Scandinavian analogues in his portrayal of the young hero, vividly portrayed several aspects of Siegfried's inherently troublesome relationship to the rest of the world. Gunther, Gernot, Giselher also remain essentially static throughout the work, although they finally come into their own again as warriors during the final confrontation in the Great Hall of Etzel (having previously left the impression of being rather indecisive, weak kings at a loss as to what to do in a variety of crises). Hagen, too, does not undergo any change, although the same cannot be said of the position taken towards him by the narrator between the end of the sixteenth *Âventiure* and the concluding scenes of the thirty-ninth. Kriemhild does appear to undergo a transformation, but it is not one that has anything to do with a process of individuation. Seen from the perspective of Dietrich, Hagen, and, it would appear, even Etzel, Kriemhild no longer has much in common with the rest of humanity by the end of the epic. The word that both Dietrich and Hagen use to describe her, *vâlandinne*, should not, however, be taken as indicative of a general condemnation of the woman by all of the poet's contemporaries. Within the framework of an ethic that lauds loyalty and which accords the highest praise to *absolute* loyalty, Kriemhild garnered more than just sympathy from some quarters, particularly the author of the *Klage* and the scribe of ms. C.

The idea of "loyalty," as Frank Gentry illustrates in "Key Concepts in the *Nibelungenlied*," was a touchstone of the work and constitutes a "red thread" in the reception of the epic from the time of its first commentary, by the author of the *Klage* (appended to most of the major manuscripts), through the first half of the twentieth century. While most versions of the

Nibelungenlied underscored the *Männertreue* of the Burgundians at the court of Etzel during the final debacle, the *Klage*-poet unabashedly holds up Kriemhild as the epitome of *triuwe*, even to the point of declaring that her unswerving loyalty to Siegfried will have earned her a place in heaven, a remarkable blending of diverse ethical premises. While in awe of the extent to which apparently total devastation predominates in the *Nibelungenlied* — although he is capable of rationalizing Kriemhild's role in the slaughter — that later poet was clearly not content to leave his audience with the image of Armageddon, but rather provided a concrete symbol of continuity through his reference to the subsequent crowning in Worms of the young Siegfried, son of Gunther and Brünhild.

In terms of both literary and extraliterary reception, few works of the European Middle Ages can boast the "staying power" of the "heroic" *Nibelungenlied* and few have generated more controversy both among scholars and the educated public. To say that the epic has always engendered interest and emulation would be patently untrue. For over two hundred years between the sixteenth and the eighteenth century, the *Nibelungenlied* lay literally obscured in the dust of monasteries and libraries, ignored by German Humanists. On June 28, 1755, what is now designated as manuscript C was discovered by the physician, Jacob Hermann Obereit in Hohenems. Two years later, Obereit's friend, the Zurich historian Johann Jacob Bodmer (1698–1783), published excerpts in his *Chriemhilden Rache, und Die Klage; zwey Heldengedichte Aus dem schwaebischen Zeitpuncte*, but confined himself solely to those parts of the epic that dealt with the conflict between the Huns and the Burgundians. The interest of the editor was squarely on Kriemhild and the revenge she exacts. This fascination with the Burgundian princess, wife of Siegfried and then Etzel (Attila), has been in evidence from the inception of Nibelungen scholarship and has continued unabated, as attested by Otfrid Ehrismann's contribution to the present volume, "'ze stücken was gehouwen dô daz edele wîp': The Reception of Kriemhild." While her detractors have tended to outnumber her defenders, Ehrismann portrays her as a multifaceted, complex individual, who defies a black-white categorization.

The "re-discovery" of the *Nibelungenlied* by Obereit and its subsequent dissemination by Bodmer were not met everywhere with the type of enthusiasm that, for example, would today greet, at least in the academic world, the announcement that a new manuscript of the epic had been located and identified. The Prussian king, Friedrich II, dismissed it and other Middle High German works he had received from Christoph Heinrich Müller (Myller), who had produced the first edition of the *Nibelungenlied* (based on mss. C and A), as "nicht einen Schuss Pulver werth."[3] It was a less than tactful response to Müller given the fact that the latter had dedicated the edition to the king. The linguist Johann Christoph Adelung viewed the occupation with older German literature as a move away from the Enlightenment, back to an age devoid of true "taste." In contrast, the advent of the Napoleonic Wars and the rise of Romanticism in Germany produced a diametrically different reaction to the literary artifacts of the German Middle Ages, in general, and to the *Nibelungenlied*, in particular. August Wilhelm Schlegel praised the epic as the German *Iliad* and *Odyssey*, a sentiment echoed a little later by his brother Friedrich in his *Geschichte der alten und neuen Literatur*. As a work of art in its own right, or as a source for the model behavior of men in battle facing overwhelming odds, the *Nibelungenlied* has had a checkered history. If it held no interest for the Humanists (being most likely unknown to virtually all of them), and was rejected by prominent representatives of the Enlightenment, Goethe, on the other hand, considered it an essential component of the cultivated individual's education and predicted that countless generations to follow would concern themselves with it. The Romanticists regarded it as the very foundation of their national poetry (Friedrich Schlegel); throughout the rest of the nineteenth century and well into the twentieth — until the end of World War II — the *Nibelungenlied* enjoyed unmitigated popularity among all sectors of society. Since 1945, however, there has been a noticeable lack of the earlier, often uncritical, acceptance of the *Nibelungenlied* as a national monument whose protagonists exuded uniquely German virtues. More often the latter have tended to be rejected in the wake of postwar realism and disillusionment. While the work is still drawn upon by modern authors for their own literary experiments, it is almost invariably used as a basis for satire and critical commentary on what is seen as an outdated ethos. There is, however, a potential, interpretive danger in such a stance, namely, that one may deliberately or inadvertently attribute a similar attitude to the original poet, even though the text itself displays no compelling evidence that the latter ever deviated from an acceptance of the warrior virtues so prominently embodied by many of his major characters.

Scholarship on the *Nibelungenlied* can be divided into four major phases. The first, concentrated in the nineteenth century, but continuing in more modest form into the twentieth, was of a technical and fundamental nature: the production of editions. These were the *sine qua non* for further scholarly investigation of the poem, but there was an inherent problem with the methodology used to produce them. While the manuscripts on which

[3] See Otfrid Ehrismann, *Nibelungenlied. Epoche — Werk — Wirkung* (Munich: Beck, 1987) 248.

editions were based evinced the texts in the versions in which the epic had been passed down, i.e., with all of their scribal errors, inconsistencies, and incongruities, nineteenth-century editors often undertook to decipher what, in their opinion, must have constituted the "original" text, to weed out the errors, real and alleged. In the process, they were not disinclined to make arbitrary changes to the text itself based on their own belief of what *should* appear there after comparing one particular manuscript with others at their disposal. Contemporary editors are more conservative with their handling of the medieval manuscripts, preferring "diplomatic" renderings which, apart from some standard normalization in orthography (and even this can be viewed as taking too much freedom with the original manuscript!), leave the text as it is to be found in the extant manuscript on which the edition is based.

The second phase dealt with the question of the "formal" origins of the epic, whether it had evolved from numerous, individual lays (Karl Lachmann), or from two basic saga traditions, the *Brünhildsage* and the *Burgundensage*, which, according to the Swiss Germanist, Andreas Heusler, had been lent "epische Breite," "Ausweitung" by the early thirteenth-century poet. Within this phase may also be included the study of the interrelationship between the diverse strands of the epic as attested by the extant manuscripts, as well as the ultimate question of the origins of its content. Research on the latter concentrated on two areas in particular: the historical and the mythological. This second phase encompasses both the nineteenth and twentieth centuries, and the highly intriguing, if complex, issues surrounding the relationship between manuscripts are still very much debated, as Joachim Heinzle illustrates below in "The Manuscripts of the Nibelungenlied." The three major manuscripts identified in the nineteenth century, A (Munich), B (St. Gall), and C (Donaueschingen) have been the basis of much speculation. Scholars have theorized on which of the three should be considered most reflective of the original *Nibelungenlied*. In the formulation of his *Liedertheorie*, Karl Lachmann (1793–1851) asserted the priority of ms. A. Karl Bartsch's preference for ms. B has enjoyed the greatest resonance among scholars, although its predominant status may gradually be giving way to ms. C, first published in its entirety in 1821 by Reichsfreiherr von Laßberg in St. Gall and Constance and in 1856 and 1857 by Friedrich Zarncke and Adolf Holtzmann respectively, prominent participants in the notorious *Nibelungenstreit* with Lachmann's defender, Karl Müllenhoff.

Will Hasty's choice of title for his contribution to this volume, "Conquest in the *Nibelungenlied*," could not be more appropriate with respect to major elements of the epic's plot. In one way or another, the *Nibelungenlied* appears to have been consistently associated with conflict and conquest, and this does not pertain solely to the plot of the early thirteenth-century epic. In

1816, Karl Lachmann, whose primary training had been in classical philology, published his treatise *Über die ursprüngliche Gestalt des Liedes von der Nibelungen Noth.* Emulating the earlier theory of Friedrich August Wolf in his *Prolegomena ad Homerum* (1795), in which the author expressed his doubt that either the *Iliad* or the *Odyssey* could be the work of one man, Lachmann postulated that the same could be asserted for the *Nibelungenlied.* He suggested that its composition had involved broader sectors of the "folk," and that it had evolved from the combining of earlier, independent lays (he would later set the number at twenty) into the longer epic. The inconsistencies in the text served as "evidence" for the suggestion that this could hardly have been the work of a single individual. For almost forty years, Lachmann's *Liedertheorie* assumed virtually sacrosanct status among philologists, who praised its exemplary methodology and convincing conclusions — which is not to suggest that criticism was totally lacking. In 1854, however, Adolf Holtzmann, Professor for Oriental Languages in Heidelberg, published his controversial *Untersuchungen über das Nibelungenlied*, in which he took Lachmann to task for the "arbitrariness" of his methodology. Lachmann could not defend himself. He had died three years earlier. Others joined the growing chorus of his detractors: Friedrich Zarncke, Franz Pfeiffer, Karl Bartsch, and Wilhelm Müller, all noted medievalists. Lachmann's defense was left to his followers, principal among them Moriz Haupt and Karl Müllenhoff. The dispute had little of the air of objectivity about it, as Müllenhoff attacked the very ethics of those who dared to deviate from the path of his revered mentor, going so far as to accuse the former of moral turpitude and professional incompetence.[4] Müllenhoff's later biographer, Wilhelm Scherer, would quite correctly proclaim that his subject's method of attack could not have been easier to repulse. Within the context of the time, however, and considering the early history of *Germanistik* prior to its solid anchoring as a discipline, there can be no doubt that Karl Lachmann's contributions, as well as those of his adversaries, were highly significant, even essential. The classical methodology and exactness which he brought to the field were indispensable in paving the way for its recognition as a bona fide *Fach* in the reformed German university of the nineteenth century.[5] The problem lay more in the absolutization of philological meticulousness to the exclusion of alternative

[4] Remarkably striking here the parallel in modern times to the tendency in some quarters to abandon all professionalism and, in a flurry of *ad hominems*, to view scholars who assume a critical stance towards the latest postmodernist fad as reprobates, racists, fascists, misogynists, and retrograde in their scholarship! In fairness to Müllenhoff, it should be noted that he was a solid scholar, irrespective of his invective against Holtzmann et al.

[5] See Rainer Kolk, *Berlin oder Leipzig? Eine Studie zur sozialen Organisation der Germanistik im »Nibelungenstreit«* (Tübingen: Niemeyer, 1990) 100.

ways of approaching texts. The *Nibelungenstreit* proved to be the catalyst for the expansion of publication vehicles and was more than merely instrumental in the founding of a new branch of *Germanistik*, namely, *Neuere Sprache und Literatur*. Its ultimate benefits for the discipline as a whole are summarized by Rainer Kolk:

> Die *Sprachwissenschaft* mit ihren herausragenden Vertretern Paul und Sievers tritt neben die *deutsche* eines Braune oder Andreas Heusler; *Neugermanistik* und *Literaturgeschichte* reflektieren philologische, ästhetische und hermeneutische Fragestellungen. Zudem wendet sich das Fach den Anforderungen der *Lehrerbildung* zu. Der »Nibelungenstreit« als der sicherlich schwerwiegendste wissenschaftliche Konflikt in der Geschichte der Germanistik erweist sich in dieser Perspektive als produktive Unordnung, aus der die Disziplin mit neuen Problemen, aber auch mit einem aktualisierten Problembewußtsein hervorgeht.[6]

Most *Nibelungenlied* scholarship — in its third phase — over the past century (beginning already in the latter part of the nineteenth century) has dealt with the work itself, its motifs and motivations, its characters, theme(s), structure, as well as its "place" among the rich tradition of Middle High German literature around 1200. The amount of secondary material on the work is vast. Goethe's prediction has been realized in the 170 years since it was uttered on the occasion of the publication of Karl Simrock's 1827 translation of the *Nibelungenlied*, and there is no indication that interest in the work, including interpretive interest, is about to let up. The approaches and foci of concern have ranged across a broad spectrum, and have included plot and character analyses against the backdrop of the historical realities of the thirteenth century, the intertwining of elements associated with both epic and romance, structural analyses, comparisons of themes, motifs, and language with other works from the period, psychological and philosophical inquiries, marxist and feminist viewpoints and, inevitably, authorship, the matter of authorial intentionality and the "message" of the *Nibelungenlied*.

The fourth phase encompasses the vast body of material subsumed under the general heading of *Rezeptionsgeschichte*. The *Nibelungenlied* has long served as a repository for aesthetic achievements in art, music, sculpture, architecture, and literature, and its characters and their actions or comportment as models for appropriate behavior in the political or military sphere. *Rezeptionsgeschichte* is, like interpretation (as which it could simultaneously be characterized), a vast field. Throughout both the nineteenth and the twentieth centuries, the medieval epic has proven to be a most fertile "source" of inspiration for scores of artists from diverse disciplines, as it has

[6] Kolk 102.

for rhetoricians from all political camps. It is no overstatement to claim that the Nibelungen theme has been ubiquitous over the past 150 years in a wide spectrum of literary and as well as non-literary endeavors. It was used by Friedrich Hebbel as the basis for one of his best psychological dramas, by Wagner, along with the Old Norse analogues, for his longest and, to some, most stirring, *Gesamtkunstwerk*, *Der Ring des Nibelungen*, and by the film maker Fritz Lang for his early 1920s two-part Expressionist masterpiece, *Die Nibelungen*, to cite only three of the more prominent examples. Its heroes provided suitable models for German troops who marched against Napoleon, a code name ("Hagen Offensive") and defensive network on the western front ("Siegfried Line") in World War I, while at the conclusion of the latter, Hagen's killing of Siegfried was compared to Germany's having been "stabbed in the back" by traitors at home. As Werner Hoffmann shows in his article on "The Reception of the *Nibelungenlied* in the Twentieth Century," the positive or negative stance on the work over the past 100 years is intimately linked to the politics or "spirit" of the times in which the commentaries originated. Largely because of the manner in which the Nibelungen theme had been harnessed for political aims throughout the first four and a half decades of this century, its reception in the post-World War II era has been decidedly non-traditional, and, as intimated above, more often than not the work has served as the basis for biting satire and criticism of societal norms as well as what had been previously considered specific traits of the Germans.

What one can derive from modern adaptations of the Nibelungen theme, particularly those that have appeared since the end of the Second World War, is that the more critical stance assumed towards the traditional concept of the "heroic," as well as the ideas of honor and loyalty, is, of course, the antithesis of the attitude that prevailed in the Middle Ages and well into the twentieth century. It would be imprudent to assume that the Armageddon-like conclusion to the *Nibelungenlied* is indicative of a critical position on the part of the poet towards those ideas which had a role in bringing about such a catastrophe. There is no *textual evidence* to support the theory that the original author of the *Nibelungenlied* was in any way critically disposed towards such virtues; an excellent case can be made, in fact, for the opposing point of view. If we assume that he is speaking through the words of the narrator — an admittedly rather modern position — the only time at which any condemnation is offered is in the commentary regarding Hagen's lack of observance of the "code," in the depiction of the latter as the epitome of disloyalty who could not have committed a more outrageous act than the killing of Siegfried while the latter was a guest of the Burgundians. Given his initially unequivocal censure of Hagen for the murder, it seems more likely that the poet worked within the framework of the ethical code prevalent at that time. The *Nibelungenlied* is not, however, a moral treatise. While accepting the general validity of the warrior's (unwritten) code of virtues, it is clear that its author was also fully capable of recognizing the entire spectrum of human emotions and of depicting figures who range above the typical to embody both the bright and the dark side of human existence.

What makes the *Nibelungenlied* a work that continues to be found in most bookshops in Europe and North America along with other classics such as the *Iliad*, the *Odyssey*, the *Aeneid*, or *El Cid*? Why is it one of only two titles from the German Middle Ages (the other is *Parzival*) listed by Harold Bloom in the appendix to his timely volume, *The Western Canon,* as having "great aesthetic interest"?[7] Is it the *Nibelungenlied's* capacity to evoke a sense of awe within the reader, whether the latter repels in horror at the devastation wrought by the warring parties upon one another or marvels at the extent to which the ideals and virtues of the respective individuals and groups are absolutized? The reasons for this fascination are undoubtedly manifold, but a major drawing card is the effectiveness with which the anonymous poet draws from a broad range of human emotions and motives to produce figures that transcend typologies. Whether the emphasis is on conquest or, as Brian Murdoch demonstrates in "Politics in the *Nibelungenlied*," on political aims and motivations, one inevitably comes back to Kriemhild, Brünhild, Hagen, Siegfried, Rüdiger, or Dietrich. Above all there is in the *Nibelungenlied*, to use one of Bloom's favorite words, one that has been used by critics to describe his own aforementioned volume, *passion*. It is apparent in the manner in which the poet allows the unique dichotomy between Kriemhild and Hagen to build to its dramatic climax in the thirty-ninth *Âventiure*. A very different approach to the concept is provided by James McGlathery in "Erotic Passion in the *Nibelungenlied* and Wagner's *Ring des Nibelungen*," and *passion* is the most appropriate word that can be used to portray the manner in which one of the greatest Nibelungen scholars, Friedrich Panzer, described his first encounter with the work as a nine-year-old schoolboy over 120 years ago: "... das Buch ließ mich nicht los. Ich ... las und las die unerhörte Mär bis zum traurigen Ende."[8]

Clearly the poet was bound to some degree by tradition, but the end product is certainly of his own making and thoroughly original. The *Nibelungenlied* is a remarkable blend of history, myth, of "epic" scenery and courtly romance; it deals with individual intrigue and combines it with "epic" consequences. There are various levels discernible in the work, as Edward R.

[7] Harold Bloom, *The Western Canon. The Books and School of the Ages* (New York: Riverhead Books, 1994) 500.

[8] Friedrich Panzer, *Das Nibelungenlied. Entstehung und Gestalt* (Stuttgart and Cologne: Kohlhammer, 1955) 7.

Haymes discusses in "Heroic, Chivalric, and Aristocratic Ethos in the *Nibelungenlied.*" As was also the case with courtly romance and *Minnesang*, the *Nibelungenlied* was, of course, *Standesdichtung*, literature for the nobility, and while we may never know precisely for whom it may have been written or who might be counted among its audience when it was orally performed, we can assume that the latter will have included some of the more powerful barons and counts, perhaps even kings and queens of the time, suitable benefactors for the minstrel-knight. Its strophes contain allusions to the splendor of the court, its action revolves around political issues, power, even gender (although it would be absurd to reduce it to any issue alone), in short, diverse human strengths and foibles, but while the poet has concentrated on precisely that "humanness" of his major protagonists, this in no way implies that he lacked any interest in the more nebulous spheres — the world of the Nibelungen treasure and the realm of the water sprites encountered by Hagen as the Burgundians/Nibelungs journey to the Hunnish court.

For the better part of two centuries, unanswered questions regarding various aspects of the *Nibelungenlied* have been posed and continue to be raised by each new generation of medieval scholars. Possibly we shall never know the identity of the hitherto anonymous "author" of the epic, in the form it was written down somewhere near the turn of the thirteenth century. Yet, as the recent discovery of six fragments of a hitherto unknown *Nibelungenlied* manuscript by Dr. Christine Glaßner in the Stiftsbibliothek Melk in Lower Austria, as well as another manuscript of the *Lied vom Hürnen Seyfrid*, demonstrate (see "Siegfried's Dragon-Fight in German Literary Tradition" by John Flood in this volume), no one can maintain with any assurance that two years, two decades, or two centuries into the next millennium another manuscript will not be resurrected containing a definitive clue as to authorship. For now, however, the hypothesis that anonymity was integral to the genre appears to be substantiated by the extant "heroic epics," although it is possible to make a case for the *Nibelungenlied* as a unicum. On the other hand, Werner Wunderlich has shown ("The Authorship of the *Nibelungenlied*") how truly unlikely it is that knowledge of the epic's author would contribute much to our understanding of the work or the manner in which we interpret it. It is quite feasible that the anonymous poet intended a specific "message" to be recognized and appreciated by his listeners or readers and there has been much speculation as to what it may have been, whether political-military: *de facto* leadership must be backed up by *de facto* power; gender-specific: the *ordo* of man and God does not accord women the formidable positions of power assumed by both Brünhild and Kriemhild; Christian sermonizing: here in this tale we have unveiled the possible consequences for those who insist on adhering to the old ethos while ignoring the message of Christ. The text itself provides only one concrete piece of evidence of the poet's "message," provided that we may assume that he is, in fact, speaking through his narrator. It is, furthermore, a message which provides a structural framework for the entire work, occurring initially at the end of the first *Âventiure* ("wie liebe mit leide ze jungest lônen kan," 17,3) and then again at the conclusion of the thirty-ninth: "als ie diu liebe leide z'aller jungeste gît" (2378,4). The poet's "message" does not concern politics, strategy, or the advocacy of Christian piety; it is philosophical in nature, and it is profoundly nihilistic.

Who were the Nibelungs? Is their story rooted in fact? Did the historical forbears of the Nibelungs actually move north rather than southeast? Was there a Latin *Nibelungias* which preceded all of the German versions? Do the vast majority of ("masculist," as one critic has put it) Nibelungen scholars hold the same views on women and their appropriate role within (at least twelfth-century) society as the male protagonists in the *Nibelungenlied*? The numerous theories on these and other questions provide ample testimony to the "belief" entertained by their advocates that either the work itself, or the approach to it, not infrequently complemented by extra-literary "evidence," will prove the veracity of said belief. Yet the *Nibelungenlied* has stubbornly refused to give up the secrets one senses it still holds, and there is good reason to believe that, despite the thousands of articles and hundreds of books that have been written on this most popular of epics, we are still generations away from answers to some of the most poignant questions, and that there may well be other lines of inquiry just as significant which we have not yet begun to contemplate. Perhaps there are no answers to many of the questions posed. The *Nibelungenlied* remains, with respect to virtually all aspects of its being hitherto examined by scholars, an enigma, but that is a good, if not the major, part of its attraction for both the academic world as well as that of the educated layman (albeit in a much more intense way during the first half of the twentieth century than is presently the case). Everything that has already been suggested regarding the discoveries of manuscripts, the attempt to decipher the intricate relationships among the various strands, as well as to the "archetype," the theories regarding origins, authorship, authorial intention(s), socio-historical background, clash of ethical systems, courtly and epic elements, etc., evoke the image of a multi-thousand-piece jigsaw puzzle, but one with enough pieces left to engage a host of generations in its reconstruction. While most of the pieces may, in fact, still exist, even if not immediately apparent, it is quite likely that some have dropped by the wayside and that the mosaic will never be entirely complete.

The *Nibelungenlied* appears to contain a variety of inconsistencies, blind motifs, and breaks in the plot, which could lead an observer to conclude that the poet was somewhat less of a master than has often been assumed. Why is there virtually no mention of Brünhild in the second half of the work? How could Dancwart claim to have been a child at the time of Siegfried's death when we know he accompanied his brother Hagen to Iceland to woo Brünhild? What, if anything, did Siegfried tell Kriemhild after having defeated the Icelandic queen in her bedchamber and depriving her of the ring and belt? Did he give his wife reason to believe that he might have deflowered her? How could "powerful" kings such as Gunther, Gernot, and Giselher remain basically inactive when Hagen kills Siegfried, confiscates the latter's *hort*, and attempts to drown the chaplain in the Danube — if they are truly averse to such actions, as they profess? What is the connection between the presence of Ortlieb, son of Kriemhild and Etzel, in the thirty-first *Âventiure* and the outbreak of fighting in the thirty-second? How could the Burgundians be told in the twenty-sixth *Âventiure* by Hagen that they will never return to Burgundy, initially react as though they believe it, and then proceed to Rüdiger's castle and on to the court of Etzel without any further indication that they are cognizant of what awaits them? How is it that Hagen occupies a greater role than Gunther following the arrival in Gran? Is the unity of the work compromised by such incongruities? This is clearly not the case. A. T. Hatto declares that it "would be wrong to think of contradictions" with respect to motives.[9] He suggests, quite correctly, that "the existence of divergent motives and characteristics attendant on additions or modifications of plot offered a challenge to the poets concerned. According to their skill and insight they made more or less of their chances."[10]

The unity of the work is not contingent upon complete cohesion between the individual parts, as Mukařovsky suggests:

> Die Einheit des Kunstwerkes, die von den Kunsttheoretikern so oft außerhalb des Werkes gesucht wurde, einmal in der Künstlerpersönlichkeit, ein andermal im Erlebnis als dem einzigartigen Zusammentreffen der Urheberpersönlichkeit mit der Wirklichkeit, die Einheit, die durch formalistische Richtungen ohne Erfolg als absolute Harmonie aller Teile und Elemente des Werkes gedeutet wurde (eine Harmonie, die in Wirklichkeit niemals existiert), kann von Rechts wegen nur in der Absichtlichkeit erblickt werden, in der im Innern des Werkes wirkenden Kraft, die auf die Überwindung der Widersprüche und Spannungen zwischen dessen einzelnen Teilen und Komponenten hinarbeitet, wobei sie deren Gesamtheit einen einheitlichen Sinn und jedem von ihnen eine bestimmte Beziehung zu den übrigen verleiht.[11]

[9] A. T. Hatto, trans., *The Nibelungenlied* (London: Penguin, 1969) 307.

[10] Hatto 308.

[11] Jan Mukařovský, *Studien zur strukturalistischen Ästhetik und Poetik* (Munich: Hanser, 1974) 36.

Mukařovský's criteria provide a basis for some reflections on the matter of authorial intentionality. What is apparent from the text is that the poet, for all of the education and training he may have received in a *Domschule* or a monastery, exuded a thoroughly pessimistic view of human existence, at least with respect to its capacity for insuring any sense of continuity subsequent to the debacle at the court of Etzel. It would be left to the anonymous poet of the *Klage* to suggest that some semblance of continuity was possible by turning to the next generation.

*

Does the *Nibelungenlied* have a future? Literary Studies, and apparently not only in America, are in something of a quandary. There is a (re)turn to blatant vocationalism on many university campuses, with a resultant downplaying of the essential value of the Humanities. The representatives of the latter have far too often been less than effective ambassadors of their disciplines with budget-conscious administrations. Catchwords replace scholarly substance and calculative thought, so integral to the hard sciences, engineering, and medicine, has tended to replace its necessary complement in the Humanities, meditative thought. It is the hour of the "buzzword," although a term such as "cutting edge," which is so very significant (and rightly so) in the aforementioned pragmatic fields, is a ludicrous way to describe literary scholarship and is indicative rather of ignorance than erudition on the part of those who employ it in this context. The *Nibelungenlied, Iliad, Odyssey* and countless other works that are viewed in some quarters as merely artifacts of "patriarchal" western culture no longer worthy of reading will, of course, survive long after the (often resentful) advocates of "cultural studies" have been laid to rest. One wonders precisely what teachers of literature at all levels have hitherto been engaged in if not precisely the latter. We need only recall the superficially devastating criticism of the *Nibelungenlied* (and other works of medieval literature) by both Friedrich II of Prussia and Adelung and note that their views stir nowadays little more than mild curiosity in passing. The fact is that there is hardly a major bookstore from San Francisco to New York, to London and Berlin, to Moscow and Tokyo, that does not provide access to some version of the *Nibelungenlied*, even if in translation, and it is reasonable, not arrogant, to assume that this will continue to be the case in the centuries to follow. Much more interesting is *why* we can feel confident making such a statement. Why does this work, eight hundred years after its commitment to parchment, continue to be read by students, their mentors, and the educated lay public? For an answer, we can return again to the wisdom of Harold Bloom as expressed in the concluding pages of his *Western Canon*: "I think that the self, in its quest to be free and solitary, ultimately reads with one aim only: to confront greatness. That confrontation scarcely masks the desire to join greatness, which is the basis of the aesthetic experience once called the Sublime; the quest for a transcendence of limits."[12] John M. Ellis puts it another way:

> Writers whose works are compelling enough to survive after their death and be read and reread by future generations have seen the essence of human situations so clearly that even profound changes in human life cannot obscure their meaning. Take, for example, the question of what it means to be exceptionally talented or to be in the company of those who are. We usually think that great talent is a blessing — something that should enable one to lead a successful life. But three great writers from different epochs saw much more in the situation. The heroic figures in Homer's *The Iliad*, in the German medieval *Nibelungenlied*, or in Tolstoy's *War and Peace* show us that exceptional talent does not make a successful life. Andrei Bolkonsky is a glittering figure for whom there is, surprisingly, no real place in the world: it is his more ordinary friend, Pierre, who survives and lives out a contented and useful life. Siegfried's extraordinary natural ability and strength allow him to get by without ever having to develop an understanding of the people around him; he is therefore surprised when those for whom he has done so much do not admire him (as he thinks they should) but instead plot to kill him at the first opportunity, using fair means or foul. In *The Iliad* the link between brilliance and unfitness for life is strongest of all, so strong that Achilles is already aware of the prophesy that one so gifted will have a short life. The three cases differ in so many ways that one can never be substituted for another, yet on occasion one illuminates the others. Coming from the *Nibelungenlied* to *The Iliad*, for example, we see immediately that the prophesy of Achilles' early death is not simply an arbitrary act of cruel gods; rather, the prophesy is about the distortion that exceptional talent inevitably brings with it....[W]hen the remarkable swimmer Mark Spitz won a record seven Olympic gold medals and then proceeded to destroy his enormous popularity through boorish behavior, no one who had reflected upon *The Iliad* or the *Nibelungenlied* could have been surprised. The shadow of Achilles and Siegfried was again visible, and even if Spitz was only a pale shadow of them, he was recognizably part of the human behavior that had inspired their creation.[13]

Although he does not use the term here, Ellis is referring to *archetypal* figures who find themselves in archetypal situations (hence the relevance of his reference to Mark Spitz), and through which universal truths (or at least

[12] Bloom 489.

[13] John M. Ellis, *Literature Lost. Social Agendas and the Corruption of the Humanities* (New Haven: Yale University Press, 1997) 39–41.

patterns) become immediately apparent to the attentive reader. Yet there is a particular fascination with those heroes and situations that end tragically, and this fascination is all the more powerful when reality in one's own time mirrors fiction, or, in the words of John Evert Härd, reality confirms myth. There is a remarkable continuity to be noted from the time of Homer, through that of the poet of the *Nibelungenlied*, and most assuredly into our own century which is manifest in the behavioral patterns and fates of major "epic" protagonists, but which also finds reflection in real life. Approximately 800 years have passed since the *Nibelungenlied* took on the literary form with which we have become familiar. Its popularity in the High Middle Ages, to which thirty-five extant manuscripts attest, has not abated. One might argue that it has, in fact, increased dramatically. The twelve essays contained in this *Companion to the Nibelungenlied* offer further evidence of the continued vitality and relevance of this monumental work of art on the threshold of the third millennium.

Otfrid Ehrismann

"ze stücken was gehouwen dô daz edele wîp": The Reception of Kriemhild

An attentive reading of the *Nibelungenlied*[1] permits the reader to develop a particular profile of Kriemhild. Our purpose here is to illustrate the role of the epic poet in the shaping of this image. The phrase, "role of the poet," remains a fiction, or rather, a heuristic construction, inasmuch as we cannot know in which form the material was available to the person to whom we are ultimately indebted for the written epic which has been passed down to us in the three versions *A, *B, and *C.

This study is not based, however, on a critique of the sources, an approach that is hardly capable of penetrating the aesthetic structure of the text. Such a method, in itself, would result in another, equally exciting game. The object is rather to arrive at a "benevolent understanding" of a written

[1] Quotations from the *Nibelungenlied* are based on the edition by Karl Bartsch, ed. Helmut de Boor, 21st ed. by Roswitha Wisniewski (Wiesbaden: Brockhaus, 1979). References to the *Klage* are based on *Diu Klage. Mit den Lesarten sämtlicher Handschriften*, ed. Karl Bartsch (1875; rpt. Darmstadt: Wissenschaftliche Buchgesellschaft, 1964). Virtually all important studies on the *Nibelungenlied* can look back on a remarkable body of prominent scholarship. I owe a great debt of gratitude to previous scholars, to my former teacher, Karl Bischoff, for the seminars and lectures I was privileged to attend, and, in particular, to the works of Werner Hoffmann, Friedrich Maurer, Bert Nagel, Friedrich Neumann, and Werner Schröder, which are not, however, discussed in detail here. In the present study I make copious references to my book, *Nibelungenlied. Epoche — Werk — Wirkung* (Munich: Beck, 1987), although I have refrained from providing a citation for every instance. The same applies to my essays: "Siegfrieds Ankunft in Worms. Zur Bedeutung der 3. Aventiure des Nibelungenliedes," in Günter Bellmann, Günter Eifler, and Wolfgang Kleiber, eds., *Festschrift für Karl Bischoff zum 70. Geburtstag* (Cologne and Vienna: Böhlau, 1975) 328–356; "Dietrich oder die Produktivität der Tränen — verhinderte Trauerarbeit am Nibelungenlied," *Diskussion Deutsch* 18 (1987): 306–320; "Strategie und Schicksal — Hagen," in Werner Wunderlich, ed., *Literarische Symbolfiguren,* Facetten deutscher Literatur 1 (Berne and Stuttgart: Haupt, 1989) 89–115; "Siegfried — Ein deutscher Mythos?" in Ulrich Müller and Werner Wunderlich, eds., *Mittelalter Mythen I* (St. Gall: UVK Fachverlag für Wissenschaft und Studium St. Gallen, 1996) 367–387; "Die Fremde am Hof — Brünhild und die Philosophie der Geschichte," in *Akten des VIII. Internationalen Germanisten-Kongresses Tokyo 1990* (Munich: Iudicium, 1991) 10: 320–331.

(generic) presentation of an epic that is based on oral tradition. We do not, however, seek to offer an interpretation aimed at "balancing out" all possible avenues of approach.

It is also not our intention to proceed along the lines of "nacherlebendes Lesen" (reenactment reading) as practiced by Friedrich Neumann,[2] and which was influenced by Dilthey's concept of life and the pedagogical philosophy that dominated Weimarian art. The object is rather to uncover feasible motives behind the action in the epic, whether they are explicit or implicit. To be sure, the implicit motives in a work of art which, by virtue of its genre,[3] is focused on the presentation of the plot, are problematic and one has to take care not to read too much into the text,[4] but they are, nevertheless, a necessary prerequisite for any attempt to explain the psychology of action — or, more exactly, to arrive at an understanding of the work. This is, in any event, the case for the recipient who, in line with the task set by epic and dramatic poetry, wishes to "sympathize" (*συμπασχειν*) with "his/her" characters and events (in the sense of Aristotelian catharsis).

Based on such a reading, we arrive at an image of Kriemhild which allows us to advance two theories that are pivotal to our understanding of the task the poet has set himself, as well as to gain an appreciation of his style: 1. he depicts only the avenging Kriemhild as a "character";[5] 2. he offers an epic which has been greatly influenced by the nature of courtly love.

[2] See Friedrich Neumann, "Das Nibelungenlied in seiner Zeit," in F. N., *Das Nibelungenlied in seiner Zeit* (Göttingen: Vandenhoeck & Ruprecht, 1967) 60–203.

[3] Note the lucid definition provided by Goethe and Schiller in their treatise, "Über epische und dramatische Dichtung," in: Johann Wolfgang von Goethe, *Werke*, Hamburger Ausgabe in 14 Bänden, vol. 12: *Schriften zur Kunst, Schriften zur Literatur, Maximen und Reflexionen*, 5th ed. by Werner Weber and Hans Joachim Schrimpf (Hamburg: Christian Wegner, 1963) 250· "Das epische Gedicht stellt vorzüglich persönlich beschränkte Tätigkeit [...] vor [...] den außer sich wirkenden Menschen: Schlachten, Reisen, jede Art von Unternehmung, die eine gewisse sinnliche Breite fordert; die Tragödie den nach innen geführten Menschen [...]."

[4] Neumann 150.

[5] I do not know of a better term to describe her appearance in this phase of individual action. Neither "role" nor "type" do justice to her ever-changing thoughts and actions. Even though, as an avenger, Kriemhild has a clear goal in mind (as defined by tradition), the *means* by which she achieves it in no way conforms to the role she has assumed, nor can it be described as typological.

I. *Love*

In all three versions of the *Nibelungenlied*, Kriemhild is the first character to be introduced, even before Siegfried and the Burgundian court, where she is the princess. The respective verses of the second stanza containing the hyperbole are to be understood as an epic stereotype and the conveyer of tradition: there is nothing in the world more beautiful than this high-born maiden, and because of her beauty many heroes were to lose their lives. One is instantly reminded of the Helena motif and, at the same time, of the genre which had already been introduced by manuscripts A and C in the preceding stanza, containing the *alten mæren*, glorious heroes, festivals, and great sadness and lamentation, thus setting the tone of the *carmen heroicum*.[6]

The Burgundian court is inextricably linked to Kriemhild because the three kings are, after all, her brothers and guardians. Moreover, the introductory *âventiure* (chapter) concludes with the dream which allegorically mirrors the first part of the epic: two eagles tear a falcon to pieces. In her interpretation of the dream, Kriemhild's mother alludes to the corresponding motif in Der von Kürenberg's song ("ich zôch mir einen valken..., der valke, den du ziuhest...,"[7] a poetical allusion to a maiden's love. The falcon's fate is in the hands of God. However, the young woman intends to renounce *minne* altogether because so many women exemplify "wie liebe mit leide ze jungest lônen kan" (17,3). Through the use of this adage, the poet immediately provides the framework and the theme for the entire epic.[8] His focus is devoted exclusively to Kriemhild in the first *Âventiure*, although — by virtue of the extensive description he provides of the court — he occasionally appears to distance himself somewhat from her. He bestows on Kriemhild the attributes of a young woman of great beauty who rebels against love — a stereotyped image of a young maiden which is, however, totally eclipsed in the following three *âventiuren*. They deal primarily with the prince who woos her from afar, and it is, metaphorically speaking, only at his side that she reappears in the epic, namely, in the victory celebrations following the war against the Saxons and the Danes. The ambience corresponds to that of the Arthurian novel:[9] "An einem pfinxtmorgen"

[6] Stanza 3, which praises the maiden's beauty, has only found its way into the critical text through manuscript A, and ought to be removed.

[7] Günther Schweikle, *Mittelhochdeutsche Minnelyrik I: Frühe Minnelyrik*, Texte und Übertragungen, Einführung und Kommentar (Stuttgart and Weimar: Metzler, 1993) 120, VIII/IX, as well as *Nibelungenlied* 14,3.

[8] See also 138,4 and 2378,4.

[9] See Otfrid Ehrismann, *Ehre und Mut, Aventiure und Minne. Höfische Wortgeschichten aus dem Mittelalter* (Munich: Beck, 1995) 91–103.

(271,1), the "scouwen" (273,3), the "scœne[n] mägede und hêrlich[en] wîp" (274,2), the "dringen" (280,2; 284,3). Like the dawn emerging out of dull clouds (381,1f.), like the bright moon before the stars (283,1), she radiates among the ladies and enchants the prince. The poet creates personality ("lîp") by drawing on biblical and courtly images.[10] In contrast to the romance, the epic places emphasis on generality. The use of such a style in this particular context makes sense because Kriemhild, by playing her role at court, signifies that, within feudal society, she is scarcely more than the mere pawn of the kings. Through her they try to acquire ("gewinnen," 289,4) the roaming hero, whatever is meant by that in the present context. Although the poet describes the scene in very general terms, he nevertheless endows the actions of his couple with traces of individuality.

The time that passes between the two scenes — the first and fifth *Âventiuren* — is left open by the poet. He only mentions the one year Siegfried spends at the Burgundian court before the war without ever being afforded the opportunity to see his love. However, this time span could also have a symbolic meaning in the sense of *zuht*: "ich zôch mir einen valken, mêre danne ein jâr," recalls the poem of Der von Kürenberg.[11] The young woman from the first adventure has become a young lady, a "vrouwe" (293, 2,4) as she is called now, when, in a courtly gesture, she welcomes him and takes him by the hand. But given the secret (293,4) and loving (293,3) looks she sends him and the friendly squeezing of his hand: "si het im holden willen kunt vil sciere getân" (294,4), this gesture may be viewed as a prelude to love, in which Kriemhild is now ready to participate. The ritualized kiss of welcome (297,3) thus gains a transritual and individualizing significance (297,4). At the same time, we observe another typical characteristic of the epic process: it is not aimed at psychological reflection. Thoughts and feelings are revealed through gestures on which the poet occasionally offers a comment, e.g., mentioning the "holden willen," as in the case above, or telling us a little later that in the days that followed, Kriemhild, in her "ze hove gân," was seen daily in the presence of Siegfried, and then his comment: "der dienst wart dem recken durch grôze liebe getân" (305,4). The epic provides the platform for great feelings, be they of love or (later) revenge.

Kriemhild is again the center of attention but now in the context of a mass scene in which she and Siegfried stand out. In contrast to the first *Âventiure*, she plays a less prominent role and becomes less and less important. She is not *the* protagonist. As the epitome of the courtly lady, she now sees to the preparation of the precious and appropriate garments needed for

[10] Compare *Hohes Lied* 6,10; Hartmann von Aue's *Erec*, vv. 1768–81; Gottfried von Straßburg's *Tristan*, vv. 7291f.; 10886f.

[11] See Schweikle, *Mittelhochdeutsche Minnelyrik I: Frühe Minnelyrik*.

the courting at Isenstein (354–366); only after Siegfried tells her the news about the arrival of Brünhild at the Burgundian court (ninth *Âventiure*), does she appear again — but then always at the side of men, playing the part of the caring woman so typical of Arthurian romance and heroic epic. As a representative character she is elevated: Siegfried leads her horse when she rides to meet her future sister-in-law (582) — a scene lifted directly from the textbook for courtly behavior.

This service leads to the first act of the marriage ceremony, which is concluded after the preliminary question is posed by the oldest brother, the *volo* of the bride, and the "ze wîbe loben" of the bridegroom, the "umbevâhen" and the "küssen" inside the circle of men (612–616). The wedding is concluded with the "bîligen" (629) and the subsequent "wîhen" in the minster (645). In the ritual of consent and in the last act, the marriage *in facie ecclesiae*, the poet demonstrates his conformity to the growing influence of the church.

Kriemhild's query regarding the sudden disappearance of Siegfried on the evening after the wedding-night (662), when he agreed to help Gunther subdue Brünhild, prompts no reaction from Siegfried (684,1). It is only after he is crowned king in Xanten that he presents her with the ring and belt (684,2f.). The poet grants his audience at this point some considerable leeway for psychological interpretation, while he himself is only interested in the inevitability of this act: "swaz er ir geben solde, wie lützel erz belîben lie!" (684,4). Although one may associate "solde" with fate,[12] it is also possible to "demystify" it and regard it as a mere game the poet is playing with the knowledge of his audience. It is not until the quarrel of the queens that the full impact of both the relevance and problematics of epic silence, as well as the liberty of reception, becomes apparent.

In the meantime, the poet draws attention to a facet of Kriemhild's personality which has not hitherto been illuminated: her awareness of the significance of representation. Until now, this has only been shown in the case of Kriemhild in connection with the performance of courtly ritual. With Siegfried having already turned down her inheritance (694f.), she expresses her desire to take at least some of the Burgundian warriors with her, namely, Hagen, Ortwin, and their relatives. Hagen, however, strenuously objects (698f.), even though she had only asked if these men would like to accompany her (698,2). She did not order them to do so, which would have been possible in accordance with Gernot's offer (697,1), but which also would have deprived Burgundy of its best heroes. What lies at the root of her question? Is there more to it than the manifestation of pride felt by the old nobility and which is clearly expressed in Hagen's words: "wir suln in langer

[12] As de Boor does in his commentary to the verse.

dienen, den wir alher gevolget hân" (699,4)? Whatever the case, the poet has again provided an opportunity for a powerful psychological interpretation that situates Kriemhild's behavior between naiveté and power consciousness, an opportunity similar to that afforded at the beginning of the *senna*, when Kriemhild initiates the conversation between herself and Brünhild.

Kriemhild's attempt to define herself not only through her husband but also through herself, her inheritance, and her dowry — feudal society did not know any other way to define a woman — is ultimately destined to fail because of love. Kriemhild renounces her rights.

Even at this point, she is not the person who determines the course of the plot. That person is Siegfried, who is accorded particular attention in the eleventh *Âventiure*, and the following *âventiuren* are dominated by Brünhild who — after a decade — is determined to unravel the events surrounding her courtship, and finally Hagen, who keeps a close eye on the mighty "vriunt" from the Netherlands. It is thus mere coincidence that Kriemhild is the one to set the dramatic action in motion, to which she will ultimately fall victim. She does this by uttering a remarkable statement in the presence of her sister-in-law, while they are watching the men at their jousting: "ich hân einen man,/daz elliu disiu rîche ze sînen handen solden stân" (815,3b-4.). It is so very difficult to justify such a remark from a psychological point of view. Its immediate effect is to destroy the peaceful atmosphere that has prevailed. Brünhild, who is "vil wæge" (812,2) towards her guests, certainly has no intention of starting a quarrel. Moreover, that Kriemhild does not set out to provoke her sister-in-law is quite apparent from the nature of her personality as it has been presented to us so far, as well as through the manner in which she comports herself during the further course of the conversation. The poet lets her paint the borrowed image of the radiant moon before the stars (817, 3), one which he had already used to portray Kriemhild during the first meeting of the lovers (283,1). This image serves to recall that meeting, i.e., the "great love"; despite Brünhild's insistence that Gunther is the more powerful man, Kriemhild reacts in a somewhat subdued manner: Siegfried is "wol Gunthers genôz" (819,4). Even Brünhild tries to restrain herself (820,1), and explains why she has good reason to assume that Siegfried is "eigen" (821,3). Kriemhild rejects this "vil friuntlîche" (822, 3). For these reasons, Brünhild ought to "die rede lâzen" (822,4), whereby "rede" could refer to "the talking," but also "the topic," as well as "the slander." Brünhild, who is by no means seeking to unleash a quarrel, insists on her rights: "zwiu sold ich verkiesen sô maniges ritters lîp..." (823,2). At this point, Kriemhild loses her patience (823,4); she puts her husband above the Burgundian king (824f.), and scornfully asks why Siegfried, were he one of Gunther's vassals, has not paid any tribute, and she even accuses Brünhild of "übermüete" (825,4). Now she is the one who has been insulted. The resolution of this conflict, a legal judgment, is not possible on a private level, but can only be effected through a "show trial":

> Du muost daz hiute schouwen, daz ich bin adelvrî,
> unt daz mîn man ist tiwerr, danne der dîne sî. (828,1f.)

Kriemhild makes careful preparations for this "trial," which consists of seeing who should enter the cathedral first.

Our understanding of the scene up to this point is based on what we view as the poet's effort to consolidate his multifaceted profile of Kriemhild: she sees her husband denigrated, she "stands by her man," and consistently demonstrates that she is the grand and power-conscious lover who rejects Brünhild's pretentious claims. The fact that she herself had used some phrases at the beginning of the discussion which at least give the impression that she entertains similar claims with respect to Siegfried, seems to have been forgotten, but it remains the crux of our interpretation. It has often been the case that readers have elected not to diminish the significance of Kriemhild's words from a psychological perspective by regarding them as naive, an expression of her love, or as somewhat flippantly expressed "wishful thinking"[13] concerning her status. In such instances, another image emerges, one that suggests that Kriemhild's words do, in fact, represent an actual claim to power,[14] and that an awareness of such power was already evident in her desire to take Hagen and his "vriunde" back with her to the Netherlands. Kriemhild may be seen as simply "showing her true colors" in the *senna.* One might also agree with the poet's later remark regarding the outbreak of fighting in the Great Hall of Etzel: "Dô der strît niht anders kunde sîn erhaben" (1912,1), or underscore the way in which he worked with his sources and the ultimate structure of his work. In any case, it would be necessary to abandon the concept of a relatively coherent character delineation (one that was particularly molded by love), or even the idea that the poet possessed either the intention or the ability to describe it.

Interpretations are determined by methodological predispositions. *We* have tried to put ourselves into the position of the poet and his (already knowledgeable) audience and, from this perspective, have attempted to read the text in a "well meaning" way. Other interpreters — and how can we take it amiss? — prefer a more "rigorous," "critical" reading of the text which is

[13] See Ehrismann, *Nibelungenlied. Epoche—Werk—Wirkung* 140.

[14] See Siegfried Beyschlag's political reading of the text: "Das Motiv der Macht bei Siegfrieds Tod [1952]," in Karl Hauck, ed., *Zur germanisch-deutschen Heldensage* (Darmstadt: Wissenschaftliche Buchgesellschaft, 1965) 195–213.

intended to show where the poet might have made his work "better," "more logical," and "more coherent."

The "show trial" in front of the cathedral ends on a particularly dramatic note for Brünhild because Kriemhild is in a position to produce the ring and belt as proof of Siegfried's superiority over Gunther. She returns the slight of being called an "eigen diu" (838,4) by insulting Brünhild through her reference to her as Siegfried's "kebse" (839,4).[15] The image that is presented of the two women is constructed in such a way that each one can perceive herself subjectively to be in the right, even if objectively, in the eyes of the audience, neither one is. By reducing Siegfried, who at Isenstein was introduced to her as a "man," to the status of "eigenman," Brünhild goes too far, just as Kriemhild does when she makes the claim in her presence: "jane was ez niht mîn bruoder, der dir den magetuom an gewan" (840,4). Siegfried later swears (858–861) that he never told his wife any such thing and he will see to it that, in accordance with his marital right to call her to task (894), she repents of her "üppeclîche[n] sprüche" (862,2). Even these exaggerations have sound subjective reasons but they cannot be justified objectively. Moreover, Kriemhild's words: "kundestu noch geswîgen, daz wære dir guot" (839,2) can be interpreted as a last attempt at reconciliation.

The mosaic-like profile of Kriemhild is rounded out by her conversation with Hagen, during which she expresses regret at the manner in which she acted in Brünhild's presence and then betrays the secret of Siegfried's vulnerable spot (892–905), as well as the parting scene prior to the hunt, from which she tries in vain to restrain her husband. Here, as well, the poet employs various borrowed motifs in an effort to paint, in warm and heartfelt colors, a picture of great love. To Kriemhild, Siegfried is the "holde[] wine" (898,2), in his eyes, she is a "holde[] triutinne" (996,4; compare also 919,1). Love makes both of them blind, especially with respect to the danger emanating from Hagen. It is out of love that they act "naively" and "thoughtlessly," not because they are "naive characters."

II. *Revenge*

The poet makes repeated, deliberate references to this great feeling of love, especially before Siegfried's death. Kriemhild's fainting spell when she learns about the dead knight lying before the door of her chamber (1009, 1), and her loud scream shortly thereafter (1009,4), as well as her wish to open the casket to kiss her dead husband for the last time (1068f.), are further indications of the depth of this feeling. It now becomes directly associated

[15] For a man to have a mistress in Germanic society was not unusual, nor did it have a negative effect on his wife's honor.

with the thought of revenge: "wesse ich, wer iz het getân, ich riet' im immer sînen tôt" (1012,4). She knows, of course, who is responsible (1010,4), but she needs proof and, above all, as a woman who, given the prevailing system of justice, did not have the right to engage in a feud, she needs men who are prepared to assist her in any attempt to avenge the death of her husband. She presents her case to the public by calling for the "Bahrprobe," the "schouwen" (the test before the bier), which reveals Hagen to be the murderer. She desires a successful outcome to her plan for revenge, and that becomes abundantly clear when she prevents Siegmund from acting recklessly and spontaneously after the death of his son.

A vendetta for murder, revenge for injured honor: such thoughts are in no way alien to Christian feudal society,[16] but Kriemhild follows a pattern of revenge with roots buried deeply in (written) Germanic tradition. This must be kept in mind if her further actions are to be understood in their historical (and not just in a general human) context:

> Die Ekstase der Germanen wird im Augenblick der Rache erreicht [...] Die Rache macht sie groß, weil sie jede Möglichkeit in ihnen entfaltet — nicht nur einige wenige blutdürstige Eigenschaften [...] Aber sie lehrt sie auch warten, sich besinnen, berechnen; jahraus und jahrein kann ein Mann warten und wägen, alle seine Pläne darauf einstellen, die flüchtigste Gelegenheit für eine Ehrenabrechnung zu ergreifen; ja sogar seine täglichen Verrichtungen in der Wirtschaft, wenn er sein Heu und sein Vieh besorgt, werden so zurechtgelegt, daß er immer nach den Wegen Ausschau halten und jeden Augenblick sehen kann, ob der erwünschte Mann vorüberreiten sollte. Die Rache lehrt ihn, mit Zeit und Raum wie mit Kleinigkeiten zu rechnen. Er wird von der Erinnerung durch die Zeit getragen, und er kann über Land und Meer getrieben werden nach einem Ziel, das er vor sich sieht.[17]

[16] See Antje Holzhauer, *Rache und Fehde in der mittelhochdeutschen Literatur des 12. und 13. Jahrhunderts*, GAG 639 (Göppingen: Kümmerle, 1997). Given the relevance of this topic even in Arthurian romance, Friedrich Maurer's identification of it with the "altgermanische[n] Wert der Ehre" (*Leid. Studien zur Bedeutungs- und Problemgeschichte, besonders in den großen Epen der staufischen Zeit*, 4th ed. [Berne and Munich: Francke, 1969] 22) is not really compelling.

[17] Wilhelm Grönbech, *Kultur und Religion der Germanen*, 11th ed., 2 vols. (Darmstadt: Wissenschaftliche Buchgesellschaft, 1991) 1: 77f.

With his application of the great theme of revenge,[18] the poet begins to imbue his subject matter heavily with basic archaic structures. He evokes the nostalgic image of an heroic age. This is not done, however, in order to play it off against courtly civilization as has been suggested by various interpretations, up to and including some that were popular during the National Socialist period. It is also not meant to propagate some sort of lesson, a horrendous deterrent, as those interpretations with a marked didactic bent would have it. In the style and spirit of the *carmen heroicum*, the poet propels his audience into what one might call an "epic frenzy." The audience is meant to take "delight" (*delectare*) in its magnificent past, to reaffirm its great history, while the "didactic" element (*prodesse*), is to be found in the catharsis, the "cleansing" process of sharing joy and pain (συμπαεια). This epic is not concerned with the sense or senselessness of heroism,[19] but focuses rather on its enjoyment by the audience. It is not the poet's intention to present an argument against the heroic world or against courtly life. (It is another matter as to how potential audiences of both sexes have "enjoyed" the work, right up to the present day.)

Immersion in the archaic structures of revenge is a gradual process. Moreover, priority is given to their "tempered" feudal equivalents. To the bitter end, Kriemhild makes an effort not to deviate from the path of legality. She asks God to help her in her quest for revenge — nothing unusual for the poetry of the time: "nu lâz ez got errechen noch sîner vriunde hant" (1046,2).

Kriemhild remains at the Burgundian court, where she has more "vriunde" than in the Netherlands, because of the special plea put forth by Giselher (1078–83). He had not participated in the hunt and had, furthermore, vehemently opposed the plan to kill Siegfried. His words: "jâ wil ich dich ergetzen dînes mannes tôt" (1080,3), contain no mention of the idea

[18] Kriemhild does not have a monopoly on acts and thoughts of revenge in the *Nibelungenlied*. One can point to the Nibelungs and to Siegmund, who would like to avenge Siegfried, to Alberich, who wished to avenge his masters Schilbung and Nibelung, to the Bavarian nobles Gelpfrat and Else, intent on avenging the death of their ferryman, the Thuringians and Danes, eager to avenge Iring, but also to Brünhild, who avenges the insult to her honor with the assistance of Hagen. When we speak of the "great theme of revenge," we are, of course, alluding to Kriemhild.

[19] See, however, Bert Nagel, *Das Nibelungenlied. Stoff — Form — Ethos* (Frankfurt a. M.: Hirschgraben-Verlag, 1965) 267f.: "Was am Ende des Liedes in den Blick tritt, ist recht eigentlich die Sinnlosigkeit der Heroik, das tragische Paradox, daß fanatische Selbstbehauptung zur Selbstzerstörung führt, die bedrückende Einsicht, daß auch konsequente Rache letztlich ins Leere stößt und menschliche Größe durch menschliche Hybris aufgehoben wird."

of revenge without, however, totally ruling it out. It becomes apparent only later that he is not thinking in terms of a vendetta: "wær' er niht mîn mâc, ez gienge im an den lîp" (1133,3). Siegmund, too, tries to influence her to come back to Xanten, where she would rule as queen, and be together with her little son: "swenne iuwer sun gewahset, der trœstet iu den muot (1087, 3). Once again the notion of revenge is avoided, although it is not excluded. Finally, Siegfried's men threaten to declare war on the Burgundians (1093). In each one of these cases, revenge is the obligation of the "vriunde." The basic structure of the epic unequivocally demands that Kriemhild remain in Worms and forego any form of immediate, direct revenge. Nevertheless, the poet is at pains to provide credible motivation for his character, whether it is a matter of believing that Kriemhild does not think the right moment for revenge is at hand (see 1030), or that she wishes to stay close to her beloved, murdered husband:

ich muoz hie belîben, swaz halt mir geschiht,
bî den mînen mâgen, die mir helfen klagen. (1088,2f.)

Great love occasions great grief (1099). In this phase of his narrative, the poet does not provide any hint as to how Kriemhild means to exact her revenge, he does not put any plan into her mind.[20] She spends her time piously and withdrawn in a building next to the cathedral and after three and a half years Giselher is successful in his effort to bring about a reconciliation between her and Gunther: "si verkôs ûf si alle wan ûf den einen man" (1115,3). She liberally distributes among the poor (1127) the gold from the hoard which Gernot and Giselher had brought to Worms and which, as we are only now informed (1116), constituted her dowry. Hagen regards this act of social welfare, something which most certainly belongs to the obligations of the aristocracy, as part of her plan of revenge (1128, 1130). While it could be considered as such, there is no compelling reason to do so. The poet speaks of "vil guoter tugende" (1127,4). In any event, Hagen takes this as a pretense to sink the hoard in the Rhine, so that Kriemhild is once again forced to bear considerable grief: "Mit iteniuwen leiden beswaeret was ir muot" (1141,1). Hagen deprived her of what we would nowadays call "life insurance," which is exactly what the dowry signifies for a woman in legal terms. Now completely without protection and thus needing a "voget," she chooses Giselher (1135,2). By elevating the hoard to the status of a dowry (and making mention of it at precisely this point) the poet accords the gold

[20] For this reason I do not believe that it is necessary to accept the theory that she spends her years of mourning "mit keimhaften Gedanken an die Rache" (Werner Hoffmann, *Das Nibelungenlied*, Grundlagen und Gedanken zum Verständnis erzählender Literatur [Frankfurt a. M.: Diesterweg, 1987] 54).

symbolic significance. On two occasions, Kriemhild has been robbed of the protection of her husband, first through his murder and then through the theft of the treasure (just as Brünhild, in accordance with the principle of epic duplication, is subdued twice, first at Isenstein and then during her second wedding night).

After ten more years have passed, a total of thirteen years following Siegfried's death (1142,2), King Etzel courts "daz vil edel wîp" (1146,3). His ambassador, Rüdiger, is only able to persuade Kriemhild, after considerable hesitation, to marry the king when he secretly (1255,2) promises to give her assistance. The poet has him use the word "ergetzen," just as earlier had been the case with Giselher: "er wolde si ergetzen, swaz ir ie geschach" (1255,3). Rüdiger assures her further: "er müeses sêr' engelten, unt het iu iemen iht getân" (1256,4). This clear offer of help tempers the widow's pain (1255,4; 1257,1) and Rüdiger swears the oath she demands of him: he and all his men shall always serve her "mit triuwen" (as the vassal does his liege lord). She will be denied nothing which might contribute to her honor: "des si êre haben solde" (1258).[21]

This is a brief, yet key, scene which provides us with significant insight into the work of the poet. He denies his audience the opportunity of surveying Kriemhild's ideas as to how she might possibly take revenge. The reader is only informed about her great suffering and of her inability to forgive Hagen (1115,3). We are told about the pious life she leads, but has she really given up? Is Rüdiger the first to rekindle within her the thought of revenge or has she simply suppressed the urge, in accordance with the Germanic custom of "biding one's time"? Is she, by nature, "lancræche" (1461,4), as Hagen describes her? By leaving open such questions, which were undoubtedly obvious even to the contemporary audience, the poet combines the mentality of Germanic *alte mæren*, heroic poetry, with that of his own new age. He also repeatedly resorts to the motif of suffering caused by love ("ich jâmerhaftez wîp," 1259,3). Can one think of a shrewder way of showing the intersection of knightly-Christian and Germanic-heroic concepts of revenge?

[21] The content of the oath demanded by Kriemhild was as follows: "sô swert mir eide, swaz mir iemen getuot,/daz ir sît der næhste, der büeze mîniu leit" (1257,2f.). From a grammatical perspective, "getuot" refers to the future (see Hermann Paul, Peter Wiehl, and Siegfried Grosse, *Mittelhochdeutsche Grammatik*, 23rd ed. [Tübingen: Niemeyer, 1989], § 306). Note, however, Ehrismann, *Nibelungenlied. Epoche — Werk — Wirkung* 163. Rüdiger's oath of service is not confined to particular deeds and he himself had, after all, included the past when considering it. How much weight should be placed on the future sense of "getuot," which harks back to the preceding "hiet getân" and rhymes with "muot"? Certainly not to the point of excluding the past deeds of Hagen, which constitute Kriemhild's "leit."

With Rüdiger's promise to protect her rights in time of need and the prospect of having at her disposal Etzel's "recken" (1260,1) and ***rîchtuom*** (note 1260,3), as well as the assurance that she may remain a Christian, Kriemhild turns her back on the Burgundian court. She departs with a large entourage of well-dressed maidens (1286),[22] escorted by Margrave Eckewart and his 500 men (1283f.), and bringing along the remains of her dowry which she has managed to preserve (1271). She is quite the ***grande dame*** and she is welcomed as such by Etzel's army on the plains of Tolna. The wedding and the consummation of the marriage take place in Vienna at Pentecost : "si wæn' sô manigen man/bî ir êrsten manne nie ze dienste gewan" (1365, 3b–4). This gives us a hint of Kriemhild's frame of mind (compare 1368), and the tears flow because she cannot help but think of Siegfried.

From the time of Rüdiger's wooing mission on, the poet focuses more and more on Kriemhild, who now becomes the major catalyst for action within the narrative. It is not the murderer Hagen, even though in the first part of the epic the action revolved around him, Siegfried, and Brünhild. He only ***reacts*** as her opponent, even if his appearances, as well as the battle scenes (which are described in great detail, in contrast to anything one finds in romance), are occasionally accorded prominence in their own right.

Kriemhild, with a power base that even Siegfried did not have at his disposal — to this extent the poet has allowed her actions to unfold in a consistent and plausible manner — is now in a position to exact her revenge. She is characterized in complete accordance with the Germanic-heroic pattern (and with clear adherence to the manuscript tradition), which does not, however, exclude Christian influences (see 1730,4). She comes into her own through the reflective and intentional manner in which she pursues her vendetta (whereby, as we already know, time has no significance). First of all, she convinces her husband to invite her Burgundian relatives to Etzelnburg (***Âventiure*** 23) after thirteen years have passed (1390), and her preliminary strategy also includes an attempt to separate Hagen from his "vriunde." However, he successfully thwarts her efforts in this regard, which ultimately results in the destruction of the entire Burgundian army and tens of thousands of Hunnish warriors. Some of the details of this heroic "show-down" are particularly significant for the characterization of Kriemhild, who is repeatedly referred to as an avenging fury, as having become, in effect, what her enemies refer to as a "vâlandinne," a "she-devil," an "inhuman witch."

Throughout all of these years, she has not forgotten the incredible suffering she has had to endure (1391–97). The poet draws a parallel

[22] 1286,1 refers to 100 maidens, 1294,1 to "Hundert unde viere," which is to be understood as "(a few) more than/just over a hundred" rather than 104.

between her in this state and Brünhild, who felt herself betrayed by Gunther. Soon after their arrival, Dietrich warns the Burgundians (now also called Nibelungs): "Kriemhilt noch sêre weinet den helt von Nibelunge lant" (1724,4), and shortly afterwards he continues:

> ich hœre alle morgen weinen unde klagen
> mit jâmerlîchen sinnen daz Etzelen wîp
> dem rîchen got von himele des starken Sîfrides lîp. (1730,2–4)

With these words, the poet's audience is once again made keenly aware of the tremendous feeling of love that motivates Kriemhild's revenge.

Kriemhild has the "gesinde" of Dancwart assigned quarters separate from the others (1735). This is the first stage in her plan for revenge and the second follows swiftly on its heels. She receives the Nibelungs "mit valschem muote" (1737,2), i.e., not according to the rules of hospitality. Only Giselher, at one time her "voget," is granted a kiss of welcome (1737,3). From Hagen she demands the return of the hoard, the loss of which she laments daily (1743,4). Everyone knows of her incessant grieving for Siegfried. The poet, clearly striving to provide a "noble" reason for Kriemhild's demand that the treasure be returned and her apparent eagerness to lay her hands on the gold, implies an identification of Siegfried and the hoard, an idea he had already developed earlier. One may reject such a rationalization, although it is often advanced by scholars. If one chooses to do so, however, Kriemhild's demand then makes no sense and can only be seen as the relic of an old source with which the poet has tried to cope in a somewhat awkward fashion. This, too, is an explanation which has often been suggested.

Kriemhild aims at an expedient and, if at all possible, bloodless resolution of the matter. This is evident in her request that the Burgundians hand their weapons over to her (1745,2f.), which is, however, promptly and defiantly rebuffed by Hagen. This signals to her that the Burgundians are aware of the danger (1747). She would like to see dead the person who has warned them, but as the latter is Dietrich, who, moreover, insults her by calling her a "vâlandinne" (1748,4), she quietly retreats in shame (1749,1). Once again she has been denigrated by Hagen and her revenge thwarted. The poet thus continues to work on this motif, with his main task being to provide a basis for the dimensions which her revenge will later assume.

He is assisted in this regard by Hagen's subsequent behavior. Hagen sits down together with Volker in front of Kriemhild's chamber: "Ez mante si ir leide: weinen si began" (1763,1). She calls upon Etzel's men, who have shown pity for her: "rechet mich an Hagene, daz er vliese den lîp" (1765,4). With these words she has expressed openly both her suffering and the goal she has set, and has appealed to the public to assist her in exacting revenge. In this respect, the only legal recourse left open to a woman in feudal society is through "instigation." Four hundred and sixty warriors offer to help (1766,1; 1769,3). Needless to say, no one ultimately dares to fight the two Burgundians, and Kriemhild is forced to endure a double insult. Once again the tears flow from her eyes (1784,3) because Hagen has placed Siegfried's sword "über sîniu bein" (1783,1) and openly identified himself as her husband's murderer (1790,2). He has also admitted to having caused her much suffering: "leides vil getân" (1791,4). Yet, he has also justified his actions, undertaken because "diu vrouwe Kriemhilt die schœnen Prünhilden schalt" (1790,4).

Kriemhild's warriors plan to attack the Nibelungs at night, a tactic that has obviously been designed by her, as "ir muot" becomes "vil grimmec" (1848,3) when she learns that it has failed. The warriors had retreated when they recognized Hagen and Volker were guarding the Nibelungs. The poet has now associated the epithet "grimmec" with the character of Kriemhild. Her vendetta has taken on a new dimension. Hagen is responsible for this escalation, but so is Dietrich, who informed Hagen of Kriemhild's plans and, by so doing, prevented her from exacting her revenge in a swift and expedient manner.[23]

Volker, in a move that is intended to provoke their enemies, kills a foppish Hunnish warrior during the tournament. Only the intervention of Etzel (1894), who is intent on observing the peace normally extended to guests (1897,1), averts the outbreak of a large-scale clash in this highly volatile situation. Nibelungs and Huns retire to the banquet in the Great Hall of Etzel's palace. In the meantime, Dietrich rejects Kriemhild's request for assistance in her attempt to avenge herself (1899–1902), and she therefore turns to Blœdel. He is easy to bribe and attacks the servants under the leadership of Dancwart, who, lodged in quarters apart from the others, are unarmed, and thus an easy prey.

In the meantime Kriemhild — shrewdly following two different tactics[24] — tries to ignite the quarrel in the hall among the "important characters" by having her six-year-old son Ortlieb brought in. Again the poet emphasizes: "(Kriemhilt ir leit daz alte in ir herzen was begraben)" (1912,2). Steeped as he is in traditional saga material, the poet has to work against the Atreus

[23] This is in keeping with the logic of epic space. I have refrained from discussing here the possibility that Hagen did not, in fact, know already what was afoot.

[24] If we accept this interpretation, then the sentence: "Dô der strît niht anders kunde sîn erhaben" (1912,1) does not represent any sort of inconsistency. The outbreak of hostilities is orchestrated on two levels, one involving the "unimportant," and the other the "important" people. In addition, the poet remains consistent with his stylistic principle of duplication.

motif, which is also well known in Norse sagas. Ortlieb is killed by Hagen, but only after word has reached the men in the Great Hall of the sneak attack on the Burgundian servants (1960f.). The verse: "wie kunde ein wîp durch râche immer vreislîcher tuon" (1912,4) raises the suspicion[25] — and it is no more than this — that Kriemhild actually intended this to happen. The poet thus ascribes to her character the cruel features of an avenger, but at the same time he distances himself from the latter as one who does not share such sentiments, and thus adopts the mood of his audience.[26] By not going into the matter of the difference, or the correspondence, between intention and result, and by not specifically saying that she truly desired Ortlieb's death, the poet tempers considerably the old image of revenge, and, however dimly, allows the softer features of the loving woman to shine through.

The struggle which is unleashed in the Great Hall following the death of Ortlieb produces yet another disaster for Kriemhild: Siegfried's murderer is still alive. Dietrich, Rüdiger, and their men did not participate in the fighting. Seven thousand Hunnish warriors have been killed.[27] She is once again insulted by Hagen (2024), Iring and his Danish warriors fall in battle, and thousands of Thuringians under Hawart are destroyed. Etzel, now in complete support of his wife, makes a futile attempt to send 20,000 warriors into battle on the evening of the same day, renouncing "vride unde suone" (2090,4). The Burgundian kings rally around their vassal Hagen: "doch wolden nie gescheiden die fürsten und ihr man" (2110,3). After all of this, Kriemhild hopes to end the misery by setting the hall on fire. She is defeated by Hagen's will power and the feudal legal system. Even the 1200 warriors who later fight against the Nibelungs — by now suffering terribly from the heat (2133) — do not change the situation.

It is only at this point that, in keeping with the pattern of epic expansion, Kriemhild (together with Etzel) asks the one man for help who once swore to stand by her regardless of the situation (2148f.), and who, at least until now, has held back out of consideration for his Burgundian "vriunde." She suggests to Rüdiger that the time has come to fulfil his promise: "des wart mir armem wîbe nie sô grœzlîche nôt" (2149,4). He provides good reasons for rejecting her request, but because the king and queen beg him on their

[25] Manuscript C frees Kriemhild of any such suspicion. Ortlieb's appearance in the Great Hall is entirely coincidental.

[26] It is wise not to associate modern mother-child feelings with this scene. Ortlieb is Etzel's heir, and Kriemhild has never loved Etzel.

[27] According to 2013,2. The number approximates the number of Burgundian servants, underscoring once again the "strategy of doubling" by the poet and the clever insertion of verse 1912,1. Manuscript C, however, ignores that strategy by reducing the number to 2000.

knees (2152) — this scene mirrors the start of the battle when Kriemhild falls to her knees before the Hunnish warriors (1765,3) — he *must* fight for them, as this gesture requires. Rüdiger's decision brings tears to Kriemhild's eyes (2166, 2). Once again the poet is at pains to portray her as "human," and this is particularly the case in her lamentation over the death of Rüdiger: "si klageten ungefuoge des guoten Rüedegêres lîp" (2234,4).

The demise of Rüdiger and his 500 men leads — also in accord with the principle of epic expansion — to the involvement of Dietrich who, like Rüdiger, loses all his men. Later, however, he is able to capture both Hagen and Gunther in accordance with protocol: first the vassal and then his liege lord. He turns them over to the queen, whose goal of bloody revenge has not yet been fully achieved. Even Dietrich cannot prevent her from exacting it.

The poet emphasizes the image of the "grimmeclîchen" avenger (2365, 3) who now demands that Hagen return the hoard (here its symbolic significance becomes quite apparent), has Gunther killed, and finally cuts down Hagen herself. While this completely flies in the face of legal propriety, it is fully in accord with the Germanic custom requiring that the weapon be wielded by the injured party.[28] She does so with the image of Siegfried before her and it is with his sword that she beheads Hagen: "daz truoc mîn holder vriedel, dô ich in jungest sach" (2372,3). Siegfried — this is the only way the symbolism of the sword can be understood — kills Hagen, and no one but Kriemhild, being one with Siegfried, could become the instrument for this symbolic action. In reality, however, it represents a blatant transgression against the prevailing law because a woman could never actively participate in a feud.

Hildebrand refers to this illegality when he cuts her "ze stücken" (2377, 2). For the last time (yet even at this late point!), the poet calls her "daz edele wîp" (2377,2). *He* does not join in condemning her as a "vâlandinne" as had Dietrich and subsequently Hagen (2371,4). Kriemhild fails in her quest for justice because those individuals whose duty it was to guarantee it have, in fact, denied it to her. She *did* have the right to seek revenge, and the poet has tried to explain to his aristocratic audience (which is beginning to acquire the tastes of courtly society) the connection between the intensity of her feelings and the depth of the love which bound Kriemhild and Siegfried to one another. He has also added depth to the legal, heroic action in accordance with the pattern of courtly psychology and, in the process, bestowed upon Kriemhild an image which is transformed from softness into hardness in reaction to the way she is treated. Her transformation, as well as the ever-increasing stoniness of her personality during the celebrations in

[28] Note Grönbech 79.

Etzelnburg, are understandably motivated by her reaction to the repeated provocations and setbacks that she is forced to endure.

Appreciation

After having spent thirteen years in Etzelnburg, Kriemhild believes that the time for revenge is at hand, and she pursues this goal steadfastly with all of the legal and political possibilities open to her. She does not come into her own as an avenger in the manner one would expect of the Germanic model.[29] The poet makes a consistent effort to underscore how much she suffers as a consequence of the course that events have taken. She takes no joy in her revenge; were she to do so, she would, in fact, be the "demon,"[30] that "she-devil,"[31] who is obsessed with a "blind ethos of revenge," or the "avenging fury,"[32] as eloquently described by some scholars. She is, however, consistent in her pursuit of revenge, and in this respect she owes much to the Germanic model. Her essence is not that of a "vâlandinne," but rather of a woman who is simply seeking justice. Revenge was a legitimate motive for action in the thinking of that time, as was the use of force. The extent of her revenge which, given Hagen's actions, Kriemhild is forced to pursue (even though at the beginning she clearly did *not* want to), can be attributed to the poetry of the *carmen heroicum.* The genre demands these dimensions and it also requires the dramatic showdown. That is not something for which a moralizing reader should take the poet to task. Moreover, *within this context,* even the question of Kriemhild's responsibility for the deaths of thousands of men is immaterial. The poet is not concerned with it.[33] He simply bears responsibility for the art of motivation and in this respect he repeatedly tempers, in a fashion reminiscent of courtly romance, the rough contours of the older material and uses psychological methods to deal with them.

[29] See Grönbech 76–78.

[30] See, for example, Bodo Mergell, "Nibelungenlied und höfischer Roman" [1950], in Heinz Rupp, ed., *Nibelungenlied und Kudrun* (Darmstadt: Wissenschaftliche Buchgesellschaft, 1976) 3–39; here 15. Also: Gottfried Weber, *Das Nibelungenlied. Problem und Idee* (Stuttgart: Metzler, 1963) 12.

[31] For example, Nagel 255. Also: Marianne Wahl Armstrong, *Rolle und Charakter. Studien zur Menschendarstellung im Nibelungenlied,* GAG 221 (Göppingen: Kümmerle, 1979) 129 and 291.

[32] See Karl Heinz Ihlenburg, *Das Nibelungenlied. Problem und Gehalt* (Berlin: Akademie-Verlag, 1969) 10 and 51.

[33] See, however, Werner Schröder, "Die Tragödie Kriemhilts im Nibelungenlied," in W.S., *Nibelungenlied-Studien* (Stuttgart: Metzler, 1968) 48–156, particularly 151. The two passages cited as evidence, 1827,4 ("von ir schulden ligen tôt") and 1024,4 ("von den mînen schulden") are to be understood in the most general sense.

The *carmen heroicum*, which deals with grand emotions (on the basis of the feudal-aristocratic ideology) is centered in itself, and, by virtue of the genre, mainly focused on the plausibility of the motivation, not on gauging "human" behavior, or the possibilities of same. In the case of Kriemhild, it is not a matter of her "womanhood" or her "humanity" or even her exemplary status. In its reception of the epic, the later, educated middle class[34] limited itself to such interests when indulging in its nostalgia for the magnificent, noble feelings of the past, and it is this nostalgia which accounts for the enormous success enjoyed by the work during this period of reception.

The image of Kriemhild which the poet gradually assembles like a mosaic does not condense into a coherent biography. There are just too many missing pieces. Kriemhild is not "from beginning to end in the center of the action."[35] The epic is not constituted so as to profile only *one* character. As Goethe remarked at the beginning of the second part of his *Wahlverwandtschaften*:

> Im gemeinen Leben begegnet uns oft, was wir in der Epopöe als Kunstgriff des Dichters zu rühmen pflegen, daß nämlich, wenn die Hauptfiguren sich entfernen, verbergen, sich der Untätigkeit hingeben, gleich sodann schon ein Zweiter, Dritter, bisher kaum Bemerkter den Platz füllt und, indem er seine ganze Tätigkeit äußert, uns gleichfalls der Aufmerksamkeit, der Teilnahme, ja des Lobes und Preises würdig erscheint.[36]

There are many *âventiuren* in which Kriemhild is not present, where she is not the motivating force. Even at the conclusion of the work, at which point she is, in fact, just that, individual warriors are singled out and accorded *their* moment on stage, *their* heroic deeds. Kriemhild's power is enormous, but it is not *the* unifying force. The *Nibelungenlied* cannot, therefore, be described as a "Kriemhild novel" as has often been done by scholars.[37] The poet has indeed endowed the work with some of the characteristics of a novel, but the "unity of the epic" is not solely or ultimately based on the unity of Kriem-

[34] The concept "educated middle class" ("bildungsbürgerlich") is taken from Ulrich Wehler, *Deutsche Gesellschaftsgeschichte*, 2 vols. (Munich: Beck, 1989) and Lothar Gall, *Bürgertum in Deutschland* (Berlin: Goldmann, 1996).

[35] Hoffmann 46.

[36] Johann Wolfgang von Goethe, *Die Wahlverwandtschaften*, in *Werke*, Hamburger Ausgabe, vol. 6: *Romane und Novellen*, ed. Benno von Wiese and Erich Trunz, 6th ed. (Hamburg: Christian Wegner, 1965) 360.

[37] See Andreas Heusler, *Nibelungensage and Nibelungenlied*, 6th ed. (Dortmund: Ruhfus, 1965) 57. On the research, see Ehrismann, *Nibelungenlied. Epoche — Werk — Wirkung* 224–228.

hild's "character."[38] The unity of the *Nibelungenlied* is achieved by means of various "unifying components." Primary among them is the theme expressed in "wie liebe mit leide ze jungest lônen kan" (17,3), which is certainly demonstrated through the death of Siegfried and the great battle at Etzelnburg. Then there is the gradual development of the images of Siegfried, Kriemhild, Brünhild, Gunther, and Hagen, as well as those persons who do not greatly influence the plot, but whose fate is portrayed in the work: Iring, Rüdiger, Dietrich, etc. In Hegel's terms:[39] the description of a "condition of the world," so typical for epic, and the "collision of characters," the "totality" — and this seduces the reader into elevating Kriemhild to the position of a "main person" who is singularly responsible for insuring unity — is not simply removed through the heavy focus placed on Kriemhild with the aim of producing a novel-like setting. The latter comes into being with the move to written texts, particularly the Arthurian courtly romances. As a consequence, "der Nibelunge nôt" and "Kriemhilden nôt" acquire a tension which is specific to the genre and which the poet makes no effort to resolve. It is for this reason that the *Nibelungenlied* cannot be viewed as representing a particular, coherent genre. It constitutes, in effect, its own genre, which was only possible because of *its* specific reception.

In the person of Kriemhild, the poet has presented the image of an unmistakably "strong" character, someone who is controlled by circumstances, but who may occasionally control them herself. Her actions are motivated by the grand sentiments of love and revenge. She does not, however, merely act out a part, because she experiences these feelings as an individual and develops her plan for revenge in an individual manner by allowing it to expand. The poet certainly does not, however, "transform" her personality from that of "a loving maiden into an avenging shrew,"[40] because the thought of revenge strikes her immediately upon viewing the dead Siegfried, as it must in keeping with the medieval concept of honor: "wesse ich, wer iz het getân, ich riet' im immer sînen tôt" (1012,4).[41]

[38] See Werner Schröder 48.

[39] See in this regard Hildegard Bartels, *Epos — die Gattung in der Geschichte. Eine Begriffsbestimmung vor dem Hintergrund der Hegelschen »Ästhetik« anhand von »Nibelungenlied« und »Chanson de Roland«*, Frankfurter Beiträge zur Germanistik 22 (Heidelberg: Winter, 1982).

[40] This formulation, or something quite similar to it, can often be found in secondary literature. The above quote is taken from Julius Schwietering, *Deutsche Dichtung des Mittelalters* (Potsdam: Athenaion, [1932]) 200.

[41] It should be emphasized that we are dealing here only with the thought of revenge, not the manner in which this revenge is developed and expanded. Thus the view that the "vengeful she-devil" has "always been there as a psychological possibility for her (i.e., Kriemhild)" (Bert Nagel, *Staufische Klassik. Deutsche Dichtung um 1200*

The epic poet does portray Kriemhild as a "developing"[42] character, as *one, differentiated* personality, but (only) as an avenger, and then specifically after Siegfried's death, and not simply in the "second part" of the work. That personality is formed by the socio-legal constrictions and the resistance that she encounters in her attempts to secure revenge. With respect to the latter, she is not the agent of the Germanic model of vengeance,[43] according to which she would "come into her own" through exacting revenge. On the contrary, when she does, in fact, follow that model, she is virtually beside herself.

The motivation for her actions is the murder of her husband. Given the tenor of the time in which the work was written, this motivation is complemented by the theme of the great love which overlaps the revenge motif aimed at restoring her honor.[44] Opinions will certainly vary as to whether the new focus, which can be traced to the Arthurian novel, is appropriate, but to argue about it from a psychological perspective: *cui bono*?

Die Klage

The image of Kriemhild that prevails in Manuscript B only partially corresponds to the image that the author of the *Klage*-B manuscript accords her. In general, he tends to side with the characterization to be found in Manuscript C. The "defense strategy" of the *Klage*-poet has been observed on numerous occasions and only a few details need to be mentioned here.

[Heidelberg: Stiehm, 1977] 466) cannot be demonstrated, quite apart from the fact that this form of psychologizing is not appropriate here.

[42] Provided that the concept of "development" is not taken too far in a psychological sense, it appears to me to be quite fitting here. I do not see any plausible semantic difference between it and the term "Wandlung" ("inner change," see Hoffmann 47). The concept "Entfaltung," on the other hand, presumes a disposition towards becoming a "merciless avenger," which contradicts the efforts of the poet to "develop" Kriemhild's actions as a reaction to the actions undertaken by the Burgundians (see fn. 40), while the term "Verwandlung" ("transformation") implies another level of being (Weber 11).

[43] Compare, however, Nagel 146: "[...] wie sehr sowohl das Ganze der Fabel als auch das episodische Geschehen durch das heroische Ehrgebot und das altheidnische Rachedenken geprägt sind."

[44] It is difficult to concur here with Friedrich Maurer, who regards "Rache für verletzte Ehre" as the basic motive for Kriemhild's actions. He interprets the state of man as being "unter dem leidvollen Schicksal [...] der Gegenstand der Dichtung" (13), and considers "Leid" to be "Beleidigung, Entehrung" (15 and 22).

From the outset, the demise of the heroes is attributed not to Kriemhild's beauty, but rather to her association with Siegfried (35–37).[45] In an indirect way, then, it is attributed to Siegfried himself, whose death has been caused "von sîner übermuot" (39). Kriemhild's efforts to exact revenge are more strongly supported by Hagen's provocative behavior ("übermüete," 230), and they are explicitly justified through Kriemhild's "riuwe" and her "triuwe":

> Des ensol sie niemen schelten.
> sold er des engelten,
> der rehter triuwe kunde phlegen,
> der hete schiere sich bewegen
> daz er mit rehten dingen
> möhte nicht volbringen
> dehein getriulîchen muot.
> triuwe diu ist dar zuo guot:
> diu machet werden mannes lîp,
> und êrt ouh alsô schœniu wîp
> daz ir zuht noh ir muot
> nâch schanden nimmer niht getuot:
> als vroun Kriemhilde geschach,
> der von schulden nie gesprach
> misselîche dechein man.
> swer ditze mære merken kan,
> der sagt unschuldic gar ihr lîp,
> wan daz daz vil edel werde wîp
> tæte nâch ir triuwe
> ir râche in grôzer riuwe. (139–158)

The basic gist of this argument corresponds to that advanced by the poet of the *Nibelungenlied* who, however, declines to express it in the above manner, something that is incumbent upon him as the narrator of an epic. By doing so, he can avoid the somewhat gaudy contours that are offered by the *Klage*-poet, who clearly had Arthurian romance in mind when he composed his elegy.

The *Klage*-poet has Kriemhild send away immediately those Burgundians whom she did not want to be killed (166–169). As for those who remain: "ich wæn si ir alten sünde/engulten, und niht mêre" (196f.). Here, Kriemhild only punishes the guilty. This rather rigid form of Christian argument, seen from the perspective of the narrative, is simply not on the same level as the more refined presentation of the epic poet, but, as an

[45] See also 546–551.

attempt to save Kriemhild in terms of Christian morality, it should be taken seriously.

The author of the *Klage* makes the insightful remark that the queen of the Huns would have been happy to have avoided the death of so many warriors (238), but was just not in a position to do so, and, for that reason, "let things take their course" (241). As a "novelist," he is again concerned about providing a good reason for this course of events: "daz kom von krankem sinne" (243). In an effort to "excuse" the death of 40,000 men (237), the poet clearly resorts to the old Ovidian topos that love makes one sick. Manuscripts A and C of the *Klage* temper this section as well.[46]

The author is concerned about Kriemhild's salvation, and so he makes it clear that she can count on "gotes hulde" (560), and that God will accept her soul (552–568):

> sît si durch triuwe tôt gelac,
> in gotes hulden manegen tac
> sol si ze himele noch geleben. (571–573)

She is a victim of the devil: "ez was alsô gebrouwen/von des tiuvels sculden" (1314f.). It is a component of Christian psychology to explain deviant behavior in such a manner.[47] Whether or not, or to what extent, this is meant to open the door to a Christian reception of the entire plot is a matter of conjecture.

The *Klage* picks up and responds to two important questions which the epic poet, as the presenter of "global events," is not obliged to answer, but which require a response from a reflecting "novelist" of the Middle Ages: how are Kriemhild's actions in exacting revenge to be gauged? And: what is the state of her soul? The author is essentially writing against a (potential or actual) type of reception of the work which condemns Kriemhild as a "vâlandinne" in the sense that the word is used by Dietrich and Hagen. In

[46] A: "daz kom von chrimhilt sinne"; C: "dô sich rechen began/Kriemhilt nâch ir sinne." See also Winder McConnell, *The Lament of the Nibelungen (Div Chlage)*, Studies in German Literature, Linguistics, and Culture, Translations from Medieval Literature, ed. Evelyn S. Firchow (Columbia, SC: Camden House, 1994) 15, fn. 11.

[47] Compare *Nibelungenlied*, 1394, where manuscripts A and B establish a connection between Kriemhild and the devil which C, however, avoids. The stanza which associates the kiss of reconciliation with Giselher (not Gunther, who is named in stanza 1114 with regard to the kiss) can be read without any serious reservations according to the tradition. It might then be possible to accept the kiss of reconciliation contained in 1115,3: "si verkôs ûf si alle." Kriemhild had taken leave of her *voget*, Giselher, "mit friuntschefte" (1394,2). However one may understand it, the departure from the Burgundian court is interpreted as a wrong move, as the devil's work.

the process, he has most certainly read or listened to “his” *Nibelungenlied* very carefully, regardless of the version that may have been passed down to him.

John L. Flood

Siegfried's Dragon-Fight in German Literary Tradition

> And when all the greatest heroes and the most famous leaders are spoken of, he is the one who will always be spoken of as foremost of all, and his name is current in all the languages spoken north of the Greek Ocean, and so it will be for as long as the world endures.
>
> *Vǫlsunga saga* , ch. 23[1]

Thus wrote the author of *Vǫlsunga saga* ("The Saga of the Volsungs") early in the second half of the thirteenth century. He was referring to Sigurd (or Siegfried in German tradition), and he seems to have been right, for even today, more than seven centuries later, Sigurd-Siegfried's exploits are still part of common knowledge, even though perhaps this may now be due more to the popularity of Richard Wagner's *Der Ring des Nibelungen* than to that of the Norse *Vǫlsunga saga* or of the German *Nibelungenlied.* When, in Dieter Schwanitz's *Der Campus* (1995), a rare example of a German "university novel" in the Anglo-American tradition, the student Martin Sommer dejectedly contemplates the awful prospect of writing a master's thesis on "Sinn und Bedeutung: Zur Rolle der phänomenalistischen Semantik in der Kunsttheorie von Nelson Goodman," he reflects on how he had got himself into this unenviable situation: he had wanted to outshine the theoreticians in the seminar, not least with a view to impressing prospective employers with his brilliance: "Er wollte im Drachenblut ihrer Hochnäsigkeit baden und sich eine intellektuelle Panzerhaut zulegen, um den Feuilleton-redakteuren der ZEIT zu imponieren. Denn wie alle Germanisten träumte Martin davon, gleich nach dem Examen bei der ZEIT einzusteigen."[2] The

[1] See R. G. Finch, ed., *The Saga of the Volsungs* (London, Edinburgh: Nelson, 1965) 41.

[2] Dietrich Schwanitz, *Der Campus* (Frankfurt a. M.: Eichborn, 1995) 125. On general knowledge of the Siegfried story in the population today, see Otfrid Ehrismann, "Siegfried. Ein deutscher Mythos?" in Ulrich Müller and Werner Wunderlich, eds., *Mittelaltermythen I: Herrscher, Helden, Heilige* (St. Gallen: UVK, 1996) 367–387, especially 370–371.

reference to bathing in dragon's blood and acquiring an armored skin is sufficient to put the reader in mind of Siegfried, even though he is not mentioned by name.

Siegfried's fight with the dragon is as much part of his legend as is the Round Table of King Arthur's. In both the Norse and the German traditions, despite differences in detail, the hero is primarily a dragon-slayer who proves himself and gains a treasure by defeating the dragon.[3] Yet, curiously enough, the dragon-fight does not feature as a primary episode in the *Nibelungenlied.* Possibly because the story was already well-known to any audience, it is marginalized and becomes a mere incidental detail, being mentioned only briefly by Hagen at the end of his résumé of Siegfried's exploits:[4]

[3] It is not possible here to discuss dragons or the theme of dragon-killers generally. There is an extensive literature on the subject covering not only the European Middle Ages, but also classical antiquity and of course the Asiatic aspects too. For a general discussion of dragons see Emil Ernst Ploss, *Siegfried-Sigurd, der Drachenkämpfer* (Cologne and Graz: Böhlau, 1966) 43–55, and with specific reference to medieval literature Claude Lecouteux, "Der Drache," *ZfdA* 108 (1979): 13–31, and Claude Lecouteux, *Les Monstres dans la littérature allemande du Moyen Âge (1150–1350) Contribution à l'étude du merveilleux*, 3 vols., GAG 330 (Göppingen: Kümmerle, 1982) 2: 183–207. The following are also useful: G. Elliot Smith, *The Evolution of the Dragon* (Manchester: Manchester University Press, 1919) 76–139; W. Lange, "Der Drachenkampf" (doctoral thesis), Munich 1939; Friedrich Wild, "Drachen im Beowulf und andere Drachen," *Sitzungsberichte der österreichischen Akademie der Wissenschaften*, philosophisch-historische Klasse 238, no. 5 (1962); Max Burkolter-Trachsel, *Der Drache. Das Symbol und der Mensch* (Berne and Stuttgart: Haupt, 1981); Uwe Steffen, *Drachenkampf, der Mythos vom Bösen* (Stuttgart: Kreuz, n.d. [ca. 1984]); and Hans Egli, *Das Schlangensymbol. Geschichte, Märchen, Mythos* (Olten and Freiburg im Breisgau: Walter, 1982), especially 194–256; Winder McConnell, "Mythos Drache," in Ulrich Müller and Werner Wunderlich, eds., *Mittelalter Mythen II: Dämonen, Monster, Fabelwesen* (St. Gallen: UVK, [forthcoming]); Joyce Tally Lionarons, *The Medieval Dragon. The Nature of the Beast in Germanic Literature* (Enfield: Hisarlik, 1997). Peter Paulsen, *Drachenkämpfer, Löwenritter und die Heinrichsage. Eine Studie über die Kirchentür von Valthjofsstad auf Island* (Cologne and Graz: Böhlau, 1966), also contains interesting material. On St. George as dragon-slayer in medieval German literature see John L. Flood, "Sankt Georg," in *Mittelalter Mythen I* 589–606.

[4] As K. C. King, "Siegfried's fight with the dragon in the *Edda* and the *Hürnen Seyfrid*," *London Mediaeval Studies* 1,1 (1937): 77–83 remarks, the fact that the stories about Siegfried's fight with the dragon and his winning of a treasure are dismissed with the briefest reference in the *Nibelungenlied* "proves nothing with regard to the extent to which the poems were known in Germany, for, in the first instance, the *Nibelungenlied* is a South German poem and the stories are of North German origin; and, in the second instance, the subject matter, at least that of the dragon-fight, was not suitable for a courtly poem of the best period" (77).

"Although I have never seen him," said Hagen, "I dare assert my belief that the knight who makes such a magnificent figure there is Siegfried, whatever his purpose. He is bringing unheard-of news to this country, for this warrior slew the bold Nibelungs, the two mighty princes Schilbung and Nibelung, and marvellous are the deeds he has done since in his great strength. Riding unaccompanied past the foot of a mountain (as I was truly told), he chanced upon a host of valiant men whom he had never seen before, gathered round Nibelung's treasure, all of which they had borne out from a cavern. Now hear the strange tale how the Nibelungs were intent on dividing it! — Siegfried marvelled as he watched them, for he came so near that he could see those warriors and they him. "Here comes mighty Siegfried of the Netherlands," said one of them; and mysterious were the things that he experienced among them. Siegfried was well received by Schilbung and Nibelung, and these noble young princes begged and implored the handsome man by common consent to make division of the treasure, and this he promised to do. He saw so many precious stones, we are told, that a hundred baggage-waggons could not have carried them, and an even greater quantity of red gold of Nibelung's country; all of which bold Siegfried was asked to divide for them. They gave him Nibelung's sword in payment, but they had scant profit from the service which the good warrior was to render them. He was unable to finish his task, so enraged were they. But although they had twelve brave men among their friends there — mighty giants they were — how could it avail them? Siegfried slew them in a fury and he also subdued seven hundred men of Nibelungland with the good sword Balmung, so that, in dread of this sword and also of brave Siegfried, a host of young warriors yielded the land and its castles to him as their lord. Furthermore he slew the mighty princes Schilbung and Nibelung, and he came in great peril from Alberich who hoped to avenge his masters there and then, till Siegfried's huge strength was brought home to him; for the powerful dwarf was no match for him. They then ran towards the cavern like raging lions, and here he won from Alberich the cloak of invisibility. Thus Siegfried, terrible man, was now lord of all the treasure.

"All who had dared fight lay slain there. Siegfried commanded the hoard to be taken back to the cave whence Nibelung's men had fetched it, and, after swearing oaths to Siegfried that he would be his humble servitor, Alberich was made lord treasurer. Indeed, he was in all ways ready to do his bidding.

"These are the deeds that he has done," continued Hagen of Troneck. "No warrior was ever so strong. But I know more concerning him. This hero slew a dragon and bathed in its blood, from which his skin grew horny so that no weapon will bite it, as has been shown time and time again. We must receive this young lord with more than usual honour, lest we incur his enmity. He is so valiant and has performed so many marvels thanks to his bodily strength that it is best to have his friendship."[5]

Exhaustive though this account is, the story of the dragon-fight takes up a mere two and a half lines:

> einen lintrachen den sluoc des heldes hant.
> er badet' sich in dem bluote: sîn hût wart hurnîn.
> Des snîdet in kein wâfen. (100,2–4a)

In the *Nibelungenlied*, the dragon-fight itself seems to be of no further relevance, only its consequence: Siegfried's almost complete invulnerability following his bathing in the dragon's blood.[6] This motif is described in *Âventiure* 15 in which Hagen goes to Siegfried's wife, Kriemhild, pretending to be solicitous for her husband's safety:

> "My lady," said Hagen, "if you have any apprehension that a weapon might wound him tell me by what means I can prevent it and I shall always guard him, riding or walking."
>
> "You and I are of one blood, dear Hagen, and I earnestly commend my beloved spouse to you to guard him." Then she divulged some matters that had better been left alone. "My husband is very brave and very strong," she said. "When he slew the dragon at the foot of the mountain the gallant knight bathed in its blood, as a result of which no weapon has pierced him in battle ever since. Nevertheless, when he is at the wars in the midst of all

[5] *Das Nibelungenlied*, *Âventiure* 3, str. 86–101. Quotations from the *Nibelungenlied* are based on the Karl Bartsch/Helmut de Boor edition, *Das Nibelungenlied*, 21st revised edition by Roswitha Wisniewski, Deutsche Klassiker des Mittelalters (Wiesbaden: Brockhaus, 1979) and are cited according to strophe and verse number. Translation from: *The Nibelungenlied*. A new translation by A. T. Hatto, rev. ed. (Harmondsworth: Penguin, 1969) 27–28.

[6] For a wide-ranging discussion of references to dragon's blood and horn as armor — in Scandinavian sources, the Old English *Beowulf*, and in German sources such as Lamprecht's *Alexanderlied*, *Orendel*, the *Kaiserchronik*, the *Jüngerer Titurel*, various poems about Dietrich von Bern, Wirnt von Gravenberg's *Wigalois*, and Heinrich von Neustadt's *Apollonius von Tyrlant*, as well as non-literary sources — see Ploss 6–12. For the motif of invulnerability see Ploss 21–28; for dragon's blood, 35–42. The idea of Siegfried's invulnerabilty of course links up well with other similar motifs. For example, Saxo Grammaticus in the early thirteenth century tells the following: "When a gigantic bear met him [Bjarki] among the thickets he dispatched it with his javelin and then told Hjalti, his comrade, to apply his mouth and suck out the beast's blood so that he might achieve greater strength; for it was believed that this type of drink afforded an increased bodily vigour." See Saxo Grammaticus, *The history of the Danes*, translated and edited by Peter Fisher and Hilda Ellis Davidson (Cambridge: Brewer, 1979) 1: 55.

the javelins that warriors hurl, I fear I may lose my dear husband. Alas, how often do I not suffer cruelly in my fear for Siegfried! Now I shall reveal this to you in confidence, dearest kinsman, so that you may keep faith with me, and I shall tell you, trusting utterly in you, where my dear husband can be harmed. When the hot blood flowed from the dragon's wound and the good knight was bathing in it, a broad leaf fell from the linden between his shoulder-blades. It is there that he can be wounded, and this is why I am so anxious."

"Sew a little mark on his clothing so that I shall know where I must shield him in battle." She fancied she was saving the hero, yet this was aimed at his death.

"I will take some fine silk and sew on a cross that none will notice, she said, and there, knight, you must shield him when the battle is joined and he faces his foes in the onrush."

"I shall indeed, my dear lady."[7]

Kriemhild's reference to the dragon-fight episode —

Dô von des trachen wunden vlôz das heize bluot
und sich dar inne badete der küene ritter guot,
dô viel im zwischen die herte ein lindenblat vil breit.
dô mac man in versnîden: des ist mir sorgen vil bereit. (902)

— adds only one new detail to what Hagen had said in strophe 100: that a leaf had fallen from a lime-tree on to Siegfried's back, so that the dragon's blood had failed to reach a spot between his shoulder blades and turn his skin into a protective coat of horn. Though the horny skin is a traditional part of the story, in the *Nibelungenlied* it is almost an irrelevance: nothing is made of Siegfried's being protected by it; it is only the unprotected patch of skin where the linden leaf fell that is important. As Ploss puts it, the motif of the unprotected patch serves only to heighten the drama of Siegfried's murder.[8] En passant, we may note that in Friedrich Hebbel's trilogy *Die Nibelungen*, which is based on the *Nibelungenlied*, Siegfried regards the fact of his incomplete invulnerability as a distinct bonus, for it protects him from the taunts of others:

DANKWART. Du bist gewiß aufs Kämpfen so versessen,
Seit du des Lindwurms Schuppenpanzer trägst?
Nicht jedermann betrog den Tod wie du,
Er findet eine offene Tür bei uns.

[7] *Nibelungenlied, Âventiure* 15, str. 897–905,1; Hatto 121.

[8] Ploss 16.

SIEGFRIED. Wohl auch bei mir! Hab Dank, du alte Linde,
Daß du ein Blatt auf mich herunterwarfst,
Als ich mich badete im Blut des Drachen,
Hab Dank, o Wind, daß du sie schütteltest!
Nun hab' ich doch die Antwort für den Spötter,
Der seine Feigheit hinter Hohn versteckt.[9]

Yet, returning to the *Nibelungenlied*, though superficially the dragon-fight episode may seem to be almost an irrelevance simply inherited from the traditional story, is this really so? Though critics tend to see mention of the dragon-fight as serving only to explain Siegfried's invulnerability, the poet emphasizing the human dimension and playing down the mythological, the one does not necessarily exclude or negate the other; as McConnell sees it, Siegfried's bathing in the dragon's blood stands as a symbol of a fusion between the human world and the world of myth, with Siegfried symbolically becoming part of the chaos that he shortly is to unleash on the courtly world. The havoc that he wreaks at Worms represents a danger for the whole courtly world. His exuberant *übermuot* is the manifestation of the chaos with which he has entered into symbiosis by bathing in the dragon's blood.[10] The final outcome is the total destruction of courtly society — in the words of the poet: "Diu vil michel êre was dâ gelegen tôt" (2378,1) — their reputation, their self-esteem lay dead there.

Outside the *Nibelungenlied* the dragon-fight is more clearly a significant episode in its own right. To return to *Vǫlsunga saga*, which is a prose harmonization of the heroic poems in the *Poetic Edda* but includes additional details about Sigurd's youth, the story of the encounter with the dragon extends over chapters 18–20. Here, as McConnell observes, the beast is conceived of as a real physical entity, rather than as a more symbolic threat as in other works.[11] Sigurd, the son of Sigmund and Hjordis, is prompted by his foster father, the dwarf smith Regin, to slay the dragon Fafnir in order to acquire his treasure. Fafnir had once been a man, a son of Hreidmar, and Regin was one of his brothers. Sigurd and Regin set out to find the track Fafnir follows when going to drink. Sigurd, awestruck by the size of the

[9] Helmut de Boor, *Friedrich Hebbel, Die Nibelungen.* Dichtung und Wirklichkeit. Deutung und Dokumention. Ullstein-Buch 5016 (Frankfurt a. M. and Berlin: Ullstein, 1966) 86, ll. 221–230.

[10] McConnell, "Mythos Drache." McConnell cites Joyce Ann Tally, *The Dragon's Progress: The Significance of the Dragon in 'Beowulf,' 'Volsunga Saga,' 'Das Nibelungenlied' and 'Der Ring des Nibelungen,'* diss. University of Denver 1983 (which I have not been able to see) as saying: "By bathing in the dragon's blood, Sîvrit becomes the monster he has slain" (143).

[11] McConnell, "Mythos Drache."

monster's tracks, is advised by Regin to dig a pit and hide in it so that he can stab the creature from underneath when it comes to drink. While he is digging, Odin, in the guise of an old man, comes up to him and advises him to dig several other pits for the dragon's blood to run into. When the dragon appears,

> the earth tremors were so violent that all the land round about shook. He breathed out poison all over the path ahead, but Sigurd was neither frightened nor dismayed by the noise. And when the dragon crawled across the pit, Sigurd thrust in the sword under the left shoulder, and it sunk in up to the hilt. Then Sigurd leapt out of the pit, wrenching back the sword, and getting his arms bloody right up to the shoulders.

Before he dies, Fafnir prophesies that Sigurd will acquire a treasure but that this gold will be the death of him and of any other man that possesses it. Regin returns and upbraids Sigurd for killing his brother. Regin drinks Fafnir's blood and tells Sigurd to cut out the dragon's heart and roast it on a fire. When the juice sputters out Sigurd touches it to see if the meat is done. He burns his finger and puts it to his mouth, "and when the blood from the dragon's heart touched his tongue he could understand the language of birds." The birds tell him of Regin's greed and treachery and they reveal to him the whereabouts of the treasure. Thereupon Sigurd slays Regin and goes and finds the treasure, before going on to waken Brynhild the valkyrie from her exhausted sleep in the circle of fire, to pledge himself to her with a magic ring.[12]

The motif of the smith's wish to rid himself of the troublesome youth occurs already in *Þiðreks saga*, a Norwegian compendium of heroic tales compiled chiefly from North German sources in the mid-thirteenth century (and at a slightly earlier date than *Vǫlsunga saga*).[13] Having been sent into the forest to prepare charcoal, Sigurd is attacked by a dragon which he kills. Hungry after his exertions, he makes a stew of the dragon, dips his finger into it and, scalding it, puts it into his mouth to cool it. As soon as the broth

[12] For the relevant passage, in Old Norse and in English translation, see Finch 30–34.

[13] On the dating see Theodore M. Andersson, *The Legend of Brynhild* (Ithaca and London: Cornell University Press, 1980) 21–22. In connection with King's remarks concerning the inappropriateness of the dragon-fight story for inclusion in the *Nibelungenlied*, we may note Finch's observation that "the conception of Sigurd-Sîfrit as a clumsy or obnoxious lout accords ill with heroic tradition" (xxviii), and Friedrich Panzer, *Das Nibelungenlied. Entstehung und Gestalt* (Stuttgart and Cologne: Kohlhammer, 1955) 245, speaks of the Siegfried of the *Nibelungenlied* as the "'Starkhans' des Märchens, und das bricht noch mehrfach durch das höfische Prunkgewand, das unser Dichter ihm umgelegt hat."

touches his tongue and runs down into his throat he is able to understand the language of the birds who reveal to him that the dragon was the brother of the smith Mimir; their advice is that Sigurd should go and kill Mimir for otherwise the smith will kill him. *Þiðreks saga* then tells how Sigurd takes the dragon's blood and rubs it on himself and his hands and everywhere he can reach, the skin it touches becoming as hard as horn. He then strips off his clothes and covers himself with the blood completely as far as he can reach, but he cannot reach between his shoulders.[14] *Þiðreks saga* thus has both motifs, the ability to understand the speech of the birds, and invulnerability bestowed by bathing in the dragon's blood. However, the saga fails to explain why Sigurd decided to cover himself with the dragon's blood. As for *Vǫlsunga saga*, this knows of the motif of Sigurd's being able to understand the birds, and while it also tells of Sigurd being covered with the dragon's blood, here it is by accident rather than by design, and furthermore in this saga the notion of the blood conferring invulnerability on him is lacking. Clearly these features are loose ends, left over during the complex development of the sagas.[15]

In Richard Wagner's *Siegfried*, the third part of the *Ring* cycle, based partly on the *Nibelungenlied* and partly on Scandinavian sources, Fafner is described as an "ungeheurer eidechsenartiger Schlangenwurm."[16] Siegfried plunges his sword Notung into the dragon's heart, and as he reaches forward to pull the weapon out of the monster's lifeless body he gets blood on his hand and draws back as though his hand were burning: "Wie Feuer brennt das Blut!" He puts his fingers into his mouth to suck off the blood, and suddenly becomes aware that he can understand the song of the birds. One of the birds in the lime-tree reveals to him:

Hei! Siegfried gehört
nun der Niblungen Hort:
o fänd' in der Höhle
den Hort er jetzt
Wollt' er einen Tarnhelm gewinnen,
der taugt ihm zu winniger Tat:

[14] *Die Geschichte Thidreks von Bern*, trans. F. Erichsen (Darmstadt: Wissenschaftliche Buchgesellschaft, 1967) 220.

[15] See Finch xxix. Andersson, *The Legend of Brynhild* 233, is certain that the motif of the bath in the dragon's blood and the invulnerability it confers in *Þiðreks saga* must have been found in the "Brünhildenlied." The evolution of *Vǫlsunga saga* and *Þiðreks saga* is too complex a matter to be re-examined here.

[16] See Wolfgang Golther, ed., *Richard Wagner, Gesammelte Schriften und Dichtungen in zehn Bänden* (Berlin: Bong, [n.d.]) 6: 136. In *Das Rheingold* Fafner is a giant, brother of Fasolt.

doch möcht' er den Ring sich erraten,
der macht ihn zum Walter der Welt![17]

Wagner thus has Siegfried putting his finger into his mouth and obtaining the power of understanding the language of the birds, as in Scandinavian tradition. It should be noted, however, that Siegfried has not actually burnt or scalded his finger, there being no fire as such: it is only that the blood burns him as though it were fire.

Leaving aside the Norse texts and their Wagnerian derivative, even within the German tradition itself the circumstances of the dragon-fight vary considerably. In the *Nibelungenlied*, as we have seen, Siegfried, who is the son of Siegmund, the king of the Netherlands, slays the dragon and, through bathing in its blood, becomes invulnerable, except for in one spot on his back. He obtains the Nibelung gold and, with the cloak of invisibility, aids the Burgundian prince Gunther to win the hand of Brünhild. He marries Gunther's sister Kriemhild, but the two queens' quarrels reveal both Siegfried's deception of Brünhild and the fact of his vulnerability, revelations which result in Siegfried's murder by Hagen.

In another German Siegfried poem, the *Lied vom hürnen Seyfrid*, the whole background to the encounter with the dragon is rather different. Here, as in *Þiðreks saga*, Seyfrid, son of King Sigmund of Niderland (as in *Nibelungenlied*, str. 20), is a hyperactive, obstreperous young man, difficult to control. His father's counselors advise that Seyfrid should be allowed to leave the court and go wherever his inclination might take him. He enters service with a smith, but proves so troublesome that his master, wanting to be rid of him, dispatches him to a charcoal burner in the forest, hoping that he will fall prey to a dragon whose lair lies behind a linden tree. However, Seyfrid tears tree-trunks out of the ground and uses then to pin down the dragons, toads, and adders he found there. Then he fetches fire from the charcoal burner and sets fire to the trees and the dragons. When their horny skin melts in the heat, he dips his finger into it and, finding that this then becomes as hard as horn, he smears his whole body with it, failing to reach a spot between his shoulders, which leads to his downfall:

Das horn der würm gund weychen
Ein bechlein her thet fließ
Des wundert Sewfrid sere
Ein finger er dreyn stieß
Do jm der finger erkalte
Do was er jm hürnein

[17] Golther 6: 139.

Wol mit dem selben bache
Schmirt er den leybe ein.

Das er ward aller hürnen
Dann zwischen den schultern nit
Und an der selben statte
Er seynen tode lidt
Als jr in andern dichten
Hernach werdt hören wol ...[18]

This passage was the basis of Sewfrid's speech in Act 2 of Hans Sachs's play *Der hürnen Seufrid*, written in 1557:

Sol ich nit von grosem glüeck sagen?
Ich hab den grossen wurmb erschlagen,
Nach dem mit esten in verprent;
Da ist zerschmolzen an dem ent
Sein horn und zusammen gerunnen,
Gleich wie ein pechlein aus eim prunnen.
Das wundert mich im herzen mein
Und daucht mit ainem finger drein,
Und als der ist erkaltet worn,
Da wart mein finger lawter horn;
Des frewt ich mich und zog zuhant
Von meinem leib all mein gewant
Und also mueter nackat mich
Mit diesem warmen horn pestrich.
Des bin ich gleich hinden und forn
An meiner hawt ganz hüernen worn,
Darauff kain schwert nit haften kan.
Des gleicht mir iz auf ert kein man.[19]

That Sewfrid has one unprotected area of "soft flesh" on his body is mentioned by Güenther in Act 7:

[18] The text is taken from K. C. King, ed., *Das Lied vom hürnen Seyfrid. Critical edition with introduction and notes* (Manchester: Manchester University Press, 1958) 106, str. 10. 1–11. 6. On the poem generally see now Volker-Jeske Kreyher, *Der Hürnen Seyfrid. Die Deutung der Siegfriedgestalt im Spätmittelalter.* Information und Interpretation 3 (Frankfurt a. M., Berne, and New York: Lang, 1986), especially 44–54.

[19] Edmund Goetze, ed., *Der hürnen Seufrid. Tragoedie in sieben Acten von Hans Sachs*, Neudrucke deutscher Litteraturwerke des XVI. und XVII. Jahrhunderts 29 (Halle/S.: Niemeyer, 1880), ll. 199–216.

Allain zwischen dem schuelter plat
Zwayer span prait waich flaisch er hat
Da selb ist er allain zu gwinnen. (ll. 1038–40)

As Andersson has remarked, all the important details in the first eleven stanzas of the *Hürnen Seyfrid* may be found in *Þiðreks saga* and can therefore be attributed to a common source.[20] The young man hews down or tears up trees and clubs the dragon or dragons to death and then cooks or burns them, but whereas in *Þiðreks saga* and *Vǫlsunga saga* Sigurd then acquires the ability to understand the birds, in the *Hürnen Seyfrid* — as in the *Nibelungenlied* and in *Þiðreks saga* — Seyfrid becomes invulnerable through discovering how, by dipping his finger in the dragon's molten scales, he can acquire a horny skin.

For all that Hans Fromm declared the dragon episode to be a "junge Fantasterei," a concession to late medieval tastes,[21] the *Lied vom hürnen Seyfrid* seems to contain ancient elements (at least as old as the *Nibelungenlied*, dating from just after 1200), yet, in the form in which we know it, is not attested earlier than about 1530, being preserved in a number of printed editions of the sixteenth and seventeenth centuries, the earliest ones being from Nuremberg.[22] The Nuremberg printers must have had access to a manuscript version, probably a late fifteenth-century one, but no manuscript of that date is known today.[23] The antiquity of stories of Siegfried's dragon-fight is indicated by scattered references to it in various medieval sources. The *Nibelungenlied* is one, but also Hugo von Trimberg's *Der Renner* (written between 1290 and 1313) alludes to "Sîfrides wurm"

[20] Again, the postulated "Brünhildenlied," according to Andersson 232.

[21] Hans Fromm, "Kap. 168 der Thidrekssaga," *DVjs* 33 (1959): 237–256.

[22] Though the earliest surviving edition is that printed by Kunegunde Hergotin, there is strong evidence that the first edition was printed c. 1530 by the Nuremberg printer Jobst Gutknecht. See Frieder Schanze, "Der verlorene Nürnberger Erstdruck des Hürnen Seyfrid mit den Originalholzschnitten Sebald Behams," *Gutenberg-Jahrbuch* 62 (1987): 301–305.

[23] As this book goes to press, news reaches us that Professor Jüri Kivimäe (University of Tartu, Estonia) has recently discovered a fragment of a manuscript version of the *Lied* in the Swedish National Archives at Stockholm. My present information is that the fragment consists of a single leaf, containing approximately the first eleven strophes. I have seen only the recto, containing str. 1.1–6.6, so far, and have formed the opinion that though the text contains variant readings which are not found in any of the printed editions, there is no reason to suppose that the manuscript offers an earlier or better version of the text. The fragment would seem to date from the mid-sixteenth century.

(Siegfried's dragon).[24] Far more significant is *Rosengarten A*, a poem dating from the late thirteenth century which matches Siegfried against Dietrich von Bern.[25] Strophe 3 tells how Sîvrit, a proud warrior, was so strong that he caught lions and hung them up by their tails:

Sie [viz. Kriemhilt] begunde vrîen ein stolzer wîgant,
der was geheizen Sîvrit, ein helt ûz Niderlant.
der pflac sô grôzer sterke, daz er die lewen vienc
und sie mit den zegeln über die mûren hienc.

This corresponds almost verbatim to str. 33 of the *Hürnen Seyfrid*, though here Seyfrid hangs the lions from trees rather than from walls:

Do was zu den gezeyten
Ein stoltzer jüngeling
Der was Sewfrid geheyssen
Eyns reychen Künigs kind
Der pflac so grosser stercke
Das er die Löwen fieng
Und sie dann zu gespötte
Hoch an die baumen hieng.

Rosengarten A also tells us that Siegfried killed a fearsome dragon, and possessed three things: a fine sword called Balmung which, it seems, he found when he slew the dragon, a breastplate made by Eckerich who brought him up in a smithy, and a horny skin:

... er ersluoc ûf eime steine einen trachen vreissam,
dem mohten alle künege niht gesigen an.

Er hât bî sînen zîten recken vil erslagen.
dannoch sint driu dinc an im, diu wil ich dir sagen:
er treit ein swert sô guot daz er ûf dem steine vant,
daz herte helme velschet und ist Balmunc genant.

Das ander ist ein brünne, daz wizze sicherlîch,
die macht aller brünnen meister der werde Eckerîch.
er hât in von kinde in der smitten erzogen,
dâvon ist der helt an der brünne unbetrogen.

[24] Hugo von Trimberg, *Der Renner*, ed. Gustav Ehrismann, Bibliothek des Litterarischen Vereins in Stuttgart 247 (1908; rpt. Berlin: de Gruyter, 1970) 2: 283, l. 16188.

[25] Georg Holz, *Die Gedichte vom Rosengarten zu Worms* (Halle/S.: Niemeyer, 1893) 3. On Dietrich see John L. Flood, "Dietrich von Bern," in *Mittelalter Mythen I*, 287–304.

Er worhte sie wol mit vlîze nâch der meisterschaft.
er wiste wol, daz er solte gewinnen grôze kraft.
goldes und gesteines lît gar vil dar an.
kein swert wart nie sô guot daz sie gewinnen kan.

Daz dritte wil ich dir nennen, daz er ist hürnîn
und wil âne sorge vor allen recken sîn ...
(*Rosengarten A*, str. 329,2–333,2)

Even in the *Ackermann aus Böhmen* (ch. XXX), written in the early years of the fifteenth century, Death mentions "den Hürnyn Seyfridt" as one of a number of German heroes he has had to deal with.[26]

But of greater interest than these passing references is the mention of the dragon-fight in manuscripts m and n of the *Nibelungenlied*. The first of these, Hs. 3249 of the Hessische Landes- und Hochschulbibliothek Darmstadt, apparently contained an account of Siegfried's fight with the dragon that captured Kriemhild, the very story which forms the core of the *Lied vom Hürnen Seyfrid*. The manuscript is, unfortunately, only a fragment listing no more than the chapter headings,[27] but even so it is quite clear that the story we know from the *Hürnen Seyfrid* formed part of it, for between the episode in which Sîvrit had his first sight of Kriemhilt (corresponding to *Âventiure* 5 in the *Nibelungenlied* as we conventionally read it) and the one in which Sîvrit goes to fetch some of his men (*Âventiure* 8), manuscript m had four chapters with the following headings:

Abinture wie gunter noch kriemilde farin wolde vnd wie sie hindert ein wildir drache

Abinture wie kriemilde nam ein wildir drache vnd furte sie uff einen hohin stein

Abinture wie siferit die juncfrauwe von dem drachin steine gewan mit manchyr groszin arbeit

[26] Karl Bertau, ed., *Johannes de Tepla, Civis Zacensis, Epistola cum Libello ackerman und Das büchlein ackerman* (Berlin and New York: de Gruyter, 1994) 1: 238, 2: 580. See Horst Brunner, "Hürnen Seyfrid," in Kurt Ruh, ed., *Die deutsche Literatur des Mittelalters. Verfasserlexikon*, 2nd ed. (Berlin and New York: de Gruyter, 1978) 4: 317–326.

[27] On the manuscript, Landes- und Universitätsbibliothek Darmstadt, Hs. 3249, see Helmut de Boor, "Die Bearbeitung m des Nibelungenliedes (Darmstäder Aventiuren-verzeichnis)," *PBB* (Tübingen), 81 (1959): 176–195. A transcription and further details are provided in Michael S. Batts, ed., *Das Nibelungenlied. Paralleldruck der Handschriften A, B und C nebst Lesarten der übrigen Handschriften* (Tübingen: Niemeyer, 1971) 799–800 and 810.

Abinture daz siferit den drachin hatte ubir wondin vnd fur mit siner juncfrauwe an dem rin

For all that the first of these headings appears to be muddled — it should surely read "Abinture wie gunter noch brunhilt farin wolde ..."! — taken together they all seem to point to the story known from the central section of the *Hürnen Seyfrid* (str. 16–172): "How Gunter intended to journey to [Brunhild] and how a ferocious dragon prevented them"; "How a ferocious dragon stole Kriemhild and took her to a high rock"; "How Sifrit won the maiden back from the dragon's rock with great effort"; and "How Sifrit overcame the dragon and journeyed with his maiden to the Rhine." Manuscript n, Hs. 4257 at Darmstadt, also contains a passing reference to Kriemhild's rescue from the dragon. Justifying her love for Siegfried, she says:

Wan er hat mich erlost vß engstlicher not
Vff dem trachen steyn da müst ich syn gelegen dot[28]

Manuscript m was written c. 1400, manuscript n in 1449. They seem to indicate quite conclusively that the story told in the *Lied vom hürnen Seyfrid* must be a century or more older than the earliest extant text of it, though Helmut de Boor warned against being too confident that we are necessarily dealing with the same story.[29]

The *Lied vom Hürnen Seyfrid* is no work of art. It has no intrinsic literary quality, but is interesting for the motifs it contains. It consists of three parts, clumsily juxtaposed rather than molded together. The main part is the central section, str. 16–172, focusing on Seyfrid's rescue of Krimhild who has been abducted by a dragon, that is, the story found in *Nibelungenlied* manuscript m. This is preceded by a short section (str. 1–15) giving a brief account of Seyfrid's adventures, largely as also related in Scandinavian sources. These two parts may even derive from separate orally transmitted stories, and as such provide interesting examples of the clothing of popular tradition in literary form. The final section (str. 173–179) represents an attempt to link the account of Seyfrid's rescue of Krimhilt to the story more or less as we know it from the *Nibelungenlied*. It tells how Seyfrid returns to Worms with Krimhilt, having meanwhile sunk the treasure he had won from the dwarfs

[28] Jürgen Vorderstemann, "Eine unbekannte Handschrift des Nibelungenliedes in der Hessischen Landes- und Hochschulbibliothek Darmstadt," *ZfdA* 105 (1976): 115–122, here 121. Vorderstemann notes that this manuscript too confuses Kriemhild and Brünhild (121f.).

[29] de Boor 177.

in the Rhine.[30] His behavior at Worms gives rise in turn to jealousy and hatred on the part of Gunther, Gernot, and Hagen who then murder him. Precisely because it is a compilation put together from disparate elements, the *Hürnen Seyfrid* is almost inevitably riddled with contradictions and inconsistencies.[31] At the beginning, for instance, we are told that Seyfrid was the son of King Sigmund, yet in str. 47 he is said to know nothing of his parents until the dwarf Eugel tells him who they were (str. 48). Furthermore, whereas str. 12 tells how, having killed the dragons and acquired a horny skin, he serves King Gybich whose daughter he marries, in str. 33 he is introduced as if for the first time:

Do was zu den gezeyten
Ein stoltzer jüngeling
Der was Sewfrid geheyssen
Eyns reychen Künigs kind ...

At this point Krimhilt has already been abducted by a dragon, and this gives rise to another dragon-fight. While out hunting Seyfrid comes upon the beast's tracks (even though according to str. 17–19 it had flown off with Krimhilt!) which lead him to the dragon's rock. First, however, he has an encounter with a giant, Kuperan (who bears a shield "hardened with dragon's blood" [str. 70, 6]) and his struggles with him are described in great detail (str. 61–114).[32] When the fight with the dragon does take place, it is dealt with very briefly (str. 143–148). Str. 147 is particularly interesting:

Er schlug so weych das horen
Mit seynem schwerdt so gut
Und auch die hitz vom Trachen
Als wer gemacht ein glut
Mit einem fuder kolen
Die alle wern ein brandt

[30] Seyfrid's reason for sinking the treasure in the Rhine is that, having been told that he is not going to live very long, he cannot see who should have a right to it (str. 167). In the *Nibelungenlied* it is of course Hagen who sinks the treasure, to spite Kriemhild. On dragons as guardians of treasure see Ploss 70–72.

[31] On the *Lied* see the introductions to the editions by Wolfgang Golther: *Das Lied vom hürnen Seyfrid*, Neudrucke deutscher Literaturwerke des 16. u. 17. Jhs. 81/82, 2nd ed. (Halle/S.: Niemeyer, 1911), and King, *Das Lied vom hürnen Seyfrid*. For the range of hypotheses advanced to account for it see Brunner, cols. 321–322, § 7.

[32] Names very similar to Kuperan also occur in Ulrich von Türheim's *Rennewart* (written c. 1250): "Kuppiron" (l. 23330), and in *Reinfried von Braunschweig* (written c. 1300): "Kuprîân" (l. 25269).

Erst ward das horn weychen
Das es ab von jm randt.

That is, Seyfrid beat the dragon's horny skin so hard with his good sword that it softened, and, coupled with the heat exuded by the dragon — it breathes "flammen blaw und rot" according to 144,4 — the effect was as though there were a roaring fire made with a load of coals, which made the horn melt so that it ran off the dragon. Underlying this account, presumably, is the idea that when the liquid cools it will turn into horn again, rather as in the account of Sigurd's dragon-fight in *Þiðreks saga* or indeed as in that of the first dragon-fight in the *Hürnen Seyfrid* itself, which strongly suggests that the two dragon-fights in the poem may really be one and the same or at least that the second is modeled on the first.

The dragon which abducts Krimhilt has, we learn, previously been human: a woman had put a spell on him (str. 125) and he was always accompanied by a devil in dragon's shape (str. 124). There is an anomaly here: either there is one dragon, the young man possessed by the devil, or there are two, the young man and the devil. At any rate, the dragon is the embodiment of the diabolical: his fire-breathing is described as devilish (str. 129,4) and hellish (str. 132,8) and he fights so devilishly (str. 145,1).[33] Krimhilt spends four years on the mountain, well-treated but lonely, then one Easter Day the dragon turns (temporarily) into a man and tells her that however much she pleads, she will never see her parents again but go to Hell. After the expiry of a further five years he will turn from being a dragon into a man and, a day later, he will deflower her and she will then be consigned to Hell (str. 22–27). As Lecouteux points out,[34] in medieval literature it is generally not dragons but giants or dwarfs who are cast in the role of abductors and violators. Lecouteux shows that underlying the account of the *Lied vom Hürnen Seyfrid* is the narrative motif of "the beast of the mountain," a genius loci from mythical and pagan times, dwelling in a wild place, defending its territory and hostile to the civilized world.[35] A feature of such figures is that they often have two facets to their character, as here: dragon and giant, guardian and destroyer of their land. Lecouteux (263) draws

[33] One is reminded of fire-breathing as a motif in the stories about Dietrich von Bern; see Flood, "Dietrich von Bern" 299.

[34] Claude Lecouteux, "Seyfrid, Kuperan et le Dragon. Contribution à l'étude de la légende," *Etudes Germaniques* 49 (1994): 257–266, here 260.

[35] Lecouteux 266, notes 10 and 11, refers to Francis Dubost, *Aspects fantastiques de la littérature marrative mediévale (XIIe-XIIIe siècles)*, Bibliothèque du Moyen Âge 15 (Paris: Champion, 1991), and his own *Démons et génies du terroir au Moyen Âge* (Paris: Image, 1995).

attention to the giant Dinabuc in Wace's *Brut* as the only case in which we find the sequence abduction—violation—death, and here it is not a dragon but a giant who carries out these deeds: Dinabuc abducts Heloine, daughter of Duke Hoel, and takes her off to Mont Saint-Michel (a place not yet integrated into civilized, Christian space). King Arthur kills the monster but the girl has succumbed to the brute's embraces. Lecouteux seems to be right to conclude that some of the apparent obscurities in the *Lied vom Hürnen Seyfrid* may be explained by seeing them in the light of these narrative traditions. At any rate, there is considerable confusion between the giant Kuperan and the dragon in the poem. For though we are told at the beginning that Krimhilt was abducted by the dragon (str. 17), in str. 59ff. it is the giant Kuperan who dwells on the mountain. Lecouteux concludes that the dragon and the giant are two sides of the same character. After all, he points out, Kuperan and the dragon never appear at the same time; the appearance of the one seems to preclude the other. Furthermore, Kuperan is guardian of the only sword with which the dragon can be slain (str. 107), that is, he is guardian of the dragon's very life. Then Seyfrid kills Kuperan, which enables him to gain access to the sword with which he will slay the dragon. Thus, Lecouteux argues, whether he was aware of it or not, the poet of the *Hürnen Seyfrid* was drawing on narrative traditions from popular folklore, attested in literary form by the thirteenth century. But it would be unwise to imagine that the *Lied vom hürnen Seyfrid* in the form that it has come down to us was of comparable age; the muddled presentation of the poem as a whole points, Lecouteux thinks, to a later period.

In the later seventeenth century the *Lied vom Hürnen Seyfrid* was recast in prose and published under the title *Historia von dem gehörnten Siegfried*. This chapbook appeared in at least three dozen editions over the next two hundred years. In the *Historia* the role of the dragon is as in the *Lied*. As there, the smith sends Siegfried into the forest to fetch charcoal, expecting him to fall prey to the dragon, but Siegfried tears out trees with which he pins the dragon and its brood to the ground. He then sets the trees alight, and in the heat the dragon's fat melts and, on cooling, turns into horn:

> Da floß das Fett als ein kleines Bächlein dahin. Siegfried tauchet den Finger in das Fett, wie dasselbe erkaltet, wird es ein hartes Horn. Als Siegfried solches gewahr wird, ziehet er sich ganz nackend aus, und überstreicht damit den gantzen Leib, ohne zwischen den beyden Schultern oder Achseln, dahin kunte er nicht wohl kommen, daß ihm dann auch endlich sein Leben an demselben Orte gekostet, wie ihr hernachmahls hören

werdet. Dieses ist die Ursache, daß man ihn den gehörnten Siegfried genennet hat.[36]

In the second dragon-fight in the *Historia*, the dragon generates such a heat that the rock became as hot as the furnace in a smithy. (We are told that over the four years or so that Florigunda — as the Krimhilt figure is named here — had been in the dragon's lair the dragon would use his heat to keep her warm in the winter!)[37] The heat is so terrible that Siegfried's own horny skin melts and he is forced to retreat until it cools down, during which time he finds the treasure that the dwarfs had hidden in the cave.[38] When battle is rejoined, Siegfried succeeds in cutting off the dragon's tail, which so enrages the beast that it directs all its heat at Siegfried. The heat was so intense that not only Siegfried's but also the dragon's own horn melts, which enables Siegfried's sword to get through to the monster's body. With a mighty blow he cuts the dragon in two.[39]

The aim of this study has been to present the details of the dragon-fights as found in the various extant sources, to provide the reader with an overview, and to offer some basic guidance regarding the interrelation of the different treatments. Detailed discussion of the complex details of the interrelationships between the various texts and between the dragon-fight and other aspects of Sigurd-Siegfried's youthful adventures is not possible here, not only because the scholarly literature on the subject is vast but also because no consensus has been reached on many of the questions which need to be addressed.

[36] Golther 65–66; K. O. Conrady, ed., *Deutsche Volksbücher*, Rowohlts Klassiker, Deutsche Literatur 24 (Reinbek: Rowohlt, 1968) 213.

[37] Cf. *Hürnen Seyfrid* 138,6.

[38] The idea that Siegfried's horn melts again is an innovation of the author of the *Historia*; in the *Hürnen Seyfrid* we hear only that Seyfrid perspired (str. 131,8), that the heat was as intense as red-hot iron in a forge (str. 132) and that Seyfrid had to flee from the blue and red flames emitted by the dragon (str. 139) and hide until the temperature had cooled (str. 140,3–4). Nevertheless the notion that the horn would melt when heated occurs already in *Rosengarten D*, str. 531,1–3, where Dietrich breathes fire at Sîvrit:

Her Dietrich wart erzürnet, riechen er began,
als ein hûs, daz dâ dimpfet und ist enzündet an.
Sîvride ûz Niderlande wart sîn gehürne weich.

[39] Golther, *Das Lied vom hürnen Seyfrid* 82–84; Conrady 228–230.

Do ſchickt jn hin der meyſter
Das er ſolt haben frag
Ein Koler ſaß im walde
Des ſolt er warten eben
Hinder derſelben Linden
Der ſolt jm Kolen geben.

¶ Hie kam Sewfrid zů der Linden da der Trach lag/ vnd erſchlug jn zů todt.

¶ Damit ſo meynt der Schmide
Der wurm ſolt jn abthon
Als er kam zů der Linden
Den wurm thet er beſton

Seyfrid slays the dragon. Woodcut by Hans Sebald Beham from *Das Lied vom Hürnen Sewfrid*. Nuremberg: Kunegunde Hergotin, c. 1530, fol. A3v.

Er thet jn bald erschlagen
Der junge küne man
Do dacht er an den Koler
Zů dem gieng er in den than.
¶ Do kam er in ein gwilde
Da so vil Trachen lagen
Lindtwürm Krötten vnd Attern
Als er bey seynen tagen
Het ye gesehen ligen

¶ Hie bedecket Sewfrid das gewürm mit baumen/vnd bringt ein fewr vom Koler/vnd will sie all verbrennen.

A iiij.

Seyfrid pins the dragons down with tree-trunks and sets fire to them. Woodcut by Hans Sebald Beham from *Das Lied vom Hürnen Sewfrid*. Nuremberg: Kunegunde Hergotin, c. 1530, fol. A4r.

¶ Das horn der würm gund weychen
Ein Bechlein her thet fließ
Des wundert Sewfrid ſere
Ein finger er dreyn ſtieß
Do jm der finger erkalte
Do was er jm hürnein
Wol mit dem ſelben Bache
Schmirt er den leybe ſeyn.

¶ Hie ſchmirt ſich Sewfrid vnd wirdt aller hürnen/dann zwiſchen den ſchultern nicht.

A v

Seyfrid smearing himself with molten horn. Woodcut by Hans Sebald Beham from *Das Lied vom Hürnen Sewfrid*. Nuremberg: Kunegunde Hergotin, c. 1530, fol. A5r.

¶ Der jungen waren dreye
Zů Künig als ich sag
Jr schwester die was schöne
Die thet vmb ein mittag
Wol in ein fenster stane
Do kam ein wilder Trach
Geflogen inn den lüfften
Vnd nam die schönen magt.

¶ Hie kumbt der Trach geflogen/vnd
füret die Junckfraw Krim-
hilden mit jm dahin.

The dragon abducts Krimhilt. From *Das Lied vom Hürnen Sewfrid.* Nuremberg: Kunegunde Hergotin, c. 1530, fol. A6v.

Da was er jm Hürnein
Vol mit dem selben Bache
Schmiert er den Leibe sein.
Das er ward aller Hürnen

Seyfrid bathes in the dragon's molten horn. From *Das Lied vom Hürnen Seyfrid*. Strasbourg: Thiebolt Berger, 1563.

Manch küner Held verlorn.
Der Jungen waren dreye
Zů König als ich sag
Je Schwester die war schone
Sie thet vmb ein mittag
Wol an ein Fenster stahne
Da kam ein wilder Trach
Geflogen in den lüfften
Vnd nam die schöne Magt.

Hie kompt ein Trach geflogen/vnd nimpt die Jungfraw Grymhilden/fürt sie mit jhm hinweg.

Die Burg war erleücht mit fewre

The dragon abducts Krimhilt. From *Das Lied vom Hürnen Seyfrid*. Strasbourg: Thiebolt Berger, 1563.

Francis G. Gentry

Key Concepts in the *Nibelungenlied*

Key concepts refer, specifically, to those ideas and motifs that inform the fundamental ethical and social structure of the *Nibelungenlied*. Of course, these concepts are not unique to the great epic, but are found in virtually all medieval German epics. This situation is not surprising, given the fact that most narratives that were composed during the classical age of medieval German literature (ca. 1160–1250) were written for patrons and audiences who shared similar aesthetic tastes and expectations. All were members of a court, for example. As such, they would expect that the literature commissioned by and produced for the court would essentially reflect its social and moral perspectives. In some respects, the works do precisely that. Nonetheless, each poet — certainly of the classical period — is not content merely to reflect the court and its practices. By a differently-angled positioning of "key concepts" of the courtly world-view, the poet is able to hold up his creation as a critical mirror for the court to view itself and, by implication, its imperfections. For by taking what seems to be familiar, but shifting the perspective just slightly, the poet forces his audience into a dialectic confrontation with its own ideals and their inadequacies. Wolfram von Eschenbach and Hartmann von Aue have long been recognized as masters of this technique. But, as we shall see, in this respect as in so many others, the anonymous Nibelungen poet is no less gifted than his illustrious contemporaries.

In the following, we shall describe several concepts and conceptual pairs in the *Nibelungenlied* in varying degrees of detail. The final part of the essay will deal extensively with the most significant key concept, *triuwe* ("loyalty") and its relationship to the concept of *vriunt* ("friend, relative, ally, lord/vassal"). We will see how *triuwe*, both alone and in association with *vriunt*, is so pervasive and so determining that it is no wonder that succeeding generations of modern readers have referred to the great epic as the *Lied von der Treue* ("the song of loyalty"). But we will also note that *triuwe* is not a static concept, but rather an extremely flexible one in the hands of the Nibelungen poet. Nonetheless, it is important to keep in mind that all the concepts which will be highlighted are to be viewed not as isolated phenomena, but rather as acting in concert, and together they constitute the complex ethical foundation of the chivalric Middle Ages. Before attempting to elucidate the meaning of the more abstract concepts and attributes, let us begin with the concrete individual about whom any heroic epic unfolds, namely, the hero.

Certain designations like *helt* ("hero"), *recke*, *degen* ("warrior"), and the very archaic *wigant* (also denoting "warrior" — occurring only twice in the epic: 61, 4; 1002,4)[1] come down from the Germanic heroic tradition and are encountered more frequently in the *Nibelungenlied* than in the Arthurian romances where the term *ritter* ("knight") is more common. Nonetheless, they all refer essentially to different facets of the same persona, an armed retainer. In the heroic epic, as would perhaps be expected, the aspect emphasized is that of the fighter, the one skilled in battle. The battles are most often mass scenes of confrontation (and destruction), although the important combats, as is usually the case in heroic epics, are presented as individual confrontations, for the simple reason that such scenes are more suitable for presenting the important lessons to be learned by the community of listeners, i.e., how one should act in a battle, how one should uphold one's own honor or the honor of one's lord, one's clan or family, etc. Of course, the *ritter* in the Arthurian romances is likewise skilled in battle, and his battles, too, are individual encounters. But the objective of a battle scene in a chivalric romance is an infinitely more self-centered one than in a heroic epic. For although it provides an opportunity for the knight to demonstrate his prowess fighting for his lord, a lady, or himself, it is also the arena in which he is forced to confront the moral and ethical implications of his calling as a knight in order to achieve, ultimately, a better insight into his proper place within society and his responsibilities to others. The heroic epic, be it the *Iliad* or the *Nibelungenlied*, is more concerned with the progress and fate of an entire people, while the romance focuses on the development and destiny of the individual knight.

Another significant concept which has come down through the ages from the ancient Germanic warrior societies, and which both epic types share and employ in approximately the same way, is *êre* ("honor"). Unlike its more modern descendant, the medieval and Germanic concept of honor is not so much an abstract, but rather describes concretely the quality of the individual to whom it is ascribed. As in the Germanic period so also in the Middle Ages honor remains primarily a visible attribute of the "outer" person, and, like its Germanic manifestation, is normative for the elite, especially for the

[1] References to the text of the *Nibelungenlied* are based on *Das Nibelungenlied*, ed. Helmut de Boor, 20th ed., Deutsche Klassiker des Mittelalters (Wiesbaden: Brockhaus, 1972).

knight/warrior.[2] Thus, *êre* most often has the meaning of "pomp" or "splendor" when referring to the external circumstances in which the individual exists. For example, the poet describes Kriemhild living among the grandeur and power of the Burgundian court: "in disen hôhen êren..." (13,1). Conversely, *êre* is used to describe that which has been lost: "diu vil michel êre was dâ gelegen tôt" (2378,1). On occasion honor ***apparently*** describes an inner quality of the individual as in strophe 2146, when Rüdiger defends his murder of a Hunnish warrior who called the bravery of the Margrave of Bechlarn into question:

> Dô sprach der ritter edele: "da beswârt er mir den muot
> und hât mir gëitewîzet êre unde guot,
> des ich von dînen handen hân sô vil genomen." (2146,1–3).

While it appears on the surface that Rüdiger is referring to a quality of his character, it is, nonetheless, clear from the context that *êre* is not used to portray an "inner" virtue of Rüdiger, but rather is intricately entangled with the external concepts of prestige, reputation, and status (cf. the discussion of "noble" below).

A ruler, for example, gains much prestige and consequently honor, and enhances his reputation, by being generous to his enemies because, by so doing, he demonstrates his superiority over them. Indeed, *milte* ("generosity"), in general, whether to friend or foe, is an attribute that enables a noble to manifest his honor (687,2). In short, *êre* is a necessary quality of any individual associated with a courtly or warrior culture.

Meaningfully connected with *êre* is the conceptual pair *liebe/leit* ("love/sorrow") which forms a major leitmotif of the *Nibelungenlied*. It is first encountered at the beginning of the work in the scene between Kriemhild and her mother Ute as the latter interprets Kriemhild's disturbing dream and prophesies that her daughter will marry a noble man. Kriemhild rejects this prediction and indicates her resolve to remain unmarried. She replies to her mother: "ez ist an manegen wîben vil dicke worden scîn,/wie liebe mit leide ze jungest lônen kan" (17,2–3). Although it is safe to assume that Kriemhild had something else in mind when she uttered this statement, namely that for women in the Middle Ages marriage was rarely an affair of the heart, the tragic events in the *Nibelungenlied* go on to demonstrate the truth of her assertion about the relationship of *liebe/leit*. The result is that *leit* meaning "sorrow" or "grief" is all too frequently encountered in the epic. But the possibility that *leit* can also carry with it the sense of insult or

[2] Otfrid Ehrismann, *Ehre und Mut, Aventiure und Minne. Höfische Wortgeschichten aus dem Mittelalter* (Munich: Beck, 1995) 65–70.

dishonor and that *leit* in this connotation is as structurally and semantically consequential as sorrow was not generally accepted until Friedrich Maurer convincingly demonstrated this thesis in his famous study from 1949.[3] Thus Kriemhild's relentless plans for revenge are much more understandable when her *leit* is viewed under the rubric of "insult." For an insult of this deadliness — after all, her husband was murdered and her treasure was stolen — humiliates and dishonors completely the person to whom it has happened. The loss of honor results in a concomitant loss of face and authority, and the dishonored individual is confronted with a shrinking, indeed disappearing power base. The only way for a member of heroic society to reclaim honor is through revenge.[4] The irony is that Kriemhild's revenge, while justified, accomplishes just the opposite of what she intended. She is brutally slain and thus even more dishonored in the eyes of the poet and the epic's surviving characters. The message is clear: revenge, no matter how great the provocation, is never acceptable.[5]

The *Nibelungenlied*, like its Arthurian counterparts, also emphasizes other less spectacular concepts than *leid*, which like *êre* serve in the process of self-identification and definition of courtly society. Among these is *zuht* ("manners, good breeding"), a fundamental component of the courtly individual's character, as strophe 105 makes clear, when Siegfried, who is unknown to Gunther, arrives at Worms. Hagen, however, identifies him correctly as a great hero, dragon slayer, and owner of the Nibelungen treasure and suggests that he be accorded an honorable greeting. Gunther and his retinue follow Hagen's advice: "Der wirt und sîne recken enpfiengen sô den gast,/daz in an ir zühten vil wênec iht gebrast" (105,1–2).

Another concept is *dien(e)st* ("service") which occurs frequently and describes the relationship of lords to vassals, men to women, as well as being used in the more general sense of "favor," as evidenced by strophe 305 when the poet relates that Kriemhild was accompanied to court twelve days in a row by Siegfried, something her brothers had arranged as a friendly gesture toward the hero ("der dienst wart dem recken durch grôze liebe getân"). Unfortunately the rather neutral concept of *dienst* has its dark side too, specifically within the *Nibelungenlied*. For the characters peopling the society depicted in the epic, much like those of the society in which the work came

[3] Friedrich Maurer, *Leid: Studien zur Bedeutungs- und Problemgeschichte, besonders in den großen Epen der staufischen Zeit*, 3rd ed. (Berne and Munich: Francke, 1964) 25–33.

[4] See Francis G. Gentry, *Triuwe und Vriunt in the Nibelungenlied* (Amsterdam: Rodopi, 1975) and Rainer Zacharias, "Die Blutrache im deutschen Mittelalter," *ZfdA* 91 (1962): 167–201.

[5] Gentry 34–43.

into being, are very conscious of their status. Strophe 724 provides a good illustration of this aspect. After many years of marriage to Gunther, Brünhild is distressed that Siegfried and Kriemhild have not appeared at court in all this time since, as far as Brünhild knows, Siegfried is a vassal of Gunther and should, by obligation, appear and attend the king periodically:

> nu gedâht' ouch alle zîte daz Guntheres wîp:
> "wie treit et alsô hôhe vrou Kriemhilt den lîp?
> nu ist doch unser eigen Sîfrit ir man:
> er hât uns nu vil lange lützel dienste getân."

This strophe also contains a concept that is of paramount importance in the work: *eigen* ("unfree vassal"). In fact, the whole conceptual complex "free/unfree" assumes an even greater thematic importance in the *Nibelungenlied* than that of *liebe/leit* and acts as the catalyst of the total tragedy of the epic. Although Brünhild's perception of the relationship between Siegfried and Gunther is mistaken, it is a misperception that was fostered both by Gunther and Siegfried himself when the latter accompanied Gunther on the journey to Iceland. In strophes 420–423 Siegfried identifies himself to Brünhild as Gunther's *man* ("vassal"), so that her attention would not be on him but rather on Gunther. In that way Siegfried could employ all his artifices to insure Gunther's victory in the three contests. Because Brünhild had no reason to disbelieve the words from Siegfried's own mouth concerning his status, she held fast to her conviction that he was a vassal. It is for that reason that she wept during her wedding feast when she saw that her sister-in-law, Kriemhild, was to become Siegfried's wife. For Brünhild, a high-born noble, this situation was nothing less than calamitous. The logical conclusion for her to draw was that Kriemhild, herself a high-born noble, was forced into an inferior social status through her marriage to Siegfried, ostensibly just a vassal, and an unfree one at that. Essentially, Kriemhild's marriage to Siegfried was socially declassé. This incident, in Brünhild's understanding, had wide-ranging implications, namely, that Gunther had so fallen in honor and prestige that he was forced to give his sister to a wealthy vassal, and as a result she, Brünhild, now Gunther's wife, was compelled to share this dishonor. The situation was not just a fiction devised by the Nibelungen poet, but was an accurate reflection of the social changes going on in Germany in the twelfth and thirteenth centuries. For around this period, the free aristocracy was either becoming impoverished or unable to reproduce male heirs (generally both conditions prevailed) and saw itself compelled to strike up alliances through marriage with wealthy members of the ministerial class, who, by the time of the *Nibelungenlied*, were among the wealthiest and most powerful nobles in the empire. But since their origins a century or more previous were unfree,[6] the conservative nobility viewed any intermarriage with even the wealthiest ministerial as a mésalliance. Thus, in spite of his marriage into an aristocratic family, Siegfried, in Brünhild's view, is a vassal and neither his wealth nor his undisputed power exempts him from performing his duties as vassal. She makes her opinion unmistakably clear in an exchange with Gunther as she is trying to persuade him to invite Siegfried and Kriemhild to Worms. In response to Gunther's objection that the distance to Worms would be too great, Brünhild plays her trump card (as she sees it) by saying: "Swie hôhe rîche wære deheines küniges man,/swaz im gebüte sîn herre, daz sold' er doch niht lân" (728,1–2). This misunderstanding on Brünhild's part, and the unwillingness on Gunther's to correct it, leads inexorably to the tragic confrontation between the two queens concerning the worth of their respective husbands. Brünhild maintains that Gunther must have priority over Siegfried in the eyes of the court because Gunther is his lord as she, herself, heard Siegfried say. Brünhild then utters the fateful word *eigen* ("unfree") to describe Siegfried's status — and, by implication, Kriemhild's as well. Kriemhild's outraged response is, of course, to be expected. Interesting for the purposes of this essay, however, is the word she uses to describe her own status, *adelvrî* ("free-born aristocracy," 828), one of the very rare if not the only occurrence of this legal term in classical medieval German literature. The scene is set: Brünhild holds fast to her interpretation of Siegfried being *eigen*, and Kriemhild intends to demonstrate that she and Siegfried are *adelvrî*. It is, of course, a dispute that has, indeed can have, no winner, and the scene degenerates into name-calling of the worst sort. Brünhild calls Kriemhild an *eigendiu* ("the woman of an unfree vassal"), Kriemhild retorts that if that is the case then Brünhild is a *mannes kebse* ("concubine of an unfree vassal"). The fact that this entire scene is being played out in public makes the dishonor to and insulting of Brünhild all the greater and cries out for revenge which must and will be taken. In the heroic environment of the *Nibelungenlied*, the only possible outcome is a tragic one.

In spite of the appalling events in the *Nibelungenlied*, the work also includes several concepts that are part and parcel of the courtly litany of positive attributes that are found in all epic works of the classical period. For the most part, they pertain to the smooth functioning of the social structure of the court as well as the interaction of its members. It is no surprise,

[6] See Marc Bloch, *Feudal Society*, trans. L. A. Manyon, vol. 2 (Chicago: University of Chicago Press, 1964); Karl Bosl, *Die Grundlagen der modernen Gesellschaft im Mittelalter: Eine deutsche Gesellschaftsdichtung des Mittelalters*, 2 vols. (Stuttgart: Hiersemann, 1972); Karl J. Leyser, *Medieval Germany and Its Neighbors 900–1250* (London: Hambledon, 1982).

therefore, to find terms like ***vröude/hôher muot*** ("joy/noble attitude"), ***hôh(ge)zît*** ("festival"), ***minne*** ("love"), ***holt*** ("favorably inclined toward"), and ***edel*** ("noble"), to cite just a few examples. The usage of these expressions in the *Nibelungenlied* conforms in large measure to that in the romances. "Noble," for example, is a designation of status and not necessarily of attitude.[7] Thus when the Burgundian kings as well as Siegfried, Kriemhild, Brünhild, Rüdiger, et al. are described as being "noble," attention is being drawn more to the circumstance of their birth. Nobles, like Rüdiger, who seems to transcend all attempts at categorization and is repeatedly addressed or referred to as "vil edel Rüedegêr," act nobly simply because this quality is part of their being. But even those who act reprehensibly are also called noble, if the circumstances of birth warrant. One example will suffice. At the end of the *Nibelungenlied,* after Kriemhild has slaughtered the bound Hagen, and after she has been savagely cut down by a berserk Hildebrand, the poet describes the grisly scene somewhat laconically: "ze stücken was gehouwen dô daz edele wîp" (2377,2). It is clear that Kriemhild's heinous actions do not reduce her nobility nor prevent her from being recognized as noble. The importance of a noble spirit as opposed to mere happenstance of birth was not seriously treated in literature until a generation later with Rudolf von Ems (*Der guote Gêrhart*) and the gnomic poets like Freidank, who wrote the memorable verse: "swer tugent hât, derst wol geborn:/ân tugent ist adel gar verlorn." Quite possibly, too, the "edele herzen" addressed by Gottfried von Straßburg in *Tristan* point in this new direction.

A necessary attribute for a member of the nobility (assuming that all nobles are *edel* in the *Nibelungenlied*) is a ***hôher muot*** (" noble attitude") and the concomitant emotion of joy which is engendered by a noble outlook. The main courtly event which fosters the development and maintenance of a noble attitude and joy is a ***hôhgezît*** ("festival"). Thus it is no accident that festivals play an important role in most epic works of the period.[8] In the Arthurian romances, for example, they are quite often the settings for major turns in the narrative, which will entail a (fortunately only temporary) reversal of the respective hero's good fortune, e.g., in Wolfram von Eschenbach's *Parzival,* when Parzival returns to Arthur after his failed visit to the Grail castle, he is denounced by the Grail messenger, Cundrie, for his failure to ask the key question. This event enables the narrative to split into two strands, the Gawain and the Parzival episodes, with Parzival beginning his long interior journey to the Grail and the meaning of God's love. Similarly, in Hartmann von Aue's *Iwein,* Iwein is a guest at Arthur's festival where he is confronted by Lunete who censures him because he did not keep his word

[7] Ehrismann 60–64.

[8] Ehrismann 91–103.

to Laudine to return to her. This causes Iwein to leave Arthur, go mad, and slowly find his way back to himself, his wife Laudine, and finally ferret out the true meaning of "adventure." The *Nibelungenlied*, too, stands firmly in this tradition, although there is no reversal of the misfortune which comes into being. There are, to be sure, several festivals in the *Nibelungenlied* that are more or less occasions of celebration (e.g., Siegfried's knighting, after the Saxon War, on the occasion of Brünhild's arrival in Worms), but the two major celebrations (at the return of Kriemhild and Siegfried to Worms and the journey of the Burgundians to Etzel) are anything but gatherings of openness and joy. On the contrary, these two key festivals are the scenes of secrecy and hidden motives and culminate, ultimately, in unrelieved sorrow with the murder of Siegfried and the annihilation of the Burgundians. Indeed, it is not mere happenstance that the first strophe identifies this paradox as a central theme of the work: "von fröuden, hôchgezîten, von weinen und von klagen,/... muget ir nu wunder hœren sagen" (1,3–4). Although the results of the intrigue and conflict surrounding the festivities are much more drastic in the *Nibelungenlied* than in the Arthurian romances, it is clear that in medieval German literature, at any rate, the *hôhgezît* is an ambivalent event and one that often becomes the crucible in which the respective heroes must prove their worth, even if, as in the case of the *Nibelungenlied*, their excellence is revealed only through their death.

The one supreme measure of the excellence of an individual's character and that which distinguishes warriors above all is their loyalty to their lords, to their society, to God, and to their own ideals. The term used to express all these attributes is *triuwe* ("loyalty, faithfulness, love"), arguably the most important concept in medieval German literature of the classical period. Wolfram von Eschenbach, for example, stretched the semantic range of the term the most. In his *Parzival, triuwe* not only connotes the spirit of loyalty and constancy that should lie at the base of all human relationships, but also is employed to express the concept of divine love. In the scene between Parzival and the Gray Knight in Book IX, the latter responds to Parzival's assertion that he has renounced service to God, because God was untrue to him, with the astonished statement:

> "meint ir got den diu maget gebar?
> ....
> ez ist hiute der karvrîtac,
> des al diu werlt sich vreun mac
> und dâ bî mit angest siufzec sîn.
> wâ wart ie hôher triuwe schîn,

dan die got durch uns begienc,
den man durch uns anz kriuze hienc."[9]

While the use of *triuwe* in the *Nibelungenlied* remains on a more mundane level, the term itself and all that it implies has long been recognized as the basic structural component of the Nibelungen narrative. It is, without doubt, the most important concept in the work. If the noun *triuwe* embodies the ethical foundation of the characters, its adjectival form *getriuwe* ("loyal") provides the defining attribute of a relationship or character. It is the most enduring and noble trait that one can have. It is the essential quality of character that nourishes all other virtues, such as steadfastness, honor, good breeding, and noble attitude, without which they would wither. In short, *triuwe/getriuwe* informs and defines every human association in the *Nibelungenlied*, whether within the feudal social structure or the structure of personal relationships.

Within feudal society, *triuwe* is the cement that holds the feudal bond together, the tenor of which is marked by the conceptual pair, *vel auxilium vel consilium* ("both aid and advice"). It is the vassal's responsibility to offer his lord protective aid and advice whenever the latter requires the one or the other. The lord, for his part, is expected to treat his vassal justly, to reward him for his services, and to protect him. If both parties perform their duties correctly, they are praised as being *getriuwe*. Both aspects of the feudal tie are frequently observed in the *Nibelungenlied*: (a) *ADVICE*: When Gunther is first apprised of the imminent attack of the Saxons and the Danes by a messenger of his enemies, he refuses to make any decision until he has discussed the matter with loyal advisors:

"Nu bîtet eine wîle", sprach der künec guot,
"unz ich mich baz versinne. ich künd' iu mînen muot.
hân ich getriuwer iemen, dîne sol ich niht verdagen
disiu starken mære sol ich mînen friwenden klagen." (147)

In this instance Gunther is doing precisely what would be expected of a wise ruler in the feudal age, seeking the counsel of his "friends," i.e., advisors, vassals, relatives. (b) *AID*: Engaging in battle on the side of one's lord dramatically illustrates the concept of *triuwe* as aid. Yet the actual use of the term in the text is found not in descriptions of combat, but rather primarily in important scenes that precede the fighting itself. The best-known illustration of this aspect of *triuwe* is found in the scene between Rüdiger and

[9] Wolfram von Eschenbach, *Parzival*, ed. Albert Leitzmann, zweites Heft: *Parzival Buch VII–XI*, 6th ed., Altdeutsche Textbibliothek 13 (Tübingen: Niemeyer, 1963) 448.2; 7–12.

Kriemhild after Rüdiger has delivered Etzel's offer of marriage. Kriemhild rejects Etzel's proposal until Rüdiger swears to serve and protect her in the land of the Huns:

> Mit allen sînen mannen swuor ir dô Rüedegêr
> mit triuwen immer dienen, unt daz die recken hêr
> ir nimmer niht versageten ûz Etzelen lant,
> des si êre haben solde, des sichert' ir Rüedegêres hant. (1258)

Of course, it is this offer of service and protection that brings Rüdiger to grief later at the ill-fated festival at Etzel's court. He evidently did not understand his pledge to include plans for avenging Siegfried's death, but Kriemhild did, as she makes clear in the following strophe when she muses: "waz ob noch wirt errochen des mînen lieben mannes lîp?" (1259,4).

The *Nibelungenlied* also offers an illustration of the reciprocal nature of the bond of *triuwe*, namely, the obligations of a lord to his vassal. Before the final battle, and when it is clear that the Burgundians will not be victorious, Kriemhild offers to let all surviving Burgundians go in exchange for the surrender of Hagen. In reply to her offer of amnesty, Giselher gives eloquent expression to the quality of the lord's obligation to his vassal:

> "Wir müesen doch ersterben", sprach dô Gîselher.
> "uns enscheidet niemen von ritterlîcher wer.
> swer gerne mit uns vehte, wir sîn et aber hie,
> wande ich deheinen mînen friunt an *den* triuwen nie verlie." (2106)

And just a few stanzas later after the Burgundians have scorned Kriemhild's demand to surrender Hagen and the final climactic battle in the hall begins, the poet underscores, once more, the importance of this bond between lord and vassal:

> Die noch hie ûze stuonden, die tribens' in den sal
> mit slegen unde mit schüzzen, des wart vil grôz der schal.
> doch wolden nie gescheiden die fürsten und ir man.
> sine konden von ir triuwen an ein ander niht verlân. (2110).

Triuwe is also used to define the character of personal relationships which, as we shall see, will have in some instances in the *Nibelungenlied* more importance than the relationships that are part of the feudal bond. Three groups comprise the spectrum of personal relationships within the *Nibelungenlied*: blood relatives, spouses, and friends. The obligations of *triuwe* imposed on the members of these groups were qualitatively the same as those of the feudal structure, and, indeed, it is often difficult to draw the line between the two groups, as far as the concept is concerned, since individuals could be members of both groups. Hagen, for example, exists in a formal relationship with the Burgundian kings, but is also a blood relative, something that is mentioned by Kriemhild in strophe 898,2 and by Giselher in 1133,3, as well as being a friend of Rüdiger. Although in the realm of friendship the concept of *triuwe* is more often implied than explicitly expressed to define vertical affinities, it is, nonetheless, the complex bond of friendship that plays the most important role in the *Nibelungenlied*. A glance at the relationship of Rüdiger to the Burgundians will serve to illustrate this point. The ties binding Rüdiger to the Burgundians are several: (1) He gives his daughter in marriage to Giselher, the youngest Burgundian king (strophe 1682); (2) The Burgundians are his guests, and he provides them with an escort to Etzel's palace; (3) He also enjoys a long-standing friendship with Hagen. An important part of the tragic poignancy of the *Nibelungenlied* is that Rüdiger's obligations of friendship come into dramatic conflict with those incurred by his pledge of personal loyalty to Kriemhild, something of which she reminds him when she states:

> ... "gedenke, Rüedegêr, der grôzen triuwe dîn,
> der stæte und ouch der eide, daz du den schaden mîn
> immer woldest rechen und elliu mîniu leit." (2151,1–3)

In addition, Etzel recalls Rüdiger's vassal loyalty and demands that the latter render the service that he owes the king. Rüdiger's quandary is surely one of the most gripping episodes not only in the *Nibelungenlied* but also in world literature. Caught between the seemingly diametrically opposed obligations of his loyalty to his lord and to his friends, Rüdiger eventually accedes to the pleas of the royal couple and fulfills his vassal loyalty, knowing that by doing so he is jeopardizing his immortal soul (strophes 2150; 2166), thereby giving dramatic emphasis to the central thematic of the *Nibelungenlied*: the paradox of *triuwe* becoming *untriuwe* ("disloyalty, faithlessness").

In general, *untriuwe* does not merely mean no *triuwe*, but rather an absence of *triuwe* where one would expect to find it. Siegfried's death provides a good illustration of this point. For the hero's death and the events surrounding it mark the first attempt on the part of the poet to indicate clearly the terrible consequences that *untriuwe* could have. On seven occasions, the poet personally intrudes into his text in order to express his outrage at the act. He repeatedly describes Siegfried's killing as one of unparalleled faithlessness (876,1–2; 887,3; 911,4; 915,4; 916,1–2; 971,4; 988,3–4). On one further occasion (1074,1–2), he has Siegmund, Siegfried's father, refer to his son's death as a faithless action. It is obvious that the poet is incensed at Hagen's deed. But it is equally as obvious that Hagen has cause to seek Siegfried's death since, as we have seen above, his lady, Brünhild, has been publicly humiliated by Kriemhild, Siegfried's wife. Another example would be Rüdiger's quandary. In the previous discussion of *triuwe* within a personal relationship, the crisis that torments Rüdiger in the thirty-seventh adventure was briefly highlighted. Just as Gunther was faced with two possibilities in the episodes leading up to Siegfried's death, i.e., to seek or to forego revenge, so, too, Rüdiger is caught on the horns of a dilemma. Should he honor his pledge of *triuwe* to his liege lord Etzel and his queen and avenge the wrongs done to the royal pair by the Burgundians, or should he honor his many ties of personal *triuwe* to the unwelcome guests? It is a conflict that Rüdiger is unable to resolve other than by agreeing to observe his vassal loyalty, even though he knows that the Burgundians are not at fault. The criticism of the poet is muted in this episode, but Rüdiger, himself, has been an eloquent judge of the wrongness of his action (2150, 2153–2154).

In both scenes the poet has put his characters into situations in which conflicting obligations of feudal and personal *triuwe* are highlighted. In both instances the issue revolves around the taking of apparent justified revenge for an injury or insult done to the king and queen. Both times the protagonists, Hagen and Rüdiger respectively, act with apparent justification, the one case involving an action to restore the honor and, thus, ruling viability of Gunther, and the other to avenge the severe losses incurred by Etzel and Kriemhild, including the slaughter of their young son Ortlieb. Yet neither reason meets with the approbation of the poet. Clearly, he is asking his characters to distinguish among conflicting obligations and not always choose to honor those that appear to be legitimized by custom (vendetta), but rather to look closely at the relationships humanized by the bond of friendship, something Gunther was unable to do with regard to Siegfried and Rüdiger with regard to the Burgundians. The answers that the Nibelungen poet offers his audience with regard to the obligations of *triuwe* are definitely not comfortable. He is asking them to make distinctions, to come to decisions that may fly in the face of accepted tradition. The tragedy of the *Nibelungenlied* is that the strict adherence to *triuwe*, the bond of society, actually sunders Nibelungen society and ultimately destroys it.

As a concluding observation, it is ironic to note that all the concepts which have been discussed in this essay should have functioned — and were meant to function — as constructive elements of society. But, as we have seen, the opposite is true: an inflexible perception of the meaning and implication of these terms brings about irrevocable destruction. In the final analysis, the *Nibelungenlied*, like the great heroic epics of Classical Antiquity, even Virgil's *Aeneid*, is a tale about loss and sundering. The Nibelungen world and its people start out at their most thriving level and progressively lose everything until they, themselves, are lost. Like Virgil's Aeneas, the Nibelungen poet's characters discover that riches, power, and status are meaningless if the cost is one's humanity and, as Rüdiger movingly recognizes, one's soul — acme and nadir occupy the same space. In this respect the *Nibelungenlied* is unique among the works of the German Middle Ages. Unlike the situation in the Arthurian tales, for example, there is no moment of "restoration," no lasting harmony. The constant flirtation with disaster that leads to an unalterable commitment to the indefensible (revenge) and culminates ultimately in irreversible tragedy constitutes the hallmark of the work as well as its great attraction for audiences throughout the centuries.

Will Hasty

From Battlefields to Bedchambers: Conquest in the *Nibelungenlied*

Conquest is inextricable from the oral and literary traditions culminating in the *Nibelungenlied*. It is present at the historical origin of these traditions in the destruction of the Burgundian kingdom on the middle Rhine, when its king, Gundaharius, attempting to expand the sphere of his power to the northwest into Roman Gaul, was defeated by the Roman leader Aëtius and Hunnish troops probably allied with him in 436.[1] It is present in Attila the Hun, the Scourge of God and ravager of most of Europe in the mid-fifth century, and in Theoderic the Great, conqueror of the western Roman empire in the late fifth century, whose deeds and death were celebrated in songs about Atli/Etzel and Dietrich von Bern that eventually became elements in the tales of the Nibelungen composed in the High Middle Ages, and it is present still in the High Middle Ages when conquering élites were invading Palestine, Greece, Andalusia, Ulster, and Prussia.[2] Conquest might properly be seen as one of the central concerns of the *Nibelungenlied*, the actions of figures such as Siegfried and Hagen being entirely consistent with the brutal, but nonetheless idealized, characteristics of the figure of the historical conqueror as this is depicted by the historian Robert Bartlett: "Vigour, boldness, brutality and greed: this was the Faustian brew that made up the conqueror."[3]

Composed during an age of conquest, the *Nibelungenlied* is, among other things, a tale of conquest: Siegfried comes to Worms with the aim of taking all the Burgundian kings have by force. The main problem with understanding the *Nibelungenlied* in terms of conquest is that it is also a tale of courtliness: Siegfried comes not with a conquering army (although with

[1] Gundaharius, along with his family and as many as 20,000 of his people died in these unsuccessful battles of conquest. The remainder of the Burgundian peoples were resettled in present-day Savoy, on the upper Rhone and Saône. This kingdom was eventually itself conquered in 534 and integrated into the realm of the Franks. See Joachim Heinzle, *Das Nibelungenlied: Eine Einführung* (Munich: Artemis, 1987) 20.

[2] See Robert Bartlett, *The Making of Europe: Conquest, Colonization and Cultural Change* (Princeton: Princeton University Press, 1993) 90.

[3] Bartlett 90.

the power of an army in his mythical strength), but as an adventuring knight with just a few comrades, and the hostile intentions he manifests upon his arrival seem to disappear upon his involvement in the courtly interest of *minne* ("love"). Despite their apparent antagonism or irreconcilability, the interest in conquest and the interest in courtliness are both consistently fostered from the moment of Siegfried's arrival in Worms. This reading of the first part of the *Niblungenlied* will endeavor to demonstrate that the interest in conquest — in the struggle for supremacy between Siegfried and the Burgundians — is not ended, but rather only temporarily contained and redirected by the *Minne*-relationship of Siegfried and Kriemhild. The murder of Siegfried, which eventually leads to the catastrophic demise of the Burgundians in the second part of the poem, does not depict the failure of courtliness in the face of darker and more compelling forces,[4] but rather the culmination of a struggle for power that has been largely dependent on courtly forms for its expression.

I

The first two *âventiuren* of the poem, which describe the kingdom of the Burgundians and that of Siegfried's father Siegmund in some detail, underscore the interdependence of armed aggression and courtly splendor. The association of aggression and courtly splendor in these descriptions, particularly in the elaborate portrayal of the festival in which Siegfried is knighted, is made programmatic in the form of a rhyme in the very first strophe of the poem, which links the terms *strîten* and *hochgezîten*.[5] *Strîten* not only alludes negatively to the catastrophic downfall of the Burgundians at the end of the poem, but also must have had positive associations among noble audiences of the poem as the activity that is necessary to obtain and consolidate the power that finds visible expression and representation in courtly festivals and in the material wealth that is necessary to stage them. The inevitability of *strîten* as an activity that is constitutive of, rather than deleterious to, courtliness is also evident in the manner in which the initial descriptions of the kingdoms of the Burgundians and of Siegmund culminate in Siegfried's arrival in Worms as both a conqueror and a suitor of Kriemhild. The aggression with which Siegfried appears at the court of the Burgundian

[4] This is basically the argument of Weber, who stresses the significance of courtliness as a system of values that goes beyond costumes and fashion. This system is destroyed, according to Weber, by demonic forces within the characters. See Gottfried Weber, *Das Nibelungenlied: Problem und Idee* (Stuttgart: Metzler, 1963).

[5] Important is the consistent connection in this poem between fighting and courtly splendor, and not whether this particular strophe was a later interpolation.

kings is consistent with these descriptions, which are more than a rich backdrop against which the events of the poem will be played out. During an age in which inequality is an "accepted premiss of almost all social and political thought,"[6] it seems likely that the juxtaposition of two such powerful realms would have given rise to fundamental questions in the minds of medieval audiences: which of these two realms, about which this tale will revolve, is the more powerful? Can two kingdoms of such immense wealth and power exist without being a threat to one another? Is armed conflict between them not inevitable?

The description of Gunther's kingdom connects the person of Kriemhild and the political power held by the Burgundians by means of the term *pflegen.* The person of Kriemhild is fostered and protected by the Burgundian kings Gunther, Gernot, and Giselher (strophe 4) in the same way that they foster and protect the integrity and power of the realm, *des hoves krefte.*[7] Kriemhild is both an embodiment of the power wielded by the Burgundians (her beauty corresponding to their power) and, to the extent that she is a beautiful young woman of marriageable age, of its vulnerability: the man who wins the hand of Kriemhild also will win a stake in the Burgundian kingdom, and thus threaten the coherence of the brothers' political power. As in the later bridal quest that wins Brünhild for Gunther, the attempt to win a lady's love, and what amounts to the conquest of a powerful foreign realm, coincide when Siegfried first arrives in Worms. Kriemhild, as is revealed at the outset of the third *Âventiure*, is destined to become Siegfried's "undertân" (46,4b), and we soon observe that the subservience denoted by this term involves more than a single marital relationship.

II

Siegfried's motivations upon his arrival in Worms are shaped by the political situation in the realm of his father. He is, on the one hand, a prince who does not wish to wear the crown of his homeland as long as his parents live, even though the people of his realm very much desire to have him as a ruler. If he is to wear a crown before the death of his father, Siegfried must apparently earn it by conquest. This situation suggests Siegfried's future ambition in Worms, even as it implies a status of political inferiority to the

[6] Susan Reynolds, *Fiefs and Vassals: The Medieval Evidence Reinterpreted* (New York: Oxford University Press, 1994) 35.

[7] Quotations from the *Nibelungenlied* are based on the edition by Karl Bartsch/Helmut de Boor, *Das Nibelungenlied*, 21st revised edition by Roswitha Wisniewski, Deutsche Texte des Mittelalters (Wiesbaden: Brockhaus, 1979) and are indicated in parentheses by strophe and verse number. Here: 12,1a.

Burgundians: as a king in the land of his ancestors, Gunther seemingly wields greater power and is of higher standing than Siegfried. Yet we also discover from Hagen, as Siegfried arrives in Worms, that the young hero is in fact already a king, even if he is not yet designated as such, because he has slain the kings Schilbung and Nibelung, along with seven hundred of their *recken* ("warriors"), and brought the land and castles — and, more important, the *hort* — of these kings into his possession (cf. strophes 87–100). One of the many functions of the *hort* is to qualify Siegfried as a conqueror when he first appears before the Burgundian power elite. Amidst the treasures, as we discover later in the poem, is a mysterious object that connects the *hort* to conquest very directly:

> Der wunsch der lac darunder, von golde ein rüetelîn.
> der daz het erkunnet, der möhte meister sîn
> wol in aller werlde über ietslîchen man. (1124,1–3)

This magic wand is among the possessions of Siegfried when he first appears before Gunther, both as a young prince out to make his own fortune before he assumes his inheritance, and as a powerful king, who could seemingly bring overwhelming power to bear against any opponent. Although riding with only eleven comrades, Siegfried confronts the feared Burgundians both as a man intent on winning the love of a lady, and as an army of one, who states his intention to take all the Burgundians have by force:

> "Nu ir sît sô küene, als mir ist geseit,
> sone ruoch ich, ist daz iemen liep oder leit:
> ich wil an iu ertwingen, swaz ir muget hân:
> lant unde bürge, daz sol mir werden undertân." (110)

At first glance, the interest in conquest seems to disappear when Gernot questions the appropriateness of Siegfried's hostility within this ostensibly peaceful, courtly setting, and when Siegfried begins to think of his love for Kriemhild. One is thus tempted to assume that Siegfried gives up his ambitions of conquest and adopts a position of subservience to Kriemhild, and through her to Gunther, within the courtly framework of *Minnedienst*, or love service. Yet this assumption fails to grasp everything that happens in this initial episode, for one need not necessarily assume that Siegfried has given up his aggressive claim: the possibility must be considered that the young hero from the Netherlands does not fight Gunther for his lands and castles, because he does not have to. Gunther, perhaps fearing a fight with the mighty Siegfried, gives him what he wants without the fight that the young hero's provocative words seek:

Dô sprach der wirt des landes: "allez daz wir hân,
geruochet irs nâch êren, daz sî iu undertân,
und sî mit iu geteilet lîp unde guot." (127,1–3)

Otfrid Ehrismann observes that the vast critical literature dealing with this episode has tended to view Siegfried's behavior either in terms of his attempt to "usurp" Gunther's power, or in terms of his love for Kriemhild, and that there has been a reluctance to explore the possibility of a single principle underlying these two seemingly different concerns.[8] Conquest provides such a principle, if we do not assume that Siegfried's aggressive ambitions have ended when his thoughts turn to Kriemhild, or that Gunther's courtly concession can be dismissed as the response of a wise and experienced ruler to the unreasonable demands of an impetuous youth. There are good reasons for taking Gunther's concession much more literally than it is generally understood. During the uneven transition from Siegfried's initial aggression to courtly forms of interaction, the reactions of some of Gunther's followers strongly suggest that the conciliatory attitude of the Burgundian kings amounts to acceding shamefully to Siegfried's demands without resistance. Gernot's mollifying words, which try to bring Siegfried from his hostile intentions by stating that the Burgundians have no aggressive intentions of their own, provoke the following response from Ortwin, who would clearly prefer to take up the gauntlet Siegfried has thrown:

Mit grimmigem muote dâ stuonden friwende sîn.
dô was ouch dar under von Metzen Ortwîn.
der sprach: "disiu suone diu ist mir harte leit.
iu hât der starke Sîvrit unverdienet widerseit." (116)

Ortwin and Hagen, although they continue to be provoked by Siegfried, are commanded by Gernot to hold their tongues and to keep their swords in their sheaths. Open conflict, like that with which the poem ends, does not occur at this point, although the words of Gernot suggest that it is conflict on a similar scale that the kings are now attempting to avoid:

"Wie zæme uns mit iu strîten?" sprach aber Gêrnôt.
"swaz helde nu dar under müese ligen tôt,
wir hetens lützel êre und ir vil kleinen frum." (124, 1–3)

Given Siegfried's previous victory over the Nibelungs, which has just been reported by Hagen, and the strength of the Burgundians in their later death

[8] Otfrid Ehrismann, *Nibelungenlied: Epoche — Werk — Wirkung* (Munich: Beck, 1987) 118.

struggle against the forces of Etzel, one might expect nothing less than a confrontation on a scale similar to that between the Huns and the Burgundians (Nibelungs) at the end of the poem if an open battle erupted at this point. Difficult to imagine, given the military qualifications of the antagonists, is a brief altercation in which the vastly superior numbers of the Burgundians would put a quick end to Siegfried's aggression.

No less than three distinct aspects are present in the relationship between Siegfried and the Burgundian kings at the moment when Siegfried's interest in conquest is apparently directed into a courtly interest in the *minne* of Kriemhild. First, Siegfried conducts himself (especially in the Saxon campaign and in the conquest of Brünhild and her land) as if his endeavor to conquer the land of the Burgundians had been successful and he himself were the Burgundian leader, which provides implicit support for what was implied by the protests of Ortwin and Hagen: too much was granted to the conquering Siegfried too fast. The second aspect is associated with subservience rather than sovereignty: Siegfried is cast as the lowly lover of the beautiful Kriemhild within the framework of courtly love service, or *hohe Minne*. Since, as we have seen in the initial *âventiuren*, Gunther looks after his sister as he does the material resources of his lands, Siegfried's love service to Kriemhild amounts to political service to the Burgundian kings. The third aspect of the relationship, circumscribed by the term *vriunt*, is the least consistently developed and most inconstant of all, perhaps because it rests on the possibility of equality in a world made up of domination and subservience. The interplay between these three aspects suggests that Siegfried's ambition of conquest has not been renounced, but rather merely complicated by the introduction of courtly forms of interaction, within which Siegfried's conquest proceeds as an assault on the heart of Kriemhild.

III

The conquest of Kriemhild by Siegfried begins with the Saxon campaign. Like Siegfried, the Saxons openly express their animosity toward Gunther and their intention to conquer his lands. Although the Saxons and Danes deliver the same kind of challenge to Worms that Siegfried did before them, they now have to face the strong young warrior from the Netherlands, whose aggressive energy has been at least temporarily integrated into the power structure of the Burgundian realm, so that it can now serve to counter the kind of external threat it once posed itself. Courtliness (i.e., in the form of *minne*) has thus served to divert aggression originally aimed at the Burgundians toward the Burgundians' enemies. Gunther is doubtful that he will have the time to muster enough men to counter the invasion of the Saxons and Danes and, upon the advice of Hagen, he turns to the young hero who is, as was established in Hagen's initial description of him and of his exploits, an army of one. In countering the Saxon and Dane threat, in transforming the threatened conquest *by* the Saxons and Danes into a conquest *of* them, Siegfried is motivated by his friendship to Gunther, although the motivating force of friendship at this early stage still seems to be weak. When Siegfried asks the Burgundian king why he is so troubled, Gunther responds that one can divulge one's deepest concerns only to true friends (155). Siegfried, however, overcomes any doubts that Gunther has, or claims to have, about the value of his friendship:

> Er sprach zuo dem künege: "ine han iu niht verseit.
> ich sol iu helfen wenden elliu iuwer leit.
> welt ir vriwent suochen, der sol ich einer sîn,
> unt trouw ez wol volbringen mit êren an daz ende mîn." (156)

The king's response indicates his happiness about Siegfried's willingness to stand for him against the Saxons because of friendship, but it also introduces another motivation that may bind Siegfried more tightly to him:

> "Nu lôn' iu got, her Sîvrit, diu rede dunket mich guot.
> und ob mir nimmer helfe iuwer ellen getuot,
> ich freu mich doch der mære, daz ir mir sît sô holt.
> lebe ich deheine wîle, ez wirdet umb iuch wol versolt." (157)

The reward Gunther promises, apparently without conditions, will eventually amount to a payment for services rendered. Although the reward does not yet explicitly have anything to do with Kriemhild, events subsequent to the Saxon campaign strongly suggest that interaction with Kriemhild is the *lôn* ("reward") that Siegfried will receive for his efforts. Thus, political expediency and the courtly interests of love will coincide.

The relationships of equality and of subservience (i.e., service) to Gunther, suggested respectively by the motivations of friendship and of reward, are juxtaposed to a relationship that is suggestive of Siegfried's superiority: when the Burgundians launch their preemptive strike against the Saxons and Danes, they do so with Siegfried as their apparent general. Upon the army's departure from Worms, Siegfried places himself at its head and commands Gunther to remain at home with the women of the court:

> "Her künec, sît hie heime", sprach dô Sîvrit,
> "sît daz iuwer recken mir wellent volgen mit.
> belîbet bî den frouwen und traget hôhen muot.
> ich trouwe iu wol behüeten beidiu êre unde guot." (174)

Siegfried's words here might be understood as consistent with his subservience within the framework of *Minnedienst.* The fact that he is willing to spare Gunther *all* of the effort involved in responding to the present military threat can be viewed as an exaggeration of his service to Gunther's power rather than a usurpation upon it. Yet such a usurpation remains implicit: Siegfried adopts the position of the conquering leader at the head of an army that includes the young king Gernot and the warrior Hagen, who might not be expected to defer to any authority other than that of Gunther. The honor and praise celebrated at court, which can only be won in battle, is won by Siegfried, who inevitably prevails in the coming conflicts against the Saxons and Danes and distinguishes himself above all others.

Victory against an external enemy by means of armed conflict marks the first step of an internal, courtly conquest, in which Kriemhild (along with the political power she embodies) will, in the end, become Siegfried's ***undertân***. Siegfried is much too rich to accept material rewards from Gunther for his services against the Saxons, so he eventually receives a different kind of ***lôn*** that maintains the integration of Siegfried into the Burgundian power structure. At the festival in celebration of the Burgundians' victory, Gunther, who knows of Siegfried's love for his sister (cf. 272), finally allows him to meet her in person. That this meeting — which culminates in a kiss that Gunther allows his sister to give Siegfried — should be understood as the reward due to the young hero from the Netherlands, becomes clear in the words of the conquered Danish king Liudegast:

> "diss vil hôhen gruozes lît maneger ungesunt
> (des ich vil wol enpfinde) von Sîvrides hant.
> got enlâz' in nimmer mêre komen in mîniu küneges lant."
> (298,2–4)

Siegfried is not yet as accomplished in courtly love as he is in the activity of conquest, at which he has no peers. It is this discrepancy that results in what seems, from a modern perspective, to be an unlikely and even comical scenario: the mighty Siegfried, who has only recently commanded the armed forces of her brothers' realm, and who strikes fear into the hearts of the stoutest kings and warriors of the world, is transformed according to the conventions of ***hohe minne*** (the unhappy and unrequited desire for a powerful and distant lady) into an abject, pining lover with no hope of ever winning the favor of his lady, whose beauty, riches, and nobility seem to put her beyond his range (cf. 285). However unlikely such a posture may be in view of Siegfried's social rank and what he has already achieved by conquest, it is more than a pose on the part of Siegfried, just as it is more than a forced employment of an inconsistent literary model by the poem's author. Love is, as has been suggested, a realm in which Siegfried has not yet won the complete and overwhelming victory to which all his other campaigns have led, although the audience may suspect that he will, despite his initial despair, eventually prevail here as well. By the time the Saxon campaign has been concluded and Siegfried has received his reward for the services he has rendered on behalf — or in the place — of King Gunther, a pattern seems to have become discernible: Siegfried's victory over the external enemies of the Burgundians amounts to an *internal* conquest of Burgundian power within the framework of a *Minnedienst*, or love service, that has transparently political implications. Although Gunther retains some power and controls Siegfried to some extent as long as he can manipulate his sister as a "resource," one suspects that there will be a fundamental shift in what seems to be a precarious balance of power when the resource is exhausted and Gunther is finally obliged to hand his sister over to Siegfried, thus apparently losing *any* claim to a superior position. Later on, when Siegfried's conquest of Kriemhild is complete, the power that he has in many respects wielded since his arrival in Worms finally provokes a resurgence of the hostility initially manifested by Ortwin and Hagen upon Siegfried's arrival in Worms.

IV

In the campaign to win Brünhild, as in the Burgundian victory over the Saxons and Danes, an external, military conquest charts the progress of an internal, courtly one, in which Siegfried is obtaining and consolidating, by means of love service for Kriemhild, an authority that appeared to be conceded to him upon his arrival in Worms. Gunther has decided to win Brünhild as his bride and is again in need of Siegfried's great strength and cunning in order to overcome the lady's ferocious resistance to all suitors. This resistance combines in the person of Brünhild the figure of the beautiful courtly lady with that of the *vâlandinne* ("she-devil"), and in Island the locus of courting with that of a realm to be conquered.[9] Siegfried tells Gunther he will help, not out of a spirit of friendship (although this may still be implicit), but because the opportunity to conquer Brünhild presents itself simultaneously as an opportunity to win Kriemhild:

> "gîstu mir dîne swester, sô wil ich ez tuon,
> die scœnen Kriemhilde, ein küneginne hêr.
> sô ger ich deheines lônes nâch mînen arbeiten mêr." (333,2–4)

[9] Here as elsewhere, Ehrismann perceives the broader political significance of the action when he points out that Brünhild's strength symbolizes the power of her land, and that the games between her and Gunther/Siegfried symbolize the defense of this land (Ehrismann 127).

Throughout this entire venture, Siegfried occupies a position of leadership. He not only brings the expedition to its destination, but also devises and executes the plan that will achieve the seemingly impossible goal of winning Brünhild. This plan has two parts: Siegfried, whose prowess is known by everyone in Island (while Gunther is an unknown stranger), *visibly* bolsters Gunther's position by pretending to be his vassal, then *invisibly* enables the Burgundian king to win Brünhild in the contests of strength. In the first part of the plan, within the courtly context of Brünhild's reception of the Burgundians, the status of political subordination that has been implied by Siegfried's love service to Kriemhild becomes a concrete and visible expression of feudal subservience when Siegfried holds Gunther's stirrup (397), a service perhaps corresponding to the *officium stratoris et strepae* mentioned in the *Sachsenspiegel.*[10] While Siegfried is visibly subservient to Gunther, invisibly he is again manifesting the leadership that he has held from the beginning of this expedition. Nothing indicates Siegfried's position of (covert) supremacy more strikingly than the fact that he provides the strength to accomplish the physical contest against Brünhild, while Gunther merely pretends to participate. To onlookers in Island, only Gunther is seen; to the audience, able to understand what is really happening, a different conclusion must be drawn about who, in fact, is conquering Brünhild and her realm. This conquest of Brünhild and her land is completed by what amounts to a re-enactment of Siegfried's conquest of the Nibelungs (cf. 482–506), as if to remind the audience that obtaining dominion over others has been and continues to be one of the poem's central concerns. The arrival of Siegfried and his Nibelungen warriors eliminates the possibility of any further resistance from Island to Burgundian supremacy.

At this point, the element of subservience in Siegfried's relationship to Gunther falls away temporarily, continuing only as a memory in the mind of Brünhild. At the same time, the element of friendship also seems to be temporarily weakened: Gunther has to beg Siegfried to bear news of the Burgundians' good fortune to Worms. The temporary weakening of these two bonds corresponds to a strengthening of the third: upon officially receiving Kriemhild, Siegfried, as a new king in the land of the Burgundians (as which he is designated by Kriemhild in 662), overtly occupies the position of power that he has long held implicitly. The last "service" performed by Siegfried on behalf of Gunther (which is, as always, also a deed he performs for himself), is a continuation and culmination of the conquest of Brünhild (now within the locus of the conjugal bed). Noting Gunther's low spirits following the night in which Brünhild ended his amorous advances by hanging him by a nail in the wall, Siegfried volunteers to help the king avoid

[10] See Heinzle 69.

a repetition of this ignominious defeat. By means of this assistance, Siegfried again seems to exercise rights officially pertaining to the Burgundian king and thus to assert his supremacy. While it is clear that Siegfried does not have sexual intercourse with Brünhild, he nevertheless violates her symbolically by taking her ring and belt after he has finally managed to overcome her resistance. A perceptive reading of this episode in terms of a metaphorical, if not literal rape of Brünhild by Siegfried is offered by Frakes.[11] Although there seems to be little doubt that it is Gunther who deflowers the weakened Brünhild, it is clearly Siegfried who overcomes her virginal strength. We may therefore say that the connection between Brünhild, Kriemhild, and supremacy in the land of the Burgundians finds yet another expression: Siegfried not only enjoys the embraces of the king's sister, but in this final "service" to Gunther, he also shares a bed with the king's wife, where he has a hand in the loss of her virginity and at the same time seizes objects that are symbolic of her power.[12] Later on, in the crucial episode depicting the railing of the queens before the portal of the Worms cathedral, Kriemhild does not speak without justification when she maintains that it was Siegfried, and not Gunther, who overcame the power of Brünhild's *magetuom*.

When Siegfried returns with his wife to Xanten, a festival is held that surpasses in its splendor the one just held in Worms and, contrary to earlier announced intentions, Siegfried receives his father's crown. The power he has managed to obtain by the strength of his hand over the Nibelungs and over the Burgundians (i.e., in the person of Kriemhild) has thus apparently translated also into the kingship over his own heritable lands. The time that transpires between the previous events in Worms and their later violent culmination, combined with the distance separating Siegfried and his wife from the Burgundians, is suggestive of a harmony that is illusory. Although the Burgundians still command the resources to compete with Siegfried in courtly splendor, it is not surprising that there is at least one powerful person, namely Brünhild, who seems to resent that the price of Siegfried's fame appears to have been paid by the Burgundians. It may be to test the validity of her suspicion, and to collect a debt she feels is owed her, that she begins to press her husband to insist upon a visit from their "vassal" Siegfried: "Swie hôhe rîche wære deheines küniges man,/swaz im gebüte sîn herre, daz sold' er doch niht lân" (728,1–2). The fame of Siegfried, and the resentment of it on the part of Brünhild, indicate that the power struggle between the young hero from the Netherlands and the Burgundian kings has not been concluded, but only temporarily suspended. Brünhild, now the strongest

[11] Jerold C. Frakes, *Brides and Doom: Gender, Property, and Power in Medieval German Women's Epic* (Philadelphia: University of Philadelphia Press, 1994) 121–126.

[12] Ehrismann 134.

advocate of Burgundian supremacy, will be satisfied only by an overt demonstration of a subservience that has not been manifested since Siegfried completed his ***Minnedienst***.

Although seemingly contradictory, the respective assumptions of Kriemhild and Brünhild about the current state of power relations in Worms are correct and consistent with earlier events in the poem. Based on the different aspects that have been present in the relationship between Siegfried and Gunther from the beginning, Brünhild has good reason to insist on the subservience of Siegfried, while Kriemhild is no less justified in considering that her husband is equal if not superior to her brothers in power, status, and fame.[13] At the moment of the queens' confrontation, and subsequent to this confrontation, courtly forms no longer seem to be able, as they were in the beginning, to absorb and redirect aggression toward an external target. The Burgundian kings no longer control a "resource" that binds Siegfried to them in a relatively pacific and constructive way. The relationship between Siegfried and the Burgundians is consequently restructured in terms of overt antagonism. Most of the figures necessary for the murder of Siegfried are drawn quickly into this antagonism, most easily Hagen, with some reluctance Gunther, and eventually even the courtly Gernot and Giselher. Siegfried's flaw, if he has one, is that he continues to count on the value of the element of friendship, and Kriemhild, despite her problems with Brünhild, also seems to build upon the weak foundation of friendship when she reveals to Hagen the spot between Siegfried's shoulders where the otherwise invincible warrior is vulnerable. If friendship can be viewed as a last remnant of courtliness in the relationship between Siegfried and the Burgundians, then courtliness enables the Burgundians to realize a plan by stealth that could not be realized in overt conflict because of Siegfried's mythic invulnerability.

The differing assumptions of Siegfried and the Burgundians find concrete expression in the hunt, which contains remnants of the aborted military conflict against the Saxons that it has seemingly replaced. Siegfried's energies are directed into the courtly aspect of the hunt as an aristocratic diversion, although his supremacy over the Burgundians continues to manifest itself, albeit in a relatively pacific form corresponding to the event in which he understands himself to be involved, in his superior prowess as a hunter. Aggression on his part against the Burgundians even occurs, although only as a jest, when he "attacks" his fellow hunters by releasing a bear into their

[13] See Siegfried Beyschlag, "Das Motiv der Macht bei Siegfrieds Tod," *GRM* 33 (1951/52): 95–108. Beyschlag also sees the words of Kriemhild in the confrontation between the queens as a "Machtanspruch" (197). A contrast to this view is offered by Ehrismann, who appears to diminish the political significance of Kriemhild's words by attributing them to a momentary, individual lapse on her part, even as he clearly remains aware of the long history of this claim to power (141).

camp, only to demonstrate his mastery again by slaying the animal when the others cannot. The Burgundians Gunther and Hagen rely on the hunt being understood as such by Siegfried, even if it is, from their perspective, something closer to the aborted military campaign. The dual nature of this final event before Siegfried's death — is it a military undertaking or a courtly diversion? — is suggested by the presence on Siegfried's hunting clothes of the mark that Kriemhild had ostensibly placed on the back of the armor he was to wear against the Saxons.[14]

What could not be achieved in open conflict, because of Siegfried's great power and strength, is achieved by means of a surprise attack, but with the same result from the perspective of the Burgundians. When Hagen drives a spear through Siegfried's back, as the latter bends down at the fountain to quench his thirst, an end is put to Siegfried's supremacy. Hagen's deed is an act of liberation from the supremacy of Siegfried, and it is cast as such by Hagen himself in his response to Gunther's belated regret about the young hero's fate:

> Dô sprach der grimme Hagene: "jane weiz ich, waz ir kleit.
> ez hât nu allez ende unser sorge unt unser leit.
> wir vinden ir vil wênic, die getürren uns bestân.
> wol mich, deich sîner hêrschaft hân ze rate getân." (993)

The killing of Siegfried has freed the Burgundians from Siegfried's supremacy, or *hêrschaft*, and transformed the entire world into a terrain of future conquest. It has brought the *hort* of the Nibelungs to Worms on the Rhine and conferred victory upon Brünhild in her courtly struggle with Kriemhild which, as we have seen, has been a continuation of the broader struggle for power between Siegfried and the Burgundians.

In the second part of the poem, the basic positions remain very similar, even as the figures who occupy them change. Where in the first part of the poem we observe Siegfried and his Nibelungs confronting the Burgundian kings, in the second part we see Hagen (bearing Siegfried's sword) and the Burgundians (Nibelungs) falling aggressively into the lands of Gelpfrat and Else, taking the sword of Eckewart (a transparent symbolic assault on the border region of Etzel's realm that Eckewart is guarding), and behaving with an offensive swagger and arrogance in the land of the Huns that is at least as consistent with the attitude of conquerors as it is with that of guests at a

[14] I am obviously assuming that such discrepancies may not simply be dismissed as the errors of an author who is more or less successfully grappling with different literary traditions (i.e., dismissed in terms of *Stoffgeschichte*). In my view, the literary and cultural significance of this poem cannot and should not be limited to what the author was (not) able to do with his sources.

courtly festival who fear they will be attacked. The Nibelungs, like Siegfried, are victims of a surprise attack (Blœdel attacks Dancwart and his men, while the strongest of the Burgundian force is dining with Etzel), and even as they defend themselves to the death against apparently insurmountable odds, they occupy Etzel's hall, the symbolic center of power in the land of the Huns. Close scrutiny of the second part, were it possible in this context, would indicate that conquest continues to be an interest of the poem, an interest that is only partially obscured by the motivational weight placed on Kriemhild's revenge.

V

The thoroughgoing interest in conquest in the *Nibelungenlied* doubtless contributed to the popularity of this poem among its medieval audiences, most of which would have been familiar not only with the mythical allure, but also with the practical aspects and material benefits of conquest. We have seen that courtliness in the *Nibelungenlied* does not stand apart from this interest in conquest, but rather is another way of giving expression to it. The involvement of courtliness in the violent business of conquest can be no surprise, given that the long history of court societies in Europe is also basically a history of conquest, and not merely the history of the gradual refinement of tastes and curbing of aggression as which courtliness tends to be understood in the interpretation of literature. Courtly forms of interaction in the *Nibelungenlied* cannot serve as a peaceful and innocent refuge to which modern readers and scholars, perhaps motivated by the ideological uses to which this poem has been put, could seek refuge.

Since there would seem to be no instance or principle in this poem that is not in some way connected to the struggle for supremacy, it is no misunderstanding or misappropriation of the poem, but simply a recognition of its interest in conquest, when nineteenth-century discussions of the *Nibelungenlied*, many of which are cited and discussed by Heinzle,[15] take a starkly militaristic tone, defining the German character in terms identifiable with conquest. The foundation of the nineteenth-century understanding of the *Nibelungenlied* was laid by Friedrich von der Hagen in the foreword of his 1807 edition of the poem, who managed to link what he viewed as typically German virtues (*Tugenden*), such as loyalty, courage, and honesty, with arrogance, defiance, revenge, and bloodthirstiness, the virtues being made even more prominent in their inextricable connection (*Verschlingung*) with these darker forces. Around the middle of the nineteenth century, Vilmar had begun in his popular literary history to focus more exclusively on

[15] See Heinzle 98–103.

loyalty, or *Treue*, as the most significant aspect of the *Nibelungenlied*, identifying it with the uncompromising attitude with which the warrior follows his leader, if necessary to the death.[16] The culmination of the nationalistic reading of the *Nibelungenlied* in terms of conquest may be found in Hermann Göring's *Wehrmachtsappell* in 1943. When Göring likens the efforts of German soldiers to those of the Nibelungs at the court of Etzel, it is clear that it does not matter that the Nibelungs lose in the end — that the secret of conquest remains unknown and perhaps unknowable — just as it does not matter that the *Wehrmacht* is about to lose catastrophically against the Red Army in Stalingrad. What seems to matter is not the eventual outcome, but rather the glory that is to be won in the passionate, single-minded, relentless pursuit of a single thing. It seems historically appropriate to view the interest underlying this attitude — the generally unstated goal behind the dedicated passion of *Treue* — as that of conquest. German nationalists did not err in recognizing this interest in the *Nibelungenlied*. If at all, they erred in identifying it as something specifically German.

[16] A. F. C. Vilmar, *Geschichte der deutschen national-literatur* (Marburg: Elwert, 1848) 60–61.

Edward R. Haymes

Heroic, Chivalric, and Aristocratic Ethos in the *Nibelungenlied*

The plot events of the *Nibelungenlied* take place in a field of tension among ethical patterns that is at least as important to the understanding of the work as the characters and their behavior as fictional individuals. Friedrich Neumann recognized what he called "Schichten der Ethik" in the epic in his classic essay, originally published in 1924.[1] He analyzed the events of the poem as taking place in a zone of tension between courtly and heroic values. Walter Haug has more recently explored the relationship between courtly and heroic under the rubric of "montage," but he still works within Neumann's bipolar scheme.[2] Haug sees the poem as essentially courtly with heroic elements "mounted" in it much as the individual elements of a photographic montage might be. As important as Neumann's essay has been to *Nibelungenlied* scholarship, I do not believe his scheme is sufficient to explain the ethical complexity of the poem.

The ethical patterns we can observe in the *Nibelungenlied* have connections to political and social history as well as being crucial to the understanding of the largely fictional world within the narrative. If we follow the usual dating of the *B-version at "around 1200," then we can see the poem arising at a time when aristocratic society was exposed to a number of different ideologies and enmeshed in several power struggles. We can observe the working out of the competition between the two major dynasties, Welf and Hohenstaufen, and we can observe a few aspects of a struggle along the horizontal fault lines between different layers of men who called themselves knights.

Our traditional pyramid image of feudal society fits fairly well as long as we are talking about hereditary nobility. The highest nobility received their fiefs from the king, the next group from them and from there on down.

[1] Friedrich Neumann, "Schichten der Ethik im Nibelungenliede," in F. N., *Das Nibelungenlied in seiner Zeit,* Kleine Vandenhoeck-Reihe 253 S (Göttingen: Vandenhoeck & Ruprecht, 1967) 9–34. First appeared in *Festschrift. Eugen Mogk zum 70. Geburtstag 19. Juli 1924* (Halle: Niemeyer, 1924) 119–145.

[2] Walther Haug, "Höfische Idealität und heroische Tradition im Nibelungenlied," *Colloquio italo-germanico sul tema: I Nibelunghi* (Rome: Lincei, 1974) 35–50.

Medieval theorists reflected this structure in the *Heerschildordnung* (*clipeus militaris*) as pictured in such presentations of medieval order as the *Sachsenspiegel*. Each overlord was forced by dynastic rights to renew the enfeoffment to the next generation so that the system remained relatively stable as long as dynastic lines did not die out. The traditional hereditary power obligated the lord to the vassal as much as the other way around and it prevented overlords, including the king, from exercising power as freely as they would have liked.

In order to gain flexibility in the exercise of military and feudal power, kings and other higher nobles began entrusting critical castles and positions to men who were not free nobles but members of the lord's household. They owed their lords *servitium* ("service") rather than the more general *fidelitas* ("fealty"). Since the monumental work of Karl Bosl,[3] we have been aware of this group of unfree knights known as *ministeriales* and of their struggle to establish themselves as a part of the nobility. Early on this struggle expressed itself in a desire to be legally declared free. Later *ministeriales* sought the rights and privileges of free nobles without seeking a patent of freedom itself. Gert Kaiser,[4] Joachim Bumke[5] and, most recently, W. H. Jackson[6] have explored possible connections between the *ministeriales*, whose position in society was defined by service (*ministerium*), and courtly romance, which seems to preach an idealization of service — even on the part of royal princes. Kaiser suggested that the service ideal was preached by the *ministeriales* in order to legitimize their status and to provide a framework for social advancement. Bumke suggested that the service ideology could just as well have been created for the *ministeriales* in order to make them accept their lot as a respectable and noble one. There can be little doubt that much courtly literature treats at least marginally questions of service and of appropriate chivalric behavior. Hartmann identifies himself as a *ministerialis* (*dienstman*) and emphasizes the service aspects of the knightly adventures through which Erec and Iwein must pass in order to reach perfect knighthood. This is echoed to a greater or lesser extent throughout the German romances. The question of chivalric service itself is problematized in Wolfram's story of Sigune and Schionatulander, in which the knight meets his death carrying out a foolish errand of service for his lady.

[3] Karl Bosl, *Die Reichsministerialität der Salier und Staufer*, 2 vols. (Stuttgart: Hiersemann, 1950–1951).

[4] Gert Kaiser, *Textauslegung und gesellschaftliche Selbstdeutung: Die Artusromane Hartmanns von Aue* (Wiesbaden: Athenaion, 1978).

[5] Joachim Bumke, *Studien zum Ritterbegriff* (Heidelberg: Winter, 1977).

[6] W. H. Jackson, *Chivalry in Twelfth-Century Germany: The Works of Hartman von Aue*, Arthurian Studies 34 (Rochester: Brewer, 1994).

Minnesang presents the knight in service to a lady. The terminology remains that of feudal service, which provides the metaphorical framework within which the complexities of erotic relationships are played out. The knight's service may consist of deeds of prowess or song, or simply of constancy, but the service is always carried out in expectation of some kind of reciprocity. The knight serves and expects payment — a greeting, a kiss, or perhaps even more — from his lady in return. Ladies who refuse to pay are sometimes criticized. There is even a narrative, *Moriz von Craûn*,[7] which parodies exaggerated courtly love service and the right of a knight to take the payment due him. The lady who refuses to play by the rules of chivalric service and reward is left alone at the end of the poem.

There was thus what one might call a service ethic closely affiliated with literary genres imported from France. These ideas were probably associated in some way with the political and social aspirations of the *ministeriales*, and the (fictional) rise of knights errant like Iwein to full kingship as a result of their knightly prowess must have implied a flexibility in questions of status that would not have been welcome everywhere in German society of the period. Karl Bosl tells about the rise of some *ministeriales* to great power, wealth and prestige, sometimes at the expense of dynastic interests. Although he was not, strictly speaking, a *ministerialis*, Otto von Wittelsbach also represented this flexibility when he was promoted from count to the hereditary rank of Duke of Bavaria at the expense of Henry the Lion. Otto earned this promotion through unswerving and often reckless service to the emperor. The message of Otto's social rise will not have been lost on the *Reichsministerialität*, many of whose members will doubtless have seen a pattern they themselves could follow if their service was of a similarly exemplary nature. Chivalric service was thus both a literary pattern and a tantalizing model for social mobility in the real political life of Hohenstaufen Germany.

In sharp contrast to this, the *Nibelungenlied* contains a strain of old-fashioned heroic behavior that must have seemed almost atavistic in the refined atmosphere of thirteenth-century literature. Hagen's actions exemplify this clearly. His murder of Siegfried is certainly a piece of heroic tradition and such rough behavior as the killing of the ferryman before the crossing of the Danube and the "attempted murder" of the chaplain during the same crossing would seem to echo an ethos that was out of place in the relatively civilized world of thirteenth-century narrative. Words like *grimme* and *ungefuoge* are used to describe his behavior. At Etzel's castle it is Hagen who takes immediate vengeance for the murdered squires by beheading Etzel's

[7] Stephanie Cain Van D'Elden, ed. and trans., *Moriz von Craûn* (New York: Garland, 1990).

young son, an act which ends all possibility of peaceful resolution. Throughout the long siege he follows a warrior ethic that keeps him in the middle of the battle and prevents his ever giving in. The logical conclusion of this behavior is seen in the climactic scene in which Kriemhild offers the captured and bound Hagen his life in return for "what he had taken from her." He refuses, saying that he had sworn never to reveal the location of the treasure as long as any of his brothers were alive. She has Gunther slain and brings his head before Hagen, who breaks out in a lamentation ending with a total defiance of Kriemhild, in which he calls her a *vâlandinne*, a she-devil, and says that the hoard will remain forever hidden from her. Kriemhild strikes off his head and Etzel laments the death of "der aller beste degen,/der ie kom ze sturme oder ie schilt getruoc!"[8] Hagen's behavior is coherent within an old-fashioned warrior ethic, an ethic that can be associated with traditional heroic poetry, with the traditions that had preserved the Nibelung story until the beginning of the thirteenth century.

The two ethical patterns described already match approximately the traditional courtly and heroic ethical patterns observed by Neumann and Haug. They do not, however, adequately cover the ethical pattern represented by the Burgundians at the beginning of the epic and by Dietrich von Bern at the end. This pattern lacks a traditional label, since it has not been recognized as an ethic on the same level as the courtly and the heroic. In fact, most of its aspects have been attributed to the courtly, an attribution that clouds over the major differences between the attitudes it represents and those represented by courtly romance and *Minnesang*. If we could start from scratch, it would be useful to call this new ethical pattern "courtly" and the pattern associated with French chivalry "chivalric," but this would mean that most of what has been considered courtly in the epic would have to be shifted to the "chivalric" rubric and "courtly" would have to be newly defined. Perhaps we will be best understood if we leave the term "courtly" behind and call the traditional courtly values represented by Gunther's court "aristocratic" and those associated with the new literature "chivalric."

The term "heroic" can still be used to designate the ethical patterns we can associate with traditional heroic literature. This is problematic, though, because we do not have any unfiltered examples of the heroic literature of the twelfth and thirteenth centuries and all attempts to reconstruct such literature are subject to question. There is, however, a genre of literature that seems to preserve many aspects of heroic behavior in a relatively unchanged form. I am referring here to the so-called *Spielmannsepen*, the bridewinning narratives

[8] Karl Bartsch and Helmut de Boor, eds. *Das Nibelungenlied*, 21st revised ed. by Roswitha Wisniewski, Deutsche Texte des Mittelalters (Wiesbaden: Brockhaus, 1979) 2374,2b–3.

that survive in versions from both the twelfth and the thirteenth centuries. Theodore Andersson has shown the indebtedness of the *Nibelungenlied* to this genre in his *Preface to the Nibelungenlied* and it extends both to the ethical patterns followed by the figures in the stories and to the narrative patterns that structure them.[9] It has long been a commonplace that the *Nibelungenlied* is structured around three bridewinning stories, but Andersson has shown us how thoroughly the traditional bridewinning pattern has informed our epic even down to the details of individual behavior. The *Þiðreks saga af Bern* contains many episodes that portray heroic behavior in stories that are certainly derived from German narrative poetry.[10] We thus have a range of literature that portrays the heroic ethos in traditional stories and can help us identify such behavior in the *Nibelungenlied*.

We can see that the two extreme ethical layers of the epic, the heroic and the chivalric, correspond to groupings of literary genres that would have been known to the Nibelungen poet. The one layer that does not have a literary formation is what I have called "aristocratic." There is no literary genre that corresponds closely to this pattern of behavior. I believe it is quite possible that this level, the one eventually idealized by the Nibelungen poet, was also his invention as a literary ethical pattern. Nelly Dürrenmatt noted in her oft-cited dissertation[11] that the *Nibelungenlied* actually has far more of what she considered "courtly" material than the courtly romances with which she compared it. This applies in particular to the presentation of "courtly" ceremonies, wealth, and finery, and to the infamous *Schneiderstrophen*. The "courtly" literature, into whose circle the *Nibelungenlied* was supposed to fit, presupposed all of this, wasting no time with what was, after all, everyday life for the audiences of the poems in question.

Stephen Jaeger has devoted a book to the question of the *Origins of Courtliness* and an article to anti-courtly attitudes in the *Nibelungenlied*.[12] His presentation shows the growth of courtly behavior and a clerical reaction to it. He quotes a number of vituperative reports of "courtly," "soft," and

[9] Theodore M. Andersson, *A Preface to the Nibelungenlied* (Stanford: Stanford University Press, 1987).

[10] Edward R. Haymes, trans., *The Saga of Thidrek of Bern*, Garland Library of Medieval Literature 56, Series B (New York: Garland, 1988).

[11] Nelly Dürrenmatt, *Das Nibelungenlied im Kreis der höfischen Dichtung* (Berne: Lang, 1945).

[12] C. Stephen Jaeger, *The Origins of Courtliness: Civilizing Trends and the Formation of Courtly Ideals 939–1210* (Philadelphia: University of Pennsylvania Press, 1985). See also his "The Nibelungen Poet and the Clerical Rebellion against courtesy," in William C. McDonald, ed., *Spectrum Medii Aevi: Essays in Early German Literature in honor of George Fenwick Jones* (Göppingen: Kümmerle, 1983) 177–205.

even "effeminate" behavior on the part of those participating in "foreign" fashion at the courts of bishops and secular nobles alike. Perhaps the most damning voice in this chorus is the Danish cleric known to us as Saxo Grammaticus, whose *Gesta Danorum* contains round condemnation of courtly behavior alongside praise for an earlier, heroic way of life. The latter is portrayed most vividly through the old warrior Starcatherus, whose rough manner, dress, and eating habits provide a powerful contrast to the fine clothing, dainty foods, and effeminate behavior of the courtiers.

Jaeger sees traces of the same attitude in the *Nibelungenlied*, particularly in such scenes as Volker's striking down of the foppish Hun and Rumold's advice to the parting Nibelungs to remain home and enjoy the comforts of courtly life. Jaeger is unable to find an unequivocal negative portrayal of courtly elements throughout the *Nibelungenlied*, however, and is forced to postulate "a great deal of unspoken, implied criticism."[13] If one realizes that the patterns of courtliness discussed in the poem are on at least two levels, then one can gain from Jaeger's observations without being drawn into the blind alley in which he finds himself as he tries to expand two or three useful observations to cover the entire epic. I cannot share his conclusion that the epic idealizes heroic behavior at the expense of courtly aberrations. The heroic attitudes finish the job begun by the chivalric as they draw the Burgundians to their destruction.

After introducing the theme of the fatal beauty of Kriemhild the poet wastes little time in establishing the Burgundian kings as of high birth ("von arde hôh erborn," 5,1b) and the orderly hereditary acquisition of their kingdom ("ir vater der hiez Dancrât der in diu erbe liez," 7,2). The orderly court is then introduced with the names of the holders of the four traditional court offices (plus the recently introduced *kuchenmeister*) along with the leading knights of the court: Hagen, Dancwart, Ortwin, Gere, Eckewart, and Volker. The image of an established and powerful court is strengthened in the third *Âventiure* when Siegfried arrives in Worms. His unprecedented challenge surprises everyone, including probably the original audience. He proposes to Gunther a single combat with nothing less than the combatants' kingdoms at stake. Critics have almost unanimously assigned this behavior on Siegfried's part to the level of a primitive heroic ethic. This seems logical until we look through heroic literature for any kind of precedent. Heroes often establish themselves at a new court through a duel or other feat of arms, but they do not challenge the ruler for his throne. The closest parallel is perhaps the story of Sir Samson at the beginning of the *Þiðreks saga*. Samson must defend himself against his lord and his lord's brother, who is king, after kidnapping his lord's daughter and making her his wife. After killing both his

[13] Jaeger, "The Nibelungen Poet" 194

lord and his king, he establishes himself in their place. There is, however, no evidence that this story is traditional and it may have more of a role in establishing the thematic role of bridewinning and violence in the saga than of providing a positive role model for the intended audience.[14]

Courtly romance, on the other hand, provides a possible model for Siegfried's challenge in the behavior of figures such as Iwein, who gains a kingdom through a duel fought as the result of a challenge. The response of the Burgundians makes it clear that Siegfried's behavior is not acceptable in polite society. Gunther points out that he has received the kingdom through orderly inheritance and that it would not be seemly to lose it "durh iemannes kraft" (112,3). Gernot responds to Siegfried's renewed challenge with a reference to the fact that their lands serve them "von rehte" (115,4). It may only be a bit of irony that the hospitality formula spoken by Gunther includes figuratively everything Siegfried had been demanding (127). Siegfried's challenge threatens not only the kingship of Gunther as occupier of the Burgundian throne, but also the entire structure on which that power is based. It is not appropriate to question dynastically established power in this world. This is not the world of the courtly romance in which power can easily be challenged by an Iwein or, for that matter, by a Siegfried. It is the real dynastic world of the twelfth century in which the Hohenstaufen kings of Germany are attempting to establish royal heredity as the guarantor of stability and peace. Challenges to this power are to be met through diplomacy and courtesy where possible and only when absolutely necessary through force and then through organized military force (as in the Saxon war) and not the chaotic force of single combat between knights errant.

Immediately after the failure of his knight-errant attack on the organized power structure of Worms, Siegfried falls into another role, this one determined not so much by courtly romance as by *Minnesang*. He moons about the court looking for all the world like a parody of Reinmar the Old, the *Minnesänger* we associate today most strongly with hopeless wooing in his poetry. His apparently hopeless love-longing for the woman he has not yet even seen leads directly to his first act of service. When the Saxons and Danes under their kings Liudeger and Liudegast declare war on the Burgundians, Siegfried is delighted at the opportunity to show his knightly prowess. His replacement of Gunther at the head of the army is an act of feudal servitude. There may also be a hint of blame directed at Gunther for

[14] Edward R. Haymes, "The Bridewinning, Seduction, and Rape Sequence in *Thidrekssaga*," in Winder McConnell, ed., *in hôhem prîse: A Festschrift in Honor of Ernst S. Dick. On the Occasion of his 60th Birthday, April 7, 1989*, GAG 480 (Göppingen: Kümmerle, 1989) 145–152.

remaining at home "bî den vrouwen." After all, even the emperor went into the field to meet his enemies himself.

Upon successful completion of the campaign, Siegfried is granted an opportunity to see Kriemhild. This scene is completely dependent on the language and imagery of *Minnesang*. The appearance of Kriemhild before the other ladies of the court is depicted "[s]am der liehte mâne vor den sternen stât" (283,1). The *Minnesang* lover Siegfried receives not only the "gruoz" from his beloved but also a ceremonial "kus."

The task Siegfried has to accomplish to win his beloved is nothing less than the winning of the supernatural princess Brünhild for Gunther. In accomplishing this task, Siegfried draws his hosts out of the safe world of Burgundian aristocracy and into the adventurous world of a bridewinning tale. The only trace left of the chivalric ethical patterns is the fact that Siegfried is rendering service in order to gain love. This fact is objectified in the public claim that Gunther is Siegfried's lord. Brünhild has no choice but to believe the claims that are made in word and deed before her. Her belief in this political relationship leads directly to the events that will end in Siegfried's death. Siegfried further demonstrates his feudal inferiority by fetching a thousand warriors to defend his "lord" in case of further resistance on Brünhild's part. During the return to Worms, Siegfried again lowers himself by playing the role of messenger to Kriemhild. She is confused by this performance and is initially unwilling to give Siegfried a reward for his service, thinking this beneath him. He insists on the reward and shows that he understands its symbolic meaning perfectly by passing it on down the feudal power chain. In the symbolic language of the aristocratic ethos, the giver is superior to the recipient. Siegfried plays fast and loose with social status, a major guarantor of domestic stability in Hohenstaufen Germany. In so doing he follows the service ideology of the chivalric romance while violating the aristocratic sense of social order called upon by Gunther and Gernot in Siegfried's arrival scene.

The traditional explanation of Brünhild's tears at the wedding is that the poet is reflecting a traditional version of the story in which Brünhild had expected to marry Siegfried and is thus brokenhearted with jealousy.[15] This interpretation of the scene runs straight in the face of Brünhild's own explanation and her clear demand to know why her new sister-in-law is marrying a vassal. This demand is sufficiently strong to justify her denying Gunther his marital rights and later for her to use it as an unspoken reason for the invitation that leads to Siegfried's murder. There is no way to connect

[15] Still implied by Joachim Heinzle, *Das Nibelungenlied: Eine Einführung*, rev. ed. (Frankfurt a. M.: Fischer, 1994) 72 and Theodore M. Andersson, *The Legend of Brynhild* (Ithaca: Cornell University Press, 1980) 158–177.

this concern with feudal status with either of the traditional poles of ethical layering in the poem. It arises clearly out of the aristocratic thinking that has been set off against both chivalric and heroic patterns throughout the poem. Brünhild stands for social stability as much as Gunther had done before. The pivotal altercation between the two queens hinges first on matters of feudal precedence and only later on the question of Siegfried's unspoken claim to have taken Brünhild's virginity. This is also a feudal concern, since the maintenance of clear dynastic bloodlines was a correlative of the dynastic solution to the problem of feudal stability. There could be no question of the paternity of an heir in this framework and this central question of the epic arises directly from the aristocratic dynastic interests of the ruling houses, including the Hohenstaufen emperors.

One of the cruxes of *Nibelungenlied* interpretation is the motivation for the murder of Siegfried.[16] Opinions are about evenly divided on whether Siegfried actually carries out the oath so carefully worded as to allow him to swear it truthfully, but the problem seems to remain for Brünhild and Hagen and the latter pushes to have Siegfried killed. The enigmatic question "Suln wir gouche ziehen?" (867,1a) suggests that Hagen does not accept Siegfried's oath and that he questions the legitimacy of someone, presumably the child Siegfried of Brünhild and Gunther, but this point is dropped in favor of the economic one of the great riches that would fall to them if Siegfried were murdered. None of these reasons is sufficient and none is really developed to the point that the reader feels that the murderers had at least a good, villainous reason to kill him. Perhaps we can best understand Siegfried's murder as the result of a collision between the chaotic chivalric patterns adhering to Siegfried and the traditional aristocratic sense of order defended by Brünhild after Gunther has allowed himself to be drawn into the alien ethos of the bridewinning adventure.[17]

The destructive power of Siegfried's entrance into Burgundian society does not end with his death. The second half of the epic involves a struggle between the heroic as represented by Hagen (and to a lesser extent by Volker and Dancwart) and the aristocratic represented by Rüdiger, Dietrich, and — to a lesser extent — Etzel. As soon as the Burgundians, now called Nibelungs, set out on their trip to Etzelnburg, it is clear that Hagen is the leader.

[16] See Theodore M. Andersson, "Why does Siegfried die?" in Stephen J. Kaplowitt, ed., *Germanic Studies in Honor of Otto Springer* (Pittsburgh: K & S Enterprises, 1979) 29–39.

[17] Cf. Edward R. Haymes, *The Nibelungenlied: History and Interpretation*, Illinois Medieval Monographs 2 (Champagne, Urbana: University of Illinois Press, 1986) esp. 63ff.

We have already discussed Hagen's behavior as an exemplar of the heroic ethos, but the persistence of the aristocratic is perhaps less obvious. Rüdiger's "courtly" reception of the Burgundians is often cited, but there is little to distinguish Rüdiger as host from Hrothgar in *Beowulf* or Sigurd the Greek in the *Þiðreks saga*. His gifts are traditional and serve to bind the guests in the net of obligations that made up traditional dynastic aristocracy.

Etzel can also be seen as a defender of traditional aristocratic ethics. He is confused by the evidence of enmity among his guests and we are given an indication of his attitude prior to the outbreak of hostilities. In an astounding strophe we are told that if anyone had told Etzel "diu rehten mære" then he would have prevented "daz doch sît dâ geschach" (1865). Etzel is, like Gunther and his brothers at the beginning of the epic, concerned with the protection of the status quo. He would have prevented the violence because it was a threat to his power and status.

The last representative of aristocratic stability is the exile king Dietrich of Bern.[18] Dietrich is a semi-permanent guest at Etzel's court and he is bound by his status as guest to support his host in matters of defense. Dietrich, however, takes a higher ground and is recognized on both sides as an independent power. When hostilities break out in the hall, it looks as if Kriemhild and Etzel will be among those falling to the demonic weapons of the Burgundians, but Dietrich is able to enforce a truce by the sheer force of his voice and personality long enough to lead Etzel and his queen from the hall under his protection. Etzel represents order in this situation and protecting him is the only way Dietrich can preserve hierarchical order in the chaotic situation that has arisen. The Nibelungs are now totally under the power of the heroic ethic. Hagen makes all of their decisions, including his personal decision not to fight Rüdiger. Kriemhild is equally bound to something like the heroic ethic in her thirst for revenge, even if it is attached to her husband rather than the more traditional vengeance for a blood relative.

The penultimate episode of the epic involves Dietrich in his last effort to salvage what little there is left of aristocratic order. He enters the fray with more justification for blood vengeance than anyone besides Kriemhild. The Nibelungs have killed not only his dear friend Rüdiger, but all of his men save Hildebrand, and Dietrich enters the battle filled with the rage brought on by these acts. He does not, however, kill his two remaining opponents, Gunther and Hagen. He accomplishes the infinitely more difficult task of binding them and delivering them as prisoners to Kriemhild, preparing the final atavistic confrontation between Hagen and the queen. Dietrich's

[18] Cf. Edward R. Haymes, "Dietrich von Bern im Nibelungenlied," *ZfdA* 114 (1985): 159–165.

behavior is always directed toward the preservation of feudal power wherever it exists and we can see in his offer of safe conduct and in the delivery of the men as prisoners rather than as corpses a respect for such orderly power, even in a situation in which chaotic forces had destroyed virtually every shred of traditional structure.

In the *Þiðreks saga* it is Thidrek who dispatches the murderous queen, but his new role as a hopeless defender of public order and public peace forces the narrator to put the vengeance for Hagen in Hildibrand's hands. At the end Etzel, Dietrich and Hildebrand stand over the ruins of a civilization that has destroyed itself at least partially through a conflict of ethical patterns and, more specifically, through a blurring of clear aristocratic patterns of order involving lordship, kingship, and fealty.

Friedrich Neumann did a great service to *Nibelungenlied* scholarship by pointing out the ethical complexity of the poem. The uncritical acceptance of his bipolar pattern, however, has blinded us to the real complexity of ethical patterning in the epos. The gap between aristocratic and chivalric values is as great as that between either of them and the heroic patterns of the traditional matter. The great attention paid to political, social, and ethical concerns in this poem is more than a function of its "epische Breite." It is a major part of the Nibelungen poet's message to his contemporaries and it is an important element in any attempt to understand "Das Nibelungenlied in seiner Zeit."

Joachim Heinzle

The Manuscripts of the *Nibelungenlied*

I

The *Nibelungenlied* has been passed down to us in thirty-five manuscripts, eleven of which are complete, or virtually complete, twenty-three are fragments, while in one case (c), there are only a few surviving traces.[1] The oldest textual evidence (C and S) originates from the second quarter of the thirteenth century, the latest (d) was written down at the beginning of the sixteenth. To these should be added the fragment of a Dutch version (T) which dates from the second half of the thirteenth century.

With respect to both the content and the form of the text, the manuscripts tend to deviate from one another, in some instances, considerably so. In general, they can be put into two categories representing two versions of the epic: the *AB- or *nôt*-version, and the *C- or *liet*-version, designated in accordance with the signatures assigned to the most important extant manuscripts (A, B, C) or with the wording of the last verse: "daz ist der Nibelunge nôt" (Bartsch/de Boor 2379, 4); "daz ist der Nibelunge liet" (Hennig 2440, 4).[2]

The letters used to designate the manuscripts (A, B, C) were introduced by Karl Lachmann,[3] who laid the foundation for subsequent scholarly

[1] The fragments include G and P, which only contain text from the *Klage*, but which probably originated in manuscripts also containing the *Nibelungenlied*. A complete list of the manuscripts appears in the appendix. Shortly after the present article had been submitted to the editor of this volume, another *Nibelungenlied* text (the thirty-fifth) was discovered by Dr. Christine Glaßner in the library of Melk Monastery, Austria. It is a fragment of a Bavarian-Austrian manuscript dating from the late thirteenth century, and belongs to the *J-tradition. The manuscript will be assigned the signature W. Dr. Glaßner will report on her discovery in a forthcoming issue of *PBB*.

[2] See Karl Bartsch and Helmut de Boor, eds., *Das Nibelungenlied*, 21st ed. by Roswitha Wisniewski, Deutsche Klassiker des Mittelalters (Wiesbaden: Brockhaus, 1979); Ursula Hennig, ed., *Das Nibelungenlied nach der Handschrift C*, Altdeutsche Textbibliothek 83 (Tübingen: Niemeyer, 1977).

[3] Karl Lachmann, ed., *Der Nibelunge Noth und die Klage nach der ältesten Überlieferung mit Bezeichnung des Unechten und mit den Abweichungen der gemeinen Lesart* (Berlin: Reimer, 1826) Vff.

research into the manuscript tradition of the *Nibelungenlied*.[4] The manner in which he used them to categorize the manuscripts is testimony to his critical appraisal of the latter as texts. Lachmann assumed that the text to be found in A was closest to the original version (on which it would have been based), that B was “eine planmässig und absichtlich verbesserte Ausgabe oder Recension” of the original text which, in turn, was subjected to a more recent and comprehensive “Bearbeitung,” represented by the text found in C.[5] Consequently, the edition that he produced in 1826, which was aimed at reconstructing the original text of the *Nibelungenlied*, was based on A. Lachmann’s appraisal of the manuscripts is clearly in line with his ideas regarding the origins of the *Nibelungenlied*. He was convinced that it was not a unified work that had been cast from one mold, but rather that it was, in the final analysis, the product of an editor who combined a series of independent lays by different authors, each of whom had dealt with an individual episode of the story. The editor had not, however, been able to remove entirely every vestige of the heterogeneous nature of the material. Under this assumption, which he defended in his treatise, *Über die ursprüngliche Gestalt des Gedichts von der Nibelungen Noth* (1816), Lachmann applied to the *Nibelungenlied* the theory regarding the genesis of Homeric epic which his teacher Friedrich August Wolf had developed in his *Prolegomena ad Homerum* (1795). Since the text contained in manuscript A is the most cumbersome of all with regard to language, metrics, and the coherence of the narrative, it most readily fits the image one must have of the original text on the basis of the genesis theory. To be sure, that does not mean that Lachmann was guilty of a *petitio principii*, as his critics maintained, by having derived his theory of origin from the text of A, only then to turn around and base the primacy of the latter on the genesis theory. The critical judgment he brought to the text is based primarily on his analysis of the variant readings.[6]

Wolf’s theory had caused quite a stir in the academic community because it called into question contemporary views on the autonomy of art and the role of genius.[7] It split Homer scholars into two groups: the “analysts,” who agreed with the theory, and the “unitarians,” who held fast to the belief in

[4] See Hendricus Sparnaay, *Karl Lachmann als Germanist* (Berne: Francke, 1948) 43ff., and Peter F. Ganz, “Lachmann as an editor of Middle High German texts,” in Peter F. Ganz and Werner Schröder, eds., *Probleme mittelalterlicher Überlieferung und Textkritik. Oxforder Colloquium 1966* (Berlin: Schmidt, 1968) 12–30.

[5] Lachmann 85f.

[6] Rochus von Liliencron, *Ueber die Nibelungenhandschrift C* (Weimar: Böhlau, 1856) 5f.; Ganz 22.

[7] Joachim Wohlleben, “Friedrich August Wolfs *Prolegomena ad Homerum* in der literarischen Szene der Zeit,” *Poetica* 28 (1996): 154–170.

the authentic poetic unity of the works as having emanated from the genius of Homer.[8] Lachmann provided the catalyst for a similar split among Nibelung scholars which, whether consciously or subconsciously, whether the "players" are aware of it or not, continues to inform the discussion even today. The aesthetic positions which are at the heart of the matter also played a role in the so-called *Nibelungenstreit.* This was a bitter conflict centering on Lachmann's hypotheses which broke out shortly after his death (1851) and which played a major part in establishing a young discipline — Germanics — on university campuses.[9] In this conflict, one after another the two theoretically possible alternatives to Lachmann's appraisal of the manuscripts were championed:[10] relatively speaking, it was most likely that either manuscript C (version *C) or manuscript B (version *B) was closest to the original. Adolf Holtzmann and Friedrich Zarncke (1854) asserted the primacy of version *C, while Karl Bartsch (1865) was the first to accord that primacy to version *B. Wilhelm Braune's study on *Die Handschriftenverhältnisse des Nibelungenliedes* (1900) came out decisively in favor of version *B.

In the meantime, Braune did not simply confirm Bartsch's model, but also modified it in important ways. Bartsch had assumed that the version *AB, as well as *C, had emanated from a common precursor and that the latter was much better preserved in *AB (and particularly in *B) than in *C. Regardless of the extent to which *C was cast into a "secondary" role, this still left open the possibility that, from time to time, *C had preserved more of the original material than *AB. According to Braune, however, and in this he concurred with Lachmann's position, *C was ultimately derived from *B, with several stages in between: "*B ist also für uns das original des Nibelungenliedes."[11] Under no circumstances could *C, given the evidence of *AB, be considered the original. Furthermore, Braune's assumption that *C had exerted a secondary influence on all of the manuscripts belonging to the *A and *B categories was of considerable consequence for the manner in which the entire manuscript tradition was viewed.

[8] Tilman Krischer, "Friedrich August Wolfs *Prolegomena ad Homerum* und die neuere Homerforschung," *Poetica* 28 (1996): 171–180.

[9] Rainer Kolk, *Berlin oder Leipzig? Eine Studie zur sozialen Organisation der Germanistik im 'Nibelungenstreit,'* Studien und Texte zur Sozialgeschichte der Literatur 30 (Tübingen: Niemeyer, 1990).

[10] Werner Hoffmann, *Das Nibelungenlied*, 6th ed., Sammlung Metzler 7 (Stuttgart: Metzler, 1992) 75ff.

[11] Wilhelm Braune, "Die Handschriftenverhältnisse des Nibelungenliedes," *PBB* 25 (1900): 1–222, here: 121.

Together with Andreas Heusler's study, *Lied und Epos in germanischer Sagendichtung* (1905), which demonstrated the untenable nature of Lachmann's "Liedertheorie," Braune's treatise put an end to the *Nibelungenstreit.* The objections which were raised here and there against the combinations he had suggested[12] were inconsequential, until Helmut Brackert addressed them in his 1963 study and subjected Braune's model to a detailed examination. The result of his criticism, which was aimed at the methodological premises for the construction of the stemma, was devastating: Braune's model, he maintained, was either untenable or unprovable with respect to its basic points. In essence, Brackert's position is based on the assumption that there was never any such thing as an "original" *Nibelungenlied* in the sense of an individual poem, and that the text that is common to all of the manuscripts only harks back to one of the earlier versions. Brackert sees the originator of this version as some sort of "editor," who cannot be differentiated in any categorial way from the "editors" who were responsible for the divergent textual versions of the diverse manuscripts. He assumes that the latter repeatedly drew upon the multifaceted saga tradition which had also formed the basis for that common text:

> Zwar gab der einzelne Redaktor einen Text, der im groben feststand, aber er opferte diesem Text nicht seine eigene Selbständigkeit. In dem sicheren Gefühl, daß dieser Text nur jeweils eine der verschiedenen Erfüllungsmöglichkeiten verwirklichte, die in den recht lockeren Gesetzen der Gattung angelegt waren, ging er überall dort eigene Wege, wo ihm — aus welchem Grunde auch immer — eine andere Möglichkeit als die bessere erschien oder auch nur geläufiger war.[13]

Brackert's investigation confronted scholars who, at that time, were completely "unitarian" in their views, with a new, "analytical" perspective. It questioned the very foundation of the dominant mode of interpretation, in accordance with which scholars took for granted that the *Nibelungenlied* was to be treated as an individual literary work of art. Reaction to his views was, as might have been expected, quite volatile. In the final analysis, the discussion led to the realization that Braune's model simply could not be sustained but, at the same time, that the critical conclusions Brackert had drawn tended to go too far.[14] We can assume that there was an "original" in

[12] See Helmut Brackert, *Beiträge zur Handschriftenkritik des Nibelungenliedes*, Quellen und Forschungen zur Sprach- und Kulturgeschichte der germanischen Völker, N.F. 11 (Berlin: de Gruyter, 1963) 4ff.; Hoffmann 78f.

[13] Brackert 169, fn. 26.

[14] See Joachim Bumke's review of Brackert's book in *Euphorion* 58 (1964): 428–438; Hoffmann 79f; Joachim Heinzle, *Das Nibelungenlied. Eine Einführung*, 2nd revised ed.,

the sense that the manuscripts are derived from a basic text, whose author we can designate as the poet of the *Nibelungenlied.* The two text groups *AB and *C, are adaptations of this basic text. The latter is relatively well preserved in *AB, while *C represents a systematic, new rendition — the view taken by Bartsch. *C has had, however, a secondary influence on the entire *AB manuscript tradition (which has been general and arbitrary in nature, and not something that can be delineated in a precise or exact manner, as Braune had assumed).[15] We basically have to assume repeated influence from the oral saga tradition upon the written versions, but this is not, as Brackert had maintained, the rule. In essence, the written tradition must be considered unified. Nevertheless, the basic text, which probably originated about the year 1200 in Passau, cannot be reconstructed any more than can the *AB-variants, and the question whether *B or *A is closer to the original text must remain unanswered.

Both the *AB-, as well as the *C-variant, must have originated fairly early on, immediately in the wake of the authoring of the basic text and in the same general area as the latter. Associated with the new variant *C is the *Klage*, an appendix in rhyming couplets, which shares the basic interpretative thrust of *C. It thus has helped to shape the impression one had in the Middle Ages of the terrible events portrayed in the *Nibelungenlied.* With the exception of two later manuscripts (k and n), the *Klage* is to be found together with all (complete) *Nibelungenlied* manuscripts and can be considered as something of a guide for readers. The question of priority, namely, whether the *Klage* is based on version *C or whether *C is based on the *Klage*, remains controversial. Bumke has recently made a good case for the priority of version *C.[16] The strongest argument for the priority of the *Klage* is the solid connection that exists between the latter and the *Nibelungenlied* in the manuscript tradition. This association suggests that the two texts were already joined before the formation of the different versions. We can be sure that in the years around 1200 there existed a sort of "Nibelungen workshop" in which, in rapid succession, perhaps even to some degree simultaneously, the basic text, the *AB-, and *C-versions, as well as the *Klage*, were composed.[17]

Fischer Taschenbuch 11843 (Frankfurt a. M.: Fischer, 1996) 53ff.

[15] Bumke 437f.; see also Ursula Hennig, "Zu den Handschriftenverhältnissen in der *Liet*-Fassung des Nibelungenliedes," *PBB* (Tübingen) 94 (1972): 113–133.

[16] Joachim Bumke, *Die vier Fassungen der Nibelungenklage. Untersuchungen zur Überlieferungsgeschichte und Textkritik der höfischen Epik im 13. Jahrhundert*, Quellen und Forschungen zur Literatur- und Kulturgeschichte 8 (Berlin and New York: de Gruyter, 1996) 495ff.

[17] Bumke, *Nibelungenklage* 590ff.

Characteristic of contemporary research is the basic agreement that exists among scholars regarding the manner in which the manuscripts or the different versions relate to one another. Yet the ensuing consequences for interpretation are usually ignored. Scholars normally interpret the text using the *B-edition by Bartsch and de Boor, without realizing, however, that this edition certainly cannot claim to be a reliable presentation of the *nôt*-version. In fact, as an edition of *B, it is not even on the same level as Braune's findings. For example, according to Braune, the famous introductory verse: "Uns ist in alten mæren ...," which leads off the text of this edition, does not really belong to version *B, but is rather derived from *C.[18] There is also a tendency to view the *liet*-text as artistically inferior to the (alleged) *nôt*-text without considering that it is really not at all possible to isolate it. Wherever *C concurs with *AB (and that is, for the most part, the case), one simply cannot ascertain whether one is dealing with the basic text or with the text of version *C. Inasmuch as the latter can be defined, it is one of the most pressing issues for scholars to take it seriously (again) as an important literary entity and to disengage the interpretation of the *Nibelungenlied* from the current fixation with the Bartsch/de Boor edition.

II

Details regarding content, as well as the linguistic and stylistic peculiarities of version C, have been repeatedly described,[19] yet the actual aim of the scribe has not been sufficently comprehended. It can be determined from the particular literary status of the *Nibelungenlied*.

The stories surrounding Siegfried's death and the demise of the Burgundians with which the epic is concerned were based on traditional narrative material that had been passed down orally over the centuries. The precise relationship between the basic text and this oral tradition is not quite clear. In other words, we do not know whether the author of the former had only the oral tradition to work with, which would then make him the grand pioneer who transformed the saga of the Nibelungs into the Nibelungen book, or whether he was already able to make use of one or even several

[18] Braune 157.

[19] See von Liliencron; Karl Droege, "Die Fassung C des Nibelungenliedes," *ZfdA* 75 (1938): 89–103; Werner Hoffmann, "Die Fassung *C des Nibelungenliedes und die Klage," in Heinz Otto Burger and Klaus von See, eds., *Festschrift Gottfried Weber. Zu seinem 70. Geburtstag*, Frankfurter Beiträge zur Germanistik 1 (Bad Homburg, Berlin, and Zurich: Gehlen, 1967) 109–143; Francis G. Gentry, "*Mort* oder *Untriuwe*? *Nibelungenliet* und *Nibelungennôt*," in Elisabeth Feldbusch, ed., *Festschrift für Ludwig Erich Schmidt zum 80. Geburtstag* (Hildesheim, Zurich, and New York: Olms, 1989), 302–316; most recently Bumke, *Nibelungenklage* 531ff.

literary predecessors. In any event, two things are clear: the tradition which precedes the *Nibelungenlied* was, like all heroic saga, multifaceted, i.e., it was not limited to one version of events, but rather incorporated several which, both in terms of detail as well as in central aspects, deviated considerably from each other in some respects. Moreover, it was considered a reliable transmission of history, a narrative of the common past of those people who had constituted it and a repository of the recollections of the collective memory.[20] In oral tradition, the existence of concurrent narrative variations did not cause any problems, or was at least tolerable, as there was, after all, no synopsis, but consistently only the actual performance text. However, the view of the person who wishes to convert the tradition into a written form is that of the collector and compiler; he sees the variations next to each other and somehow has to come to terms with the problem of contradiction. The result, the *nôt*-text that has been handed down to us, demonstrates that the *Nibelungenlied*-poet made a rather impressive effort to construct a structure of motivation that was suitable for the book form. It is also clear, however, that he was not at liberty to execute this in a consistent manner because the tradition simply was considered sacrosanct and could not be manipulated at will. Consequently, his work was filled with inconsistencies and incongruities. It might be said that, just like the *nôt*-text, it had not yet become a proper book. This is clearly the juncture at which the *C-scribe set to work. Moving along the same path taken by the author of the basic text, he contributed to the transformation of the oral Nibelungen saga into a Nibelungen book. In other words, the basic text/*nôt*-version and the *liet*-version represent for us two stages or phases in the development of the text, as the subject matter of the Nibelungs was transformed into written form as the *Nibelungenlied.*

The advanced book status of *C is evident first of all in the fact that the editor has either removed or tempered a considerable number of the incongruities and weaker motivations. This has to do, on the one hand, with the microstructure of the text, whereby individual phrases or stanzas have been enhanced through rephrasing, elimination, or augmentation. The following two examples should provide a convincing illustration of how this has been achieved. When Kriemhild is told that the Burgundians are approaching the court of the Huns, according to the *nôt*-version (Bartsch/de Boor 1716f.), she keeps watch:

[20] See Jan Assmann, *Das kulturelle Gedächtnis. Schrift, Erinnerung und politische Identität in frühen Hochkulturen* (Munich: Beck, 1992); Joachim Heinzle, "Konstanten der Nibelungenrezeption in Mittelalter und Neuzeit," in Klaus Zatloukal, ed., *3. Pöchlarner Heldenliedgespräch. Die Rezeption des Nibelungenliedes*, Philologica Germanica 16 (Vienna: Fassbaender, 1995) 81–107.

Kriemhilt diu vrouwe in ein venster stuont.
si warte nâch den mâgen, sô noch friunt nâch friunden tuont.
von ir vater lande sach si manigen man.
der künic vriesch ouch diu mære; vor liebe er lachen began.

"Nu wol mich mîner vreuden", sprach Kriemhilt.
"hie bringent mîne mâge vil manigen niuwen schilt
und halsperge wîze: swer nemen welle golt,
der gedenke mîner leide, und wil im immer wesen holt."

Kriemhild's words constitute an irritating contradiction to the context of the plot. After all, she means to kill her relatives and certainly has no reason to rejoice over the fact that they are heavily armed. She ought to wish that they would arrive without weapons. The contradiction can be explained once one understands the way in which the material was developed. We are obviously dealing here with a relic from an older version — probably the original one — in which the treacherous invitation did not emanate from Kriemhild, but rather from Etzel, who sought to rob his brothers-in-law of the famous Nibelungen treasure. In this version, one in which the murder of Siegfried plays no role, Kriemhild had warned her brothers and thus her joy at seeing them in their armor is quite understandable.[21] The scribe of *C removed the contradiction by replacing the two stanzas above with three new ones (Hennig 1755–1757):

Dô diu küniginne vernam diu mære,
ir begunde entwîchen ein teil ir swære.
von ir vater lande kom ir vil manic man:
dâ von der künic Ezele vil manigen jâmer sît gewan.

Si gedâhte tougenlîche: "noch möhte is werden rât.
der mich an mînen freuden alsô gepfendet hât,
mag ich daz gefüegen, ez sol im leide ergân
ze dirre hôchgezîte: des ich vil guoten willen hân.

Ich solz alsô schaffen, daz mîn râche ergê
in dirre hôchgezîte, swiez dar nâch gestê,
an sînem argen lîbe, der mir hât benomen
vil der mînen wunne: des sol ich nu ze gelte komen."

In this case, the entrance of the Burgundians fits perfectly into the revenge plot.

[21] Andreas Heusler, *Nibelungensage und Nibelungenlied. Die Stoffgeschichte des deutschen Heldenepos*, 6th ed. (Dortmund: Ruhfus, 1965) 132f.

The second example is the famous demand at the end of the work that the Nibelung treasure be returned.[22] Hagen and Gunther are in Kriemhild's hands. She promises to let Hagen go if he will turn over the hoard which the Burgundians have previously sunk in the Rhine. Hagen refuses to divulge the hiding place as long as Gunther is still alive. Kriemhild promptly has her brother decapitated, and now Hagen enjoys his triumph: he is the only one left who knows where the treasure is hidden and he prefers to die rather than betray the location. The scene does not fit the context at all. It is inexplicable why Kriemhild should suddenly be ready to spare Siegfried's murderer in return for restoration of the treasure and thus turn her back on the revenge to which she had hitherto devoted her entire existence. It is also incomprehensible how Hagen, the most loyal of all vassals, suddenly reaches a point where he effectively brings about the murder of his lord. Once again, we are dealing here with a vestige of the supposedly original version of the tale, in which the king of the Huns was the one who demanded the treasure. By having Kriemhild step into Etzel's role, and allowing the invitation to serve the objective of taking revenge on Siegfried's murderers, the queen's demand for the treasure becomes senseless. Yet, as a spectacular highpoint of the tale relating the demise of the Burgundians, it appears in the meantime to have become indispensable, so that the editor of *C as well was forced to show his limitations at this point: he simply could not eliminate the motif. However, he did find an explanation for Hagen's behavior which was well motivated in the original version, in which Gunther was the one from whom the hoard was demanded. In a supplemental stanza (Hennig 2428), the scribe affords us some insight into Hagen's way of thinking:

> Er wiste wol diu mære, sine liez in niht genesen.
> wie möhte ein untriuwe immer sterker wesen?
> er vorhte, sô si hête im sînen lîp genomen,
> daz si danne ir bruoder lieze heim ze lande komen.

A more damning image of Hagen as a scoundrel is hardly conceivable. He cannot stand the idea that he has to die while his lord has a chance to escape and so he brings about Gunther's death in a most malicious and insidious manner. This is the culmination of a long series of intervening commentaries to be found in the text, by means of which the editor portrays Hagen in a

[22] See Joachim Heinzle, "Gnade für Hagen? Die epische Struktur des Nibelungenliedes und das Dilemma der Interpreten," in Fritz Peter Knapp, ed., *Nibelungenlied und Klage. Sage und Geschichte, Struktur und Gattung. Passauer Nibelungengespräche 1985* (Heidelberg: Winter, 1987) 257–276; Alois Wolf, *Heldensage und Epos. Zur Konstituierung einer mittelalterlichen volkssprachlichen Gattung im Spannungsfeld von Mündlichkeit und Schriftlichkeit*, ScriptOralia 68 (Tübingen: Narr, 1995) 418ff.

negative light. These intrusions upon the text are part of the strategy he uses to balance out a basic contradiction in the macrostructure of the work.

It is simply a matter of fact that the images of Hagen and Kriemhild which prevail in the first part of the work do not correspond with what we find in the second — a consequence of the fact that each of the two parts can be traced back to an independent tale.[23] Hagen appears in the first part as the treacherous murderer and Kriemhild as the victim; the second part, on the other hand, depicts Hagen as the great hero and selfless protector of the Burgundians, while Kriemhild appears as a dehumanized murderess. Just like the poet of the *Klage*, the *C-scribe interpreted events from the constellation apparent in the first part of the epic. He portrayed Hagen as the faithless ("ungetriuwen") catalyst for all of the misery that ensued. Kriemhild, however, is seen as a suffering and loving woman whose actions, despite their terrible consequences, are motivated by loyalty ("triuwe"), i.e., by the loyalty of her love for Siegfried, even beyond death. Thus, Hagen is repeatedly referred to as being disloyal ("ungetriuwe"), whereas the *nôt*-version offers a neutral formulation (for example, *AB [Bartsch/de Boor] 903,1 and 1001,1: "von Tronege Hagene" = *C [Hennig] 910,1 and 1012,1: "der ungetriuwe," or *AB [Bartsch/de Boor] 984,4: "des künic Guntheres man" = *C [Hennig] 993,4: "der vil ungetriuwe man"). Particularly weighty is the manner in which he is condemned as "morder ungetriuwer" by the chaplain, whom he had thrown into the water while crossing the Danube (Hennig 1621, in a supplemental stanza). Furthermore, Hagen's self-serving and shabby behavior was already underscored by his sinking of the treasure in the Rhine. An additional stanza (Hennig 1153) informs the reader that he intended to cheat his lords out of the hoard. In contrast, Kriemhild is characterized as "triuwe," whereas the *nôt*-version contains a neutral description: *AB (Bartsch/de Boor) 1105,4: "sît rach sich wol mit ellen des küenen Sîfrides wîp" = *C (Hennig) 1116,4: "sît rach sich harte swinde in grôzen triuwen daz wîp." And once again, in a supplemental stanza (Hennig 1159,4), she is praised as the most loyal of all women: "getriuwer wîp deheine ist uns selten ê bekant." She is, however, intentionally excused as the one who unleashes the slaughter at the Hunnish court: she explicitly gives the order to kill only Hagen and to let the other Burgundians live (Hennig 1882, along with 1947). The fact that everyone meets the same fate is attributed to the work of the devil (Hennig 2143).

[23] See Joachim Heinzle, "Zweimal Hagen oder: Rezeption als Sinnunterstellung," in Joachim Heinzle and Anneliese Waldschmidt, eds., *Die Nibelungen. Ein deutscher Wahn, ein deutscher Alptraum. Studien und Dokumente zur Rezeption des Nibelungenstoffs im 19. und 20. Jahrhundert*, suhrkamp taschenbuch 2110 (Frankfurt a. M.: Suhrkamp, 1991) 21–40.

Emendations to the story that occurred when it was transformed into book form included the care taken to insure that the events of the plot adhered to basic logic, as well as the evaluation of those events from the standpoint of Christian morality using the categories of guilt/sin and innocence/guilt. An evaluation of this sort signifies, at the same time, a certain distancing from tradition. This, too, is a characteristic of literality. In oral tradition, the narrative appears as the past which has been directly brought into the present,[24] while in written form, on the other hand, it is regarded as preserved antiquity. It is only here that the category "old" takes on significance, where the narrative derives value and authority from its age, but where it can also become the object of reflection and criticism.[25] It is thus noteworthy that in *C (as well as in the *Klage*) the key word "alt" is placed at the beginning of the report and in a phrase which allows a distancing pathos to set the basic tenor of the narrative: "Uns ist in alten mæren wunders vil geseit...."

This "distance" expresses itself not least of all in the fact that the authenticity of the historical element becomes a problem. The editor felt obligated to protect it from possible doubts through repeated commentary. Thus his rationalization in two supplemental stanzas (Hennig 518f.) following the claim that Siegfried recruited in an instant three thousand (in A the reference is even to 30,000), respectively, a thousand Nibelungen warriors:

> Nu sprichet lîht ein tumber: "ez mac wol lüge wesen.
> wie möhte sô vil ritter bî ein ander sîn genesen?
> wâ nâmen si die spîse, wâ nâmen si gewant?
> sine kundenz niht verenden, und ob in dienten drîzec lant."
>
> Sîvrit was sô rîche, als ir wol habt gehôrt:
> im diente daz künicrîche und Nibelunge hort.
> des gaber sînen degenen vil vollelîch genuoc,
> wande sîn wart doch niht minre, swie vil man von dem schatze truoc.

A fine example of how the editor was concerned that the narrative might not be taken seriously is also provided by the description of the fighting that takes place at Etzel's court. In an extra stanza (Hennig 2178) he declares that all

[24] Ursula Schaefer, "Zum Problem der Mündlichkeit," in Joachim Heinzle, ed., *Modernes Mittelalter. Neue Bilder einer populären Epoche* (Frankfurt a. M. and Leipzig: Insel, 1994) 361f.

[25] See Assmann 100f., and Heinzle, "Konstanten der Nibelungenrezeption..." 92f.

of the Burgundians could have survived the firing of the Great Hall because the edifice was built of stone arches which would have withstood the flames.

In the same vein, the editor also "verifies" in a supplemental stanza (Hennig 1013) precisely where Siegfried was killed:

> Von dem selben brunnen, dâ Sîvrit wart erslagen,
> sult ir diu rehten mære von mir hœren sagen:
> vor dem Otenwalde ein dorf lît Otenhein,
> dâ vliuzet noch der brunne, des ist zwîfel dehein.[26]

We learn in subsequent supplementary stanzas (Hennig 1161; 1164) that Ute and Siegfried were buried in Lorsch Monastery, where even today their coffins can be seen.[27]

It should be emphasized that the editor changed virtually nothing with respect to the "facts" of the external plot. He, too, considered them sacrosanct. However, he was willing to eliminate troublesome motifs and was more adept in creating links among the various motivations. But by no means was he, as one can read time and time again, obligated to a different "world view" or a different poetics when compared to the author of his source. The latter himself — inasmuch as the *nôt*-version allows us to arrive at any judgment — did everything in his power to insure a logical sequence of events in the plot. The redactor of *C did not deviate from the line taken by his predecessor, he simply pursued it further in a consequential manner. In the process, he was not concerned with the propagation of a moral position, nor was he interested in aesthetic questions in the sense of a modern view of art, but rather with the factual imparting of "ancient lore."[28]

III

From the outset, the *liet*-version has dominated *Nibelungenlied* tradition as that text which is the most developed in terms of a literary book form. The earliest literary echo of the work with which we are familiar, a passage in Wolfram von Eschenbach's *Parzival*, probably dating from ca. 1204–1205,

[26] See Heinzle, "Konstanten der Nibelungenrezeption..." 91.

[27] Heinzle, "Konstanten der Nibelungenrezeption..." 91; also Bumke, *Nibelungenklage* 502ff.

[28] Otto Höfler, "Die Anonymität des Nibelungenliedes," in Karl Hauck, ed., *Zur germanisch-deutschen Heldensage*, Wege der Forschung 14 (Darmstadt: Wissenschaftliche Buchgesellschaft, 1961) 387f.; Heinzle, "Konstanten der Nibelungenrezeption..." 89.

refers to the *liet*.[29] Moreover, the undoubtedly oldest textual evidence of the *Nibelungenlied* itself is precisely manuscript C, which was written down in the second quarter of the thirteenth century.

The significance of the *liet*-version in the initial phase of the tradition is further underscored by the fact that the first evidence we possess of the *nôt*-version is directly connected to it. We are referring here to the fragment complex S, the vestiges of a manuscript that may, perhaps, be somewhat later than C. It contains a text that, for both the sections of the *Nibelungenlied* and the *Klage*, follows *C for a short segment and *AB for the remainder. (In the *Nibelungenlied*, the cutoff point is situated in the area of strophes 270/271 in Hennig's edition.) There are reasons to assume that the mixing of texts already took place in a precursor of manuscript S. This mixing is evinced in an entire group of manuscripts, of which, however, only D and b have survived in (almost) complete form. The parent manuscript that needs to be reconstructed is, therefore, referred to as *Db. The only way it is likely to have come into being was for two scribes sitting next to each other to have begun work on a copy of the *Nibelungenlied* and *Klage* sections based on a *C-manuscript (which had been accordingly divided up). After a brief period of time, this manuscript was no longer available to them, so that the work had to be continued using a precursor of *AB.[30] The fact that the *nôt*-version was handed down in this branch of the tradition could be attributed to a makeshift solution: what one actually wanted was the *liet*-version.

The *nôt*-version was first retained in its entirety in manuscript B, which originates from the middle of the thirteenth century (perhaps about 1260).[31] The codex, which has been written on exquisite parchment, beautifully adorned with initial letters composed in byzantine-venetian style, also contains, besides the *Nibelungenlied* and the *Klage*, Wolfram von Eschenbach's *Parzival* and *Willehalm*, Stricker's *Karl*, Konrad von Fußesbrunnen's *Kindheit Jesu*, and Konrad von Heimesfurt's *Mariae Himmelfahrt*. At least six different scribes can be discerned. That means that the manuscript was composed in an unusually large *scriptorium* where the *liet*-version was also available. We have a fragment of this version (E), the text of which came from a scribe who was involved in writing down the *Nibelungenlied* in

[29] Bumke, *Nibelungenklage* 572ff.

[30] Bumke, *Nibelungenklage* 298ff.

[31] Nigel F. Palmer, "Der Codex Sangallensis 857: Zu den Fragen des Buchschmucks und der Datierung," in Joachim Heinzle, L. Peter Johnson, Gisela Vollmann-Profe, eds., *Wolfram-Studien 12: Probleme der Parzival-Philologie. Marburger Kolloquium 1990* (Berlin: Schmidt, 1992) 15–31; Bumke, *Nibelungenklage* 147ff.

manuscript B.[32] Once again we have direct evidence that the two versions could come into contact with one another in the course of their transmission. The inclusion of the *Nibelungenlied/Klage* complex within an extensive collection of narrative texts representing a variety of genres in B is remarkable. Inasmuch as the fragmentary nature of the manuscripts allows any sort of conclusion, it is by far more often the case that the latter are passed down individually (an association, in each instance, with another text or complex of texts can be seen with J and h, an affiliation with several texts is evident with n, k, and d; there is evidence of a connection with a supplementary text in the case of K and c, but the possibility exists that the manuscripts did contain some other texts). Above all, however, the fact that the *B-version was chosen for the exquisite collection is an exception; it has not been passed down in this form anywhere else.

Manuscript A, the third of the three main manuscripts, is approximately three to four decades later than B. As for the rest, the *liet*-version also dominates in the second half of the thirteenth century. Apart from fragment E, it is represented by the fragments Z (third quarter of the thirteenth century),[33] F, G, and X (all in the fourth quarter), as well as R (about 1300).

Fragment O appears in the last quarter of the thirteenth century. It is the oldest testimony to another hybrid variant which basically exhibits the *nôt*-version *B, while also containing, however, a series of stanzas from *C. Among the latter are to be found several of the typical "commentary stanzas" (in Hennig 822: the devil as adviser; 923: condemnation of Siegfried's murder; 1013: reference to the spring at Odenheim; 1947: vindication of Kriemhild). The interpolater was obviously interested in emphasizing the position taken by the editor of *C. The hybrid version is contained in its entirety in the latest manuscript d, to which manuscript O could have served as the immediate forerunner.[34] One other complete manuscript also containing these stanzas is J, composed about 1300. However, since the manuscript which also contains, besides the *Nibelungenlied* and the *Klage*, the *Winsbeckischen Gedichte*, has a different text when compared to (O)d; it is more appropriate not to speak of a hybrid variant, but rather of a hybrid complex *Jd consisting of the groups *J and *d. One can imagine that the manuscript from which they are derived was one of the *nôt*-manuscripts belonging to either the *J or *d type. This manuscript was modernized by

[32] Karin Schneider, *Gotische Schriften in deutscher Sprache. I. Vom späten 12. Jahrhundert bis um 1300, Textband* (Wiesbaden: Reichert, 1987) 136.

[33] Erroneously dated by earlier scholars to the beginning of the thirteenth century; see Schneider 144f., fn. 109.

[34] Braune 135f. An opposing view is offered by Hermann Schmidt, "Die Nibelungenhandschrift O," *ZfdA* 54 (1913): 88–98.

adding the stanzas from *C in the margins, and was then used to augment once again a manuscript from the other type. (It is unlikely that the correspondence between the hybrid forms in *J and *d is based on pure coincidence.)[35] The fragment complex K can also be associated with J about 1300. It is derived from a manuscript which, just as with B, still contained (at the very least) Konrad von Fußesbrunnen's *Kindheit Jesu*. The Berlin fragment E of Konrad's work belongs together with the three K fragments of the *Nibelungenlied*, something which has hitherto not been recognized.

Thus, by the beginning of the fourteenth century, the most important *Nibelungenlied* texts were in existence, namely:

1. the *nôt*-version *A (manuscript A)
2. the *nôt*-version *B (manuscript B)
3. the *liet*-version (manuscript C, fragments E, F, G, R, X, Z)
4. the hybrid version *Db (fragment complex S)
5. the hybrid complex *Jd (manuscript J, fragment complex K, fragment O).

It is striking that the manuscripts cited above originated, without exception, in Bavaria or Austria, i.e., in the southeastern section of the German-speaking area. Of the great narrative works of the Middle High German *Blütezeit* ("classical period"), only Gottfried's *Tristan* displays a similar "provinciality" with respect to its geographical dissemination in the thirteenth century (in Gottfried's case, his work was confined to the southwest).[36] Yet, it can be determined from quotations in Wolfram,[37] from its (presumed) use in the Norwegian *Þiðreks saga* dating from ca. 1250,[38] and from the Dutch variant,[39] that the text was early on far more widely disseminated than the provenance of the manuscript might allow us to believe. With these five text forms, the paths which the manuscript tradition

[35] Brackert 116f.

[36] See Thomas Klein, "Ermittlung, Darstellung und Deutung von Verbreitungstypen in der Handschriftenüberlieferung mittelhochdeutscher Epik," in Volker Honemann and Nigel F. Palmer, eds., *Deutsche Handschriften 1100–1400. Oxforder Kolloquium 1985* (Tübingen: Niemeyer, 1990) 124ff.

[37] As well as from the *Klage* and in *Willehalm*, see Bumke, *Nibelungenklage* 572ff., 588ff.

[38] Heinzle, *Das Nibelungenlied. Eine Einführung* 37f. We can assume that both Wolfram and the author of the *Þiðreks saga* used a manuscript from the *C tradition as their basis. See Bumke, review of Brackert, fn. 37.

[39] See Norbert Voorwinden, "Die niederländischen Nibelungen-Fragmente (Hs.T)," *AbäG* 17 (1982): 177–188.

of the *Nibelungenlied* would take in the following centuries were clearly defined.

The *nôt*-version *A is represented in the fourteenth century by the fragment M and the fragment complex L and, in addition, in the fifteenth century by the extensive fragment g, the vestige of a copy of manuscript L. We have already pointed out that the *nôt*-version *B, in the form passed down by Manuscript B, is otherwise not attested. The only thing we have at our disposal that can be used to check the manuscript tradition is the *d-group of the hybrid complex *Jd. Previously, scholars associated fragment I (fifteenth century), which only contained slightly more than fifteen stanzas, as well as manuscript c, with B, but in both cases such a link is highly questionable.[40] Manuscript c otherwise deserves particular attention. We are dealing here with a codex dating, perhaps, from the fourteenth century, but which is no longer extant. In the sixteenth century, the Viennese scholar, Wolfgang Lazius, published some of the verses from the *Nibelungenlied* and the *Laurin* which were contained therein. It is possible that c was a more extensive collection of heroic poetry, a *Heldenbuch*, which may have been connected to the d strand of the manuscript tradition.[41]

Only one fragment (U) of the *liet*-version has survived from the fourteenth century. This is compensated for by the *Wallensteiner Handschrift* a (named after the place where it was discovered), which was written down in the second quarter of the fifteenth century. From the perspective of textual history, this manuscript is very important because it fills in some of the larger (technical) gaps to be found in C. It is also an illuminating document with respect to the matter of how contemporaries understood the text. A short, historical preface, written in prose, precedes the *Nibelungenlied*, which does not begin until the sixth *Âventiure*. We are told that, in the year 740, Pipanus of France was Roman Augustus and how, because of the disobedience of the Romans, he withdrew to Constantinople while appointing Dietrich von Bern as his deputy. During the latter's rule, the "auenteur dez pueches vonn denn Rekchenn vnd vonn Kreymhilldenn" supposedly took place. This historical locating of the action, which utilizes data lifted from scholarly historiography,[42] provides direct evidence of the conviction that the Nibelungen legend was based on history, which, we have assumed, played a major role in its transition to a written form, particularly in *C.[43]

[40] Braune 132f., fn. 1; also Hermann Menhardt, "Die Nibelungenhandschrift c, der Laurin und die Historia Gothorum des Lazius," *ZfdA* 84 (1952/53): 152–158.

[41] Menhardt 156.

[42] Hennig, "Zu den Handschriftenverhältnissen..." 115ff.

[43] Heinzle, "Konstanten der Nibelungenrezeption..." 99f.

The hybrid version *Db is represented in the fourteenth century by manuscript D itself (written down sometime during the first three decades), as well as by three fragments (N, P, V). There follows in the fifteenth century the *Hundeshagen Handschrift* b (named after its former owner and written down between 1436 and 1440). With thirty-seven (of probably an original thirty-nine) colored ink drawings, it is the only continuously illustrated manuscript of the *Nibelungenlied* (Manuscript k contains a frontispiece).

Likewise, the *J-Group of hybrid complex *Jd is represented in the fourteenth century by three manuscripts (Q, Y, l). Here as well we have a complete manuscript from the fifteenth century, namely, h, written about 1450–1455. Like J, it contains the *Winsbeckischen Gedichte*. Finally, there is the *d-group: in the fourteenth century we have a fragment (H), as well as manuscript d, the famous *Ambraser Heldenbuch*, an extensive collection of heroic epics, courtly romances, and minor epics, composed in South Tyrol between the years 1504–1515 (or 1516) by Hans Ried for Emperor Maximilian I.

If we survey the manuscript tradition described here since the fourteenth century, we have the impression that the hybrid versions have gained prominence over the "pure" versions. It is, however, difficult to say whether this impression corresponds to historical reality or is really just a matter of coincidence. As striking even now as was the case earlier is the extent to which the geography of the manuscript tradition is limited: apart from Lg (Rhenish-Franconian), the manuscripts originate, now as before, from Bavaria or Austria and the surrounding areas (D quite likely from Lower Bavaria or Bohemia, N and P perhaps from Franconia, U and l possibly from the Alemannic area, b perhaps from Augsburg). A certain block-like concentration in the manuscript tradition can be seen as well in the fact that, in two cases, we (possibly) have "mother" and "daughter" manuscripts (O–d, L–g). A marked tendency, which can be observed throughout the centuries, to preserve the structure of the manuscripts in the transmitting of individual texts, points in the same direction. Thus, all *A-manuscripts (A, L, M, g) set off verses and stanzas, while the three *d-manuscripts (O, H, d), which originated in Tyrol, evince a continuous text.[44]

IV

The three hitherto uncited manuscripts do not fit into the aforementioned description of the manuscript tradition. They evince radical adaptations of the text, whereby the editors have also fallen back on the oral tradition of the epic material, which is still very much alive.

[44] See Bumke, *Nibelungenklage* 215ff.

The Darmstadt manuscript m, which dates from the middle or second half of the fourteenth century, is a fragment which only contains a list of the *âventiuren* (*Darmstädter Aventiurenverzeichnis*). We can determine from this table of contents that the story of the abduction of Kriemhild by a dragon and her rescue by Siegfried, recorded in the *Hürnen Seifried*, has been incorporated into the text.[45]

The adaptation found in the second Darmstadt manuscript, n, also reminds us of this story. This manuscript, which was only discovered in 1976, originated in a codex composed in 1449 (or around 1470–1480?), which also included the Darmstadt manuscript by Johanns von Würzburg, entitled *Wilhelm von Österreich,* and the Berlin manuscript of *Alpharts Tod*. The text only takes up the matter of the Burgundians' demise. It is preceded by an introduction, which provides a précis of the prior history and, with the Bartsch/de Boor stanza 1520, joins the text at the twenty-fifth *Âventiure*. The *Klage* is missing. The editor has been fairly free with the manuscript text, partly following *B, to some degree *C. He has restructured it, abbreviated it, and also expanded it. The introductory section evinces reflexes of the oral tradition, for example, the aforementioned recollection of Kriemhild's abduction,[46] but above all, the statement that Siegfried's body was placed into the arms of the sleeping Kriemhild[47] (in the *Nibelungenlied*, Hagen has the dead hero placed before Kriemhild's chamber). That the n-version is old can be seen from the fact that it corresponds to the report that is provided by the *Þiðreks saga*; it is also striking that the murderer is depicted as Siegfried's brother-in-law: Hagen and Gunther were originally brothers and that is the manner in which they have been portrayed in the *Þiðreks saga*.

The two manuscripts originated, as had L and g, from the Rhenish-Franconian region which, in the fourteenth and fifteenth centuries, began to rival the southeast as a second center for the transmission of the tradition. It is, perhaps, no coincidence that the two centers correspond to the geographical area of the narrated world (in the southeast the Danube basin, as well as indirectly the Alpine area of the Dietrich stories, and in the west the Rhenish Burgundian empire in the area of Worms). The *Nibelungenlied* could be considered in both places as a local tradition. Such an interest in the Nibelungs can be established directly for Worms: since the late fifteenth

[45] See Heinzle, "Konstanten der Nibelungenrezeption..." 97.

[46] Heinzle, "Konstanten der Nibelungenrezeption..." 97.

[47] Peter Göhler, "Bemerkungen zur Überlieferung des Nibelungenliedes," in Klaus Zatloukal, ed., *3. Pöchlarner Heldenliedgespräch. Die Rezeption des Nibelungenliedes*, Philologica Germanica 16 (Vienna: Fassbaender, 1995) 67–79.

century there is evidence of the existence of a local legend revolving around Siegfried.[48]

The k-version is to be found in a *Heldenbuch*, i.e., a collection of heroic epics, which was most likely commissioned by the Nuremberg townsman Lienhart Scheubel and put together between 1480 and 1490 (*Lienhart Scheubels Heldenbuch*, also designated as the *Piaristenhandschrift* after the place where it was found, the Piarist Monastery in Vienna). In this particular rendition, parts of which are based primarily on *C and other parts on *B, the *Nibelungenlied* has been subjected to an intense stylistic and metrical restructuring aimed at adapting it to the literary conventions of the time.[49] It remains to be investigated whether or not the oral tradition figured in this restructuring. Intriguing in this regard are, for example, the name of the father of the Burgundian kings,[50] as well as the report concerning Iring's death, which once again accords with the *Þiðreks saga* and not with the *Nibelungenlied*.[51] The *Klage* is also missing in this version, but it can be demonstrated that the author of the manuscript was familiar with it.[52]

[48] Heinzle, "Konstanten der Nibelungenrezeption..." 98.

[49] Margarete Springeth, "Beobachtungen zur Nibelungenrezeption in der Wiener Piaristenhandschrift (k)," in Klaus Zatloukal, ed., *3. Pöchlarner Heldenliedgespräch. Die Rezeption des Nibelungenliedes* 173–185.

[50] Heinzle, "Konstanten der Nibelungenrezeption..." 95 and 97.

[51] Hilkert Weddige, *Heldensage und Stammessage. Iring und der Untergang des Thüringerreiches in Historiographie und heroischer Dichtung*, Hermaea, N.F. 61 (Tübingen: Niemeyer, 1989) 108.

[52] Weddige 109; Bumke, *Nibelungenklage* 257, fn. 1.

Appendix

List of Manuscripts[53]

Capital letters are used to designate the parchment manuscripts of the thirteenth and fourteenth centuries, small letters the parchment and paper manuscripts of the fourteenth through the sixteenth century (d, m, and probably c are parchment, the others paper). The letters W, e, and f have been replaced by other designations: those fragments which used to be referred to as e and f are now under L (=L_1), the fragment formerly designated W is now to be found under S (=S_3). The abbreviation T is reserved for the Dutch version. Stars indicate fragments.

A Munich, Bayerische Staatsbibliothek, Cgm 34

B St. Gall, Stiftsbibliothek, Cod. 857

C Donaueschingen, Fürstlich Fürstenbergische Hofbibliothek, Cod. 63

D Munich, Bayerische Staatsbibliothek, Cgm 31

*E Berlin, Staatsbibliothek, Fragm. 44

*F Alba Julia (Karlsburg), Rumania, Bátthyáneum (lost; what has been preserved is a strap [ms. number: R III 70 = Hadamar von Laber, *Die Jagd*, Hs. C] with an impression of the front page of the first leaf on the front inside cover)

*G Karlsruhe, Badische Landesbibliothek, Cod. Donauesschingen 64

[53] On individual manuscripts see Willy Krogmann and Ulrich Pretzel, ***Bibliographie zum Nibelungenlied und zur Klage***, 4th ed., Bibliographien zur deutschen Literatur des Mittelalters 1 (Berlin: Schmidt, 1966) 11ff.; Michael S. Batts, ed., ***Das Nibelungenlied. Paralleldruck der Handschriften A, B und C nebst Lesarten der übrigen Handschriften*** (Tübingen: Niemeyer, 1971) 801ff.; Peter Jörg Becker, ***Handschriften und Frühdrucke mittelhochdeutscher Epen*** (Wiesbaden: Reichert, 1977) 140ff.; Karin Schneider (see Register); Göhler; Bumke, *Nibelungenklage* 141ff. On manuscript L, see also Joachim Heinzle and Kurt Hans Staub, "Neue Bruchstücke der Nibelungenhandschrift L," *PBB* 115 (1993): 66–85. On manuscript Q, see Hans-Friedrich Rosenfeld, "Neue Nibelungenfragmente aus Rosenheim und München," *PBB* 109 (1987): 14–50. On manuscript c, see Gerard Jaspers, "Die deutschen Textfragmente in den lateinischen Werken des Wolfgang Lazius," *AbäG* 20 (1983): 56–73.

*H Formerly Munich (lost), copy by Bernhard Joseph Docen in Berlin, Staatsbibliothek, Mgq 825a

J(I) Berlin, Staatsbibliothek, Mgf 474

*K Group of four fragment sections: (1) Berlin, Staatsbibliothek, Mgf 587 (*Nibelungenlied* K_1); (2) Berlin, Staatsbibliothek, Mgf 814 (*Nibelungenlied* K_2); (3) Dülmen, Herzoglich von Croy'sche Verwaltung, Hausarchiv Nr. 54 (*Nibelungenlied* K_3); (4) Berlin, Staatsbibliothek, Mgf 923 Nr. 13 (Konrad von Fußesbrunnen: *Kindheit Jesu* E)

*L Group of two fragment sections: (1) Cracow, Biblioteka Jagiellońska, Berol. Mgq 635 (*Nibelungenlied* L_1); (2) Mainz, Bibliothek des Bischöflichen Priesterseminars, maculature from and a glued copy in incunabulum FB II Nr. 712, partially lost (*Nibelungenlied* L_2)

*M Linz, Oberösterreichisches Landesmuseum, Ms. 122

*N Group of three fragment sections: (1) Würzburg, Universitätsbibliothek, Deutsche Fragmente 2 (N_1: *Nibelungenlied*); (2) Nuremberg, Germanisches Nationalmuseum, Hs. 2841a (N_2: *Klage*); (3) Nuremberg, Germanisches Nationalmuseum, Hs. 4365a (N_3: *Nibelungenlied*)

*O Cracow, Biblioteka Jagiellońska, Berol. Mgq 792

*P Cracow, Biblioteka Jagiellońska, Berol. Mgq 1895 Nr. 8

*Q Group of three, respectively four, fragment sections: (1) Freiburg, UB, Hs. 511 (Q_1); (2) Rosenheim, Stadtarchiv, HS-g 1, designated (Q_2 [previously under the manuscript call number: Abt. B/H Nr. 1211] + Q_3); (3) Munich, Bayerisches Staatsarchiv, Fragmentensammlung Nr. 2 (Q_4)

*R Nuremberg, Germanisches Nationalmuseum, Hs. 22066

*S Group of three fragment sections: (1) Prague, UB, Fragm. germ. 2 (S_1: *Nibelungenlied*); (2) Prague, Nationalmuseum, I Ea 1 (S_2: *Nibelungenlied*); (3) Prague, Nationalmuseum, I Ea 2 (S_3: *Klage*)

*U Group of two fragment sections: (1) Nuremberg, Germanisches Nationalmuseum, Hs. 42567 (U_1: *Nibelungenlied*); (2) Sterzing, Kapuzinerkloster, no manuscript number (U_2: *Klage*)

*V Vorau, Stiftsbibliothek, folded strips from Hs. 138

*X Vienna, Österreichische Nationalbibliothek, Cod. 14281

*Y Trient, Municipal Library, Ms. 3035

*Z Klagenfurt, Universitätsbibliothek, Perg.-Hs. 46

a Geneva-Cologny, Bibliotheca Bodmeriana, Cod. Bodmer 117

b Berlin, Staatsbibliothek, Mgf 855

*c Lost manuscript belonging to Wolfgang Lazius

d Vienna, Österreichische Nationalbibliothek, Cod. Series nova 2663

*g Heidelberg, Universitätsbibliothek, Cpg 844

h Berlin, Staatsbibliothek, Mgf. 681

*i Cracow, Biblioteka Jagiellońska, Berol. Mgq. 669

k Vienna, Österreichische Nationalbibliothek, Cod. 15478

*l Basel, Öffentliche Bibliothek der Universität, Cod. N I 1 Nr. 99a

*m Darmstadt, Hessische Landes- und Hochschulbibliothek, Hs. 3249

n Darmstadt, Hessische Landes- und Hochschulbibliothek, Hs. 4257

(Translated by Winder McConnell)

Werner Hoffmann

The Reception of the *Nibelungenlied* in the Twentieth Century

Any depiction of the history of the influence and the reception of the *Nibelungenlied* in the twentieth century in Germany (the nature of the topic necessitates that the area of inquiry be geographically restricted) should distinguish between the different areas in which this reception has manifested itself in the past and in which it is currently in evidence. First and foremost, that would involve the academic research that has hitherto been conducted on the subject and the interpretations that have been based upon such research. This would be followed by the more popular, non-specialist, journalistic areas of publication. These publications address a broader range of readers by imparting the results of research in a comprehensible and, in general, more simplified manner. Included here are public lectures and speeches which, over a long period of time, have addressed the *Nibelungenlied* more frequently than any other work of German medieval literature. Thirdly, there is the reception that takes place in schools, which naturally plays an important role in imparting basic and detailed knowledge about literary works. Fourthly, one has the artistic sphere, which has produced very diverse variations on the Nibelung theme, ranging from relatively close adaptations of the epic to freer interpretations, from recounting the entire plot to concentrating on individual characters or scenes, and this would include literature and film, music, and fine art (paintings, illustrations, sculptures). Finally, there is the political arena, in the broadest sense of the term, which, especially in the nineteenth and the first half of the twentieth century, is especially illuminating with respect to the reception of the *Nibelungenlied*. This category needs to be seen in a different light than the ones mentioned before, inasmuch as journalists, teachers, authors, artists, and even scholars, along with politicians, have attempted to achieve a political effect by harnessing the epic *Nibelungenlied* for ideological purposes. For a Middle High German poetic work to have such an enormous political resonance is unusual; perhaps comparable in significance, even if on a much more modest scale, to the work of Walther von der Vogelweide for the German population of South Tyrol.

It should not be surprising, therefore, that it is precisely this aspect of *Nibelungenlied* reception that has attracted the most attention and which will also constitute a major area of focus in this article. The popular, non-specialist, journalistic area, on the other hand, where it has not been responsible for the misuse of the *Nibelungenlied* for political purposes, as well as the reception of the epic in schools, are not included in the present study. An investigation of the pedagogical sphere would entail a detailed examination of the curricula, the essay topics assigned pupils, and the textbooks used, inasmuch as the latter expose students to passages of the Nibelung saga and the *Nibelungenlied*. It needs to be stressed at this juncture, however, that since the early 1970s the *Nibelungenlied*, as well as most medieval literature, has only played a minor role, if any at all, in the German school curriculum. Nevertheless, there are compelling reasons to review, even in the form of a somewhat rough sketch, the course of Nibelung research during the twentieth century. First of all, despite all the simplification and even possible distortions, such research establishes the guidelines which other cultural mediators follow, thanks to the attention granted it by various areas of reception. Secondly, this research contradicts the impression occasionally (or, perhaps, intentionally?) evoked that the reception of the *Nibelungenlied*, at least up to the middle of the twentieth century, could be reduced to the misuse of the epic for political-ideological purposes. Likewise, the artistic reception of the *Nibelungenlied* cannot be excluded from this paper, but it is necessarily restricted to the literary sector. In all probability, this form of the epic's reception is more significant in arriving at an understanding of the *Nibelungenlied* and the subject matter of the Nibelungs than knowledge of the epic itself. Even the political reception of the *Nibelungenlied* has often been based on these reinterpretations in the literary sphere.

Academic Reception

The year 1900 saw the end of a long and bitter discussion which had tended to dominate *Nibelungenlied* research in the second half of the nineteenth century: the dispute surrounding the assessment of the three main manuscripts (A, B, C) and, simultaneously, the priority of the different versions represented by them (*nôt*-version: *A, *B; *liet*-version: *C). It seemed as if Wilhelm Braune, in his very detailed and astute contribution, *Die Handschriftenverhältnisse des Nibelungenliedes*,[1] had finally demonstrated the priority of version *B, as recorded in the St. Gall manuscript. In the following decades, the problem of the manuscripts, once so vehemently discussed, became much less of an issue. It was not until the appearance of Helmut Brackert's *Beiträge zur Handschriftenkritik des Nibelungenliedes* in

[1] Wilhelm Braune, "Die Handschriftenverhältnisse des Nibelungenliedes," *PBB* 25 (1900): 1–222.

1963[2] that the scholarly dispute again became relevant, especially since Brackert offered a radical criticism of the premises underlying Braune's argument. He questioned the applicability of the usual methods of text criticism with regard to the tradition of the *Nibelungenlied*. Brackert seems to have missed the point when he argues that there is basically no original of the *Nibelungenlied* in the sense of a definitive, single text produced by one individual. He is certainly right, however, in the presumption that we can reconstruct neither its exact wording nor that of the archetype, i.e., the manuscript from which the entire tradition originates. In more recent times, individual scholars (for example, Rolf Bräuer) have claimed that version *C is the original, which is, however, a most unlikely theory.

Twentieth-century research on the *Nibelungenlied* was for decades characterized by an emphasis upon its genealogy, i.e., the history of its subject matter. This line of research is primarily associated with the name of the Swiss Germanist, Andreas Heusler. In his short essay, *Lied und Epos in germanischer Sagendichtung*,[3] Heusler offered a detailed explanation of the basic difference between lay and epic. This difference precludes any attempt to view the origin of the epic *der Nibelunge nôt* as a composite of individual lays, as had been suggested in 1816 by Karl Lachmann, the original founder of strictly philological Nibelung research, with his so-called *Liedertheorie*.[4] Heusler seems to have finally put this hypothesis to rest with his "accretion theory," according to which the epic evolved from the expansion, the "accretion" of the tale, which already exists in its entirety in the narrative song. "Ballad-like brevity" is replaced by "epic breadth." Even more influential were Heusler's theories on the genesis of the *Nibelungenlied*, which, he claimed, dated to the fifth and sixth centuries. The work was complete after a few stages, i.e., as the product of a relatively small number of poets. Separate strands of the legend (*Brünhildsaga* and *Burgundensaga*) formed the core and were finally all brought together around the year 1200 by one single poet and set down in writing in the form of the *Nibelungenlied* known to us today.[5] Heusler's theories were widely acclaimed and enjoyed almost canonical validity until after World War II. The occasional detail was

[2] Helmut Brackert, *Beiträge zur Handschriftenkritik des Nibelungenliedes*, Quellen und Forschungen zur Sprach- und Kulturgeschichte der germanischen Völker, N.F. 11 (Berlin: de Gruyter, 1963).

[3] Andreas Heusler, *Lied und Epos in germanischer Sagendichtung* (Dortmund: Ruhfus, 1905).

[4] Karl Lachmann, *Über die ursprüngliche Gestalt des Gedichts von der Nibelungen Noth* (Berlin: Dümmler, 1816).

[5] Andreas Heusler, *Nibelungensage und Nibelungenlied. Die Stoffgeschichte des deutschen Heldenepos*, 6th ed. (Dortmund: Ruhfus, 1965). [First published in 1921.]

modified, but the basic concepts were never fundamentally challenged. This not only represented an analysis of the *Nibelungenlied* from a genealogical standpoint, but as often as not also a preference for the poetic import of the Germanic songs over and above the Christian and courtly influences on the High Medieval *Nibelungenlied*.

The attempt to understand the *Nibelungenlied* in and from the historical context of the period around 1200, based on a rigorous interpretation of the text, was not *the*, or, for that matter, even *an* aim of research around Heusler's time. This approach to the *Nibelungenlied* was rather left to "outsiders." To be sure, even in the 1920s there were some individual studies devoted to the interpretation of the historically recorded *Nibelungenlied*, for example, the work of Josef Körner in 1921 (whose main area of interest was actually modern German literary history) and Ernest Tonnelat in 1926 (who, as a French critic, was not particularly influenced by the trends of German scholarship, which tended to take their cue from Andreas Heusler).[6] Friedrich Neumann (1927) demonstrated quite methodically that the *Nibelungenlied* must also be viewed as a poem of the High Middle Ages, just like the contemporary courtly romances, and not as the last link in a chain of plot variations reaching far back into the past, about which neither the poet nor the contemporary audience could know anything.[7] Neumann himself was not able to meet this theoretical challenge until forty years later (1967), and then only in a very disappointing manner.[8] By this time several more recent, extensive interpretations of the *Nibelungenlied* had been published, the first by Gottfried Weber (1963),[9] which was followed shortly thereafter by Bert Nagel's study (1965).[10] Central to Weber's interpretation is the work-immanent approach to poetry, which was very popular at the time. However, his consequent overlooking, particularly of (constructed) pre-stages of the *Nibelungenlied* and, even more, of other surviving heroic poems, precluded an adequate understanding of the *Nibelungenlied*. Inasmuch as Weber was at all interested in an historical approach, if one can call it that, he limited himself almost exclusively to intellectual history. This perspective is also

[6] See Josef Körner, *Das Nibelungenlied* (Leipzig and Berlin: Teubner, 1921), and Ernest Tonnelat, *La chanson des Nibelungen. Etude sur la composition et la formation du poème épique* (Paris: Societé d'édition: Les belles lettres, 1926).

[7] Friedrich Neumann, "Das Nibelungenlied in der gegenwärtigen Forschung," *DVjs* 5 (1927): 130–171.

[8] See Friedrich Neumann, *Das Nibelungenlied in seiner Zeit*, Kleine Vandenhoeck-Reihe 253S (Göttingen: Vandenhoeck & Ruprecht, 1967).

[9] Gottfried Weber, *Das Nibelungenlied. Problem und Idee* (Stuttgart: Metzler, 1963).

[10] Bert Nagel, *Das Nibelungenlied. Stoff – Form – Ethos* (Frankfurt a. M.: Hirschgraben-Verlag, 1965).

legitimate when examining a work of poetry like the epic *der Nibelunge nôt*, but it cannot play a central role. The necessary addition of a concrete historical approach, the integration of the *Nibelungenlied* into the political, social, and legal context of the High Middle Ages, has occurred against the backdrop of the re-orientation of literary as well as medieval studies since the late 1960s and 1970s. This has, needless to say, sometimes been characterized by the same one-sidedness and exaggeration of what was basically a justified point, just as had occurred a few years earlier with Weber. About this time there also appeared the first complete interpretation of the *Nibelungenlied* by a Germanist in the German Democratic Republic: a monograph by Karl Heinz Ihlenburg (1969).[11] He viewed the epic as a reflection of feudal-courtly society about the year 1200, with all of its concrete, socio-historical constellations and conflicts. More recent interpretations of the *Nibelungenlied* are totally free of such biases. We can mention here the comprehensive work by Otfrid Ehrismann (1987),[12] the subtitle of which — *Epoche – Werk – Wirkung* — concisely delineates the three main areas of contemporary interest concerning the *Nibelungenlied*, as well as three notable works by Germanists in the United States: Winder McConnell (1984),[13] Edward R. Haymes (1986),[14] and Theodore M. Andersson (1987).[15] Andersson's book stands out because its author, more than the other interpreters, inquires into the background of the epic and, to a certain degree reviving Heusler's ideas, covers in detail the "Sources and Analogues" of the *Nibelungenlied*.

About the same time as socio-historical approaches to the *Nibelungenlied* were being undertaken, oral-formulaic analysis, which in fact pre-dates the former, was also being applied to the epic. Since 1967 its main advocate has been Franz H. Bäuml.[16] Even if the high concentration of formulae and formulaic expressions and the undeniable recurrence of traditional story patterns in the *Nibelungenlied* (e.g., courting the bride, advice-giving scenes, etc.) justified the presumption that the heroic epic of the Middle Ages was

[11] Karl Heinz Ihlenburg, *Das Nibelungenlied. Problem und Gehalt* (Berlin: Akademie-Verlag, 1969).

[12] Otfrid Ehrismann, *Nibelungenlied. Epoche – Werk – Wirkung* (Munich: Beck, 1987).

[13] Winder McConnell, *The Nibelungenlied*, Twayne's World Authors Series 712 (Boston: Twayne, 1984).

[14] Edward R. Haymes, *The Nibelungenlied. History and Interpretation*, Illinois Medieval Monographs 2 (Urbana and Chicago: University of Illinois Press, 1986).

[15] Theodore M. Andersson, *A Preface to the Nibelungenlied* (Stanford: Stanford University Press, 1987).

[16] Franz H. Bäuml and Donald J. Ward, "Zur mündlichen Überlieferung des Nibelungenliedes," *DVjs* 41 (1967): 351–390. See also Edward R. Haymes, *Mündliches Epos in mittelhochdeutscher Zeit*, GAG 164 (Göppingen: Kümmerle, 1975).

a product of oral composition, we know today that this was the wrong path to take. Bäuml explicitly states that the phenomenon of "the 'pseudo-oral' formula in written Middle High German texts, that is, of formulicity as written style"[17] (1986) or, as one could also put it, formulicity as an element of epic language, occurs even outside the framework of oral poetry. But independent of the specific ideas that are associated with this form of expression, the research that has been undertaken into the *Literarisierung* ("literarization") of the Nibelung subject matter has proven to be very fruitful in our attempt to come to terms with the text of the *Nibelungenlied*. This is also true in general with respect to the problems associated with the transition of oral forms into written in medieval German poetry — together with the recognition that both of these types of poetry co-existed over a certain period of time. It is also indisputable that the oral tradition of lays and short epics continued for some time alongside the written tradition of *der Nibelunge nôt*.

Another important turning point in *Nibelungenlied* research, again around the year 1970, was the emergence of interest in the history of its reception, an interest which continues unabated to the present day. There had been earlier studies on the history of research,[18] but they were confined to, and only traced the progress of, specialized fields of scholarly research. The reassessment of reception as a central object of literary studies (whether in the sense of a more empirically oriented reception history or in the sense of reception aestheticism) was advanced by the Romanist Hans Robert Jauß (1967), who was very interested in questions of literary theory.[19] We are indebted to Helmut Brackert (1971) for providing the impulse to reassess the reception of the *Nibelungenlied* from a critical point of view and to examine the prerequisites, manifestations, and effects of monopolizing it for political and ideological purposes.[20] The tendency to enlist the *Nibelungenlied* in the service of patriotism, nationalism, chauvinism, and even racism, is a dominant feature of its reception from the era of Romanticism up through National

[17] Franz Bäuml, "The Oral Tradition and Middle High German Literature," *Oral Tradition* 1 (1986): 398–445; here 432.

[18] Mary Thorp, *The Study of the Nibelungenlied. Being the History of the Study of the Epic and Legend from 1755 to 1937*, Oxford Studies in Modern Languages and Literature (Oxford: Clarendon, 1940).

[19] Hans Robert Jauß, *Literaturgeschichte als Provokation* (Frankfurt a. M.: Suhrkamp, 1970). The essay entitled "Literaturgeschichte als Provokation der Literaturwissenschaft" had already appeared in 1967.

[20] Helmut Brackert, "Nibelungenlied und Nationalgedanke. Zur Geschichte einer deutschen Ideologie," in Ursula Hennig and Herbert Kolb, eds., *Mediaevalia litteraria. Festschrift für Helmut de Boor zum 80. Geburtstag* (Munich: Beck, 1971) 363–364.

Socialism, and demonstrating this constitutes an integral part of more recent research. Yet, it would be just as one-sided and false to absolutize what are, in reality, various types of reception. There have always been strictly philological, scholarly studies on the *Nibelungenlied* — sometimes even from those scholars who, before a larger audience, took the opportunity of stating their nationalistic views by using the epic as their point of reference (e.g., Gustav Roethe and Friedrich Vogt).

It need hardly be emphasized that contemporary *Nibelungenlied* scholars, in particular, have turned their attention to a vast number of individual aspects of the work, for instance, specific *âventiuren*, motifs (the treasure, dreams, etc.), and characters who appear in the epic, as well as to questions of narrative technique, structure, time frame, language, genre, the relationship between the *Nibelungenlied* and the *Chansons de geste* (Alois Wolf), and, as ever, the search for the unknown author. If one were to hazard a guess as to the common feature in the veritable flood of recent studies on the *Nibelungenlied*, then it would, perhaps, be that the diversity of questions and interests in discoveries corresponds to a diversity of methodological approaches which, in their own right, are then accepted even by those scholars who do not practice them. This was not always the case.

Literary Reception

It is only on occasion that the scholarly reception of the *Nibelungenlied* betrays elements of a political or doctrinaire nature, and even then to a much lesser extent than in other areas. On the other hand, the artistic, and especially the literary reception of the work, proved to be considerably less resistant to ideological intrusion. One has to differentiate between authors who were quite happy to have their Nibelung works used for political purposes, as was often the case with popular literature, and other authors whose adaptations were only later used in that way by those who succeeded them.

In the history of the reception of the *Nibelungenlied*, the turn of the century did not signify any decisive change in the literary sphere, anymore than it did in the political, a dimension which was there from the start. For many years, the story of the Nibelungs was passed on in one predominant form: the drama. It was, from the outset, the genre that was preferably, or even exclusively, used for adaptations of both Nordic and medieval sources (songs of the *Edda*, *Vǫlsunga saga*). Most of these dramas from the nineteenth and the early twentieth centuries have been forgotten. But Richard Wagner's *Ring des Nibelungen* (premières of the individual parts took place in 1869, 1870, and 1876 respectively) and Friedrich Hebbel's trilogy, *Die Nibelungen* (première 1861), were not the only works to have exerted the greatest influence (Hebbel's drama until the end of World War II). Both were also paradigmatic for the exploitation of the theme of the Nibelungs and the *Nibelungenlied* for political purposes, which reached its apex during the Third Reich. Considerations of space preclude a separate treatment of Richard Wagner's musical drama, which it certainly does deserve. Friedrich Hebbel's *Die Nibelungen* proved to be a great success for several decades. It was never performed more often, however, than during the National Socialist era. According to William John Niven (1984),[21] the *Nibelungen* was the second most performed play by Hebbel during the Weimar Republic (the first being the clear favorite *Maria Magdalena*), followed by *Gyges und sein Ring*. During the Third Reich, Hebbel, because of his supposedly Nordic nature, became one of the preferred poets, even to the point of being regarded as something of a cult figure. With 1,094 performances, the *Nibelungen* was unquestionably the most popular of Hebbel's dramas, outdoing *Agnes Bernauer*, which could also be interpreted politically. While the latter had not played a major role in the theater repertoires during the Weimar Republic, during the Third Reich it provided a ready example for the thesis of the absolute primacy of the state over the rights of the individual. On occasion it was even claimed that Hebbel's *Nibelungen* constituted *the* German "national drama," analogous to the assessment of the *Nibelungenlied* as the German national epic, a view which, even at that time, was no longer taken very seriously. Typical for the manner in which the play was regarded at the time was the comment made in 1942 by Fritz Martini, one of Germany's leading literary scholars after World War II, when he described the destruction of the Burgundians in Hebbel's drama as a "gewaltiges dramatisches Heldenlied auf deutsches Mannentum." In addition to the prevailing unfamiliarity with the Middle Ages in general, it was undoubtedly just this misuse of Hebbel's *Nibelungen* as a propaganda instrument to promote the Nordic-Germanic-German character, along with the heroic virtues personified in the drama, that was responsible for the latter's widespread disappearance from the stage following World War II, despite some spectacular new performances in the last few years.

None of the Nibelung dramas written in the twentieth century have ever come close to matching the significance of Hebbel's *Nibelungen* — and this is not only true from the perspective of its historical impact. Some of them are, nevertheless, worthy of attention, even if they hardly proved effective on stage. It thus seems appropriate at this time to point out especially those elements which underscore the way in which these dramas were a product of their time. Interestingly enough, Samuel Lublinski, known today as one of

[21] William John Niven, *The Reception of Friedrich Hebbel in Germany in the Era of National Socialism* (Stuttgart: Heinz, 1984).

the fathers of literary sociology, placed Gunther at the center of his rather long drama *Gunther und Brunhild* (1908). Hagen does not make an appearance at all, thus leaving it up to Gunther to stab Siegfried. Obviously Lublinski's drama has an inherently political dimension and the statement it contains does not pertain solely to conditions in the Middle Ages. Gunther rules during a time of radical change and, as king, is caught between the knights and the townspeople. He wants to be a king "of the people," who tries to achieve goodness and peace, but he is unable to prevent the outbreak of violence, nor is he in a position himself to avoid the use of force.

Paul Ernst, the leading representative of Neo-Classicism, used parts of the *Nibelungenlied* on two occasions as the basis for his dramas: *Brunhild* (1909, première 1911) and *Chriemhild* (1918, although the première did not take place until 1924).[22] Both dramas, and especially the first, are burdened with overly intellectual dialogues that are even heavier than the plot. The fact that, in the first of the two dramas, Ernst accords the figure of Brunhild more attention than had the author of the *Nibelungenlied*, reflects a tendency in the reception of the work that was already quite apparent in the nineteenth century. Ernst follows a well-beaten path with respect to his basic idea. Written towards the end of the war, the *Chriemhild* drama, on the other hand, evinces a novel and surprisingly critical approach. The German defeat caused the poet to comment on those virtues that, especially during the war, had been praised as typically German, such as loyalty and the absolute adherence to one's duty — virtues which had precluded any other outcome than the senseless holding out to the bitter end. Rüdiger responds as follows to Chriemhild's demand that he intervene in the fighting: "Nun tu ich meine Pflicht. Verfluchte Pflicht,/Verfluchtes Sklavenwort. Ich bin ein Sklav" (Act III). Hagen's last words, moreover, are not concerned with his loyalty towards his king and towards himself, nor, for that matter, his triumph over the *vâlandinne* Chriemhild; rather they have a distinct ring of disillusionment about them:

> Ich glaubte, daß ich Diener bin. Ich glaubte,
> Treu muß ein Diener sein. Ich war nur feig.
> Aus Treue hab ich Göttliches getötet;
> Ich wollte nur die Treue sehn, ich log
> Von meinem Blick des Gottes Antlitz fort.
> Aufrührer mußt ich sein. Jetzt töte mich.
> Fall ich von Weiberhand, es ist verdient. (Act III)

[22] Paul Ernst, *Brunhild. Trauerspiel in drei Aufzügen* (Leipzig: Insel, 1909) and *Chriemhild. Trauerspiel in drei Aufzügen* (Munich: G. Müller, 1918).

In an "Afterword" to the play written in the year 1919, Paul Ernst associated Hagen's insights with Germany's immediate past: the disaster was caused by unquestioning loyalty to the emperor.

During the Weimar Republic as well as the era of National Socialist tyranny, there was not a single Nibelung drama written that could be considered even marginally satisfactory from an aesthetic viewpoint, with one late exception. The overwhelming majority are nothing more than attempts to manifest and propagate contemporary *Weltanschauungen*, including racism. Towards the end of the Third Reich, however, there did appear a Nibelung drama which enjoyed much acclaim in its time, but which today is virtually unknown, except among experts: Max Mell's dramatic poem in two parts, *Der Nibelunge Not.*[23] Both parts were staged for the first time in the *Burgtheater* in Vienna: the first in 1944, the second after the war in 1951. Mell, who had a strong Christian background, stresses the Christian features of the *Nibelungenlied.* It is thus only logical that he accords the figure of Dietrich of Bern, who serves as a representative of the humane, Christian way of thinking, more importance in the second part of his work than Hebbel ever did in his drama. While at the conclusion of Hebbel's drama, Dietrich assumes control over Etzel's kingdom "[i]m Namen dessen, der am Kreuz erblich," in Mell's drama the king of the Huns returns to the steppe. At the same time, Dietrich, as has been recounted in the Norwegian *Þiðreks saga* (mid-thirteenth century), mounts a black horse which carries him off. The historic-philosophical optimism of the nineteenth century, the conviction that even after a catastrophe history continues in a sensible way, cannot be reiterated by a poet of the mid-twentieth century, given the impressions left by the horrible events of World War II. It is clear that the conservative author Max Mell intended to counter the distortions of the *Nibelungenlied* by the Nazis with a more faithful reading of the text, as he understood it. In actuality, however, Mell's viewpoint was already passé. In this regard, it is significant that the drama *Die Tarnkappe* by Reinhold Schneider,[24] who was also rooted in Christian tradition, was published in 1951, although it was never performed on stage (which may, of course, also have been due to the poetic weaknesses of the play).

Axel Plogstedt's drama *Nibelungen*, which was performed in 1975–1976 in several cities, was completely different from any of the former dramatizations.[25] It was a satire of the *Nibelungenlied* (a number of which have appeared in narrative form over the last few decades — see below); it could even be regarded as pure slapstick. Apparently it is no longer possible to

[23] Max Mell, *Der Nibelunge Not* (Salzburg: O. Müller, 1951).

[24] Reinhold Schneider, *Die Tarnkappe* (Wiesbaden: Insel, 1951).

[25] Axel Plogstedt, *Die Nibelungen*. (Copyright Axel Plogstedt, 1975)

provide a serious description in dramatic form of the potential meaning of the *Nibelungenlied*, one that extends far beyond the time it was created, or even to use drama to counter its distorted reception. Confirmation of this is offered by two plays, whose authors entertained high ambitions which were, however, never realized beyond the stage of pure experimentation: Heiner Müller, *Germania Tod in Berlin* (1978)[26] and Volker Braun, *Siegfried Frauenprotokolle Deutscher Furor* (1986).[27]

The number of film versions of the *Nibelungenlied* is rather sparse, but a few deserve mention here: Fritz Lang's famous, if not unproblematic, film from the year 1924 (based on a script by Thea von Harbou) and Harald Reinl's purely entertaining film from the year 1966. The much more demanding script for the feature film *Der Nibelunge Not*, written by the East German author Franz Fühmann in the early 1970s, was never produced.

Narrative texts have increasingly provided the focal point for reception of the Nibelung theme over the past few decades, and even today this genre appears to be particularly well represented. One reason for the change of emphasis in "reception genre" may be that contemporary authors are no longer content with making the plot of the *Nibelungenlied* accessible to readers and theatergoers, regardless of the "message" they may wish to impart. They are more interested in penetrating deeply into the substance of the work, reflecting upon the narrative in a way that is impossible to do in the drama. At the same time, they want to examine the reception of the *Nibelungenlied* more thoroughly and critically than is feasible in a drama with its short and often poignant scenes. It also appears that for some authors the *Nibelungenlied* comes burdened with so many layers of reception that they are no longer able to discern the origin of reception per se, namely, the epic tale of the High Middle Ages. Rather, they remain chained to certain stages of its reception.

The first novel based upon the *Nibelungenlied* was Werner Jansen's *Das Buch Treue. Nibelungenroman*, published in 1916.[28] Already the title leaves no doubt as to the manner in which the *Nibelungenlied* is to be revitalized. The fundamental German virtue of loyalty is celebrated and propagated in the middle of World War I. In other words, the "message" of the Middle High German epic, as Jansen understands it, is to be applied to the present situation. The author explicitly states the goal of his novel in the preface, namely, the desire to extract "den fernen Spiegel des edelsten Deutschlands

[26] Heiner Müller, *Germania Tod in Berlin* (Berlin: Rotbuch-Verlag, 1977).

[27] Volker Braun, *Siegfried Frauenprotokolle Deutscher Furor* (Halle: Mitteldeutscher Verlag, 1992). [Première 1986]

[28] Werner Jansen, *Das Buch Treue. Nibelungenroman* (Braunschweig: Westermann, 1916).

der schmählichsten Vergessenheit,"[29] which is somewhat surprising considering the many translations and adaptations of the *Nibelungenlied* that had appeared in the interim. The figure who most personifies the idea of unconditional loyalty, to the point of meeting a heroic death, is Hagen, whom Jansen consistently calls the Chancellor, sometimes even the Iron Chancellor. This inevitably evoked associations with Bismarck among Jansen's contemporaries, even to the point of effecting an identification of the fictitious with the historic character. Hagen is the dominating figure in Burgundy. Gunther, on the other hand, is a weak king. It is the unconditional loyalty towards the king but also towards the people, towards the fatherland, towards *Heimat* (an ahistorical, emotionally charged concept in the novel) which prompts the *Realpolitiker* Hagen, an advocate of power politics, to act. If necessary, this may also be done in an unscrupulous, even criminal way, as is the case with the murder of Siegfrid. In contrast to the manner in which values allegedly peculiar to Germans are exalted to the point of idealization, the Huns are portrayed as degraded and degenerate. They are not alone in this respect; similar treatment is meted out to the representatives of the State Church, here in the person of Bishop Johannes. However, Jansen does introduce — this undoubtedly intended as another bridge to the present for contemporary readers — Chaplain Ratbert as a counter-figure to Bishop Johannes and the representative of true German Christianity. The latter combines religious conviction with love of the fatherland and with a willingness to defend it by force, if necessary. *Das Buch Treue* proved to be a great success, and retained its popularity throughout both the Weimar Republic and the Third Reich (in 1943, the year of the author's death, sales of the work reached between 181,000 and 195,000 copies).

Other Nibelung novels that were published up to the end of World War II evince similar affinities to the ideological tenor of their times, even if not as poignantly as Jansen's *Buch Treue*.[30] The first Nibelung novel that appeared after the war, *Der Stern von Burgund*, by Martin Beheim-Schwarzbach (1961),[31] underscores the radical change in attitude towards both the *Nibelungenlied* and the Nibelung legend. The Nibelungs no longer embody the supposedly typical Germanic-German characteristics, such as heroism, sense of duty, unconditional loyalty, and willingness to make sacrifices. Rather they are endowed with general human traits and are not without their

[29] Jansen, preface.

[30] See Herbert Erich Buhl, *Krone der Frauen. Roman der Königin Brunhild* (Berlin: Reichel, 1939) and also Buhl's *Auf fremdem Thron. Roman der Königin Kriemhild* (Berlin: Reichel, 1941).

[31] Martin Beheim-Schwarzbach, *Der Stern von Burgund. Roman der Nibelungen* (Hamburg: Rütten & Loening, 1961).

weaknesses. Beheim-Schwarzbach used the plot of the *Nibelungenlied* to write a popular novel, omitting what up to that point had been the usual elevation of the figures and the resulting veneration of them and the heroic epic in general. The *Nibelungenlied* simply provides an effective narrative just like other earlier works of literature. If one is so inclined, it is possible to see in Beheim-Schwarzbach's work the first phase in the dismantling of a heroic monument. Yet for all that, it still is not an explicit attempt to come to terms with the ideological claims that were staked against the *Nibelungenlied*, as they were usually to be found in poetic adaptations. It could not, therefore, be considered a literary contribution to the much discussed concept of *Vergangenheitsbewältigung*.

Such was, however, quite clearly the goal of the author of the by far most successful Nibelung novel of the postwar period, Joachim Fernau's *Disteln für Hagen* (1966).[32] The book owes its success mainly to Fernau's narrative style, which is extraordinarily reader-friendly, catchy, witty, and disrespectful, even playful, if perhaps also somewhat affected. Readers may find the book extremely entertaining. The author has much greater ambitions, however. As the subtitle proclaims, he intends to take inventory of the German soul. This is effected through the use of reflections which are introduced at regular intervals. With the help of the *Nibelungenlied*, consistent, timeless qualities of the Germans are to be underscored. Yet, despite all the ironic distortions of the heroic stance, Fernau retains traditional stereotypes and clichés. He thus explains characteristics of the Germans as being rooted in the German soul and therefore inevitable. It follows that Hagen and Siegfried are both similarly characterized as personifications of the latter. *In this respect*, they are, in the final analysis, no different from Hitler who, Fernau claims *expressis verbis*, would eventually be transformed into myth. From a contemporary perspective at least, the latter prophecy turned out to be quite incorrect.

Georg Zauner was even more radical in his efforts to strip the Nibelung heroes (particularly Siegfried) of their aura of heroism and ideology.[33] With the concept of reincarnation as his point of departure, Zauner resurrects his Sigfrid, who originated during the period of mass migrations in the fourth and fifth centuries, in the body of a convicted murderer and rapist of the nineteenth century. The resplendent German hero is portrayed as criminal in nature and ruled only by his compulsive desires. Just as the glorification of the youthful hero is here turned into his exact opposite, the often exaggerated, empty pathos that can be found in some adaptations of the Nibelung

[32] Joachim Fernau, *Disteln für Hagen. Eine Bestandsaufnahme der deutschen Seele* (Berlin, Munich, and Vienna: Herbig, 1966). It appeared in a softcover edition in 1978 and sold almost 100,000 copies within three years.

[33] Georg Zauner, *Die Erinnerungen des Helden Sigfrid* (Zurich: Benzinger, 1985).

topic is replaced by language which does not even spare the reader vulgarities.

Judging by authorial intention, the contents, the narrative perspectives, and the language, the spectrum of postwar Nibelung novels, particularly those of the last decade, is exceptionally broad. Apart from works whose authors wish to introduce the medieval epic to contemporary readers, such as Armin Ayren's 1991 novel,[34] or Wolfgang Hohlbein's *Hagen von Tronje*,[35] with its more extensive plot changes and which is directed particularly at young readers, there have also been attempts to situate the events of the *Nibelungenlied* in the present. This is a transposition based on the conviction that the epic not only deals with historical events but also with constant factors of human behavior, such as "den Gegensatz zwischen Frau und Mann, um männliche Unbekümmertheit, Herrschsucht und Prinzipientreue, um Frauenliebe, Frauenstolz und Frauenrache," as Bernhard Schnellen puts it in the prologue to his novel *Nibelungenleid* (1986).[36] Even the subject matter of the Nibelungs of old Scandinavia, which differs greatly from the *Nibelungenlied*, and the rejuvenation of which is inextricably linked to the name of Richard Wagner, has undergone an extensive adaptation by Stephan Grundy (*Rheingold*, 1992), the German translation of which has enjoyed greater success than the English original.[37]

The most ambitious Nibelung novel in recent years is Jürgen Lodemann's *Siegfried* (1986).[38] From a formal point of view, the revised edition evinces a shift in perspective from a third person narrative to an imaginary chronicle of a monastery, the latter ostensibly a translation of Giselher's eyewitness report. Lodemann not only claims to be able to specify exactly the time and place of Siegfried's murder, i.e., the "historicity" of the event. He also vehemently defends the thesis that with his (Siegfried's) death — a result of the conspiracy involving the Roman-infected Hagen and the repulsive

[34] Armin Ayren, *Meister Konrads Nibelungenroman* (Munich: Deutscher Taschenbuch Verlag, 1991), first published in 1987 under the pseudonym *Meister Konrad*.

[35] Wolfgang Hohlbein, *Hagen von Tronje. Ein Nibelungen-Roman* (Vienna: Ueberreuter, 1986).

[36] Bernhard Schnellen, *Nibelungenleid. Roman* (Frankfurt a. M.: Haag + Herchen, 1986).

[37] Stephan Grundy, *Rheingold*, trans. Manfred Ohl and Hans Sartorius (Frankfurt a. M.: Wolfgang Krüger, 1992). English original: *Rhinegold* (New York: Bantam, 1994).

[38] Jürgen Lodemann, *Siegfried. Die deutsche Geschichte im eintausendfünfhundertsten Jahr der Ermordung ihres Helden nach den ältesten Dokumenten erzählt* (Stuttgart and Vienna: K. Thienemanns, 1986). Later a revised edition appeared under the title *Der Mord. Das wahre Volksbuch von den Deutschen* (Frankfurt a. M.: Büchergilde Gutenberg, 1995).

Bishop Ringwolf — the possibility of a better future for the Germanic and Celtic peoples had been destroyed. Destroyed as well were the hope of freedom for the oppressed, the love of this world, the integration of mankind into nature, and the unity of body and soul. The institution which did prove victorious, however, was the Roman State Church which had supposedly perverted the true Christian doctrine. What, from Lodemann's perspective, was to have had an enlightening function, proves to be (although this was not Lodemann's intention) a remythologization of the Nibelung plot. It is yet another instance of its being used for ideological purposes in a manner which echoes suspiciously National Socialist ideas. According to Lodemann, the Germanic soul had been deprived of its unique nature through its adoption of institutional and mental structures from foreign sources. Moreover, it had been suppressed by the Christian religion. All of this had already been noted by Bernhard R. Martin in his comments on the first version of the novel in 1992.[39] Lodemann's novel demonstrates once again that prejudice and antipathy constitute a poor basis for creative (poetic) work.

Any description of the more recent narrative adaptations of the *Nibelungenlied* would be inappropriate and incomplete if one did not mention the travesties and the satires. Their aim is to dismantle any idea of heroism as well as those traits associated with the concept which had long been considered characteristic of Germans. This process of dismantling could also be described as a form of de-ideologization. It is doubtful, though, whether the travesties really exercise a benevolent function, considering the relatively minor presence of the *Nibelungenlied* and Nibelung legend in public awareness. Are we not dealing here primarily with a rather superficial and simplistic form of entertainment for the reader?

We have already pointed to a parallel in drama, namely, Axel Plogstedt's *Nibelungen*. In this respect, we should also recall the burlesque operetta *Die lustigen Nibelungen* by Oscar Straus from the year 1904.[40] Herbert Schneider's rather thin volume, *Die Nibelungen in Bayern* (1974), has also become quite popular.[41] The Burgundians (Nibelungs) have no intention of riding to the land of the Huns, where death awaits them, but only move down as far as Bavaria and settle there. However, as the alluring charms of the Bavarian women cause them to tarry far too long in sending for their wives, it falls to the Bavarian dukes to arrange for their emigration. These dukes have the names Alfons and Franz Josef — as did the leading politicians of the CSU-

[39] Bernhard R. Martin, *Nibelungen-Metamorphosen. Die Geschichte eines Mythos* (Munich: Iudicium, 1992).

[40] Oscar Straus, *Die lustigen Nibelungen* (Berlin: Harmonie, 1904).

[41] Herbert Schneider, *Die Nibelungen in Bayern* (Pfaffenhofen an der Ilm: Ilmgau, 1974; 4th edition 1983).

party at the time Schneider wrote his book (the Bavarian Minister President was Alfons Goppel and the CSU-Chairman Franz Josef Strauß). It is essential that this rather satirical little work be set in the present. Giselher, for instance, who is introduced as a womanizer, becomes a well-known gynecologist in Munich and Siegfried, the son of Gunther and Brunhild, becomes a director at the Siemens Corporation. As a further example one might mention the little book by Uta Claus and Rolf Kutschera: *Total krasse Helden. Die bockstarke Story von den Nibelungen* (1986).[42] In this instance, a work on the Nibelungs is presented in the language of juveniles, but in such an exaggerated way that, although the authors probably did not intend it as such, this type of language becomes a parody in itself. Finally, one needs to mention adaptations of the *Nibelungenlied* that have appeared in various dialects. The most recent example is the spontaneous and abbreviated adaptation into the Palatinate dialect by Paul Tremmel (1994).[43] Whatever the motivation, it definitely replaces with a form of language that is intimately known to the speakers of the dialect not only the difficult language of the medieval epic, which is accessible to only a very few readers, but also the often melodramatic and excessive language of the adaptations in circulation from the nineteenth through to the mid-twentieth century, including the old-fashioned but still widely disseminated earlier translations. From the outset, the *Nibelungenlied* is stripped of everything heroic and monumental. More often than not, this work, which was once heralded as the German national epic, is nowadays approached with little attention to distance or respect. However questionable these endeavors may be from an aesthetic point of view, there is something refreshing about them and they can serve as a corrective of the erroneous idealization and idolization which have strongly shaped the history of the reception of the *Nibelungenlied*. This corrective is much less necessary today, however, than it would have been in former times.

The Nibelungenlied in the Service of Politics

Many adaptations of the Nibelung theme make it abundantly clear that its reception was not confined to an inner-literary dialogue. Apart from this, the *Nibelungenlied* also has a more direct connection to politics. As the supposed German national epic, it has repeatedly provided certain patterns of identification, it has accompanied and even stimulated the development, establishment, and exaggeration of a German sense of national identity. Of

[42] Uta Claus and Rolf Kutschera, *Total krasse Helden. Die bockstarke Story von den Nibelungen* (Frankfurt a. M.: Eichborn, 1986).

[43] Paul Tremmel, *Die Nibelungesag'. Wie se in Worms un drumerum bassiert is* (Forst/Weinstraße: Published by the author, 1994).

all the specifically Germanic-German characteristics that are said to have found expression in the *Nibelungenlied*, none has been more greatly emphasized than loyalty. We cite here two of many such examples from the popular sector: the enthusiastic comments to be found in the highly successful and popular literary history by the Protestant theologian and literary historian August Friedrich Christian Vilmar,[44] and the speech, "Deutsche Treue in Dichtung und Sage," by the renowned Germanist Gustav Roethe in 1923.[45] However, the loyalty which one finds manifested in the Middle High German epic could also become a political slogan. In a speech given in the *Reichstag* on March 29, 1909, the Imperial Chancellor, Fürst von Bülow, coined the now famous expression *Nibelungentreue* ("loyalty of the Nibelungs"), when referring to the relationship between the German Reich and Austria-Hungary:

> Meine Herren, ich habe irgendwo ein höhnisches Wort gelesen über unsere Vasallenschaft gegenüber Österreich-Ungarn. Das Wort ist einfältig. Es gibt hier keinen Streit um den Vortritt, wie zwischen den beiden Königinnen im Nibelungenliede. Aber die Nibelungentreue wollen wir aus unserem Verhältnis zu Österreich-Ungarn nicht ausschalten, die wollen wir gegenseitig wahren.[46]

It obviously slipped the Imperial Chancellor's mind, as would be the case with many others who subsequently used the term, that this concept of loyalty is not only linked to the idea of unconditional alliance and standing by each other even unto death, but also to the downfall of all the Nibelungs and almost everyone else involved in the events that unfold, i.e., the total demise of entire peoples. It seems that the slogan, whether this is due to a somewhat inaccurate knowledge of the *Nibelungenlied*, or a deliberate repression of the ultimate consequence of *Nibelungentreue*, becomes independent and develops a life of its own once removed from its literary context.

One who was conscious of the consequences was Franz von Liszt, a member of the *Reichstag* and, in his time, a highly respected lawyer. In his

[44] August Friedrich Christian Vilmar, *Vorlesungen über die Geschichte der deutschen National-Literatur* (Marburg: Elwert, 1845). The 27th edition appeared in 1911.

[45] Gustav Roethe, *Deutsche Treue in Dichtung und Sage* (Langensalza: Beyer, 1923). [Reprinted in: Gustav Roethe, *Deutsche Reden* (Leipzig: Quelle & Meyer, 1927) 19–47.]

[46] See Herfried Münkler and Wolfgang Storch, *Siegfrieden. Politik mit einem deutschen Mythos* (Berlin: Rotbuch-Verlag, 1988) 70 and Werner Wunderlich, *Der Schatz des Drachentödters. Materialien zur Wirkungsgeschichte des Nibelungenliedes* (Stuttgart: Klett-Cotta, 1977) 63.

speech “Von der Nibelungentreue,” delivered on November 18, 1914, he expanded on the expression used by the Imperial Chancellor von Bülow. After stating that the *Nibelungenlied* had been designated “mit Fug und Recht als das Hohelied von deutschem Heldenmut und deutscher Treue,” he described the relationship between Germany and Austria-Hungary using the figures of Hagen and Volker, whose bond of *triuwe* was not of a feudal sort but rather had the character of comrades-in-arms or even of friendship:

> Der waffengewaltige, stolze, grimme Hagen auf der einen Seite, das Sinnbild Preußen-Deutschlands, und der heitere Spielmann auf der anderen Seite, der in Kampf und Lied gewandte Volker, das Sinnbild des sangesfrohen und kampfeslustigen Österreich-Ungarn. Ich weiß nicht, ob es gerade dieses Bild war, das dem Reichskanzler vorgeschwebt hat. Aber mit dem einen Worte von der Nibelungentreue hat er treffend und schön das Bündnisverhältnis bezeichnet, wie es zwischen dem Deutschen Reich und Österreich-Ungarn besteht.[47]

(In a variation on Liszt’s theme, Wilhelm Scherer — not to be confused with the famous Germanist of the same name — rearranged the constellation of figures in the *Nibelungenlied* in his poems *Nibelungentreue. Kriegsgesänge* [1916][48] and placed Rüdiger, who only appears in the second part of the epic, as a representative of the East German Mark [Ostmark!], at the side of Siegfried, “wonderfully united” in loyalty.) Later on in his speech, Liszt did not conceal the fact that Hagen and Volker (regarded as symbolic of Prussia-Germany and Austria-Hungary, respectively) eventually go to their deaths. Nevertheless, he still clings to the image of *Nibelungentreue*. This is the explanation provided for the death of the two heroes: “Hagen von Tronje und Volker von Alzey, die hatten Blutschuld auf sich geladen durch die Ermordung Siegfrieds, und darum waren sie dem Untergang trotz aller Tapferkeit geweiht.” (Strictly speaking, it is incorrect to claim that Volker had blood on his hands from having murdered Siegfried.) In the historical context in which Liszt delivered his speech, he was able to lay the guilt at the doors of the enemies of those nations which were bound together in *Nibelungentreue*, “den serbischen Mördern des österreichischen Thronfolgers Franz Ferdinand,” as well as those countries that were allied with them. He thus prophesies for the German Reich and the Austro-Hungarian Empire: “Nicht der Untergang, sondern der Sieg wird das Ende des gemeinsamen Kampfes sein.”

[47] Franz von Liszt, *Von der Nibelungentreue. Rede am 18. November 1914*, Deutsche Reden in schwerer Zeit (Berlin: Heymann, 1914).

[48] Wilhelm Scherer, *Nibelungentreue. Kriegsgesänge* (Regensburg: Kösel und Pustet, 1916).

The fact that the Central Powers did not win, but rather lost the war — despite their supposed innocence — has in no way diminished the popularity of the slogan *Nibelungentreue*, even to the present day. To be sure, its origins, along with its inherently tragic implications, are, for the most part, completely forgotten. As a contemporary example, one might cite a report carried by the press agency AFP which appeared on February 18, 1996 in the *Frankfurter Allgemeine Zeitung* Sunday paper. According to this article, German Chancellor Helmut Kohl's visit with Russian President Boris Yeltsin shortly before the recent elections in Russia was referred to and criticized by a politician of the opposition SPD as *Nibelungentreue.*

The German virtue of loyalty was chiefly exemplified by Hagen (see Jansen's novel *Das Buch Treue* above) and also by the Burgundian kings who demonstrate the same kind of loyalty when they stand by their vassal and refuse to turn him over to Kriemhild in order to save their own lives. On the other hand, it is Hagen's loyalty which, in the first part of the *Nibelungenlied*, gives rise to a clear injustice, a heinous crime, committed in the interest of the sovereign or of the dynasty, or more abstractly: the state. Loyalty can accord legitimacy even to a crime for "reasons of state." It is a conclusion reached by many who, over the years, have tried to make use of the *Nibelungenlied* for political purposes. Gustav Roethe, for instance, has specifically stated in the aforementioned speech: "Ungetreu war er [Hagen], denn meuchlings ermordete er den arglosen Siegfried. Aber er schlägt ihn aus Treue: er kennt keinen Zweifel, da die Ehre seines Königs und seiner Königin auf dem Spiel steht." However, the extent to which biased clichés can, at the very least, preclude an accurate appraisal, is demonstrated by Roethe when he clearly compares "German loyalty" with "foreign deceit" without also characterizing Siegfried's murder by Hagen as a deed of (not simply foreign!) duplicity. In addition to Hagen, Siegfried has also been declared the incarnation of the German soul, or at least of certain German virtues. In the Wilhelminian era this resulted in the rather curious phenomenon of Bismarck's being represented symbolically by both Hagen and Siegfried, depending on the aspect used to associate him with the *Nibelungenlied.*[49] It was quite natural that Siegfried, the resplendent, young hero of incomparable strength and valor, of respectable and noble intentions who, however, goes his own way in an innocent and carefree manner, would be perfectly suited to serve as a role model for those young people who became acquainted with his image through legends and juvenile literature. Moreover, it follows that he represented, in every respect, the antithesis of foreigners, especially the French, who were viewed through xenophobic eyes. The faith that was extended to this strong and indomitable hero when it came to open battle,

[49] See Münkler/Storch, *Siegfrieden.*

a man endowed with a name which, in itself, seemed to promise victory, certainly appears to be the reason why, in 1917, the German fortifications in France (constructed to accommodate a strategic retreat) were named the Siegfried Line. This certainly did not impress the English, who expressed their contempt of the structure with the song: "We're going to hang out our washing on the Siegfried Line." During World War II, the English again ridiculed German defenses in the west as the Siegfried Line. Apart from this, the *Nibelungenlied*, as well as Richard Wagner's *Ring des Nibelungen*, were the sources for other military code names during World War I, such as the Hagen Offensive.

Of much greater political consequence was the opinion expressed by conservative circles after Germany lost the war in 1918, namely, that the soldiers at the front had been betrayed by those at home, and that the German defeat had been caused by the latter's disloyalty and perfidy. This was regarded as analogous to the underhanded way in which Siegfried had been killed in the *Nibelungenlied*. The explanation they offered came to be known as the *Dolchstoßlegende* ("the stab in the back myth"). The initial image of the *Dolchstoß* apparently arose without any connection to the *Nibelungenlied*. As early as October 28, 1918, i.e., prior to the armistice, Theodor Wolff, the chief editor of the liberal *Berliner Tageblatt*, wrote that the warmongering press was telling "den Truppen, daß man ihnen verräterisch in den Rücken gefallen sei."[50] As far as we can ascertain, the weapon itself (a dagger) was first implicitly mentioned in the *Neue Zürcher Zeitung* on December 17, 1918, which expressed the opinion that the German army had been "von der Zivilbevölkerung von hinten erdolcht." Shortly thereafter, on December 31, 1918, the conservative *Kreuz-Zeitung* carried the following comment: "Unseren kämpfenden Truppen haben wir den Dolch in den Rücken gestoßen."[51] An explicit allusion to the *Nibelungenlied* is to be found in a speech which Albrecht von Graefe, a prominent member of the *Deutschnationale Volkspartei*, delivered on October 29, 1919 before the German National Assembly (which is not to suggest, however, that von Graefe was the first to connect the *Dolchstoßlegende* with the *Nibelungenlied*):

> Sie [die deutsche Armee] liegt am Boden, das Bild wiederholend, das uns die alte Heldensage von Siegfried und dem Hagen als ein immer wiederkehrendes Symbol der deutschen Geschichte vorahnend verkündet hat; und

[50] Quoted from Anneliese Thimme, *Flucht in den Mythos. Die Deutschnationale Volkspartei und die Niederlage von 1918* (Göttingen: Vandenhoeck & Ruprecht, 1969) 78.

[51] Thimme 82.

> der Speer, der von dem Hagen dem Siegfried von hinten in den Leib gestoßen worden ist, ist von langer Zeit vorher geschmiedet worden.[52]

In the same year, Field Marshal von Hindenburg, Chief of the Supreme Army Command during the last years of the war and later President of Germany, wrote in his so-called political testament: "Wie Siegfried unter dem hinterlistigen Speerwurf des grimmigen Hagen, so stürzte unsere ermattete Front." There are numerous obvious reasons why a *Speerwurflegende* did not arise, two of which might be mentioned here. First of all, there is the linguistic reference to the verb "erdolchen" ("to stab"). Secondly, we have the figure of speech "Dolch im Gewande" ("dagger [hidden] under the cloak") which is well known to all Germans from Schiller's ballad, *Die Bürgschaft*. This dagger is not only drawn to get rid of a tyrant, but can also be directed in a malicious way against one's own people. The image of the dagger, a contemporary weapon, had replaced that of the medieval spear in political discussions and in the arena of political agitation. The debate as to whether or not the homeland, and particularly the revolutionaries of 1918, had caused the German defeat, even led to a trial, the so-called "Dolchstoß-Prozeß" in Munich in 1925. This slogan, which can be traced to the plot of *Nibelungenlied*, proved to be remarkably tenacious, demonstrated by the fact that, during World War II, warnings were issued that a second *Dolchstoß* had to be avoided at any cost.

The painful experiences suffered by the Germans during and after World War I were scarcely inclined to put an end to nationalistic abuse of the *Nibelungenlied*. The conventional clichés were still cultivated — during the Weimar Republic by conservative and reactionary circles, and during the Third Reich by the official party line. Not surprisingly, the hope for renewal during the Weimar Republic was connected to the figure of Siegfried and one might even suggest that this hope had been realized at one point during the Third Reich. At the same time, German loyalty was still being invoked through allusions to the Nibelungs and particularly Hagen. It is hardly necessary to describe in detail the reception of the Nibelung theme during this twenty-five year period. (The examples chosen by Werner Wunderlich in his 1977 study provide sufficient evidence of numerous literary texts which are rather unpalatable from the point of view of language, judged both by the standards of today as well as those of the time in which they were written.)[53] It is perhaps remarkable that, during the Third Reich, there was an increasing tendency to draw not only upon the *Nibelungenlied*, but also upon the Nordic versions of the Nibelung legend (the lays of the *Edda* as well as the

[52] Thimme 76.

[53] See Wunderlich, *Der Schatz des Drachentödters*.

Vǫlsunga saga). These present the idea of heroism, including its horrifying consequences, in a more poignant and less compromising manner than the High Medieval epic, which was characterized by a courtly and Christian ambience. Aside from that, the Nordic texts were quite "useful," because even the geographical area in which they originated seemed to convey the aura of the Nordic person, that "Nordic spirit," which the adherents to racist Nazi ideology considered the quintessence of the true German. Nordic, Germanic, German and, wherever possible, even Aryan became virtually interchangeable terms. The use of the *Nibelungenlied* as well as the Nibelung legend in this way did not, however, originate with the National Socialists, just as very little in their ideology could claim to be original. Such appropriation was already in vogue a long time before 1933. To cite one example from many: in 1919, Bruno Tanzmann, in his *Versuch einer neuen Deutung des Nibelungenliedes*, had already interpreted this allegedly German national epic as a "Spiegel des Kindheit- und Jugendschicksals der germanischen Rasse."[54]

Instead of citing dozens of names and titles which would be meaningless to the reader, it is more revealing to examine in detail two comments which particularly underscore the political misuse of the *Nibelungenlied* during World War II. On February 3, 1943, the *Völkische Beobachter* published, in slightly amended form, the speech which Hermann Göring had delivered on January 30, 1943, the tenth anniversary of Hitler's rise to power, before selected members of the *Wehrmacht* at the Reich Ministry for Aviation (and not in the Berlin Sport Palace as one can sometimes read, even in more recent Germanistic publications). Göring's intent was to celebrate the anniversary of the National Socialist *Machtergreifung* and, at the same time, to provide (in the interest of propaganda) a reappraisal of the catastrophe that was already becoming apparent at Stalingrad. In his comments on the battle, which, at that point, had already entered its final phase, Göring also referred to the *Nibelungenlied*. The often quoted passage in the original version of the speech reads as follows:

> Und aus all diesen gigantischen Kämpfen ragt nun gleich einem gewaltigen, monumentalen Bau Stalingrad, der Kampf um Stalingrad heraus. Es wird dies einmal der größte Heroenkampf gewesen sein, der sich jemals in unserer Geschichte abgespielt hat. Was dort jetzt unsere Grenadiere, Pioniere, Artilleristen, Flakartilleristen und wer sonst in dieser Stadt ist, vom General bis zum letzten Mann, wer da jetzt kämpft gegen eine gewaltige Übermacht um jeden Block, um jeden Stein, um jedes Loch, um jeden Graben, immer wieder kämpft, ermattet, erschöpft — wir kennen ein gewaltiges, heroisches Lied von einem Kampf ohnegleichen, das hieß "Der Kampf der Nibelun-

[54] Bruno Tanzmann, *Versuch einer neuen Deutung des Nibelungenliedes*, Blätter vom Hakenkreuz [Neue Folge] 7 (Hellerau bei Dresden: Hakenkreuz-Verlag, 1919).

> gen". Auch sie standen in einer Halle von Feuer und Brand und löschten den Durst mit eigenem Blut — aber kämpften und kämpften bis zum letzten. Ein solcher Kampf tobt heute dort, und jeder Deutsche noch in tausend Jahren muß mit heiligen Schauern das Wort Stalingrad aussprechen und sich erinnern, daß dort Deutschland letzten Endes doch den Stempel zum Endsieg gesetzt hat![55]

The only element that can actually be derived from the *Nibelungenlied* as a model, from the 36th *Âventiure* to be precise, is the heroic battle to the bitter end, and this means heroic death. The image used by Göring in the last sentence of this passage (one that was changed when the speech was printed in the newspaper) is quite inappropriate: a comparison of the deaths suffered by tens of thousands with what he suggested was the onset of a final German victory (*Endsieg*), rings hollow and is hardly more than rather cynical propaganda. Little note has hitherto been taken of Göring's reference to the *Nibelungenlied* as "The Battle of the Nibelungs." This undoubtedly is an allusion to the last half-verse of the epic (which, from the perspective of literary history, is not really a "song") as it appears in the *B version: "daz ist der Nibelunge nôt" (2379,4). In Middle High German, *nôt* can actually mean battle. In an edition and translation of the *Nibelungenlied* which appeared thirty years after Göring's speech, Ulrich Pretzel elected to translate *nôt* as *Heldenkampf* ("heroic battle"), and this compound would have been more to Göring's liking had it occurred to him. However, the term *nôt* simultaneously calls to mind the word field that conveys the idea of "suffering." It means "hardship, trouble, need, grief, sorrow," and, in the present context, "defeat, demise." Needless to say, Göring had to avoid this semantic component and, with the rendering of *nôt* as "battle," opted for an often-used, and positively charged concept in National Socialist propaganda.

It should at least be mentioned that Göring shortly thereafter alluded to a second historical and literary parallel to the heroic battle waged by German soldiers in Stalingrad: that of the Spartan Leonidas and his 300 warriors, whom Göring, without much ado, transforms into "Nordic [!] people" who stop the onslaught from the Asiatic East, with which the Soviet armies are clearly identified. He thus complements the medieval example with one from the Classical period. Göring was only able to quote both of these examples because he could presume that his audience would be aware of them, regardless of whether their knowledge of either was highly sophisticated or relatively vague.

[55] Quoted by Peter Krüger in Joachim Heinzle and Anneliese Waldschmidt, eds., *Die Nibelungen. Ein deutscher Wahn, ein deutscher Alptraum. Studien und Dokumente zur Rezeption des Nibelungenstoffs im 19. und 20. Jahrhundert* (Frankfurt a. M.: Suhrkamp, 1991) 180.

Göring's appropriation of the *Nibelungenlied* as a medieval work portraying a situation analogous to that of the German soldiers in Stalingrad, who were facing the choice between capitulation (signed on January 31 and February 2, 1943) or total destruction, is the ignominious climax of the ideological-propagandistic misuse of the *Nibelungenlied*. Death is viewed as the inevitable consequence of German loyalty. Vilmar, in his literary history, had expressed it in what were then relatively harmless words: "Für den lieben [!] König und Herrn wird alles gethan, wird treulich gekämpft, wird willig geblutet, wird freudig in den Tod gegangen."[56] These "harmless words" had, however, become a bitter and brutal reality for the 160,000 men who were trapped in Stalingrad, and who most certainly did not joyfully sacrifice their lives for the *Führer*. The often repressed, or consciously ignored, result of heroic loyalty could no longer be concealed.

This was also evident, although from a very different perspective and using a completely different line of argument, in the 100th wartime lecture ("Das Nibelungenlied eine staufische Elegie oder ein deutsches Nationalepos?"), delivered by Hans Naumann at the University of Bonn just a few months before Göring's speech.[57] Hans Naumann was one of the most renowned Germanists of the interwar period, a scholar who had excelled through his studies on early Germanic history, the Middle Ages, folklore, and modern German literature. He was an early adherent to National Socialism and was not capable of detaching himself from it, even when, to some degree, he became disillusioned. Since the time of Friedrich Heinrich von der Hagen (1810), people had generally understood the *Nibelungenlied* to be the German national epic, although this view had long since been abandoned by serious academics. Taking the idea of *Nibelungentreue* as his point of departure, Naumann repeats in his lecture the usual cliché of the *Nibelungenlied* as "ein Hoheslied des Heldentums und der Treue,"[58] but at the same time questions its appropriateness as the German national epic. In fact, Naumann explicitly rejects this interpretation because of the dark side of the *Nibelungenlied*, its tragic substance, the demise of the kings and virtually their entire people. Thus, Naumann regards *Der Nibelunge nôt* not only as the "battle" of the Nibelungs, but also as their destruction. The "überreiche Todesernte dieser Dichtung, die mit einem hoffnungslosen [!] Massentode alles germanischen Kriegsvolkes endet"[59] contradicts, according to Naumann,

[56] Vilmar 61.

[57] Hans Naumann, "Das Nibelungenlied: Eine staufische Elegie oder ein deutsches Nationalepos?" *Dichtung und Volkstum* (= *Euphorion*) 42 (1942), part 4: 41–59. Also appeared as a separate edition (Bonn: Scheur, 1942).

[58] Naumann 53.

[59] Naumann 54.

the status of the *Nibelungenlied* as a national epic, the fundamental nature of which should be "glückverheißend, optimistisch und heilverbürgend."[60] Moreover, it is imperative that the people should recognize themselves in the work: "Gerade das deutsche Volk hat sich doch gerettet aus dem germanischen Untergang mit Hilfe der Kaiser- und Reichsidee."[61] We can agree, nonetheless, with Naumann when he characterizes the *Nibelungenlied* as an "epische Elegie des Stauferreichs."[62] The political interpretation of the *Nibelungenlied*, which, in recent years, has received renewed attention from the historian Heinz Thomas,[63] is compatible with Naumann's characterization of the *Nibelungenlied*, even if Thomas's interpretation most assuredly has nothing to do with Naumann's outdated argumentation. Naumann discredits even the debatable part of his argument by fantasizing about a future German national epic which was already actually in the making:

> Im Dritten [Reich] wird gewiß die erlösende Stunde schlagen, es besitzt ja bereits in dem einzigen Manne und in der Geschichte seiner Erscheinung ein Nationalepos urältester Struktur, dem verlorenen des Ersten Reiches verwandt; man brauchte es nur in Verse zu gießen.[64]

The national epic of the First Reich is a product of Naumann's rather active imagination: a Dietrich epic from the time of Friedrich Barbarossa. At the end of 1942, while the battle of Stalingrad was being waged and was, in fact, already lost, the dictator Adolf Hitler, who had ordered that it be fought to the last man, is designated as the future hero of a German national epic. Hans Naumann was obviously unable to see that the history for which Hitler was responsible would also end in chaos and a disaster which went far beyond the *nôt* of the Nibelungs that he had emphasized.

In the last months of the war, Hitler gave orders aimed at the intentional destruction of Germany, which, he believed, had proven unworthy of his ideas. It is feasible that the concept of *Ragnarök* to be found in Richard Wagner's *Ring des Nibelungen* also played a role in his decision. It is in keeping with such a scenario that German radio, according to John Evert Härd, broadcast music from Wagner's *Götterdämmerung* without interruption throughout the last days of the war.[65] Herfried Münkler states: "Von

[60] Naumann 44.

[61] Naumann 54.

[62] Naumann 57.

[63] Heinz Thomas, "Die Staufer im Nibelungenlied," *ZfdPh* 109 (1990): 321–354.

[64] Naumann 58.

[65] John Evert Härd, *Das Nibelungenepos. Wertung und Wirkung von der Romantik bis zur Gegenwart*, trans. from the Swedish by Christine Palm (Tübingen and Basel:

einer militärischen Lebenslüge am Ende des Ersten Weltkriegs [der *Dolchstoßlegende*] war der Mythos zur politischen Handlungsanweisung am Ende des zweiten Weltkriegs avanciert."[66] This marked, however, the end of its "fatal" potential. The unrelenting national fascination with the *Nibelungenlied* after 1918 came to an end in 1945.

There can be no doubt that the *Nibelungenlied* and the analogous Scandinavian poems were often misused for ideological purposes by both scholars and politicians. We have no idea whether or not, however, the desired effect was achieved by falling back on these texts. It would be a mistake to overestimate their significance in this regard, and certainly no soldier sacrificed his life during either World War I or World War II because the Nibelungs had been held up to him as a role model. The *Nibelungenlied* has probably always appealed to certain listeners and readers solely as one element among a conglomeration of pseudoarguments when audiences are wooed by irrational appeals. This, in itself, is regrettable, and one can only welcome the fact that, in general, the *Nibelungenlied* and its subject matter are approached today in a relatively objective and sober manner.

Francke, 1996) 18f.

[66] Münkler/Storch 106.

Joyce Tally Lionarons

The Otherworld and its Inhabitants in the *Nibelungenlied*

Every reader of the *Nibelungenlied* soon recognizes that there are at least two different worlds, and perhaps two different times, coexisting within the poem. The first is the "real," historically conceived society of Worms and Xanten: this is a chivalric, courtly world in which normal human beings — albeit sometimes kings and princesses — are born, live, marry, compete for influence and political power, and finally die. The second may be termed the "Otherworld."[1] Not all its inhabitants are human, and those who are seem preternaturally strong, with knowledge and power far surpassing the denizens of the "real" world. The non-human inhabitants of the Otherworld come straight from myth and *Märchen*: there are giants and dwarfs, dangerous dragons, and beautiful elf-like women inhabiting rivers and springs. The Otherworld is a place of essences, in which appearance and reality, intrinsic worth and external status coincide; it has neither politics nor political intrigue, but a hero, if he is both strong and lucky enough to prevail over his adversaries, may win treasures there: gold, land, a specially wrought sword or a magical talisman. And yet the Otherworld is not simply a place for fairy-tales: its depiction in the poem repeatedly sounds a somber and somewhat disturbing note in suggestions that the Otherworld may in fact be a manifestation of the Underworld, the land of the dead.

Precisely how to characterize the relationship between the two worlds has caused some critical dispute. Many scholars see the dividing line as one of ethos: a "heroic" or "mythic" world is contrasted to the everyday historical world. Walter Johannes Schröder states the opposition clearly: "Dem mythisch-märchenhaften Norden steht der geschichtliche Süden gegenüber."[2] Some also emphasize a difference in time, finding the Otherworld to

[1] Although the term "Otherworld" is a general one, in this context I am borrowing it from Winder McConnell, *The Nibelungenlied*, Twayne's World Authors Series 712 (Boston: Twayne, 1984) 28ff.

[2] Walter Johannes Schröder, *Das Nibelungenlied: Versuch einer Deutung* (Halle: Niemeyer, 1954) 22. See also McConnell 28–45, and Edward R. Haymes's essay in this volume.

represent a more archaic age than that of its courtly counterpart. Jan de Vries argues that the Otherworld "seems to belong to the remotest past."[3] Still others see the difference as primarily psychological: Walter Falk, for example, draws a distinction between an external world of physical reality and "eine traumhafte, psychische Innenwelt,"[4] where all the supernatural events of the poem occur. Despite their differences, however, most contemporary students of the *Nibelungenlied* would probably agree with Otfrid Ehrismann's assessment of the situation: "Die neue Welt ist politischer, und sie macht den alten Zauber symbolfähig."[5] This essay will examine the poem's "old magic" and its practitioners, both as they relate to the mythic and folkloric contexts from which they arise, and as they function, symbolically or otherwise, within the textual world(s) of the *Nibelungenlied* as a whole.

The primary point at which the Otherworld intersects with the historical world is in the character of Siegfried.[6] Siegfried belongs equally to both worlds, and in fact, he seems to have had two different upbringings, one in each. In Xanten, he is a courtly young prince ("eins edelen küneges kint," 20,1b), educated in the mannered and diplomatic customs of an idealized medieval German society.[7] He is not allowed to ride out alone, being always in the company of his tutors or other wise counselors who are conscious of protecting his honor ("... wîsen, den êre was bekant," 25,3). He is initiated into knighthood at a spectacularly lavish *Schwertleite*, at which he gives away land and cities to others but refuses the crown of the Netherlands for himself because his parents, Siegmund and Sieglind, are still alive (29–43). Yet as Hagen's description of Siegfried's youthful adventures in *Âventiure* 3 makes clear, at this point he has already undergone another sort of heroic initiation in the Otherworld. There Siegfried does ride out alone ("al eine," 88,1a) to find two princes, Schilbung and Nibelung, engaged in dividing their treasure (91). The princes offer him Nibelung's sword Balmung as a reward for his help (93), and although we are given no explicit account of what follows, it

[3] Jan de Vries, *Heroic Song and Heroic Legend*, trans. B. J. Timmer (London: Oxford University Press, 1963) 64.

[4] Walter Falk, *Das Nibelungenlied in seiner Epoche: Revision eines romantischen Mythos.* (Heidelberg: Winter, 1974) 120.

[5] Otfrid Ehrismann, *Nibelungenlied. Epoche — Werk — Wirkung* (Munich: Beck, 1987) 126.

[6] In Ehrismann's view, Siegfried is "der personifizierte Schwebezustand zwischen Gegenwart und Vorzeit" (113).

[7] Quotations from *Das Nibelungenlied* are from the Karl Bartsch/Helmut de Boor edition, 21st edition by Roswitha Wisniewski, Deutsche Klassiker des Mittelalters (Wiesbaden: Brockhaus, 1979) and are identified within the text by strophe and verse number.

is clear that when Siegfried fails to divide the treasure to their satisfaction, a violent conflict erupts and the young hero must fight for his life against the princes, twelve giants, seven hundred warriors, and the dwarf Alberich (93–96). By the end Siegfried has won the land, the hoard, and Alberich's cloak (or literally "hood") of invisibility, the *tarnkappe* (97,3a). Moreover, in a seemingly unrelated incident, Siegfried kills a dragon ("einen lint-rachen," 100, 2a) and bathes in its blood, acquiring horn-hard skin and thus virtual invulnerability in battle. Later, Kriemhild reveals to Hagen that his invulnerability is not total: a leaf fell onto the hero's back, shielding one spot from the dragon's blood (902) and leaving him unprotected against anyone who knows the secret.

Both incidents have ample precedent in Germanic myth and legend, and it is important to examine their motifs individually. When Siegfried first finds the two princes, they have brought the treasure, called "Nibelung's hoard" ("Hort der Nibelunges," 89,1a) out from its resting place in a hollow mountain ("ûz einem holen berge," 89,2a). This would seem to indicate that the treasure once belonged to an earlier King Nibelung, most likely the father of Schilbung and Nibelung II, who has died and been buried with his treasure in a mountain cavern. "Hollow hills" of this kind have a long history in Germanic legend, where they are most often represented as habitations of the dead, either as burial mounds or as entrances to the underworld; thus, a hero's entry into such a hill or mound, or his winning of a hoard associated with a hollow hill, can be interpreted as a symbolic journey into the world of the dead. Ancient Scandinavian folk beliefs, for example, include the idea of "dying into the mountain" to be welcomed by one's departed friends and ancestors, and there are mountains in southern Sweden that were once believed to be the homes of the dead and therefore given the name *Valhǫll* (Valhalla), "hall of the slain."[8] Moreover, in *Njals saga,* after the Icelander Svan dies during a storm on a fishing expedition, it is reported that "[e]nn fiskimenn þeir er vóru í Kaldbak þóttust sjá Svan ganga inn í fjallit Kaldbakshorn, ok var honum þar vel fagnat ("some fishermen at Kaldbak thought they had seen Svan being warmly welcomed into the innermost depths of Kaldbakhorn Mountain").[9] Closer and perhaps more relevant to the specifically German context of the *Nibelungenlied* may be South and West Germanic stories of buried and entranced kings waiting inside mountain caverns for the day on which they will be called upon to save the world: both

[8] Rudolf Simek, ed., *Dictionary of Northern Mythology*, trans. Angela Hall (Cambridge: Brewer, 1993) 347.

[9] Magnus Magnusson and Hermann Pálsson, eds. and trans., *Njal's Saga* (Harmondsworth: Penguin, 1960) ch. 14. Other notable examples occur in *Gisla saga*, *Eyrbyggja saga*, and *Landnamabók*.

Friedrich Barbarossa and Charlemagne are reputed to be inside the Untersberg in Austria, while Friedrich II is in the Kyffhäuser in Germany, and King Arthur in Cadbury Hill in Somerset.[10]

Those beings who dwell inside actual burial mounds are neither so heroic nor so well-intentioned. In the Northern tradition such mounds can be inhabited by the corporeal ghosts of their buried occupants — called ***draugar*** in Old Norse — who at certain times, generally at midwinter, leave their barrows to ravage the countryside. Even mounds that appear outwardly peaceful can turn out quite otherwise, for some ***draugar*** remain quiescent as long as the gold and weapons they are buried with are untouched. Nevertheless, anyone entering a mound to steal its treasure will find the ***draugr*** more than able to fight viciously if disturbed. Stories of ***draugr***-quellings are found throughout the Scandinavian saga tradition, with notable examples occurring in *Grettis saga*, and in the story of Þórstein Uxafótr in *Flateyjarbók* I.[11] Thus, while the ***draugar*** have no specific counterparts in the South Germanic tradition of the *Nibelungenlied*, they illustrate graphically the terror and danger a "hollow hill," filled with the treasure of a (possibly un)dead inhabitant, can possess.

Of course Germanic burial mounds can also be inhabited by dragons, whose nature it is to lie on piles of treasure left in the earth. The most famous mound-dwelling dragon is probably the one Beowulf fights, and there is an Old English gnomic verse which states that barrows full of gold are the proper places for dragons in general: "Draca sceal on hlæwe, frod, frætwum wlanc" ("The dragon should be on the grave-mound, old and wise, proud of the treasure").[12] Sometimes a man or giant enters a barrow alive and transforms himself into a dragon to guard his gold, but even those dragons that do not inhabit grave mounds *per se* are almost always found dwelling in mountain caverns or on mountainous cliffs high above the sea.[13] Because a dragon is commonly regarded as the most formidable adversary a warrior can encounter, in general only the greatest heroes of Germanic legend become dragon slayers. The rewards are as great as the dangers: in addition to giving up its treasure, a dragon may disclose secret or esoteric knowledge to a

[10] Simek 50.

[11] The best study of the ***draugar*** remains Nora K. Chadwick, "Norse Ghosts: A Study in the *Draugar* and the *Haugbúi*," *Folk-Lore* 57 (1948): 50–65, 106–127. Other sagas featuring troublesome ***draugar*** include *Eyrbyggja saga*, *Flóamanna saga*, *Hávarðar saga Ísfirðings*, *Laxdæla saga*, and *Svarfdæla saga*.

[12] "Maxims II," in Elliott Van Kirk Dobbie, ed., *The Anglo-Saxon Minor Poems* (New York: Columbia University Press, 1942) 26a–27b.

[13] For two examples of Norse grave mound battles that feature dragons rather than ***draugar***, see *Játmundar saga ljúfa* and *Gull-Þóris saga*.

victorious hero, as Fáfnir does in the Eddic poem *Fáfnismál*, and wisdom, as well as the ability to understand the language of birds, can be gained by eating the dragon's heart. Finally, as has already been seen, the touch of a dragon's blood makes a person's skin turn hard as horn.[14]

It is also worth noting that although they are not often linked explicitly to the world of the dead, in both the Scandinavian and German traditions dwarfs are reputed to live under mountains or inside rocks, where they hoard the gold and silver they mine and use their extraordinary skill as smiths to make wonderful swords and other valuable, often magical items. Norse myth credits the dwarfs with making most of the marvelous possessions of the gods, including Odin's Gungni, Thor's hammer Mjǫllnir, and Freyr's marvelous ship Skíðblaðnir, which is said to be large enough for all the gods to sail in, but can be folded up like a piece of paper and carried in a pocket. However, the specific nature and provenance of the dwarfs is uncertain. In *Gylfaginning*, Snorri Sturluson describes the *døkkálfar* ("dark elves") as if they were dwarfs, hinting that the two may be related; he says that (like dwarfs) the dark elves live *niðri í jǫrðu* ("down in the earth").[15] In fact, many dwarf-names — such as "Alberich," which translates as "elven-power" — incorporate a form of the word "elf" (ON. *álfr*, MHG. *elbe*) as one of their components. Snorri gives his characterization of the dwarfs a more ominous note when he asserts in the same work that they "kviknat í moldunni ok niðri í jǫrðunni svá sem maðkar í holdi" ("quickened in the soil and down in the earth like maggots in flesh")[16] — a simile that is literalized when Snorri goes on to say in the next sentence that in reality the dwarfs actually *were* maggots in the flesh of the giant Ymir, from whose body the world was made. They were transformed into dwarfs when the gods gave them human shape and reason, but because of their origin they still prefer to live "í jǫrðu ok í steinum" ("in the earth and in rocks"). Of particular interest is the fact that Snorri names some dwarfs as having come from a grave mound in Jǫruvellir,[17] a detail that links them with other mound-dwellers and by implication once again with the realm of the dead.[18] It is sometimes assumed

[14] For a more extensive account of the *Nibelungenlied* dragon and its analogues, see John L. Flood's essay in this volume, as well as Joyce Tally Lionarons, *The Medieval Dragon: The Nature of the Beast in Germanic Tradition* (Enfield Lock, Middlesex: Hisarlik, 1997).

[15] Anthony Faulkes, ed., *Edda: Prologue and Gylfaginning* (Oxford: Clarendon, 1982) 19.

[16] Faulkes 15.

[17] Faulkes 15–16.

[18] Simek (68) says that the concept "dwarf" may have arisen either from the idea of nature spirits or that of "demons of death."

that because the dwarfs were created from rocks, they can be turned into rocks again: in the Eddic poem *Alvíssmál*, the purportedly "all-wise" dwarf Alvíss turns into stone when he is tricked by Þórr into remaining outside when the sun rises.

Most German sources agree, however, that if one is clever enough to capture a dwarf by lying in wait outside his cavern, the dwarf will bargain for his release by promising his captor items from his own treasure or even the treasure of another. An example occurs in the twelfth-century *Ruotlieb*, in which the hero surprises a dwarf and thus manages to seize him unawares: the dwarf negotiates for his freedom by promising to reveal the whereabouts of a vast treasure. Like the Nibelung hoard with its two princes, this treasure is guarded by two kings, Immunch and Hartunch, who must be fought before the hoard is won. The episode is plainly an analogue of the hoard-winning scene in the *Nibelungenlied,* and although the two poets were most likely simply working from the same tradition in different centuries, it is tempting to speculate that *Ruotlieb* could be a source of the later poem.[19]

The final Otherworld beings associated with Siegfried's youthful adventures are the giants. As noted above, one Old Norse creation myth describes the earth as having been made from the body of a giant, Ymir, and giants generally play a more important role throughout Norse mythology than do dwarfs or dragons. In the medieval German tradition, however, giants have diminished in both prominence and intelligence. They are considered to be at once dangerous and stupid, not to be matched in size and strength by most men, but relatively easy to outsmart.[20] Certainly neither the giants guarding the Nibelung hoard in the *Nibelungenlied* (*Åventiure* 3), nor the giant Siegfried fights in *Åventiure* 8, are a match in intellect or strength for the hero.

It is a hero's job, of course, to acquire a treasure by overcoming its supernatural guardian — whether *draugr* or dwarf, giant or dragon — through cunning and martial prowess. The defeat of the monstrous hoard-guardian traditionally represents an almost ritualized initiation into a new stage in the hero's life, symbolized by his appropriation of the treasure and often of an instrument of power, such as a sword or magical talisman, as well. This kind of fictional initiation sequence can be profitably compared to real-life initiation rituals, such as those studied by anthropologist Arnold van Gennep, who states that although the details may vary according to the society, a typical initiation ritual comprises three distinct parts: (1) temporary

[19] For this suggestion as well as for information on *Ruotlieb* as an analogue, I am indebted to an unpublished paper presented by Paul Battles at the 32nd International Congress on Medieval Studies, held in May, 1997 at Kalamazoo, Michigan.

[20] Simek 107.

expulsion from ordinary society into a so-called "liminal" or "threshold" state, where (2) the initiand undergoes certain prescribed tests to prove his or her worthiness in order to (3) re-enter the social world at a new, higher level of societal and ontological existence.[21] The tests may include a confrontation with a monstrous adversary like a dragon, and often the initiand is forced to undergo a mock death and symbolic rebirth as a sign that the initiation, in Mircea Eliade's words, "is equivalent to a basic change in existential condition."[22] Obviously Siegfried's solitary visit to a liminal place outside of the world and society of Xanten, his victory over the dragon, his acquisition of sword, *tarnkappe*, and hoard from the denizens of a "hollow hill" that is also a grave mound, and finally his successful return to Xanten, provide a good example of the initiation process transformed into heroic narrative. Siegfried's youthful adventures in the Otherworld may thus be seen as a rite of passage, corresponding in narrative function to his *Schwertleite* in the historical world, but altering his ontological condition in a deeper and more decisive fashion than his knighting, which is a promotion in social status alone, could do. Siegfried's experiences serve to set him apart from those characters in the *Nibelungenlied* who have been initiated into knighthood in the courtly world alone, without having undergone the tests of worthiness an Otherworld initiation entails, and whose merits may therefore be only skin-deep. The contrast between the rites of passage in the two worlds provides a clear rationale for Siegfried's superiority over the Burgundians, a superiority symbolized by his possession of the sword Balmung, the treasure, and the *tarnkappe*. Hagen's report of Siegfried's adventurous past should therefore not be dismissed as mere fairy-tale ornamentation or the slightly embarrassing traces of an outmoded tradition in an otherwise historical and political epic; the hero's Otherworld initiation is clearly more potent and more significant than any *Schwertleite*, no matter how lavish, and its effects carry over into the courtly world with disastrous results.

The substantive acquisitions that provide evidence for Siegfried's Otherworld initiation — the sword, the *tarnkappe*, the hoard, and the services of the dwarf Alberich as vassal and hoard-guardian — repay closer examination. The idea of a hero's having a special and sometimes magical sword is close to universal in heroic literature, not only in the Germanic tradition but throughout the corpus of Indo-European myth and legend: notable analogues to Balmung include Beowulf's sword Nægling in the Old English

[21] Arnold van Gennep, *The Rites of Passage*, trans. Monika B. Vizedom & Gabrielle L. Caffee (London: Routledge & Kegan Paul, 1909); see also Victor Turner, *The Ritual Process: Structure and Anti-Structure* (Ithaca: Cornell University Press, 1969).

[22] Mircea Eliade, *Rites and Symbols of Initiation: The Mysteries of Birth and Rebirth*, trans. Willard R. Trask (New York: Harper, 1958) x.

poem, Þiðrekr's sword Nagelring and Viðga's sword Mímung in the early Norwegian *Þiðreks saga af Bern*, and Sigurd's sword Gram in *Vǫlsunga saga*. The *tarnkappe* is less common and therefore more interesting. It appears in connection with dwarfs and dwarf-treasures frequently in the German poetic tradition: an example occurs in the thirteenth-century *Laurin und der kleine Rosengarten*, in which the eponymous hero is a dwarf-king who wears a *tarnkappe* (along with armor dipped in dragon's blood and a magic belt) to fight off intruders into his realm, in this case Dietrich von Bern and his companion Witege.[23] Moreover, certain strophes from the seventh *Âventiure* of the *Nibelungenlied*, normally considered to be later interpolations and thus omitted in modern editions of the poem, state:

> von wilden getwergen hân ich gehœret sagen,
> einz, heizet tarnkappen, von wunderliche art:
> swerz hât an sîme lîbe, der sol vil gar wol sîn bewart.
> Vor slegen unt vor stichen; in müge ouch niemen sehens
>
> wenn er sî dar inne. beide hœren unde spehen
> mag er nâch sînem willen, daz in doch niemen siht;
> er sî ouch vrre sterker, als uns diu âventiure...[24]

One North Germanic counterpart to the *tarnkappe* would seem to be the *huliðshjálmir* ("concealing helmets") mentioned in a number of Old Norse sagas.[25] These "helms" are not associated with dwarfs, and sometimes not even with actual helmets, for by the time the sagas were written down in the twelfth and thirteenth centuries, the term *huliðshjálmr* was apparently used for any magical means of producing invisibility. At one time, however, the word must have denoted some sort of hat or helmet that was used, like its German counterpart the *tarnkappe*, to make its wearer disappear.[26] A second, more specific analogue to Siegfried's *tarnkappe* in the *Nibelungenlied* is the

[23] Karl Müllenhoff, ed., *Laurin und Walberan, Deutsches Heldenbuch*, 5 vols. (1866; rpt. Berlin: Weidmann, 1963) 1: 201-257.

[24] Karl Bartsch, ed., *Das Nibelunge Nôt* (Leipzig: Brockhaus, 1870) 53n.

[25] Hilda Ellis Davidson, "The Hoard of the Nibelungs," *Modern Language Review* 37 (1942): 477. Davidson cites examples of *hulipshálmir* occurring in *Ólafs saga Tryggvasonar*, *Fóstbrœðra saga*, *Þorskfirðinga saga*, and *Bósa saga*.

[26] Jacqueline Simpson, "Olaf Tryggvason versus the Powers of Darkness," in Venetia Newell, ed., *The Witch Figure* (London and Boston: Routledge and Kegan Paul, 1973) 169.

ægishjálmr ("helm of terror")[27] which Sigurd wins by killing the dragon Fáfnir in the Old Norse versions of the Siegfried story. Judging from the name alone, this is an actual helmet used to terrify the opponents of its wearer. The precise nature of the power of the *ægishjálmr*, however, remains a matter of conjecture, since although Siegfried does not hesitate to wear the *tarnkappe* in his adventures, Sigurd is never explicitly reported to use the *ægishjálmr* at all.

Nor does either hero make use of the hoard in any significant way. Siegfried, of course, officially gives it to Kriemhild as her *Morgengabe* (1116), but the treasure apparently remains untouched in its hollow mountain in Nibelungenland until Kriemhild is coerced by Hagen into bringing it to Worms. It is at this point in the narrative, as the hoard is about to make its final passage from the Otherworld into the historical world, that its contents are described for the first time: the hoard of the Nibelungs is made up entirely of gemstones and gold, and is so large that twelve fully loaded wagons have to make three trips a day for four days in order to remove it from the mountain (1122). More astounding than the hoard's size is its ostensible inexhaustibility, for we are told that "unt ob man al die werlde het dâ von versolt,/sîn newære niht minner einer marke wert"(1123,2–3). This quality may provide the reason why Schilbung and Nibelung, even with Siegfried's help, are unable to divide the hoard satisfactorily, for a hoard that cannot be diminished in value most likely cannot be divided either. The idea of the hoard's indivisible nature is further strengthened by the poet's final revelation concerning the treasure's contents: unnoticed by any of the characters in the poem, the hoard contains a tiny golden rod ("ein rüetelîn," 1124,1b) that, were it to be found and recognized, would give its owner power over the entire world (1124,2–3). The "rüetelîn" is doubtless the Otherworldly embodiment of the political power that possession of the hoard bestows on its owner in the historical world, and such absolute power can be wielded by only one person at a time. If Siegfried is aware of the "rüetelîn," however, he is entirely uninterested in its use, for his political aspirations throughout the poem are focused solely on gaining the love of Kriemhild, not on power for its own sake. Kriemhild's interest in the hoard is as a reminder of Siegfried, not as a means to gain absolute power, and its loss simply provides an additional reason for revenge against her brothers. Hagen and Gunther are another matter, for they are indeed interested in political power *qua* power — that is why they believe they must steal the hoard from

[27] Interestingly enough, the *ægishjálmr* may ultimately have classical roots: Simek points out that the function of the Greek *aigis*, like the *ægishjálmr*, is to terrify, and Greek *aigis* might easily have become attached to Fáfnir's "helm of terror" by a phonetic conflation with Old Norse *œgr*, "terrible" (2).

Kriemhild, to prevent her from using it to gain a political power base in Worms. Nevertheless, without the "rüetelin" the Burgundians are as incapable of utilizing the power of the hoard as Schilbung and Nibelung, and they are finally reduced to sinking it in the Rhine to avoid trouble. Still, Hagen plans to return alone and make use of the hoard — and its power — if he can (1137).

If anyone in the poem is both cognizant of the hoard's attributes and able to use them, it is most likely the dwarf Alberich, but like Siegfried, Alberich seems to have no interest in ruling the world. His function is to guard the treasure in the Otherworld for its rightful owner, whoever that owner might be. He makes the transition from serving Nibelung and Schilbung to serving Siegfried fairly easily, convinced that the hero's superior strength entitles him to appropriate the treasure. After Siegfried's murder, he serves Kriemhild as he had her husband. When she orders the hoard removed to Burgundy, Alberich obeys her wishes, remarking that he "dare not" ("turren ... niht," 1118,3) withhold the treasure from Kriemhild since as Siegfried's gift it is legitimately hers. Nonetheless, the dwarf hints that he might not have been so acquiescent about moving the hoard to Worms if he had not lost the *tarnkappe*, his "guoten tarnhût," to Siegfried and could still take advantage of both invisibility and supernatural strength (1119).[28] Certainly he makes no effort to accompany the hoard and its owner to the historical world; Alberich's place is in the Otherworld, and once the hoard has been removed he disappears from the poem.

Alberich reappears, however, in other works relevant to the *Nibelungenlied*, most often in connection with the Dietrich story.[29] As "Álfrekr" in *Þiðreks saga af Bern* he is characterized as "inn mikli stelari, er allra dverga var hagastr" ("a great thief and the most skillful of all the dwarves," ch. 16),[30] but surprisingly he has no connection either to Sigurd or to the Nibelung hoard in the saga, nor does he own a *tarnkappe* or enjoy extraordinary strength. Instead, in a scene analogous to both *Ruotlieb* and the hoard-winning episode in the *Nibelungenlied*, the dwarf is captured by Dietrich (i.e., Þiðrekr) and Hildebrand; he promises them the sword Nagelring along

[28] Alberich remarks that if he had the *tarnkappe*, this would never have happened ("[d]och wurdez nimmer ... getân" 1119.1). The *tarnkappe* does not reappear in the poem after Siegfried subdues Brünhild in the famous bedroom scene, and is never mentioned again after strophe 1119.

[29] Once again I am indebted throughout this account of Alberich's history to Paul Battles' 1997 presentation at Kalamazoo.

[30] See Guðni Jónsson, ed., *Þiðreks saga af Bern*, 2 vols. (Reykjavík: Íslendingasagnaútgafan, 1954). A modern English translation is available by Edward R. Haymes, *The Saga of Thidrek of Bern* (New York & London: Garland, 1988).

with information about where they can find a treasure in return for his release. As might be expected, to win the treasure the heroes must fight its two guardians in yet another hollow hill, here called a "jarðhús" ("earth-house"). The guardians are Grímr, a man with the strength of twelve, and his even stronger and more formidable troll-wife Hildr. It is a difficult contest; nevertheless, the two heroes eventually prevail, winning the hoard itself and a helm, called "Hildegrímr" after its ill-fated owners. This helm has no special powers like its counterparts the *ægishjálmr* and *tarnkappe*, but it is said to be a valuable treasure in itself, and Dietrich is reported to wear in it battle for a long time afterward.

Alberich plays a more extensive role in the thirteenth-century poem *Ortnit.*[31] Here he is a king of the dwarfs and clearly a more supernatural figure than in either the *Nibelungenlied* or *Þiðreks saga af Bern.* He has no need of a *tarnkappe*, since he is invisible by nature and has strength far beyond his physical size; moreover, he is preternaturally wise and at times can predict the future. Only Ortnit, who is wearing a magical ring given to him by his mother, is able to see the dwarf-king. At their first meeting the two fight furiously but are later reconciled, as is also true with Siegfried and Alberich in the *Nibelungenlied.* In fact, it turns out that Alberich is Ortnit's father, and just as the dwarf and his *tarnkappe* help Siegfried during and after Gunther's wooing of Brünhild, Alberich here helps Ortnit in his own bridal-quest, in part by using his skill as a master smith to forge a marvelous sword and impregnable armor for his son.

The most curious element of Alberich's role in the *Nibelungenlied*, however, has no obvious parallels in the analogues to Alberich's story or in other versions of the Siegfried legend: in our poem the dwarf and the hero fight *twice*, once in *Âventiure* 3 when Siegfried first wins the hoard, and again in *Âventiure* 8 when Siegfried returns to Nibelungenland to fetch a thousand warriors for Gunther. In each episode Siegfried arrives on the scene in the guise of a stranger, literally so in *Âventiure* 3 and invisibly with a disguised voice in *Âventiure* 8; in each he fights both a giant or giants and Alberich — almost to the death — before obtaining a reconciliation and an acknowledgment that he is the dwarf's master and the owner of the hoard. While it has often been recognized that the events of *Âventiure* 8 are simply another version of Siegfried's experiences in *Âventiure* 3,[32] precisely why the poet would choose to double the episode in this way has puzzled many readers of the *Nibelungenlied.* Joachim Bumke suggests that the solution lies

[31] J. W. Thomas, trans. and ed., *Ortnit and Wolfdietrich: Two Medieval Romances* (Columbia, SC: Camden House, 1986).

[32] Joachim Bumke credits the initial insight to a 1909 article by Karl Droege; see Bumke, "Sigfrieds Fahrt ins Nibelungenland," *PBB* 80 (1958): 255.

in the fact that the events of *Þiðreks saga af Bern*, ch. 168, are more closely related to Siegfried's Otherworld journey in *Âventiure* 8 than his hoard-winning in *Âventiure* 3 seems to be.[33] In *Þiðreks saga*, Sigurd arrives at Brünhild's door as a stranger and immediately fights with her door warden, literally breaking down the locked doors of her stronghold, before Brünhild, who apparently does know who he is, intervenes and invites him in. In context, this fight before Brünhild's gate seems just as gratuitous as Siegfried's fight with his own door-wardens. However, if the source of the *Nibelungenlied*, like *Þiðreks saga af Bern*, included a truncated version of the traditional fight with a hoard-guardian within its narration of Siegfried's first visit to Brünhild, the *Nibelungenlied* poet may in turn have regarded such a battle as an integral part of the episode, and so have created Siegfried's battle with Alberich and the giant in Nibelungenland directly after his visit to Brünhild on that basis.[34] It may be useful, therefore, to discuss the events of *Âventiure* 8 in combination with Gunther's bridal-quest to win Brünhild.

Brünhild is the only character besides Siegfried to make a transition from the Otherworld to the historical world. Unfortunately, like Siegfried she finds that her Otherworldly characteristics spell disaster in her new environment. Like many inhabitants of the Otherworld, Brünhild is preternaturally strong, and she has therefore devised tests for her potential suitors based on physical strength rather than on the mannered and artificial rituals of *Minnedienst* currently in fashion in the courtly world at Worms. As long as she is secure in her position as queen of her Otherworld island, Brünhild cares little about the real-world social standing or political power of her suitors; even the vassalage deception becomes important only in the historical world of the Burgundians. In her world Brünhild simply demands a husband whose personal physical prowess can match her own "riesensterke" ("giant-strong")[35] abilities. Of course only Siegfried can hope to do so, and Brünhild is even stronger than he is: Siegfried barely overcomes her despite having the help of the *tarnkappe*, which adds the might of twelve men ("wol zwelf manne sterke," 337,3a) to his own already formidable strength. It would seem that in the symbolic realm of the Otherworld, personal strength is — or should be — an external manifestation of inner virtue: the man who is strong in the Otherworld will be superior in the historical world as well. The deceptive strategy employed by Siegfried to make Gunther *appear* strong despite his underlying weaknesses has no legitimate place in Brünhild's world;

[33] Bumke 258. Cf. Helmut de Boor, "Kapitel 168 der Thidrekssaga," in Hermann Schneider, ed., *Edda – Skalden – Saga* (Heidelberg: Winter, 1952) 157–172.

[34] Bumke 261.

[35] Neumann 76.

it is a practice imported from the historical world of half-truths and political intrigue.

Siegfried knows and understands the rules of Brünhild's realm, and he knows that Gunther has no chance of winning her on his own. Because of his "real-world" desire to obtain Kriemhild, however, Siegfried uses his knowledge against the queen. He advises Gunther to leave at home his warriors and courtly retainers, symbols of the king's purely political strength, for he knows that in Isenstein only personal strength will matter. Instead of trying to impress Brünhild with an army, therefore, Gunther sets out to sea in a small boat, accompanied only by Hagen, Dancwart, Siegfried (who alone knows the way to Brünhild's land), and twelve sets of magnificent clothing (341–344). Apparently, even though Brünhild's court exists in the Otherworld, it is still a court, and the courtly virtue of magnificence, unlike military might, retains its influence.[36]

Most modern readers of the poem are aware of the fact that in the Old Norse analogues, Siegfried and Brünhild have declared their love and vowed to marry each other before Siegfried's memory of her is destroyed by a magical potion and Brünhild is deceived into marrying Gunther. The fact that in the *Nibelungenlied* Brünhild recognizes Siegfried at first sight and greets him by name, plainly assuming that he is her suitor and with no knowledge of who the Burgundians are, would seem to indicate that the *Nibelungenlied* poet — and thus possibly his medieval audience as well — also knew of the love relationship in other versions of the tale and may even have been hinting at its existence here. The poet makes no explicit reference to a prior relationship between the two; there is simply another layer of irony added to the description of Gunther's bridal quest for anyone aware of the tradition. Less critical attention has been given to the fact that in the same analogues Brünhild is a valkyrie, and anyone aware of the prior love relationship would also be aware of this aspect of her character.[37] Once again Germanic tradition provides a tacit correlation between the Otherworld of the *Nibelungenlied* and the world of the dead, for the valkyries (literally "choosers of the slain") are servants of Odin, the Norse god of battle and death, and their function is first to decide which fighters will die in battle and then to escort the fallen warriors to the god's Otherworld paradise, Valhalla. The valkyries are said to choose only the best and strongest warriors for an afterlife in Valhalla, and the fact that Brünhild uses the same criteria in her

[36] Cp. Ehrismann 126: "Archaisches Ambiente heißt niemals eo ipso *unhöfisches Ambiente.*"

[37] For a discussion of Brünhild's history in Germanic legend and literature, see Theodore M. Andersson, *The Legend of Brynhild* (Ithaca and London: Cornell University Press, 1980).

choice of a suitor may indicate that the *Nibelungenlied* poet knew of the valkyrie tradition and modified it for his own, very different, uses.

The modification includes a drastic revision in tone, however, for Brünhild's contests with Gunther (and, unbeknownst to her, with Siegfried in the *tarnkappe*) play out as pure farce. The scene looks backward to Siegfried's own earlier tests of worthiness in the Otherworld, which certainly gain in stature by the comparison, as well as forward to his second use of the *tarnkappe* in his almost equally farcical battle with the giant and Alberich in the next *âventiure*. Nonetheless, there is a bitter edge to the comedy, and it lies in the unfeeling attitude which the other characters, and most likely the poet himself, have towards Brünhild. All are clearly unsettled by her prodigious strength; the poet's decision to make the bridal tests comedic reflects his unease. The male characters express their dismay openly: upon seeing Brünhild's initial prowess in the tests, Hagen exclaims, "waz hât der künic ze trût!/jâ sol si in der helle sîn des übeln tiuvels brût" (450,3b–4). Siegfried is simply rude when he tells her at the end of the contests, "Sô wol mich dirre mære ... daz iuwer hôhverte ist alsô hie gelegen,/daz iemen lebet, der iuwer meister müge sîn"(474,1–3). Even Gunther will declare that Brünhild is an "übeln tiuvel" when, alone with his bride on his wedding night, he is confronted by her Otherworldly strength (649,2a).

In the events following the wedding night, the insensitivity on the part of both poet and characters turns vicious. The poet amplifies the farcical tone of the bedroom scenes in his depiction of the hapless Gunther hanging from a nail on the wall, but he describes, and with evident satisfaction (cp. 675-76), what is in fact a violent marital rape. McConnell has suggested that Siegfried's attitude toward Brünhild is based in the hero's stated belief in male dominance, pointing out that as he wrestles furiously with Brünhild in Gunther's bed, Siegfried is explicitly said to think that by forcing her to submit he is somehow preventing other women from following the queen's example and therefore advancing the cause of men in general (673). McConnell adds that "it is quite possible that Siegfried considers Brünhild to be a threat to society in her 'Amazon-like' state."[38] But a belief in male dominance is not simply part of Siegfried's characterization; the poet clearly shares the hero's views, and we may assume that at least half of his audience did as well.

Brünhild's Otherworldly strength disappears with her loss of virginity in yet another folktale motif that acquires symbolic importance in the *Nibelungenlied*. Not only must the former queen of an Otherworld realm accommodate her behavior to the rules of a male-dominated, courtly society, but she discovers in addition that if she is to have any influence — or pose

[38] McConnell 30.

any threats — within that society she must learn to play the games of duplicity and political machination that prevail in the historical world. She therefore competes for precedence with her rival Kriemhild, conceals her motives for persuading Gunther to invite Siegfried and Kriemhild back to Worms, and possibly even conspires with Hagen in Siegfried's murder. Kriemhild at any rate assumes collusion between the two when she hears of Siegfried's death and cries out, "ez hât gerâten Prünhilt, daz ez hât Hagene getân" (1010,4). Once she is forced by her loss of virginity to become an active participant in Burgundian power politics, Brünhild's outward appearance no longer matches her inner reality, and it is this more than anything else that is symbolized by her forfeiture of her Otherworldly strength.

It is therefore fitting that Brünhild's initial defeat in Isenstein is followed in the next *âventiure* by a display of Siegfried's strength in the Otherworld in a graphic demonstration of what Gunther never had and what the queen will lose by her marriage. Parallels to the earlier episode include the fact that in each *âventiure* Siegfried acts while invisible in the *tarnkappe*, and in each he defeats an opponent whose strength is equivalent to (or even greater than) his own. The element of farce continues into *Âventiure* 8 as well, since Siegfried's disguise in Nibelungenland seems prompted by high spirits rather than a serious attempt at deception, and the image of Alberich having his beard tugged by an invisible opponent (497) parallels that of Brünhild's defeat: it is simultaneously comic and humiliating. But although Bumke is no doubt correct in suggesting that the scene seems to have been modeled on an analogue to Siegfried's first visit to Brünhild and is best considered as part of the bridal quest, its full function is more complicated. In addition to incorporating parallels with the earlier *âventiure*, the *Nibelungenlied* poet structures *Âventiure* 8 as the counterpart of a later scene as well, namely, Hagen's fight with the ferryman before crossing the Danube into Etzel's land in *Âventiure* 25.

Like Siegfried and Brünhild, Hagen, too, has ties to the Otherworld. Those ties are implied in the *Nibelungenlied* by the fact that Hagen not only knows who Siegfried is at first sight (86), but also knows enough about him to tell the Burgundians the story of his youthful adventures in the Otherworld (87–100). By way of contrast, in *Þiðreks saga af Bern* Hagen's relationship to the Otherworld is made explicit: there he is the son of an elf who found the Burgundian queen asleep in her garden and fathered a child on her, thus making Hagen half-brother to the Burgundian princes. Still, in both the saga and the poem, Hagen's most significant encounter with the forces of the Otherworld takes place as he is leading the Burgundian forces into Etzel's Hungary, and it is in this episode that the parallels to *Âventiure* 8 are to be found.

In *Âventiure* 8, Siegfried travels alone to Nibelungenland in a small boat to retrieve a thousand of his Nibelung warriors; to do so, he must cross a boundary or "threshold" separating the historical world from the Otherworld. As we have seen, the literal threshold of Siegfried's stronghold in that world is guarded by a giant doorkeeper and the dwarf Alberich. Both are Siegfried's servants and would be expected to recognize him, so Siegfried disguises himself as a stranger in order to indulge in a playful, but still quite dangerous and apparently unnecessary battle with them. He then ferries the thousand warriors back to Isenstein to accompany Gunther and Brünhild to Worms. In *Âventiure* 25 Hagen is similarly trying to take a thousand "Nibelung" warriors (as the Burgundians are now called) to Etzel's land, but he finds himself faced with the physical boundary of the Danube, which functions here as a symbolic threshold between the familiar world of Worms and the more remote and exotic world of Etzel's realm. Like Siegfried, Hagen battles a recalcitrant and violent threshold guardian in the person of the ferryman, and he also resorts to a disguise, albeit in precisely the opposite manner in which it is used by Siegfried: rather than impersonating a stranger in order to avoid recognition as a returning friend, Hagen impersonates a returning friend in order to avoid recognition as a stranger. The resulting violence is serious rather than slapstick, and the scene ends in Hagen's murder of the ferryman, which forces him to ferry all one thousand warriors across the river himself in an astounding display of almost Otherworldly strength. It is worth pointing out that in describing the folktale qualities of *Âventiure* 8, Bumke asks wryly if we are really to believe the preposterous idea that all one thousand Nibelung warriors made the trip back to Isenstein in the same boat that Siegfried had arrived in.[39] When Siegfried's actions are compared to Hagen's behavior in *Âventiure* 25, however, the absurdity of the idea is lessened by the force of the parallel.

It is in *Âventiure* 25 as well that Hagen encounters the last inhabitants of the Otherworld to appear in the poem, in the form of two beautiful women, the "merwîp," whom he discovers bathing in a clear spring. These figures do not arise from a clearly discernible or widespread tradition in Germanic legend, and scholars are often uncertain of precisely how to translate the word "merwîp" into English: a quick survey reveals "water sprites," "water-fairies," "nixies," and "mermaids."[40] Their counterparts in *Þiðreks saga af Bern* are designated by the simple Old Norse equivalent to the Middle High German word, *sjókonur* ("sea-women"). Nonetheless, the function of the

[39] Bumke 254.

[40] The translations are from McConnell 32, Hatto 193 and 194, and Edward R. Haymes, *The Nibelungenlied: History and Interpretation* (Urbana and Chicago: University of Illinois Press, 1986) 76 respectively.

merwîp in the poem — to prophesy the outcome of the Burgundian expedition — is one that is widely attributed to female figures in general within the Germanic tradition, from Tacitus through the Middle Ages.[41] The prophetic knowledge of the two *merwîp* is both surprising and specific: they know Hagen by name and ancestry, calling him Aldrian's son ("Aldrîânes kint," 1539,2b), they give him specific directions as to how to find and handle the ferryman (which Hagen only partly follows), and most importantly, they tell him that none of the Burgundians will return from their journey alive, excepting only the chaplain. Hagen immediately tests the prophecy as best he can by attempting to drown the priest. When he nevertheless survives and swims safely back to the Burgundian side of the river, Hagen becomes certain that the *merwîp* are telling the truth, and in a final grand gesture he sinks the ferryboat, thereby destroying the possibility of anyone else turning back to Worms.

Clearly the two episodes are meant in part to provide a comparison of Siegfried's and Hagen's dealings with the Otherworld and its inhabitants; such a comparison serves to emphasize the distinction between what Edward R. Haymes has called the "bright" hero Siegfried and the "dark" hero Hagen in both character and behavior.[42] As a "bright" hero, Siegfried typifies the traditional Indo-European conception of heroism: he slays the evil dragon, wins the beautiful princess, lives his life in accordance with societal standards, and dies nobly but tragically at a young age; he can be identified not only with Sigurd and Beowulf, but also with the god Baldr. By way of contrast, "dark" heroes like Hagen work evil as easily as good; Haymes remarks that although the hero's "participation in the dark side of life makes him a questionable model for behavior ... it does not disqualify him from being both the structural hero of a narrative and an object of awe and admiration."[43] Thus Hagen, like Siegfried, participates in the archetypal "monomyth" of the hero, first articulated by Joseph Campbell and most often used to interpret stories of "bright" rather than "dark" heroes. McConnell likewise sees Hagen as a heroic counterpart to Siegfried, asserting that in his encounter with the Otherworldly figures of the *merwîp* and the events that follow, Hagen has "undergone a kind of initiation" that may be compared to Siegfried's earlier experiences in the Otherworld and that serves to designate Hagen as the true hero of the rest of the poem.[44]

[41] See Jacob Grimm, *Deutsche Mythologie*, vol. 1 (Göttingen: Dieterich, 1835) under the heading *Weise Frauen*, 328–407. For seeresses in the Norse tradition, see Simek 279.

[42] Haymes, *Nibelungenlied* 80, 87.

[43] Haymes, *Nibelungenlied* 87.

[44] Haymes 74–77; McConnell 37. For Campbell, see *The Hero with a Thousand Faces* (1949; rpt. Princeton: Princeton University Press, 1968).

In fact, Hagen's experiences with the *merwîp* and the ferryman as threshold guardians, his crossing of the Danube with all his companions, and his final sinking of the boat behind them, would seem to symbolize the Nibelung warriors' passage into the Otherworld as surely as do the trip to Isenstein or Siegfried's voyage to Nibelungenland. The difference, and it may not be as great a difference as it initially appears, is that the earlier crossings are seemingly into a daylight world of magic and marvels, while the passage over the Danube leads only to darkness and death.

It is easy to see *Âventiure* 25 as representing, if not a literal journey into the Otherworld, at least an incursion of Otherworldly motifs into the historical world. Gottfried Weber has described the episode as "von der Dunkelheit und Wildheit übernatürlicher Kräfte durchzogen,"[45] and it is in fact the last truly supernatural episode of the poem. It is less easy to see the events which follow in Etzelnburg as transpiring in a world significantly different from that of Worms or Xanten. Perhaps the poem's original audience found the differences easier to perceive: Hatto points out that while much of the geography of the Burgundians' journey would have been "intimately known" to a contemporary audience, as they approach Etzel's Hungary the Burgundians would have seemed to "draw away into a distant past ... in a place grown shadowy and remote."[46] The major transition, however, and one discernible by medieval and modern audiences alike, is in atmosphere. Once both Hagen and the audience realize fully that the annihilation will be absolute, that *no one* will survive the journey, nothing looks the same. Any vestige of ordinary life in the historical world — such as the marriage of Rüdiger's daughter to Giselher in *Âventiure* 27 — becomes acutely ironic, while the progress of events leading to the final destruction takes on an almost mythic air of inevitability. The Burgundians have here entered an Otherworld in which they are not dead, yet are no longer alive in any meaningful way.

Some of this has been suggested before, most notably by Stephen L. Wailes, who states baldly that "in the fall of the Burgundians we are dealing with the Journey to the Other World," and then proceeds to formulate a mythological allegory equating Etzel to "the giant, ogre, or fiend who rules that world" and the Burgundians to "the god who makes the journey."[47] But although the *Nibelungenlied* poet certainly draws on myth in both his plot and his descriptions of the Otherworld, there is no consistent mythological

[45] Gottfried Weber, *Das Nibelungenlied: Problem und Idee* (Stuttgart: Metzler, 1963) 136.

[46] Hatto 399.

[47] Stephen L. Wailes, "The *Nibelungenlied* as Heroic Epic," in Felix J. Oinas, ed., *Heroic Epic and Saga* (Bloomington: Indiana University Press, 1978) 138.

allegory in the poem. Rather, the mythic elements serve to intensify the darkly sinister atmosphere which infuses the last few ***âventiuren***, and to underscore the idea that the events that transpire there take place in a symbolic "realm of death"[48] that will become literal by the final strophes.

Thus, although at first glance Etzel's Hungary may seem to have more in common with the historical world of Burgundy and Xanten than with the Otherworld of Isenstein or Nibelungenland, its poetic representation as a literal kingdom of the dead places it firmly in the realm of the Otherworldly. As has been seen, both Nibelungenland and Isenstein have their own connections to the world of the dead in the motif of the hollow hill and in Brünhild's status as a valkyrie, and certainly the ***merwîp*** on the borders of Etzel's land would not be out of place in either location. Perhaps the relationship between the "bright" Otherworld of Nibelungenland and Isenstein and the "dark" Otherworld of Etzelnburg is best seen as analogous to the relationship between the poem's "bright" and "dark" heroes: each is the equivalent and yet mirror image of the other. Each version of the Otherworld provides a symbolic embodiment of the essence of one character's disposition and experiences, and they are thus structurally equivalent despite differences in specific characteristics. Finally, to paraphrase Ehrismann's comment once again, the poem's representations of the Otherworld also serve to provide the *Nibelungenlied* with enough of the "alten Zauber" of myth and *Märchen* to create a symbolic structure on which the poet's courtly epic, traditionally based yet newly conceived, can be built.

[48] Haymes 77.

Winder McConnell

The *Nibelungenlied*: A Psychological Approach

Science, particularly as evinced in the work of the British biologist, Rupert Sheldrake, as well as in the research of the Swiss physician and psychoanalyst, Willy Obrist, has produced yet further evidence of the validity of core ideas postulated almost a century ago by Carl Gustav Jung, foremost among them the concept of the archetypes of the collective unconscious.[1] It seems reasonable to assume that, as a consequence, greater links, if not cohesion, might have arisen between such (apparently) diverse areas as comparative mythology and religion, literature, biology, and psychology. Yet, despite the far-reaching ramifications of such studies, the disciplines, especially the Humanities and Social Sciences and the Natural Sciences, seem further apart today than ever before. Scientists are often enough skeptical of the forays of their humanist colleagues into physics, chemistry, biology, and psychology. Regrettably, with good reason. Rarely do the latter have any formal training in these areas and the modesty incumbent upon anyone approaching such disciplines as a non-initiate is often precluded by a zeal to promote socio-political agendas which ultimately hampers any real effort at understanding where actual points of intersecting among the disciplines can and do occur.[2] What is touted so often these days as interdisciplinary study is little more than a euphemism for watered-down, baseless curricula fashioned to serve some vague political purpose at the expense of students too young and gullible to recognize the dilettantism and political agendas of their "mentors" and lacking the power to undertake measures to counter it should they recognize the deception. There is certainly a real danger to true interdisciplinary study in such an atmosphere. The latter deserves a better

[1] See, in particular, Rupert Sheldrake, *A New Science of Life. The Hypothesis of Formative Causation* (Los Angeles: Tarcher, 1981); The *Presence of the Past. Morphic Resonance and the Habits of Nature* (New York: Vintage, 1989); Willy Obrist, *Archetypen. Natur- und Kulturwissenschaften bestätigen C. G. Jung* (Olten and Freiburg im Breisgau: Walter, 1990).

[2] Note Paul R. Gross and Norman Levitt, *Higher Superstition* (Baltimore: The Johns Hopkins Press, 1994). I am grateful to my (scientist) colleague, Richard Falk, a humanist in his own right, for first having made me aware of this work and for the opportunity to discuss with him on numerous occasions the potential for true interdisciplinary work between the Sciences and the Humanities.

forum and should be encouraged, albeit with the caveat that literary scholars with secondary (or even tertiary) interests in subjects often far afield of their major area of specialization should take care to defer to the recommendations and emendations of experts in those respective fields.

The application of analytical psychology and psychoanalysis in literary exegesis dates back a century. It is not a new methodology, but it has rarely been a popular one.[3] It is impossible to determine precisely why this has been the case, why psychological interpretations of literary works have not enjoyed, for example, the same support as New Criticism or Structuralism. Part of the reason may lie in the danger of reductionism, which, whether the approach be psychological or deconstructionist, invariably culminates in an intellectual cul-de-sac.[4] There is also the question of whether the application of such criteria is unjustifiably anachronistic. Psychological interpretations of literary works in the Freudian and post-Freudian era must necessarily take into account that the creators of such works were aware of the existence of the subconscious and that the primary text itself may revolve around a plot in which clear distinctions are made between the conscious and subconscious. Such was not the case — or so it would seem — in the Middle Ages.

The differentiation between "outer" and "inner" is relatively new. What is obvious, exposed, in short the *persona*, is, in the year 1200, for all intents and purposes, in conformity with *inner* reality. When Hartmann von Aue's protagonist in *Der arme Heinrich* is afflicted with leprosy, he can assume that those who observe him in this state are not merely fearful of becoming infected, or simply repulsed by his appearance, but that they also will have concluded that he has offended against God, that the external affliction is

[3] Nonetheless, the frequency with which the word "psychology" (or one of its cognates), as well as specific terms grained from that discipline are used in literary interpretations of medieval works is remarkable. As one example I cite the recent German translation of John Evert Härd's book, *Das Nibelungenlied. Wertung und Wirkung von der Romantik bis zur Gegenwart*, trans. from the Swedish by Christine Palm (Tübingen and Basel: Francke, 1996): "Die archetypische Struktur der Sage von *Tristan und Isolde...*" (22); "Im *Nibelungenlied* ist die Intrige psychologischer Art..." (30); "... die schöne höfische Welt wird zerschlagen, indem die elementaren, destruktiven Triebe des Menschen losgelassen werden, das ist das Grundthema des *Nibelungenlieds...*" (35); "In der Schilderung von Kriemhilds Verhalten während dieser Begegnung [between her and Hagen prior to the fatal hunt] ... liegt eine eigenartige Zweideutigkeit, eine psychologische Unwahrscheinlichkeit..." (43); "... ein psychologisch motiviertes Intrigenspiel" (83); "Es sind die psychologischen Bindungen zwischen den Menschen, die sich überschneidenden Loyalitäten, die nach Dilthey dem Werk seine Spannungstruktur geben..." (117); "... er ersetzt übernatürliche Erklärungen durch psychologische..." (119). Such examples could be augmented at will.

[4] See John M. Ellis, *Against Deconstruction* (Princeton: Princeton University Press, 1989).

simultaneously a reflection of internal decay or disorder. Beautiful women of the court and handsome knights mirror the inward purity of individuals and the inherent goodness of the court itself.

If one comes to the *Nibelungenlied* from the perspective of analytical psychology, it is thus wise to approach the work with the conscious realization that the terms one will use to describe its characters, action, motivations, motifs, are derived from a terminology unknown to the western world — in the way it is commonly used today — until the last decades of the nineteenth century.[5] Anyone who might have suggested to a thirteenth-century courtier that the Burgundians/Nibelungs were given to "repressing," perhaps even "denying," their irrevocable fate after they had crossed the Danube on the way to Hungary, that an *animus* had taken hold of Kriemhild who was truly no longer *herself*, would undoubtedly have been met with a vacuous stare. Yet it is quite conceivable that one might have turned to a contemporary as a minstrel-performer held forth on the betrothal of Gotelind and Rüdiger's daughter to Giselher and queried aloud whether the Burgundians, who had wept over the message of doom imparted to them by Hagen just hours previously, had forgotten in the interim that they have no future to which to look forward. The contemporary might even have offered an explanation: "daz wollen si jâ niht hœren!" Moreover, the narrator of ms. B of the *Nibelungenlied* clearly attributes the workings of the devil to Kriemhild's act (see 1394,1), a pre-psychological explanation of the psychological phenomenon of giving in to the shadow. My point is that, while objective psychology — and psychologizing — as we understand them today, were foreign to the Middle Ages, the psychological phenomena themselves were present and may well have occasioned more than just passive acceptance on the part of the more astute observers of the time. This is, of course, to attribute to the poet of the *Nibelungenlied* himself a talent for depicting aspects of the human psyche in a way that could well be considered unparalleled in his time. Such a suggestion is not new; it was expressed, in other words (and, in fairness to the author, perhaps with more caution than I might be apt to exercise), in an article written by Walter Haug over ten years ago and which represents, in my view, one of the most insightful contributions to *Nibelungenlied* scholarship that has appeared in the past half century.[6] It also provides an excellent starting point for an analysis of

[5] A noteworthy psychological contribution to the field of Nibelungen reception is to be found in Jean Shinoda Bolen's *Ring of Power. The Abandoned Child, The Authoritarian Father, and the Disempowered Feminine. A Jungian Understanding of Wagner's Ring Cycle* (San Francisco: Harper, 1993).

[6] Walter Haug, "Montage und Individualität im *Nibelungenlied*," in Fritz Peter Knapp, ed., *Nibelungenlied und Klage. Sage und Geschichte, Struktur und Gattung. Passauer*

probably the most complex figure within the work: Kriemhild, Princess of Burgundy, Queen of the Netherlands and Nibelungenland, and Queen of the Hungarian Empire.[7]

The present essay is intended as a *prolegomenon* to a larger study planned on German heroic epic and the *Nibelungenlied*, in particular, which will examine these works from the perspective of analytical psychology. I am principally concerned here with the motivations of main characters and the dynamics of their relationships. The terminology employed is largely that developed by Carl Gustav Jung, although it is not exclusively confined to the latter. I believe it is also possible to view the work as a whole from such a vantage point, particularly with respect to the obvious contrast it presents with the vast amount of literature otherwise predominant at that time. Finally, there are some intriguing psychological aspects to be noted regarding the manner in which the *Nibelungenlied* has been received in the twentieth century; in fact, one might suggest that certain manifestations of its *Rezeptionsgeschichte*, particularly over the past nine decades, offer considerable insight into the psyche of twentieth-century man (on this point see Werner Hoffmann's contribution to this volume and pertinent comments in the Introduction).

*

> Die Staubwolken der Reiter, Zeichen des freudigen Aufbruchs, Zeichen der Hoffnung, daß ein riesiges Reich sich aus seiner Trauer erheben wird, Zeichen des Glücks, das man sich von der neuen Königin erwartet, sie werden im Vergleich durchsichtig auf das, was diese Königin tatsächlich bringen sollte: den Feuerbrand, der alles vernichten wird.... Was damit geschehen ist, erfaßt man in seiner literaturhistorischen Bedeutung nur völlig, wenn man bedenkt, daß es zuvor in der mittelalterlichen Literatur eine Trennung von Innen und Außen nicht gegeben hat. Das Äußere ist gewissermaßen das Innere.[8]

Walter Haug's description of the Hunnish welcome prepared for Kriemhild reads, in its first part, almost like a film script, and is, in fact, somewhat reminiscent of the activity of the Hunnish scouts in Fritz Lang's 1924 production of *Kriemhilds Rache* when they become aware of Kriemhild's

Nibelungengespräche 1985 (Heidelberg: Winter, 1987) 279–293.

[7] Although the movement away from an automatic assumption of a correspondence between the outer and the inner is incidental to her argument, Joyce Tally Lionarons has also intimated that such a split has occurred with respect to the figure of Brünhild in the *Nibelungenlied*. Note p. 167 above.

[8] Haug 277, 281.

approach. The dichotomy between unrestrained optimism on the part of Etzel and his horde and the "reality" that lies behind the motivation for the queen's removal to Gran and the camp of Etzel is simultaneously unique and devastating. Virtually everything relating to the essence of courtly society that would have meant something to Kriemhild at Worms prior to her marriage to Siegfried and at Xanten prior to her fateful return to Worms, has lost its significance by the time she arrives in the land of the Huns. In his depiction of Kriemhild, the poet of the *Nibelungenlied* has sprung the bounds of medieval expectations; his character is modern, driven by emotions that defy the standard ideal of the time, the pursuit of *mâze*.

I have examined the figure of Kriemhild elsewhere from the viewpoint of animus possession and the significance of the *Klage*-poet's defense of the queen.[9] My contention in that earlier study was to suggest that Kriemhild's isolation and self-isolation within the work, combined with her tendency to repress or deny her shadow while simultaneously turning her back on both motherhood and her obligations as queen, led, in the absence of any real leadership on the part of the men in her life, to an inversion of the *ordo* of things and with Kriemhild completely dominated by the animus. The issue is less one of morality than psychology.[10] Here, too, one can consider the poet of the *Nibelungenlied* to have been unique. The issues raised in the work, along with the motivations of characters, do not tend to be treated solely from the binary perspective of good and bad. To be sure, there is moralizing — consider the manner in which Hagen's killing of Siegfried is

[9] Winder McConnell, "Animus Possession in Kriemhild: A Medieval Insanity Plea?" *Journal of Evolutionary Psychology* 11.1–2 (1990): 22–33.

[10] In this respect, I cannot concur with Jerold Frakes, whose 1994 work, *Brides and Doom*, a marxist-feminist approach to the *Nibelungenlied, Klage,* and *Kudrun*, completely avoids the possibility of any explanation for Kriemhild's behavior which is not rooted in the socio-political sphere. I do think that his criticism of the moral(istic) approach that has been taken by scholars (and, perhaps, the poets themselves) towards Kriemhild and other prominent females in the epics of the period is justified — albeit without the ad hominems which lead Frakes into the paradox of moralizing on moralizing — insofar as it points to a rather one-sided limiting of possibilities for interpretation of the figures' actions. However, where scholars, attempting to view the plots from the perspective of thirteenth-century audiences, have agreed with the poets, narrators, and figures within the epics themselves who have labeled Kriemhild and Gerlind (in *Kudrun*) as *vâlandinnen*, they have not been incorrect (although Kriemhild most certainly had her admirers as well as detractors, as the *Klage*, and undoubtedly the scribe of ms. C, have so aptly demonstrated). They may simply have not gone far enough, namely, to have also considered the male protagonists as being just as responsible for the onset of chaos (once again with the obvious exception of the *Klage* poet). See Jerold C. Frakes, *Brides and Doom. Gender, Property, and Power in Medieval German Women's Epic* (Philadelphia: University of Pennsylvania Press, 1994).

recorded by the narrator: "Hagen sîne triuwe vil sêre an Sîfriden brach" (971,4) or "sus grôzer untriuwe solde nimmer man gepflegen" (915,4), as well as the way in which Gunther's role in the whole business is depicted: "swie harte sô in durste, der helt doch niene tranc,/ê daz der künic getrunke; des sagt er im vil bœsen danc" (978,3–4).[11] Yet it is also quite clear that such moralizing with respect to the court at Worms is of limited duration, and that, by the time of the arrival of the Burgundians at the court of Etzel in Gran, the narrator could just as easily have been among the Huns eager to catch a glimpse of the man who had slain Siegfried. Any revulsion that may have previously existed over the manner that the hero of the Netherlands met his death has given way to wonder over his victor:

....
dô wunderte dâ zen Hiunen vil manegen küenen man
umbe Hagen von Tronege, wie der wære getân.

Durch daz man sagete mære (des was im genuoc),
daz er von Niderlande Sîfriden sluoc,
sterkest aller recken, den Kriemhilde man.
des wart michel vrâge ze hove nâch Hagene getân. (1732,3–4; 1733)

Morality, when it comes to the murder of Siegfried, is relative. By the twenty-eighth *Âventiure*, no one, including the narrator, is holding Hagen morally responsible for Siegfried's death, other than Kriemhild, of course.[12] It is telling that Kriemhild garners such great praise from the *Klage*-poet for the unrelenting loyalty she demonstrates towards her murdered husband:

swer ditze mære merken kan,
der sagt unschuldic gar ir lîp,
wan daz daz vil edel werde wîp
tæte nâch ir triuwe
ir râche in grôzer riuwe. (154–158)

[11] Quotations from the *Nibelungenlied* are based on the edition by Karl Bartsch and Helmut de Boor, 21st revised ed. by Roswitha Wisniewski, Deutsche Klassiker des Mittelalters (Wiesbaden: Brockhaus, 1979).

[12] Even the author of the *Klage*, who is otherwise ill-disposed towards Hagen and basically views him as responsible for the catastrophic events in which the *Nibelungenlied* culminates, attributes Siegfried's death to his arrogance. See *Diu Klage. Mit den Lesarten sämtlicher Handschriften*, ed. Karl Bartsch (1875; rpt. Darmstadt: Wissenschaftliche Buchgesellschaft, 1964), vv. 38–39: "unt daz er selbe den tôt/gewan von sîner übermuot."

Quite clearly, this first commentator on the *Nibelungenlied*, who assumes a position towards Kriemhild that is much closer to what we find in the *C-version than in the manuscripts of the *AB-tradition, chose to focus on *triuwe* as a gender-unbounded concept, in contrast to many of his contemporaries. The latter tended to adhere to the idea of *Männertreue*, most likely harking back to a pre-Christian Germanic ethos, but also combined this with an aversion to any defiance of the courtly ideal of *mâze*, and appear to have reflected a deeply-held belief that women and revenge do not mix, at least with respect to the former becoming instruments of the latter.

There is one thing that can hardly be doubted about Kriemhild — her love for Siegfried.[13] It is not, however, a love in any way comparable to that of, for example, Isolde for Tristan. Neither Siegfried nor Kriemhild is overtaken by the archetype of romantic love, as much as they may appear to pine for each other prior to the marriage. After all, this is a socially acceptable love, legal prior to and certainly *within* marriage, not opposed to the institution, not forbidden, and, for both medieval and modern sentiments, scarcely a romantic love at all. Although a convincing argument could be made that Siegfried and Kriemhild are incompatible partners, particularly with Brünhild in the wings, there is nothing about the union from a socio-political standpoint which might be considered inappropriate, other than the circumstances — the deception of Brünhild — which made it possible. Kriemhild's relationship to Siegfried is, nonetheless, not without its problematical side.

Most important, there is Kriemhild's dream, which occupies the last seven strophes of the first *Âventiure*, thus underscoring its pivotal significance for the subsequent unfolding of the plot. No other motif is accorded similar weight in the *Âventiure*. We need not spend an inordinate time on its interpretation, which is delivered in a fairly straightforward, if incomplete, manner by Ute, Kriemhild's mother.[14] The falcon of which she dreams and

[13] Noteworthy here are Gottfried Weber's comments: "Dass Kriemhildens, der ursprünglichen und ungewandelten, Wesen Liebe ist, daß sich ihre weibliche Art ganz und gar erfüllen wird in dem *undertân*-Sein gegenüber dem Geliebten ... was es überhaupt mit der Kriemhilden-Minne auf sich hat, erzählt der im Seelischen verhaltene und karge Dichter nirgends unmittelbar; das wenige, was er überhaupt sagt, gestattet vorerst kaum einen Einblick in die unbegrenzten Tiefen von Kriemhildens Liebesmöglichkeiten.... Worauf der Dichter hinzielt, ist gleichwohl überaus deutlich: es soll offenkundig werden, daß sich Kriemhilt nicht in sich, sondern nur in dem Manne ihrer Liebe erfüllt — in dem grenzenlosen Hingegebensein ihrer Seele an Sîvrit." See Gottfried Weber, *Das Nibelungenlied. Problem und Idee* (Stuttgart: Metzler, 1963) 5.

[14] See the comments by Theodor Reik in his short article, "Kriemhilds Traum," *Zentralblatt für Psychoanalyse. Medizinische Monatsschrift für Seelenkunde* 2 (1912): 416–417: "Der Vogel als Penissymbol wird hier von der kundigen Ute bestätigt.... Es

which she "raises," is a nobleman, who will surely be lost to her (as the falcon is torn apart by two eagles) if God does not protect him. It is, of course, on one level a prediction of things to come with regard to Siegfried and his disastrous relationship to the Burgundian royal family. What is particularly striking about the dream on another level, however, is a) Kriemhild's radical reaction to her mother's interpretation of it and b) the total lack of any further reference to it on her part throughout the rest of the epic. It should also be noted that Kriemhild's first impulse is to protect *herself* from the suffering she now also associates with the "message" of the dream. In apparent contrast to Hagen's dismissal of Ute's dream of the dead birds prior to the departure of the Burgundians for the land of the Huns, Kriemhild takes her dream and her mother's explanation of it very seriously.[15] She believes in its auguring power. Yet, that belief is suspended, or, psychologically speaking, repressed, when Siegfried comes into her life and the possibility looms large for a union between the two of them. It is hard to believe that the dream is simply "forgotten." It served, after all, as the basis for a prolonged period of isolation on Kriemhild's part with respect to the "wooing circuit." Kriemhild's belief in the efficacy of the dream is, perhaps, outmatched by her belief in her husband-to-be's (near) invulnerability. Like Siegfried, she succumbs to *übermüete* which, from a Christian perspective, may be equated with *superbia*, overweening pride, or in terms of analytical psychology — inflation. Kriemhild is by no means the only figure in the *Nibelungenlied* who reads astutely ominous signs provided by various means and who may initially react instinctually — and correctly — to such signs, but who subsequently demonstrates remarkable inconsistency in acting in accordance with this previous knowledge. A similar situation prevails in the second half of the epic with respect to the behavior of the Burgundians

ist wahrscheinlich, dass sich in der reifen Jungfrau die Libido regt und verdrängt wird.... Der ungestillte Trieb schlägt in sadistische Tendenzen um.... [D]as Zerfleischen des Vogels zeigt sadistische Tendenzen und ist zugleich der Wunsch nach der höchsten Lust. Der Angstaffekt ist aus dem Bewusstsein, das die verbotenen Wünsche kontrolliert, leicht zu verstehen.... Und am Schlusse bricht die angeborene und durch ungenügende Sexualbefriedigung verstärkte sadistische Komponente sich elementar Bahn." It might be noted at this point that the editor of the *Zentralblatt für Psychoanalyse* was Sigmund Freud and that one of the individuals listed under "Unter Mitwirkung von" was C. G. Jung.

[15] Hagen appears to be disinclined to pay any attention to the dream that Ute has prior to the Burgundians' departure for the land of the Huns, but his "rejection" is possibly posturing for the benefit of the kings and may not necessarily reflect his true attitude towards what is, after all, one of the most common forms of prophecy in his time. He will certainly take very seriously the next prophecy, that offered by the water sprite prior to crossing the Danube.

following their arrival on the eastern shore of the Danube and the revelations provided to them by Hagen of their inevitable fate.

Kriemhild is not given to complete repression, however, as her anxiety prior to Siegfried's departure to combat the alleged insurrection of Liudeger and Liudegast in the sixteenth *Âventiure* would indicate. This is one of the most complex sections of the *Nibelungenlied* when considered from the perspective of motivation. It seems that there are two views that can be taken of Kriemhild's actions at this point: she is patently naive, or she is remarkably capable of repressing the extent to which she has contributed to besmirching the collective image of Worms and demonstrating, in an almost treacherous manner, her total disregard for its welfare. When she elects to inform Hagen of Siegfried's vulnerable spot, she reverts to the role of the devoted family member, reduces the quarrel between herself and Brünhild to little more than a somewhat nasty familial squabble, and appears to reflect once again the unity between the outer and the inner. It is difficult to conceive of Kriemhild as being naive, but she has already, through the reversal of her initial reaction to the falcon dream, displayed a tendency to reject certain signs. In this particular instance, it would appear that the two dreams she has of Siegfried's demise, no longer in the metaphor of a falcon, but *as Siegfried*, are fatally *misinterpreted* by her. While Kriemhild envisions the (strong) possibility of Siegfried's death, she imagines it at the hands of the invading Saxons and Danes, and does not appear to consider for a moment that her brother Gunther and *oheim* Hagen, the two eagles of her first dream, have more than enough reason to want the hero of Xanten dead.

It might be contended, however, that Kriemhild is, in fact, quite naive, that she fails to recognize the seriousness of her altercation with Brünhild before the minster and its consequences for the Burgundian court, that she could not conceive of the sanctity of hospitality towards guests being defiled, particularly not in the case of her husband, a loyal military ally of Worms. Does she not, after all, approach Hagen as "family"? Quite true, but then why the doubts expressed later in 920ff., on the heels of her two dreams (in the first, Siegfried is hunted down by two wild boars; in the second, he is crushed by the collapse of two mountains), dreamt *after* her conversation with Hagen? A *Vorahnung* of what is brewing clearly has her in the direst straits, and the reader can well imagine what she is actually thinking when the narrator comments: "Do gedâhtes' an diu mære (sine torst' ir niht gesagen),/diu si dâ Hagenen sagete" (920,1–2a), and this is more starkly underscored two stanzas later: "ich fürhte harte sêre etelîchen rât,/ob man der deheinem missedienet hât,/die uns gefüegen kunnen vîentlîchen haz" (922,1–3). There is an interesting sequence of events here, beginning with the so-called "treachery" of the Saxon and Danish kings, Hagen's seeking out Kriemhild and her betrayal of his vulnerable spot, Kriemhild's dreams on that same night (i.e., *prior* to her hearing about the change in plans), the transformation of the military campaign into a hunt, Siegfried's seeking out Kriemhild to say his good-byes, and finally, Kriemhild's relating to her husband of her two dreams and her fruitless effort to dissuade him from participating in the hunt — stopping short, of course, of actually admitting to him the very sound reasons for her anxiety. Up until the point that Kriemhild herself learns that there is not to be a renewal of the war against the Saxons and the Danes, she could justifiably have identified the two boars and the two mountains with Liudeger and Liudegast. Once she realizes that a hunt has taken the place of the campaign, it is clear that she senses the potential for disaster emanating from much closer to home; her words in stanzas 920 and 922 allude to members of her own family. This is certainly how (a truly naive) Siegfried interprets them: "ine weiz hie niht der liute, die mir iht hazzes tragen./alle dîne mâge sint mir gemeine holt" (923,2–3).

If Kriemhild had initially reacted only out of selfish interests to the first dream, and then, after having met Siegfried, repressed the "message" of that dream, and if she had, in fact, shown herself to be rather naive in her dealings with Hagen, at this juncture there is clearly no doubt as to the basis of her fears and anxiety. But this raises the highly poignant question: why, as a loving and devoted spouse, does she not make it clear to Siegfried prior to his departure that she has betrayed the one secret that can keep him alive and that he is now *very* vulnerable? The text supplies an answer, although few will be particularly satisfied with it: "(sine torst' ir niht gesagen)" (920,1b). Is it truly *fear* that prevents Kriemhild from taking the one step that might have saved Siegfried's life? She had, in fact, sustained a rather severe beating from Siegfried for the fiasco she had helped to perpetrate before the minster. Is it, then, the fear of a second beating that precludes her divulging her betrayal of her husband? This would appear, in fact, to be the case. The narrator's explanation for Kriemhild's reluctance to say anything to Siegfried can be accepted verbatim: she simply did not dare to tell him. It would seem that Kriemhild has broken a sacred trust between herself and her spouse by having imparted his "ultimate" secret to Hagen, and potentially to many others, a secret brought back from the Otherworld to which only she in the courtly world, as far as we know, was privy. The betrayal of Siegfried begins with Kriemhild,[16] who allows fear to conquer love, although her original intention

[16] Unless we wish to contend that Siegfried had already betrayed himself through having helped Gunther to procure Brünhild, instead of recognizing that he was the one destined to defeat her in the trials in Iceland and thus, in keeping with the rules of the game, should have been the one to wed her. The question may certainly be posed: would not Siegfried and Brünhild have constituted a much more suitable pair than Siegfried and Kriemhild? Even were we to ignore the Norse analogues (which may well have been known to the German scribe), a union between Brünhild and Siegfried would

in telling Hagen of Siegfried's weakness was entirely honorable and focused on preserving her spouse's life.[17]

In a psychological sense, the second half of the *Nibelungenlied* is of less interest than the first, at least insofar as Kriemhild's motivations are concerned. Her course has been plotted from the moment that Siegfried is killed and it is simply re-confirmed with the theft of the *hort*. The narrator, reader/listener, Hagen, Dietrich, the Burgundian kings, Etzel, and Rüdiger — in this approximate order — eventually realize the true/only reason for Kriemhild's marriage to Etzel. Political marriages in the Middle Ages were a matter of course, and, more often than not, involved the creation of alliances, but Kriemhild's union with the Hunnish ruler has only one purpose and that is to secure a power base from which she may eventually be able to avenge the killing of Siegfried as well as the other outrages she has suffered at the hands of her brothers and Hagen. Before turning our attention to other members of the "cast," however, several points warrant comment.

Kriemhild's designation as a "vâlandinne" in the second part of the epic can certainly be justified *from a medieval point of view*. To be sure, injustices have been committed against her, no "champion" has stepped forward to take up her case, she is isolated, but at the same time, she has never comprehended the extent to which her murdered husband, with his "ganz

scarcely have led to the compromising situation in which the hero finds himself in the sixteenth *Âventiure*. Brünhild and Siegfried would have complemented each other in a way that could never be possible for Siegfried and Kriemhild.

[17] One occasionally encounters the suggestion that Kriemhild subconsciously wished to "remove" Siegfried, assume his power and possession of his *hort*. Such an interpretation would be predicated upon an *a priori* desire on the part of the queen for absolute power, as well as possible resentment over Siegfried's rejection of the lands to which she was entitled upon marrying and the beating he gave her after her indiscretion before the minster. The text, however, offers no support for any interpretation that Kriemhild *consciously* contemplated such a move. Siegfried may even fit the pattern of the average medieval knight when it comes to wife-beating, but this arouses, at the most, fear within Kriemhild, not fury. Siegfried, whether as a symbol or as a person, is an integral part of Kriemhild's life. On a subconscious level, it might be contended that, in the wake of Siegfried's murder, she may attempt to find some sort of compensation in the *Nibelungenhort* with its *Wünschelrute* (note below), and the power it endows which, as Hagen fully realizes, could prove dangerous for Worms. Her daily lamenting in the land of the Huns would lead one to believe that the love she still held for Siegfried was as sincere as the remorse felt over his death and the fury directed at the perpetrators of the deed, undoubtedly intensified all the more through the ever-present realization of her own part in the affair. Note, however, Härd's brief and intriguing allusion to possible ulterior motives on the part of Kriemhild: "Streng genommen wird Siegfried von ihr verraten, und geschieht das wirklich völlig unabsichtlich und ahnungslos?" (43).

unkontrollierte Naturkraft"[18] constituted a perpetual problem for courtly society as a whole.

It is less Kriemhild's understandable desire for revenge that is striking or alarming than the manner in which this is allowed to consume her as an individual over more than two decades and the extent to which the absolutization of her resolve results in catastrophe for entire nations. Kriemhild's plan could never have been realized, however, without the complicity of various males and the naive or inept leadership of specific rulers who are given more to repression of the obvious, and dangerous than to assuming an active role in preserving their peoples from a cataclysm. What had been characteristic of Kriemhild subsequent to her marriage to Siegfried — an imprudent turning away from her intuition, and then not acting upon it at *the* decisive moment (prior to her husband's final departure) — now holds true for all of the major male players in the work, with the exception of Hagen.

Given the reception of the *Nibelungenlied* in the twentieth century, it may seem almost blasphemous to suggest that, *from a psychological perspective*, Siegfried initially appears to be one of the least interesting characters in the *Nibelungenlied*. He is the archetypal hero: strong, to the point of near invincibility, the "perpetual" friend, or at least aspiring friend (note stanza 155) who manages, however, to create chaos rather than to instill order and stability within society. Siegfried was certainly a hero to the majority of those who heard his praises sung in the Middle Ages. While that is the image that has also tended to prevail through the first half of the twentieth century, it is noteworthy that late medieval depictions of Siegfried — as an irritating apprentice and eventually, in Hans Sachs's *Lied vom Hürnen Seyfrid* (1557), as a poor second to Dietrich in terms of prowess in combat, who even has to seek protection from the latter's wrath in the lap of Crimhilt! — were scarcely as flattering. One should not forget as well the remark made by the anonymous author of the *Klage*, already quoted above: "unt daz er selbe den tôt/gewan von sîner übermuot." This thirteenth-century commentator on the *Nibelungenlied* had relatively little to say about the hero of Xanten and astutely attributed his death in large part to his own failing.

Siegfried may have his vassals and fellow-knights, whether they hail from Xanten or the Otherworld of Nibelungenland, but he is, in the final analysis, *confidant* to no one and, with the possible exception of Kriemhild, has no one to be his *confidant(e)*. The hero's solitariness is striking, particularly when we consider the relationship that exists between Hagen and Volker later in the epic, or that between Roland and Oliver in the *Rolandslied*. In marked contrast to the youthful Parzival, who has both male and female

[18] Weber 24.

mentors to help him in a process of maturation and individuation/transformation which eventually culminates in his ascension to the Grail throne, Siegfried neither encounters, nor does he seek out, older, wiser figures of either sex. He is rather a "loner," although he is given to self-deception when it comes to the matter of friendship. There are indications, however, that Siegfried is not entirely in a psychological vacuum when it comes to knowledge regarding his actual relationship to the Burgundians, specifically Gunther. Prior to informing Siegfried of the attack by Liudeger and Liudegast, Gunther declares:

> "Jane mag ich allen liuten die swære niht gesagen,
> die ich muoz tougenlîche in mîme herzen tragen.
> man sol stæten vriwenden klagen herzen nôt."
> diu Sîvrides varwe wart dô bleich unde rôt. (155)

Siegfried's reaction to Gunther's declaration is to blanch and then to blush. It is clearly a sensitive response to the implication that Gunther does not necessarily consider him among the "stæten vriwenden" but rather that he is counted more among "allen liuten." The very fact that Gunther did not see fit to approach Siegfried immediately with his concerns over the impending Danish-Saxon war should be a sign to the hero of Xanten that he does not belong to the "inner circle." There is much meaning in Siegfried's blanching and blushing, an indication of his "inner" knowledge that he is an outsider. This knowledge is, nonetheless, continually repressed by Siegfried and even denied when he lies dying after being struck down by Hagen. For all of his desire to become a good friend to the Burgundians, and to Gunther, in particular, Siegfried's "otherness," and, in particular, his incapacity to recognize and deal with the darker side of his personality, preclude any "normal" male bonding between himself and, as it appears, anyone else.

The dynamics between Siegfried and Hagen are, in some respects, more subtle than those between Hagen and Kriemhild, but they have led, in at least one instance, to a remarkable bit of scholarly speculation. Prior to examining the latter, however, let us consider the following. Upon arriving at Worms, Siegfried demonstrates no concern whatsoever for the honor of the Burgundians and must certainly offend Hagen (whom he addresses directly), in particular, with his overt declaration of intended conquest. Hagen nonetheless attempts to derive whatever assistance possible from Siegfried in his efforts to enhance the status of Worms, whether that is putting the thought into Gunther's head that he should inform Siegfried about the Danish-Saxon crisis (the clear intention being to engage his help in the forthcoming battle), or "conscripting" him for the wooing mission to Island to procure Brünhild (whereby Hagen fully realizes that Gunther, by himself, is not up to the task). It is his manipulation, after the mission has been successfully completed, that sees Siegfried sent on ahead to Worms to announce, messenger-style, the arrival of the victorious party from Island. Hagen may not have been able to, or even interested in, establishing close, personal ties to Siegfried, but he is fully aware of how valuable the hero could be for Worms if Kriemhild is held out as the ultimate prize. In sum, the relationship, at least from Hagen's standpoint, is one of pragmatism (in contrast, for example, to the affinity developed between Hagen and Volker in the second half of the epic). Even if, as in the case of the wooing of Brünhild, the goal is ill-advised, Hagen's intentions are consistently aimed at the enhancement of Burgundian power and prestige. If the latter is compromised, he will do whatever is necessary to rectify the situation. Hagen's motivation for killing Siegfried is undoubtedly multifaceted in nature, but the major reason is certainly the damage done to Worms, its royal family, their reputation and honor, through the indiscretions of the hero of Xanten and his spouse. It is thus possible to concur to some degree with D. G. Mowatt and Hugh Sacker when they suggest that the murder came about as "Sifrid's punishment for not caring about Worms."[19] Less easy to accept, however, is the Freudian interpretation they accord to the hunt which provides the backdrop for the murder and to the symbolism accorded the act itself: "Is perhaps the whole hunt scene a homosexual hunt, with Hagen and Sifrid the two wild boars of Kriemhilde's dream (921,2), and fatal penetration from the rear Sifrid's punishment for not caring about Worms?"[20]

The matter of Siegfried's sexuality is by no means without interest. He is undoubtedly aware of the attention he receives from the opposite sex in general (note 131,1–3 where the women are always delighted to see Siegfried among the sporting knights, or 135,3–4, in which his looks cause "manec frouwe" to adore him), and, despite his initial qualms about wooing Kriemhild, he is from all indications a successful sexual partner. When sex is alluded to in conjunction with Siegfried, scholars are most likely to concentrate on the bedroom scene in which Siegfried "tames" Brünhild for a hapless Gunther. Mowatt and Sacker maintain that "he is essentially responsible for her loss of maidenhood," but that "he left her to Gunther to deflower."[21] Siegfried is no Tristan, however, as the reservations he expresses in stanza 136 regarding the possibility of even seeing Kriemhild indicate. The Burgundian princess is Siegfried's ***anima***, just as he, in many ways, represents her ***animus***. As the epitome of courtly existence, Kriemhild in essence becomes the focus of Siegfried's effort to reintegrate himself into society,

[19] D. G. Mowatt and Hugh Sacker, *The Nibelungenlied. An Interpretative Commentary* (Toronto: University of Toronto Press, 1967) 92.

[20] Mowatt/Sacker 92.

[21] Mowatt/Sacker 71.

undertaken subconsciously after his youthful adventures in the otherworldly sphere. Paradoxically, he will adapt less easily to the court than Kriemhild does to his more aggressive sphere. Even the vocabulary used to describe the contemplated sex act (in the case of both Siegfried and Gunther) is not devoid of some bellicose vocabulary: "Die herren kômen beide, dâ si solden ligen./do gedâht' ir ietslîcher mit minnen an gesigen/den minneclîchen vrouwen" (628,1–3a). The perspective provided by the narrator is solely that of Siegfried's satisfaction, however: "Sîfrides kurzewîle diu wart vil grœzlîche guot" (628,4) and we learn nothing of how Kriemhild fared, although there is no reason to doubt that the pleasure enjoyed was mutual. The desirability of Kriemhild as a lover is not lost on others. The obvious attraction that she and Siegfried have for each other once Kriemhild has appeared physically before him, the image painted of their coming together, prompts many an observing knight to contemplate the pleasures of "being" together with Kriemhild, of making love to her (296,1–3). Siegfried has a sexual persona, and his superiority also in this arena is not to be underestimated when it comes to understanding the relationship between himself and Gunther and hence, through association, to Hagen. It is a persona, however, which is decidedly heterosexual and, from every indication, monogamist: "er næme für si eine niht tûsent anderiu wîp" (629,4; see also 656,2b–3).

There are, of course, obvious sexual overtones to Siegfried's "taming" of Brünhild for Gunther and one can certainly concur with Mowatt and Sacker that Siegfried's bears responsibility for the Icelandic queen's loss of her virginity. Siegfried seems to have anticipated that his help would be needed, as we read in 648,1–2: "Im [= Gunther] unt Sîfride ungelîch stuont der muot./wol wesse, waz im wære, der edel ritter guot." Psychologically, this must be an almost unbearable situation for the Burgundian king. Politically, it could become disastrous, should the antics of the preceding night become widely known. Gunther's sexually inferior status when compared to Siegfried is painfully "rubbed in" through a remark by the latter which may seem to be relatively harmless on the surface: "ich wæne uns ungelîche hînat sî gewesen" (652,2). Gunther is fully aware of Siegfried's sexual prowess and the potential, after the latter's offer of assistance to subdue Brünhild, for a violation of his royal prerogative, hence his rather pathetic statement: "Âne daz du iht triutest" (655,1a). Once assured that, for Siegfried, there is no other woman but Kriemhild, Gunther is quite relieved, although terribly anxious for the day to pass. When it does, however, the poet provides his audience with some excellent insight into the mental state of the Burgundian monarch: "daz was dem künige Gunther beidiu liep unde liet" (665,4). Gunther realizes that there is no other way to "win" Brünhild, but it is a torturous fact that his wife must be "tamed" by another man and there is certainly more than a little ambiguity in his thought: "Den künic ez dûhte lange, ê er si betwanc" (675,1). Gunther remains throughout fully cognizant of the fact that Siegfried held true to his oath not to "violate" Brünhild sexually.[22] He is, however, a medieval sovereign who cannot completely repress the symbolic significance of the later public display of his spouse's ring and belt by his sister after she has declared (lied?) to all and sundry, and more with a sense of pride than of shame, that it was her husband, Siegfried, who first bedded Brünhild.

Previous scholarship has occasionally seen the *Nibelungenhort* — as well as the sword Balmung — as symbolic of Siegfried, hence the added significance of Kriemhild's demand that the hoard be returned to her when she confronts Hagen in the final scenes of the epic and her decapitation of the latter using Siegfried's sword. If this is a correct interpretation, then it is worth noting that the one item in the treasure that is singled out as having particular significance is the magic wand, the *Wünschelrute*: "Der wunsch der lac darunder, von golde ein rüetelîn./der daz het erkunnet, der möhte meister sîn/wol in aller werlde über ietslîchen man" (1124,1–3). While this can certainly be taken verbatim as the equivalent of the wizard's magic wand,

[22] Scholars have always assumed that Brünhild was a virgin until bedded by Gunther following the wrestling match with Siegfried. The assumption makes perfectly good sense, as one would otherwise expect an earlier "deflowering" to have occurred (in Isenstein) only had a worthy suitor appeared before Siegfried/Gunther, in which case Brünhild would have already been married. Provided, then, that we may assume that Brünhild remained chaste while a sovereign in Island (i.e., that she was not given to using men for her own sexual gratification), Gunther would have had physical proof on the second wedding night of his wife's "purity" (and thus his "friend's" integrity). He would objectively *know* that Siegfried had not overstepped his bounds, at least in the sexual arena. That knowledge, however, will not necessarily compensate for the psychological realization (and frustration) that, were it not for Siegfried, he would conceivably never have been able to consummate his marriage to Brünhild. Unlike Gunther, Brünhild can never enjoy complete assurance that it was not, in fact, Siegfried who "deflowered" her, following a brief interlude subsequent to the taming episode, and the *timing* of his removal of her ring and belt, namely, *prior* to intercourse, could provide her (as it must later those in attendance during the quarrel before the minster) with symbolic evidence that it could only have been Siegfried, in the guise of Gunther, who bedded her. Siegfried, in his arrogance, may have deprived Brünhild of both objects as though they were "war booty," but for Brünhild (and everyone else, including Kriemhild) they are sexual trophies. In this sense, the *Nibelungenlied* differs radically from the *Vǫlsunga saga*, in the thirty-second chapter of which Brynhild urges the death of Sigurd and his son in full cognizance of the fact that the hero had kept his vows and not violated her (having placed his sword between them in bed). From Brünhild's perspective, the realization that Siegfried was with her at all on her second wedding night, with all of the ramifications it holds for prior events in Island, can only have shattered forever any illusions she may have entertained of a correspondence between inner and outer reality.

used principally to preclude any diminishing of the treasure, it is intriguing to note that the term *wünschelruote* or *wünschelstap* was also used in the Middle Ages as a euphemism for the male member.[23] The *hort* represents vitality, including sexual vitality,[24] and it is thus possible to view Siegfried himself as the epitome of such vitality, a man who has not only the potential to become "meister" over all men, but also all women, in the world.

We must be cautious, however, about extending this imagery too far. Suffice it to say that Siegfried outdoes Gunther not only in battle — note their respective roles in the Saxon-Danish war, and also the struggles against Brünhild — but also in the bedroom, irrespective of the fact that both produce sons. It should be underscored once again that Siegfried is not Tristan, he is no Don Juan, although there are certainly aspects of the archetypal *puer aeternus* about him, in the sense that he "remains too long in adolescent psychology."[25] At no time is there any indication that Siegfried himself understands the delicate psychological position in which Gunther must find himself through the very presence of the hero of Xanten and Nibelungenland. Siegfried is simply in every way but one (the ability to form a deep and reliable relationship to his peers) "the better man," and, because it is impossible for him to become any one else's true friend (irrespective of how he may regard himself in the eyes of others), his success in the sexual sphere will inevitably impede a closer relationship to the Burgundian king.

Siegfried is desired by women (possibly including Brünhild), loved by Kriemhild, and himself indicates unequivocally on a number of cases that the princess of Worms is the only woman in his life. At no time is there a hint of homosexuality in his behavior or demeanor. While Mowatt and Sacker have any number of valuable points to make in their commentary, this is one that leads nowhere. What has been said of Siegfried applies as well to Hagen. There is no homosexuality in the Nibelungenlied, either symbolically, or otherwise. There is sexual tension between Siegfried and Gunther, Kriemhild

[23] Note Konrad von Megenberg, *Das Buch der Natur. Die erste Naturgeschichte in deutscher Sprache*, ed. Franz Pfeiffer (1861; rpt. Hildesheim: Olms, 1962) 38 "Von den Zaichen ob ain fraw swanger sei oder niht": "daz ander zaichen ist, daz diu wünschelruot oben trucken ist an dem haupt und daz si die muoter vast seugt," and 399 "Von dem weizen Senif": "aber daz wilde [Kraut] pringt daz harmwazzer und erweckt die unkäusch, wan es sterkt den wünschelstab und daz würkt allermaist des krautes sâm."

[24] C. G. Jung, in a reference to Kluge's *Etymologisches Wörterbuch*, has suggested that the original Indo-European root of the word *hort*, **kuth*, is "possibly related to κεύθω and κύσθος, 'cavity, female genitals'" (*Symbols of Transformation*, 2nd ed., Bollingen Series XX [Princeton: Princeton University Press, 1976] 364).

[25] Marie-Louise von Franz, *Puer Aeternus. A Psychological Study of the Adult Struggle with the Paradise of Childhood*, 2nd ed. (Boston: Sigo, 1981) 1.

and Brünhild, possibly also between Siegfried and Brünhild, and there is sexual (although not necessarily psychological) compatibility between Siegfried and Kriemhild. Sex is used by Kriemhild to sway Etzel, as is fatherhood, it may be used by the Hunnish queen to entice Blœdel to commit treacherous acts against the Burgundians (by offering him the widow of the highly acclaimed hero Nuodung [see also *Alpharts Tod*, 78–79]), but it is, at best, one of several motivating factors within the dynamics of relationships between the various main characters in the *Nibelungenlied*, and it is never anything other than heterosexual in nature.[26]

A number of years ago, Theodore M. Andersson posed the complex and provocative question, "Why does Siegfried die?"[27] He concluded that there was no good reason provided in the *Nibelungenlied*; the Old Norse versions of the tale, on the other hand, offered convincing motivation for the act. Yet we do have the statement made by the *Klage*-poet that the hero of Xanten was killed as a consequence of his *übermuot*. Siegfried's murder — and it will always remain that, regardless of whether one finds it justified or condemnable — can, however, be explained psychologically from the text itself, without recourse to analogues (although this is by no means intended to dispute the possibility that the latter were known to the *Nibelungenlied*-poet and that he, too, like some modern interpreters, saw the potential for an ambiguous interpretation of Brünhild's tears at the sight of Kriemhild sitting next to Siegfried). One might even go so far as to say that the killing was inevitable, given the static nature of an adult child[28] who remains stubbornly oblivious to the serious (negative) ramifications of both his words and deeds on the society around him. Siegfried is not simply Burgundy's "problem." He poses a threat to the stability of the rest of the "epic" world, specifically because of his incapacity to adhere to the norms of the latter, his spontaneity, and his apparent ignoring of the "rules" according to which that world functions. Even in his last moments, Siegfried never demonstrates the capacity to confront his shadow. When he proclaims to Gunther and Hagen: "ich was iu ie getriuwe" (989,3a), he is technically quite correct. He had, from his perspective, and perhaps even from the audience's, always been loyal

[26] Note, in this regard, the article by C. Stephen Jaeger, "Mark and Tristan: The Love of Medieval Kings and their Courts," in Winder McConnell, ed., *in hôhem prîse. A Festschrift in Honor of Ernst S. Dick*, GAG 480 (Göppingen: Kümmerle, 1989) 183–197.

[27] Theodore M. Andersson, "Why does Siegfried die?", in Stephen J. Kaplowitt, ed. *Germanic Studies in Honor of Otto Springer* (Pittsburgh: K & S Enterprises, 1978) 29–39.

[28] See my article, "Inflation and the Gifted Child: The Case of Siegfried," *Journal of Evolutionary Psychology* 9 (1988; nos. 1/2): 127–140.

towards the Burgundians, because he had never *intentionally* or, more accurately, *consciously*, undertaken anything to their disadvantage. Siegfried can look back on his participation in the Danish–Saxon war, his indispensable role in procuring Brünhild, the "service" performed for Gunther in "taming" her, as acts performed on behalf of Gunther and the Burgundians and yet none of these are events that can be designated so simply. Prior to leaving on the Danish-Saxon campaign, Siegfried encourages Gunther "... sît hie heime ... belîbet bî den frouwen" (174,1a; 3a). Siegfried's assurances to Gunther that he will protect "beidiu êre unde guot" (174,4b) are sincere, and there is no reason to believe that he *intends* a slight against the monarch with his recommendation that he remain home with the women. One might contend that it is fitting for Gunther to let his liegemen and allies deal with this problem and remain removed from the actual battlefield, but Gunther is not Arthur, sending out knights on *âventiuren*. The specific reference to "staying home with the women" is remarkable. Liudegast is king of Denmark and an active participant in the campaign against Burgundy. It is inconceivable that Etzel would remain "at home with the women" once his hordes have begun to march. Nor do we find Hagen in *Kudrun*, written within three or four decades after the *Nibelungenlied*, or King Hetel, or his adversary King Ludwig, entrusting either their offensive or defensive wars to vassals while they enjoy the relative security of remaining "at home with the women." Yet it is a recommendation to which Gunther accedes and not a word of his reaction is recorded in the text. The reader/listener is left to decide for himself what Gunther must be feeling in this moment. It is not indicated whether or not Siegfried's statement is made before several of the king's liegemen, but even if said to him privately, it casts a rather hapless Gunther into an even more unenviable psychological position as he is forced to realize who is, at this point, the *de facto* power in Burgundy.

When Siegfried accompanies Gunther, together with Hagen and Dancwart, to Island to woo Brünhild — although he originally advised Gunther against it, while Hagen urged the mission with Siegfried's assistance — he is most certainly providing an invaluable service (albeit with the direst consequences) to Worms and its sovereign. Yet, here again, the situation is psychologically volatile. From the outset, it is clear to all and sundry that the entire mission could not be seriously contemplated without the help of the "initiate" Siegfried, and this becomes patently obvious when the Burgundians eventually confront the "devilish" Brünhild. Moreover Siegfried, who has wished so much to demonstrate his "friendship" towards Gunther and the others (note 156), allows himself a throughly unnecessary remark which can hardly fail to offend the king and his men: "Jane lob' ichz niht sô verre durch die liebe dîn/sô durch dîne swester" (388,1–2a). Once again, there is no response from Gunther and what could he have possibly replied? In short, any potential for real friendship or comradeship is precluded by the unnerving proclivity of Siegfried to say precisely the wrong thing at the wrong time. Let us recall again Siegfried's query of Gunther following the wedding night, one that is made in *full awareness* of what has undoubtedly happened (648,2). The terrible dichotomy is time and time again apparent: Gunther and the Burgundians need Siegfried, he is more than willing to help, but that help is invariably provided in ways as to remind them consistently of the extent to which they are, individually and collectively, inferior to him. In this respect, he provides a striking contrast to a figure such as Beowulf, on whom Hrothgar and the Danes depend, but who never creates the impression that he is a threat to the latter, a hero who is sensitive to the Danish king's position, and also willing to learn from the latter's wisdom and experience, and who leaves for his own homeland before the suspicion of any usurpation of Danish power could be contemplated. In the case of Siegfried, however, there is the ever-present, gloomy realization that Gunther and his men are not up to accomplishing any of these goals themselves and that, from the moment that Siegfried arrived at Worms, they have become "obliged" to him and aware that they are entirely at his mercy.

Why, in fact, does Siegfried die, if one is not prepared to accept the perfectly good explanation to be derived from the text, namely, that one cannot let rest his responsibility for the public humiliation of the Burgundian court? One might cite Jung's explanation as provided in his *Symbols of Transformation* — here referring to Wagner's opera but it can just as easily be applied to the situation in the *Nibelungenlied*: "The subsequent fate of Siegfried is the fate of every archetypal hero: the spear of the one-eyed Hagen, the Dark One, strikes his vulnerable spot."[29] The poet is thus following an established pattern (not just tradition passed on from the oral-formulaic forebears of the epic or its immediate written source) that transcends epic aesthetics and expectations and which finds its origins in mythology. Another explanation might be proposed, one that may be feasible from the perspective of medieval thinking (or psychology). In contradistinction to the expectation of conformity prevalent at the time, Siegfried's archetypal features are not confined to heroic acts which are intended to benefit society, but also include a remarkable measure of *individuality* that confronts and defies the interests of the collective. Furthermore, it is into this realm of individual achievement and self-assertion that Kriemhild is inextricably drawn when she weds Siegfried and which causes her to move further and further away from the clan and the interests and welfare of her family. Quite in keeping with this emergence of the individual is the overweening pride, the *übermuot* which exacerbates Siegfried's independent, *spontaneous*

[29] Jung, *Symbols of Transformation* 389.

tendency towards unreflected action.[30] The reasons for Siegfried's death may well be seen as multifaceted, but the inflationary, unpredictable nature of this transgressor against the prevailing *ordo* of the world constitutes, at the very least, a major subconscious impetus to his removal. His transgressions have in large part to do with the affinity he displays to the Otherworld and the power he has acquired through his successes in that realm. We are reminded here of a *Spruch* by Nietzsche: "Wer mit Ungeheuern kämpft, mag zusehen, daß er nicht dabei zum Ungeheuer wird. Und wenn du lange in einen Abgrund blickst, blickt der Abgrund auch in dich hinein."[31] Siegfried defeats the dragon, but acquires in the process some of what it symbolizes, particularly the capacity for unleashing chaos. If the Otherworld is viewed as a metaphor for the unconscious, it should be recalled that the latter is also the repository for some things best left "below the surface." Siegfried's inability to discern between what should be allowed to emerge from the depths, what might benefit him and society as a whole, and what should justifiably — and wisely — be repressed, can be regarded as a major factor in the unfolding of his own personal tragedy.

Siegfried's nemesis, Hagen, is a highly complex figure who may, however, on the surface at least, create the impression of being relatively one-dimensional in terms of his motivation. He, as well as his clan, appear to have one purpose in life, namely, to serve the Burgundian royal household. All of Hagen's actions take Worms and the welfare of Burgundy as represented by its kings as their point of departure. He will later be designated by the narrator as "ein helflîcher trôst" (1526,2b) and also by Dietrich as the "trôst der Nibelunge" (1726,4a), an allusion that should be understood in both a physical and spiritual sense. It is worth noting from the outset that Hagen is not accorded overtly *personal* ambitions by the poet. For all intents and purposes, any hopes, dreams, wishes, that he may have are identical to what he would consider to be the best course of action for Burgundy, which is not to suggest, however, that Hagen does not jealously guard his own particular position within the hierarchy of the court, one that he has clearly assumed in accordance with a venerable tradition. He is the quintessential "company man," who sees his purpose in enhancing and upholding the stature of Worms. Hagen subscribes to, and upholds, the traditional code of honor and loyalty, albeit defined within the context of the clan. As such, he is the

[30] Inflationary tendencies are, of course, by no means limited to the individual, as is demonstrated by the later allusion to the collective *übermuot* (1865,4a) of the Burgundians by declining to inform Etzel of the true state of affairs.

[31] Ivo Frenzel, ed., *Friedrich Nietzsche. Werke in zwei Bänden*, based on the three-volume Hanser edition by Karl Schlechta (Munich: Hanser, 1967) 2: 70.

avowed enemy of anyone or anything which might compromise the physical or "metaphysical" welfare of the Burgundians.

Hagen enjoys a unique position at the Burgundian court among other things because of his wide knowledge of the world outside its immediate confines: "Dem sint kunt diu rîche und ouch diu vremden lant" (82,1). As his later encounter with the water sprites on the way to Etzel's camp illustrates, this knowledge extends to the Otherworld, not surprising given the connection Hagen has in Norse analogues to the world of lower mythology, his father having been an elf. He knows of Siegfried, and correctly surmises that the magnificent "recke" who appears in Worms in *Âventiure* 3 is none other than the legendary hero. For all of his "otherness," however, and his somewhat solitary nature — we have no reason to believe that Hagen enjoys any sort of "personal" life outside his relationship to the royal household; a wife and family are never mentioned in connection with him. Hagen is well integrated into Burgundian society and is fully aware and, for the most part, respectful of, the rules that govern the often delicate relationship to peers and superiors. Siegfried's arrival in Worms is not the occasion for unreserved rejoicing. Hagen recommends that he be accorded the appropriate reception, but the motivation behind his advice to Gunther in this respect may well betray more than understandable caution and prudence, namely, fear:

> "Wir suln den herren enpfâhen deste baz,
> daz wir iht verdienen des jungen recken haz.
> sîn lîp der ist sô küene, man sol in holden hân.
> er hât mit sîner krefte sô menegiu wunder getân."
> (101)

From the outset, that fear precludes any real possibility that Siegfried and Hagen might eventually develop a warriors' friendship. There is anxiety in Hagen's voice when he continues: "er stêt in der gebære, mich dunket, wizze Krist,/ez ensîn niht kleiniu mære, dar umb' er her geriten ist" (103,3–4). In four brief stanzas, Siegfried essentially justifies the anxiety that Hagen has hinted at, as he moves from recognition of the great "recken" associated with Worms, to its kings, his own status within society, and his intention to earn a name for himself by seizing Burgundian vassals and property. This confrontation, initiated by the intended "guest," sets the essential tone for the relationship which will evolve between Siegfried and the Burgundians. Although Hagen (along with Gernot) is reported as having countered Siegfried's claims in 114,4, it is not until stanza 121 that his words are actually recorded:

> Dô sprach der starke Hagene: "uns mac wol wesen leit,
> allen dînen degenen, daz er ie gereit
> durch strîten her ze Rîne; er soltez haben lân.
> im heten mîne herren sölher leide niht getân."

The reader notes that Hagen's words do not constitute a threat against Siegfried, that they are not indicative of an angry, indignant outburst, but are rather more a reflection of the anxiety he had earlier demonstrated when commenting on Siegfried's stature and reputation. Gunther had been somewhat dismayed over the relative silence demonstrated by his liegeman in the face of Siegfried's challenge (119,3: "daz der sô lange dagete, daz was dem künege leit"). Why had, in fact, Hagen not stepped forward? Why is it left to Ortwin, his nephew, to take up the gauntlet? This is not lost on Siegfried, who provokingly remarks: "War umbe bîtet Hagene und ouch Ortwîn,/daz er niht gâhet strîten mit den friwenden sîn" (125,1–2). Gernot apparently makes it clear to Hagen and Ortwin that they are not to respond to Siegfried's obvious provocation and it is he who extends, despite the latter's arrogance, a warm welcome to the hero. One wonders, however, precisely how Hagen would or could have responded, had Gernot not intervened. He is fully aware of Siegfried's near-invulnerability, and a clash of arms at this juncture could well leave not only himself and his nephew slain, but also the entire Burgundian royal family decimated. Consider Hagen's position; it has already been pointed out that Gunther is somewhat disappointed with his lack of action, he is openly challenged by Siegfried, but dare he move against him, even if not restrained by Gernot? Inasmuch as Hagen's *raison d'être* centers around his ability to protect and enhance the Burgundian monarchy, he cannot undertake a thing at this moment without the possibility that the devastating consequences alluded to above will become fact. That means, however, that he must suffer the indignity of leaving Siegfried's challenge unanswered, at least for now.

From the outset, Hagen is cast into an adversarial relationship with Siegfried that is not of his making, and forced to endure an outrage that cannot help but compromise both his individual sense of honor as well as the collective image of the court. Yet Siegfried possesses a remarkable talent for dissipating — on the surface — the understandable resentment he has undoubtedly evoked among the Burgundians present at this arrival scene, for the narrator comments in 129,4: "in sach vil lützel iemen, der im wære gehaz." To what extent we may take the litotes "vil lützel" to apply to everyone is, however, debatable. Hagen may slip temporarily into the background as Siegfried whiles away his time for a year at the Burgundian court hoping to catch a glimpse of Kriemhild, but this does not mean that he will have necessarily forgotten (or trivialized) the significance of Siegfried's initial appearance at Worms. Given the circumstances that prevail subsequent to Kriemhild's move to the land of the Huns, it is most likely that her brothers, at this point, adapt to Siegfried's presence at court to such an extent that they are able to repress the unpleasantries of the initial encounter. Hagen will not forget; when he asks Gunther, following the announcement of the approaching war with the Saxons and the Danes, "wan muget irz Sîvride sagen" (151,4b), it is completely in accord with the role of the competent royal advisor. On another level, however, it is just as feasible to see Hagen's "advice" as calculated to place Siegfried, at least on the surface, into the role of someone serving Worms, in compensation for the manner in which the Burgundians have been relegated into second-power status by his overbearing, if youthful, "naturalness." Stanza 331 (Hagen's suggestion that Siegfried be engaged for the wooing mission to Iceland) and 532 (Hagen's urging of Gunther to have Siegfried take the message to Worms that they are returning with Brünhild) provide further evidence of a manipulative, perhaps compensatory, effort by Hagen to have Siegfried not only serve Worms but also be controlled by what he, Hagen, has recommended. Once again, we are dealing with different levels of motivation and purpose.

Hagen has not actively contemplated the death of Siegfried from the moment it became clear that he would always remain a potential threat to Burgundian power and prestige. It appears that as long as he can be contained or controlled, as in the above instances, Hagen, something of a medieval *Realpolitiker*, is content to let matters stand. The quarrel of the queens before the minster, however, precludes a continuation of such a policy. Containment is no longer an option. Nothing, up to that point, had approximated the damage done to Burgundian image, including Siegfried's arrogant behavior upon his arrival. The public suggestion that Gunther had been cuckolded by the upstart from Xanten is not something that can be repressed or for which some sort of compensation can be found. Yet, it provides — at Brünhild's urging — only the immediate impetus for the murder.

Highly revealing is Hagen's statement to the despairing Burgundian kings after the deed has been done:

> Dô sprach der grimme Hagene: "Jane weiz ich, waz ir kleit.
> ez hât nu allez ende unser sorge unt unser leit.
> wir vinden ir vil wênic, die getürren uns bestân.
> wol mich, deich sîner hêrschaft hân ze râte getân." (993)

Several things can be established from this statement: 1) Hagen feels no remorse about having killed Siegfried and is somewhat chagrined over the fact that the kings do; 2) he appears to believe, paradoxically, that all of the worries and cares of the Burgundians are at an end — precisely what these are will need further elucidation; 3) the act of killing Siegfried brings with it enhanced political and military stature for the Burgundians for no one will dare challenge them now; 4) Hagen takes a considerable degree of personal satisfaction for having been the one to have put an end to Siegfried's *hêrschaft*. Precisely what Hagen means by "unser sorge unt unser leid" is not explained in any detail, although the obvious immediate reference would be to the sense of helplessness perceived by the Burgundians in the face of the dishonor done their court by Kriemhild's indiscretion in front of the minster. It is quite possible, likely, in fact, that the significance of the comment is much more far-reaching. There is a sense of relief that is conveyed by 993,2 and underscored by the presence of "allez." From Hagen's perspective, the Burgundians have long suffered under Siegfried's *hêrschaft*, his overbearing demeanor, unpredictability, his thoughtlessness, recklessness, his *übermuot*. But Hagen uses the first person plural in his comment and the reader/listener can be sure that while his murder, in Hagen's view, ought to remove the collective anxiety created by his very presence, Hagen himself is relieved to be rid of the man who, on numerous occasions, has cast him into the shadows and relegated him (and his king, in fact, if not in theory) to secondary status. It is thus quite understandable that Hagen immediately follows this comment with an assertion of new-found (or restored?) Burgundian (military/political) power. Particularly revealing is the emphasis he places on the fact that it was *he* who has put an end to the hero's *hêrschaft*, a term which has a range of meaning extending from "dominion, control, power" to "pride, arrogance."[32] It is one of the few instances in the *Nibelungenlied* when we are afforded some insight into Hagen's innermost feelings.

While the argument can be made that Hagen's killing of Siegfried was ultimately a necessity for society as a whole, the immediate consequence of his death is a sense of re-established *individual* and *collective* power, but this is viewed almost exclusively from Hagen's vantage point. His words in stanza 993 are, of course, remarkably ironic: the real troubles of the Burgundians are only about to begin. While it is questionable whether a true reconciliation with Kriemhild could ever have been effected without some action being taken against Hagen, the unchecked inflationary stance of the latter following Siegfried's death, together with the fact that no one of stature steps forward to champion her cause, contributes directly to the queen's increased isolation from her family (irrespective of her decision to remain in Worms rather than journey back to Xanten to raise her son) and distance from courtly norms.

[32] See Matthias Lexer, *Mittelhochdeutsches Handwörterbuch*, 3 vols. (1872; rpt. Stuttgart: Hirzel, 1974) 1: cols. 1261–1262. Hagen's remark in 993,4 is reminiscent of the biting comment made by Siegfried to Brünhild in 474,1–3 following his victory over her in Island.

Hagen makes it quite clear from the outset that he is unconcerned about Kriemhild's reaction: "ez ahtet mich vil ringe, swaz si weinens getuot" (1001,4), but he goes further and takes deliberate steps to intensify her suffering. The narrator states succinctly the motivation for Hagen's provocation of Siegfried's widow: "Von grôzer übermüete muget ir hœren sagen,/und von eislîcher râche" (1003,1–2a). Kriemhild is targeted by Hagen not only for the manner in which she compromised Burgundian honor in her confrontation with Brünhild. Hagen has clearly not forgotten the (as he must view it, reckless and provocative) way in which, in total disregard for a long-standing and virtually sacrosanct tradition, Kriemhild expressed her wish that he, along with Ortwin and various other knights from Worms, return with her to Siegfried's homeland (note 697–699). Once again, we have a "transgression" on two levels, the individual and the collective. From the moment she had become Siegfried's spouse, Kriemhild had turned her back on the interests of Worms and demonstrated abject callousness towards Hagen's pivotal role as chief counselor to the Burgundians. Where wisdom is called for, Hagen now allows a psychological need for revenge to prevail. Nor is the act done openly, but rather: "Er hiez in tougenlîchen legen an die tür" (1004,1), although one wonders why he bothers, for it is certainly clear to Kriemhild who has been behind the act: "ez hât gerâten Prünhilt, daz ez hât Hagene getân" (1010,4).

It is, of course, the Hagen-Kriemhild dichotomy/antagonism which has particularly fascinated generations of scholars. From the moment of Siegfried's murder, the epic appears to revolve around the two of them, even if they themselves are frequently relegated to the background. From a psychological point of view, it can be asserted that Hagen remains relatively consistent, static, throughout the plot; we at no time can discern a change in personality or in motivation, irrespective of the lack of wisdom we may ascribe to some of his actions or advice given the Burgundians. He is, as ever, committed to the physical and spiritual welfare of Worms. On occasion, he may also demonstrate an (understandable) degree of self-interest, as in his initial, negative reaction to the invitation from Etzel and Kriemhild to the Burgundians to visit the Hunnish court, but there can never be any doubt that his top priority remains his resolve to serve Worms, even to the point of insuring that they die with honor.

In this highly personal feud, Kriemhild may also be seen as adhering consistently to her principles (regardless of whether or not they fly in the face of the accepted norms of a basically warrior-oriented society), certainly as much as is the case with Hagen. If the latter is concerned with preservation (of Burgundian power, prestige, but above all, honor), Kriemhild's focus is on restoration of those things of which she has been deprived: honor, power, the *hort* (which has frequently been seen as symbolic of Siegfried himself). In both instances, the respective goals are to be achieved at any price. Hagen leads the entire Burgundian warrior class along with his kings into a foretold death, and he certainly knows that this is their fate once the chaplain has survived his attempt to drown him. Kriemhild is just as prepared to sacrifice any and all, including her son Ortlieb, to the realization of her aim. If we adhere to ms. B in our interpretation of the work, it seems that the poet/narrator's sentiments towards the conclusion of the tale lie squarely with Hagen and the Burgundians, even if he includes references to their "übermuot" in refusing to let Etzel know the true state of affairs. Yet his voice is not the only one that must be noted in this regard. The scribe of ms. C was most certainly at pains to avoid any "demonization" of Kriemhild such as we experience in B, while the author of the *Nibelungenklage* went so far as to insist that Kriemhild's place in heaven is assured, given the loyalty she has demonstrated towards Siegfried: "sît si durch triuwe tôt gelac,/in gotes hulden manegen tac/sol si ze himele noch geleben."[33] Opinions on Kriemhild's behavior were undoubtedly quite diverse in the early thirteenth century, with some contemporaries basing their judgment on the queen's association with the devil (note 1394,1–2: "Ich wæne der übel vâlant Kriemhilde daz geriet,/daz sie sich mit friuntschefte von *Gunthere* schiet"), and, from their perspective, her own "transformation" into a "vâlandinne" (as proclaimed by both Dietrich [1748,4a] and Hagen [2371,4a]), in complete conformity with a traditional patriarchal stance towards the appropriate role of the female in feudal society. Others, however (and they were most likely males), laid the blame for the cataclysm squarely at Hagen's door (and to a lesser degree at Gunther's) and, while not repressing the extent to which Kriemhild was clearly ready to achieve her aim, demonstrated sympathy with the situation in which she found herself, condemned the injustices done her — the murder of Siegfried and the theft of the *hort* — and were even prepared to express admiration for her absolute adherence to the principle of loyalty.

There is a noteworthy difference between Hagen and Kriemhild with respect to their psychological states as manifested in the second half of the *Nibelungenlied* and it is here that we return to the thesis propounded by Walter Haug. Whereas Hagen is decidedly overt in his actions from the time that he steals the *hort* on, Kriemhild's are patently covert. Her machinations, as Haug as pointed out, do not simply constitute the often laudable trait of *list*, but rather serve to underscore a basic transformation of her personality. While the medieval narrator has ascribed the latter in pre-psychological terms to the workings of the devil, the post-Freudian, Jungian literary critic might suggest that Kriemhild has succumbed to the *animus* or the *shadow*. As

[33] Karl Bartsch, ed., *Diu Klage mit den Lesarten sämtlicher Handschriften* (1875; rpt. Darmstadt: Wissenschaftliche Buchgesellschaft, 1964) vv. 571–573.

autonomous archetypes, both have, in fact, something in common with the earlier concept of Satan. Kriemhild's re-ascent to a position of power as the spouse of Etzel does not function as a compensatory balance for the inner turmoil and fury she has nurtured since the murder of Siegfried and which she is not always successful in concealing, as Dietrich's comments to the Burgundians upon their arrival in the land of the Huns would indicate: "Kriemhilt noch sêre weinet den helt von Nibelunge lant" (1724,4); "ich hœre alle morgen weinen unde klagen/mit jâmerlîchen sinnen daz Etzelen wîp" (1730,2–3).[34] Rather, it serves solely to allow the shadow greater control over her psyche. Thus, while Kriemhild may still symbolize a new beginning for Etzel and the Huns, in reality her nurturing, mothering, "feminine" side has been completely subsumed beneath the aggressive aims of the *animus/shadow*. Nowhere is this more in evidence than in her apparently complete lack of grief over Hagen's decapitation of her son Ortlieb (the second offspring on whom she has turned her back), whose head lands in her lap (1961,3). External and internal features no longer correspond, whereas with Hagen they could not be in greater accord as the epic moves inexorably towards the final debacle.

The scenes of confrontation between Hagen and Kriemhild following the arrival of the Burgundians at Gran are masterpieces of dramatic technique. While Kriemhild may greet (only) Giselher with a kiss, the welcome is done "mit valschem muote" (1737,2b). There is nothing "false," however, about Hagen's retort to Kriemhild's query regarding the status of the *hort*: "Jâ bringe ich iu den tiuvel" (1744,1a) which is followed up by a specific reference to his sword, none other than Siegfried's Balmung: "daz swert an mîner hende des enbringe ich iu nieht" (1744,4). Kriemhild's request that all weapons be handed over to her is also rejected outright — by Hagen, not by Gunther or any of the other kings. They have yet to speak. What is most intriguing about this scene is one comment by the narrator that would indicate Kriemhild's conscious awareness that her plans for revenge are not

[34] The pattern-like quality of this lamenting underscored by Dietrich's reference to "alle morgen" makes it virtually inconceivable to believe that Etzel is not aware of his wife's state of mind. One has the impression, however, that Etzel is given to repressing the obvious, whether it is the state of Kriemhild's psyche, the significance of Volker's slaying of the garish Hun, the appearance of the Burgundians at his court in full armor, or even the biting comment by Hagen concerning Ortlieb's (lack of a) future. He is not alone in this respect. The Burgundians themselves, with the notable exception of Hagen, fail to read — or simply deny — any of the signs of their impending doom, demonstrate remarkable lack of intuition with regard to the motivations of their sister, and, even when informed by Hagen that they will not return from the land of the Huns, appear to repress this information as they continue on to Bechelaren and Gran. How else can one explain their obvious joy over the betrothal of Rüdiger's daughter to Giselher?

within the parameters of acceptable behavior towards guests. When Dietrich publicly refers to her as a "vâlandinne" (1749,4a), she feels such shame that, speechless, she has no recourse but to retreat: "Des schamte sich vil sêre daz Etzelen wîp" (1749,1). Kriemhild still retains awareness of what is right and what is no longer within the framework of accepted, courtly behavior, but the sparring between herself and Hagen creates its own dynamic which will eventually occasion the deaths of tens of thousands. The poet proceeds quite rapidly to the next encounter, the scene before Kriemhild's palace, to which only Hagen and Volker advance ("Noch liezen si die herren ûf dem hove stân," 1760,1) and where they sit down on a bench in full view of Kriemhild's window. This is deliberate provocation on Hagen's part, which is further intensified by his refusal to stand up in her presence, electing instead to remain seated with Siegfried's sword placed across his lap. The narrator himself suggests that this was done precisely by Hagen to cause her distress: "... weinen si began/ich wæne, ez hete dar umbe der küene Hagene getân," 1784,3b–4). While this may be attributed to "übermüete" (note 1783,1a), it can simultaneously be regarded as testimony to Hagen's "inner" sovereignty, for we should not forget that he *knows* full well that neither he nor the others will ever leave here alive. He openly admits that he killed Siegfried and associates this directly with Kriemhild's insulting of Brünhild (1790, 3–4). All of this transpires before some assembled Huns, who quickly recognize that it is suicidal to attack Hagen and Volker and whose withdrawal causes Kriemhild even greater grief (1799,2).

What we witness here is Hagen in relative control, not only of the Burgundians, whom he has served as *de facto* leader on the journey to the land of the Huns, but also, if temporarily, of the situation in Gran, Kriemhild's "home ground," so to speak. It is not correct to suggest that Hagen no longer has anything to lose. His honor and his sense of (inner) sovereignty are to him paramount and in the current situation — he realizes he has absolutely no control over its (external, physical) outcome — both can only be maintained by refusing to concede to Kriemhild on a single point. Once again, power is at the heart of it all, albeit for Hagen now internalized, as the Burgundians do not have a chance of emerging victorious in a conflict against the Huns. In this respect, one might well maintain that he ultimately proves victorious over Kriemhild at the conclusion of the epic, yet the reaction of Etzel to his death would indicate that externally, at least, from the perspective of the male survivors of the catastrophe, his demise was less than "honorable":

> "Wâfen", sprach der fürste, "wie ist nu tôt gelegen
> von eines wîbes handen der aller beste degen,
> der ie kom ze sturme oder ie schilt getruoc!
> swie vîent ich im wære, ez ist mir leide genuoc." (2374)

Walter Haug has declared that the *Nibelungenlied* is one of the most "modern" works of its time. It transcends contemporary expectations, dissolves the assumed uniformity between inner and outer (particularly in the person of Kriemhild, but also with regard to the epic as a whole), depicts a world in which forces that fester below the surface are decisive and it is the latter which ultimately determine man's fate. In this respect, the dreams of the *Nibelungenlied* should be accorded the highest significance, not for the transformative influence they have on individuals — too often their meaning(s) are repressed by the recipients of the dream-material — but for the manner in which they herald a rather black future involving the demise of both individuals and societies. Understood and acted upon, the dream can effect a positive transformation on various levels. Repressed or ignored, it may remain simply the harbinger of catastrophe.

*

The transformative power of the dream, in this instance, a dream based on the Nibelungen theme, can be demonstrated for the father of analytical psychology himself, Carl Gustav Jung. On December 18, 1913, less than a year prior to the outbreak of World War I, Jung had a dream, subsequently recorded, in which, together with the assistance of a "brown-skinned man, a savage," he killed the approaching hero, Siegfried.[35] Jung, convinced that the latter must die, shoots Siegfried with a rifle as the latter rushes down the side of a mountain in a chariot that has been fashioned from the bones of the dead. Given Siegfried's standing (at the time) as a relatively unproblematic hero in the German-speaking regions of Europe, Jung's killing of him understandably appalled him in his dream and caused him concern over the possibility of discovery. This was alleviated somewhat by a heavy downpour which Jung believed would eradicate any traces of the "crime" he had committed. His guilt, however, was not purged. Jung provided his own interpretation of the dream, which is worth noting:

> When I awoke from the dream, I turned it over in my mind, but was unable to understand it. I tried therefore to fall asleep again, but a voice within me said: "You *must* understand the dream, and must do so at once!" The inner urgency mounted until the terrible moment came when the voice said, "If you do not understand the dream, you must shoot yourself!" In the drawer of my night table lay a loaded revolver, and I became frightened. Then I began pondering once again, and suddenly the meaning of the dream dawned on me. "Why, that is the problem that is being played out in the

[35] Carl Gustav Jung, *Memories, Dreams, Reflections*, recorded and edited by Aniela Jaffé, rev. ed., trans. Richard and Clara Winston (New York: Vintage Books, 1965) 180.

> world." Siegfried, I thought, represents what the Germans want to achieve, heroically to impose their will, have their own way.... I had wanted to do the same. But now that was no longer possible. The dream showed that the attitude embodied by Siegfried, the hero, no longer suited me. Therefore it had to be killed.[36]

Jung's interpretation of his Siegfried dream as recorded in this biography requires, however, some augmentation. The year 1913 was one of crisis for Jung. It was the year in which he broke with Freud, gave up his professorship at the University of Zurich, and toyed with the idea of suicide. David Rosen provides some of the "missing pieces":

> [O]n December 18, 1913, Jung went through a suicidal crisis and underwent what I would call "egocide." ... Jung dreamed that he teamed up with a dark-skinned savage and they shot and killed Siegfried.... Jung tells that he was frightened because in the drawer of his night table lay a loaded revolver. Fortunately for him, and us, Jung committed egocide, not suicide.... Jung and his "primitive shadow" psychically murdered this negative side of Jung's ego-image and identity. Of course, Siegfried also sounds like Sigmund, which affirms that this is a killing of the heretofore dominant Freudian ego-image or Jung's *false self*.[37]

The interpretations offered by both Rosen and Stevens are convincing, but Jung's dream is also significant in another way. Siegfried had to be killed, yet the killing evoked a sense of revulsion in the killer. In the *Nibelungenlied* there can be little doubt that, apart from the relief, perhaps even enthusiasm shown by Hagen after committing the murder, there is, to be sure, little joy among anyone else over what has transpired (note, in particular, 991–992). Yet there is the unstated "understanding" on the part of the Burgundian royal family (and perhaps, in the wake of the killing, by figures such as Dietrich and Rüdiger) that it had to be done. Jung could no longer accept

[36] Jung 180.

[37] David Rosen, *The Tao of Jung. The Way of Integrity* (Arkana: Penguin, 1997) 65–66. See also 4–5. Note as well Anthony Stevens, *Private Myths. Dreams and Dreaming* (Cambridge, MA: Harvard University Press, 1995) 124: "... Jung omits to say that it also represented what Freud wanted to achieve — heroically to impose *his* will, have *his* own way. And now *that* was no longer possible. In this dream, Jung is finally sacrificing Freud as his heroic role model and replacing him by a willingness to undertake his own descent into the underworld.... Siegfried was thus a complex figure in which were condensed (1) the heroic mentor, Freud; (2) the young sun-god, the aged sun-god's 'Son and Heir' and 'Crown Prince'; and (3) a transcendent symbol capable of reconciling the differences between the two men. His death meant that Jung had finally put all that behind him and committed himself to his *own* process, the discovery of his own psychological truth."

Freud's dogma, particularly with respect to the sexual complex, and his rejection of the idea of the collective unconscious. Worms, and the rest of the courtly world, would likewise have been hard pressed to tolerate further the unpredictability and (albeit naive) arrogance of Siegfried.

*

The contemporary literary scholar is hardly in a position to approach the *Nibelungenlied* and its major protagonists from a black-white viewpoint. Kriemhild will continue to have her detractors, but they will also concede that, even if transformed into a she-devil, she is not entirely to blame for the metamorphosis. Her defenders can hardly ignore the manner in which absolute adherence to her goal of revenge allows events to hurtle out of control. Siegfried will scarcely be seen at the turn of the third millennium as the apotheosis of a sun-god, a reflection of Baldr, or simply a decent, if naive, hero who makes some fatal errors of judgment. He has partaken of the Otherworld and the dragon's blood, and his inability to re-integrate himself fully into the mores and expectations of courtly society augurs ill for his own future as well as that of everyone else, particularly if his unpredictability and spontaneity are not kept in check.[38] He carries the seeds of chaos within him. He can be malicious, as when he unnecessarily chides Brünhild for having lost in Island, consciously or subconsciously demonstrating at the same time the pride he takes in having been the one to defeat her at her own game. His lack of foresight and his arrogance in retiring from Gunther's bedchamber with his "booty" prove the catalyst for his ultimate demise. Hagen will most assuredly avoid nowadays the unequivocal condemnation he suffered at the hands of the poet of the *Klage*. In the earlier part of this century he served in Germany either as a symbol of treachery — after World War I — while he was later depicted, during World War II, as the quintessence of bravery, loyalty, and honor. Gunther may continue to experience a "bad press" as a weak king in the medieval tradition, but he will also have his advocates who can point to his laudable (if fruitless) efforts to maintain stability in a highly precarious and finely-balanced world and who, when combat became inevitable, certainly gave an excellent account of himself from the perspective of the warrior ethics prevalent at the time. Much the same thing could be said of Etzel, as it could of Rüdiger, Dietrich, Gernot, and Giselher. In short,

[38] Something Gunther may well recognize and hence his hesitation to accede to Brünhild's request that her sister-in-law and her husband be invited to Worms, to which Gunther can offer only the lame reservation that Kriemhild and Siegfried live far away! Intriguingly, Siegfried offers the same excuse to Kriemhild, who is eager to take advantage of the invitation. Both men appear to "know" intuitively that it is best if these particular constellations are kept apart!

they are all — whether prominently profiled or of a more secondary nature — figures which defy a black-white categorization.

If one were to select a key term from the vocabulary of analytical psychology which pertains to characters, actions, motifs, and even the major theme of the *Nibelungenlied*, then this could certainly be repression, on the part of Siegfried with respect to his "otherness," which so often results in arrogant, reckless behavior; on the part of Kriemhild, who refuses to recognize the true significance of her public quarrel with Brünhild before the minster and later "buries" the fact that without her (albeit inadvertent) assistance, Siegfried would hardly have met his death. It also applies to the reception of dreams in the *Nibelungenlied*. Kriemhild "forgets" her initial dream and acts against what she realized (in 17,4) to be in her own best interests; Siegfried pays no attention whatsoever to the two dreams Kriemhild has had on the night before the hunt. The Burgundians, including (initially) Hagen, repress Ute's dream in which all the birds of the land were dead. Having crossed the Danube, the vast majority of the Burgundian force appears to put behind it rather quickly the confirmation from Hagen that they will not return alive from the land of the Huns; other than Hagen and Volker, none of them show any visible reaction to the information passed on by Dietrich upon their arrival that Kriemhild continues to mourn for her murdered Siegfried. Etzel never appears to acknowledge the unrelenting grief expressed by Kriemhild for her first husband.[39] Both Etzel and Kriemhild — although the former is visibly shaken — remain inactive following Hagen's prophecy that their son Ortlieb does not appear long for this world (1918, 3–4). These are only some of the more poignant instances of repression within the work. But it is *not* apparent in the narrator/author of the epic, an individual who never falls into the trap of assuming a correlation between the "inner" and the "outer," but who is rather constantly aware, and reminds his audience of the fact, that "Sein" and "Schein" are not in accord with one another.

But what of the epic *Nibelungenlied* as a whole? In his own right the poet was — in thirteenth-century terms — a highly astute *Menschenkenner*, whose characters may well have mirrored actual historical personalities, but who certainly, in several instances, transcended the image of typical, fictionalized kings, queens, margraves, and vassals to become individualized personalities designed to impart the entire range of human emotions. Yet the *Nibelungenlied* does not give up conclusively any of its secrets with regard to authorial intentionality. It is left to the reader to decide. Certainly it may be contended

[39] This was not lost, however, on Fritz Lang, whose portrayal of Etzel in his film, *Kriemhilds Rache*, was that of a ruler fully aware of the inability of his spouse to put the past behind her and to turn to the future.

that the "message" of 2378,4: "als ie diu liebe leide z'aller jungeste gît" (which harks back to Kriemhild's words in 17,3: "wie liebe mit leide ze jungest lônen kan," albeit in this earlier reference pertaining specifically to the relationship of women to men) constitutes the major thrust of the epic, a philosophical (and psychological) countering of the cyclical structures of courtly romances with their happy endings and emphasis on continuity. Perhaps it was intended as a lesson for rulers, in specific or in general, that the reins of power must be grasped tightly, that kings must be kings in fact as well as in name. The antagonistic relationship between the feminine and the masculine is amply attested to throughout the work, whether in the wooing of Brünhild in Island (note Siegfried's biting remark to Brünhild in 474,1a, 3: "Sô wol mich dirre mære ... daz iemen lebet, der iuwer meister müge sîn"), the unacceptable idea that occurs to Siegfried during his wrestling match with Brünhild, that, should he lose, all women ("elliu wîp") would become arrogant ("tragen gelpfen muot") towards their spouses (673), or in the drastic reaction of both Etzel and Hildebrand (as well, we may assume, as Dietrich and any other warriors of stature who have not been killed in the preceding slaughter) to the death of a defenseless Hagen by the hand of a woman (2373ff.). Yet it does not culminate in any programmatic declaration of the "proper" place of the sexes within society. As we have witnessed from both the manuscript tradition as well as the appended *Klage*, Kriemhild was most assuredly not without her sympathizers in the thirteenth century.

Finally, we may also have in this anonymous author a cynic, even a nihilist, who was highly influenced by the tragic lays of the past and who (in contrast to the authors of the romances of the period) felt no need to temper the "message" of irrevocable fate through a vision of a better world to come. Even if we can believe that his audience of eight hundred years ago was intended to recognize the "model" comportment and virtuous bearing of those facing their doom — something which more modern audiences have, in fact, also done throughout the past two hundred years — this poet ultimately concentrated squarely on one particular archetype: the "shadow" side of man and his proclivity to destruction.

James McGlathery

Erotic Passion in the *Nibelungenlied* and Wagner's *Ring des Nibelungen*

The *Nibelungenlied*, in literature, and Richard Wagner's *Ring des Nibelungen*, in music, represent two renowned German cultural monuments. Perhaps for that reason, scholarly critics have accorded a relatively minor place to erotic passion as the motivating force in either of these great classics. The madness to which love proverbially leads is readily thought to be rather more a fit subject for comedy than tragedy, for humorous as opposed to serious depiction. The widespread tendency has been to treasure the *Nibelungenlied* as reflecting the glories of a largely no longer extant heroic poetry of the Germanic peoples and Wagner's *Ring* operas as a modern-day recovery of and tribute to the spirit of an heroic past, each adapted and recast to address the needs of a new age. To look on the medieval epic poem and the modern operatic treatment of related material as mere love stories, much less as depictions of erotic passion per se, would, in the eyes of most, diminish their stature and importance as cultural icons. We do no honor to a great classic, though, by failing to understand it, to grasp what is central to the portrayal, what is the focus of the depiction. Unquestionably, the *Nibelungenlied* tells us a great deal about the society of its time and undoubtedly also contains elements dating from an earlier Germanic past; and Wagner's *Ring* certainly involves an attempt to draw on stories from the Germanic past for current cultural, social, and political purposes, at least in the early conceptions of the work. Here it will be argued, however, that the chief driving force in the action of both the epic and the operatic tetralogy is indeed none other than erotic passion, a focus that may have rendered the *Nibelungenlied*, among Wagner's various sources, decisive for the *Ring's* focus in the text that Wagner ultimately set to music. (In his essay on the *Nibelungenlied* and the *Ring*, Wapnewski focuses on influences of the epic on Wagner, but does not deal with matters of interpretation much less with the role of erotic passion in the two works.)[1]

[1] Peter Wapnewski, "Siegfried im Spiel der Götter, oder Wasser und Gold: Zur Nutzung und Verwandlung des Nibelungenliedes durch Richard Wagner," in Hansgerd Schulte, ed., *Spiele und Vorspiele: Spielelemente in Literatur, Wissenschaft und Philosophie. Eine Sammlung von Aufsätzen aus Anlaß des 70. Geburtstages von Pierre Bertaux*, Suhrkamp

The relative lack of attention paid to the role of erotic passion as such in the *Nibelungenlied* is owing partly to the moralistic approach characteristic of much criticism on the work. McConnell faults Kriemhild for abandoning her son out of grief over her husband's death: "... by rejecting her son, Kriemhild has symbolically turned her back on the concept of a productive (and consoling) future; she has, in essence, lapsed into a type of nihilism."[2] Mowatt and Sacker criticize her for "a preoccupation with domination and power and a (typically Burgundian) inability to act openly and directly."[3] Kuhn complains about her seeming greed in worrying about recovery of her Nibelung treasure and in sacrificing her brother to try and get it when she is supposed to be preoccupied with gaining revenge for the murder of her beloved husband Siegfried.[4] Curschmann agrees that in the last analysis Kriemhild is portrayed negatively.[5] Haymes does give surrender to erotic passion its due, but only as a moral flaw: "Siegfried is led astray by the power of *minne* and he eventually dies because of his error."[6] Mahlendorf and Tobin find the work's theme to be "law and form being denied its rightful place."[7] Bekker believes that the poet's intent was "to depict the world of the *Nibelungenlied* as dedicated to the principles of would-be order, peace and harmony."[8] And in a similarly moralistic vein, Gentry concludes that

> unlike the romances in which the individual is set apart from his society and achieves his own higher, more intimate calling, the individual in the *Nibelungenlied* is seen as an integral part of his society. And for that society to function, to be considered a just and moral organization, it is the duty of

Taschenbuch 485 (Frankfurt a. M.: Suhrkamp, 1978) 99–122.

[2] Winder McConnell, *The Nibelungenlied*, Twayne's World Authors Series 712 (Boston: Twayne, 1984) 18.

[3] D. G. Mowatt and Hugh Sacker, *The Nibelungenlied. An Interpretative Commentary* (Toronto: University of Toronto Press, 1967) 14–15.

[4] Hans Kuhn, "Der Teufel im Niblungenlied [sic]: Zu Gunthers und Kriemhilds Tod," *ZfdA* 94 (1965): 294.

[5] Michael Curschmann, "Zur Wechselwirkung von Literatur und Sage: Das 'Buch von Kriemhild' und Dietrich von Bern," *PBB* 111 (1989): 396.

[6] Edward R. Haymes, *The Nibelungenlied. History and Interpretation*, Illinois Medieval Monographs 2 (Urbana and Chicago: University of Illinois Press, 1986) 103.

[7] Ursula R. Mahlendorf and Frank J. Tobin, "Legality and Formality in the *Nibelungenlied*," *Monatshefte* 66 (1974): 237.

[8] Hugo Bekker, "The Nibelungenlied: Rüdeger von Bechlaren and Dietrich von Bern," *Monatshefte* 66 (1974): 239.

each member to behave in a moral and responsible manner, not merely for his own good but for that of society as a whole.[9]

Another main line of inquiry about the *Nibelungenlied* concerns the extent to which it derives from the tradition of heroic epic. Much of this criticism has revolved recently around the figure of Siegfried's murderer, Hagen. Thus, for Krausse the issue is how Hagen can be portrayed so negatively in his assassination of Siegfried in the epic's first part, then so positively as Kriemhild's victim in the second and concluding part, Krausse's answer being that in the sources for the *Nibelungenlied* Hagen must originally have been a hero as he is in part two.[10] Haymes, indeed, sees Hagen, not Kriemhild, as the focus of poetic interest, as exemplified by his "heroic defiance" of Kriemhild's demand of the return of her Nibelung treasure.[11] By contrast, Northcott argues against seeing Hagen as a hero even in part two: "[I]n the closing stages of the epic, Hagen is frequently placed by the poet in an unheroic 'posture' and ... the critics who suggest that he finally finds his warrior role at the end of the poem have overlooked a number of salient points."[12] And Wailes, in viewing the poem as heroic epic, finds unsatisfactory the explanation that the inclusion of the episode of the Saxon war "shows Siegfried ingratiating himself with the Burgundians in order to bring closer to reality his dream of marrying Kriemhild."[13]

Aside from continuing moralistic views about the *Nibelungenlied* or about its stature as heroic epic evidenced above, the feminist approach of the past several decades, too, has been uninterested in erotic passion as the action's driving force. Anderson is happy to find that

[i]n comparison to the women in the works of Hartmann, Gottfried, Wolfram, and the poems of the minnesingers, where women are generally

[9] Francis G. Gentry, "Hagen and the Problem of Individuality in the Nibelungenlied," *Monatshefte* 68 (1976): 11.

[10] Helmut K. Krausse, "Die Darstellung von Siegfrieds Tod und die Entwicklung des Hagenbildes in der Nibelungendichtung," *GRM* 21 (1971): 370–378.

[11] Edward R. Haymes, "A Rhetorical Reading of the 'Hortforderungsszene' in the Nibelungenlied," in Werner Wunderlich and Ulrich Müller, eds., *'Waz sider da geschah': American-German Studies on the Nibelungenlied. With Bibliography 1980–1990/91*, GAG 564 (Göppingen: Kümmerle, 1992) 86.

[12] Kenneth J. Northcott, "Actions and Reputations in the Nibelungenlied," in *Medieval German Studies [Festschrift for Frederick Norman]* (London: University of London Institute for Germanic Studies, 1965) 117.

[13] Stephen L. Wailes, "The Nibelungenlied as Heroic Epic," in Felix J. Oinas, ed., *Heroic Epic and Saga: An Introduction to the World's Great Folk Epics* (Bloomington and London: Indiana University Press, 1978) 126–127.

> portrayed as passively waiting for things to happen to them, Kriemhild consistently acts upon her own initiative, regardless of the cost.... What fascinates and horrifies the poet simultaneously is her obstinate will to defy society and take charge of her life.[14]

Wynn considers Kriemhild to be focused ultimately on power as exemplified by her reaction to Hagen's taunting her with Siegfried's sword: "[I]t is in fact the insignum of Sifrit's power which here opposes her insignum of power, namely the Hunnish crown on her head, that makes this scene into one of unbearable and heartrending humiliation for Kriemhilt."[15] Washington and Tobol, too, see Kriemhild as striving to be "empowered":

> Daughters seeking personal power evidently have ancient roots in Kriemhild and Clytemnestra, who both first tried the passive resistance patterns of their mothers in a restrictive environment.... Their violence carries a warning of the disaster which threatens those who frustrate the need for total fulfillment found only in the full range of the positive female potential.[16]

Newman, meanwhile, is not concerned with Brünhild's physical attraction to Siegfried, but instead with the question of whether

> social considerations played the major role in the author's depiction of Brünhild at Worms. Brünhild, as she is depicted in Islant, must indeed become *verhöflicht*; otherwise, she would appear to the Burgundian court, and to the poet's audience as well, as a monster, outside of the bounds of accepted female behavior.[17]

Nelson's focus is that the women in the *Nibelungenlied* "must lend — actually give — their bodies in the service of patriarchal political and economic sovereignty."[18] And Classen argues that this taming of Brünhild

[14] Philip N. Anderson, "Kriemhild's Quest," *Euphorion* 79 (1985): 5.

[15] Marianne Wynn, "Hagen's Defiance of Kriemhilt," in *Medieval German Studies [Festschrift for Frederick Norman]* 112.

[16] Ida H. Washington and Carol E. Washington Tobol, "Kriemhild and Clytemnestra: Sisters in Crime or Independent Women?" in Cathy N. Davidson and E. M. Broner, eds., *The Lost Tradition: Mothers and Daughters in Literature* (New York: Ungar, 1980) 20.

[17] Gail Newman, "Two Brunhilds?" *AbäG* 29 (1989): 76.

[18] Charles G. Nelson, "Virginity (De)Valued: Kriemhild, Brünhild, and All That," in Wunderlich/Müller 127.

reflected "a disastrous development for women at the end of the archaic age and/or at the beginning of historical time."[19]

Other critics have not ignored the role of erotic passion in the *Nibelungenlied*, yet they have not been entirely willing to give it its due. Wailes argues that the poet did indeed have free choice about including the scene in which Siegfried subdues Brünhild for Gunther but views it simply as episodic "bedroom comedy" not in relation to an omnipresent erotic theme.[20] Krausse sees Kriemhild as motivated by a love that has more to do with faithfulness than sexual passion.[21] Similarly, Ehrismann argues that the poem is about love as marital love and as such a criticism of love as depicted in the courtly epics.[22] Andersson, too, finds the point to be "marital fidelity of the sort encouraged by ecclesiastical emphasis on the permanent union of hearts."[23] Thelen sees Brünhild and Kriemhild as motivated not by erotic passion but by a need "to resolve their inner turmoil and to learn the truth."[24] Schottmann argues that Brünhild is not outraged because Siegfried deceptively subdued her for Gunther, but because Kriemhild's rebuke of her as Siegfried's "concubine" is made publicly.[25] Boehringer is interested in the issue of power, the role of sexual desire in Kriemhild's persuading her second husband King Etzel to do her bidding: "Kriemhild's complete control of Etzel's power is necessary if she is to carry out her revenge. Without the 'Eros-factor,' such complete dominion would be difficult to justify."[26] In his monograph on the figure Rüdiger von Bechelaren, who courts Kriemhild for Etzel, Splett notes Rüdiger's recommendation of Kriemhild to Etzel for her

[19] Albrecht Classen, "The Defeat of the Matriarch Brünhild in the *Nibelungenlied*, with Some thoughts on Matriarchy as Evinced in Literary Texts," in Wunderlich/Müller 110.

[20] Stephen L. Wailes, "Bedroom Comedy in the Nibelungenlied," *MLQ* 32 (1971): 366.

[21] Helmut K. Krausse, "Die Darstellung des Todes im Nibelungenlied," *Neophilologus* 61 (1977): 254.

[22] Otfrid Ehrismann, "Siegfrieds Ankunft in Worms: Zur Bedeutung der dritten Aventiure des Nibelungenlieds," in Günter Bellmann, Günter Eifler, and Wolfgang Kleiber, eds., *Festschrift für Karl Bischoff zum 70. Geburtstag* (Vienna: Böhlau, 1975) 353–355.

[23] Theodore M. Andersson, *A Preface to the Nibelungenlied* (Stanford: Stanford University Press, 1987) 166.

[24] Lynn D. Thelen, "The Vassalage Deception, or Siegfried's Folly," *JEGP* 87 (1988): 481.

[25] Hans Schottmann, "Der Streit der Königinnen," in Helmut Rücker und Kurt Otto Seidel, eds., *'Sagen mit Sinne': Festschrift für Marie-Luise Dittrich zum 65. Geburtstag*, GAG 180 (Göppingen: Kümmerle, 1976) 152.

[26] Michael Boehringer, "Sex and Politics?: Etzel's Role in the Nibelungenlied: A Narratological Approach," in Wunderlich/Müller 163.

incomparable beauty, but does not see that praise in the context of a pervasive theme of erotic passion.[27]

The presentation offered here is in essential agreement with Nagel, who appears to have remained alone among critics in judging the poem to be about erotic passion or "minne," terming the work the "novel of a love" ("Roman einer Liebe").[28] Nagel's special interest is to view the *Nibelungelied* in the context of the portrayal of erotic passion in the lyric poems and epics of its time, in which courtly poets

> [e]inhellig verkünden ... daß Minne Macht bedeutet, Macht, gegen die Herz und Wille des Menschen nichts auszurichten vermögen, die beide, jung und alt, bezwinge und als Schicksalsgewalt das Leben bestimme.... Als die große Unruhestifterin der Welt, als die unwiderstehliche Nachstellerin der Herzen wird sie zugleich gepriesen und angeklagt.[29]

As we shall see, however, in the *Nibelungenlied* there is only the barest evidence of struggle against erotic passion on the part of the characters themselves; nor does the narrative voice appear to view surrender to that passion in a negative light. The poem would seem rather to be the celebration of a great erotic love.

While there is anything but universal agreement on the matter, a certain consensus now exists that Kriemhild is the *Nibelungenlied*'s central figure. As is easily recognized, the epic as we have it opens with our introduction to her and ends with her demise. More important, what we first see of her is evidence of her awakening adolescent desire to wed and we last see her in middle age finally able to accomplish the slaying of the murderer of her passionately adored first husband Siegfried.

The case with Siegfried, whose death before the halfway point of the epic disqualifies him as its central figure, is much the same. We first meet him as he is feeling the urge to wed and has become passionately devoted to the idea of making Kriemhild his bride, about whose great beauty he has heard much but whom he has not yet seen. It may be argued that everything Siegfried does henceforth right up to his murder by Hagen is motivated by his passion to win Kriemhild and to remain a hero worthy of her passion. We find the action driven, moreover, by a love triangle, if only of sorts. Siegfried and Kriemhild have eyes strictly for one another, though Siegfried is not blind to

[27] Jochen Splett, *Rüdiger von Bechelaren: Studien zum zweiten Teil des Nibelungenliedes* (Heidelberg: Winter, 1968) 44.

[28] Bert Nagel, *Das Nibelungenlied: Stoff — Form — Ethos* (Frankfurt a. M.: Hirschgraben, 1965) 186.

[29] Nagel 187.

Brünhild's exceptional beauty and appeal and indeed seems perhaps to have had some contact with her in the course of his earlier youthful adventures. Were Brünhild, meanwhile, ever to conceive a passion for a man, and surrender to it, that man would have to be Siegfried.

Our attention is directed to the matter of erotic desire immediately at the outset by young Kriemhild's report of her dream in which the strong, beautiful, and wild falcon she has trained is torn apart by two eagles (13).[30] Her mother, Queen Ute, interprets the dream for Kriemhild as meaning that she may lose the man she has won if God does not protect him. Kriemhild responds that she does not want to hear of marriage. The reason does not appear to be simply fear that she might lose the man she loved; she seems rather to associate preserving her beauty with refraining from marriage. Her mother, at any rate, appears to interpret her rejection of the idea of marrying as involving youthful virginal vanity, since she counters with the argument that a woman cannot be truly happy without a man's love and, indeed, a man's love will make her beautiful as well as happy. As we then hear, a number of years pass without young Kriemhild having found any man she wanted to marry.

We are thereupon introduced to Siegfried and made witness to the ceremony of his passage to knighthood (*Âventiure* II) and immediately thereafter (III) his passion to wed Kriemhild, the praise of whose beauty is on everyone's lips, but who is considered to be unattainable in view of the unsuccessful efforts of many suitors. Siegfried's parents, King Siegmund and Queen Sieglind of the Netherlands, moreover, do their best to dissuade him because of their dislike of the Burgundian court at Worms. Perhaps precisely because of his parents' warnings, Siegfried sets out determined to take the Burgundians' lands from them, presumably convinced by his father's attempt at dissuasion that any other approach would be to no avail in his passionate quest to make Kriemhild his bride. The same driving force, Siegfried's erotic passion, explains his ready acceptance of the terrified Burgundians' attempt to win him as an ally by according him the utmost in hospitality. What matters is winning Kriemhild. Now that he sees the possibility of winning her with her family's consent, instead of by defeating them in battle, he patiently waits for his chance to see and meet her, which comes only after he has been residing as a guest of the Burgundians for a whole year (138).

As Siegfried likely recognizes, his volunteering to lead the Burgundians into battle against the Saxons and Danes offers perhaps a chance for him to

[30] References to the *Nibelungenlied* in the text are based on *Das Nibelungenlied. Nach der Ausgabe von Karl Bartsch*, ed. Helmut de Boor, 18th ed., Deutsche Klassiker des Mittelalters (Wiesbaden: Brockhaus, 1965). *Âventiuren* are indicated by Roman numerals, stanzas by Arabic.

be introduced finally to Kriemhild. To be sure, it appears that Siegfried is content to go back to the Netherlands when the other warriors are returning home from the ensuing celebrations of the victory; but this apparent nonchalance may be feigned to help produce the desired result of being introduced to the woman of his dreams, as then happens.

What we have heard of Kriemhild in the meantime has to do with her same passion for Siegfried, from the very moment she spies him from afar (132–137). She appears not only to have eyes solely for him but to be fully and completely occupied with thoughts of him. She is unhappy whenever he rides off with her brothers and the other knights, she being thereby deprived of the opportunity to watch him from her windows. When messengers arrive in Worms to report to King Gunther about the course of the battle with the Saxons and Danes, Kriemhild bids one of them to a secret audience with her so that she can learn about the fate and deeds in battle of the hero she adores from afar and unbeknownst to him (224). Her passion for Siegfried can only be heightened by the messenger's account; virtually his whole report is devoted to Siegfried's great heroism. What matters most to her, though, is that Siegfried suffered no bodily harm in the battle (241). The moment Siegfried is then allowed to meet her, as a result of his great service to her family in defeating the Saxons and Danes, Kriemhild lets him see immediately that she is more than merely kindly disposed toward him (294). To Siegfried's great joy, and hers as well we can be sure, she is allowed to give him a kiss (297). And when they are then leaving the minster and Kriemhild speaks to him of his great deeds, it is clearly sweet music to her ears to hear him confess that he has done it all in order to gain her favor (304).

Siegfried's agreement to help King Gunther win the Icelandic princess Brünhild as his bride is made on the promise that if they are successful Kriemhild will be his (333). This ill-fated adventure, against which Siegfried at first strongly advises and which later leads to his death, is thus the product of his passionate desire to wed Kriemhild. The ill-fatedness of the adventure, however, is owing not least to Brünhild's strong attraction to Siegfried, to passion engendered by erotic desire. Whether or not there was a prehistory to this attraction, as seems hinted at (e.g., 411), Brünhild, like Kriemhild earlier, has eyes only for Siegfried once he appears on the scene in front of her castle. Indeed, even before she sees him but has heard that he may be one of the four men who has been spotted arriving, she assumes that it is he who has come to win her as his bride and quickly adds, perhaps only for the benefit of her ladies in waiting, that she is not so afraid of him that she would surrender without a fight (416). Although Brünhild appears to be a good sport on finding that it is Gunther instead who has come to woo her and on being defeated by him in the contests of strength to which she challenges him, once Kriemhild has become engaged to Siegfried, Brünhild's secret wish that she were his bride instead is indicated by the tears she sheds on seeing Kriemhild sitting next to him (618). To be sure, when asked by Gunther, her intended, why she is crying, she declares that it is because she hates to see Kriemhild wasting herself on a mere vassal of Gunther's, which Siegfried had pretended to be in helping Gunther win Brünhild by defeating her in the games with the aid of his magical coat that renders him invisible. Obviously, though, Brünhild can hardly confess to Gunther the actual reason for her tears, which is, we suspect, that she wishes she were marrying the "vassal" Siegfried instead of his supposed liege lord.

Whether Brünhild first conceived a passion for Siegfried merely by hearing of his godlike beauty and strength or only upon having seen him with her own eyes, her attraction to him is decidedly physical. He is the man of her dreams in that her tomboyish passion is to marry a terribly handsome man who is more than a match for her in tests of strength. In other words, she is the sort of proud virgin whose desire is to be conquered if she is to be wed at all. Her attraction to Siegfried indicates that she is attracted only to a man who might be able to fulfill that dream. Were Siegfried her bridegroom, as she appears secretly to wish, we can imagine that she might not simply have surrendered on the wedding night without a fight, even if her attraction to him made her feel compelled to do so; she would perhaps have tested his strength.

Gunther's physical appearance being no match for Siegfried's and being such as to make Brünhild wonder how he could ever have managed to muster the strength to defeat her in the contests at her castle, it is no surprise that she refuses to surrender to him in the bridal chamber, thereby testing his ability to subdue her physically (633–639). The ease with which Brünhild subdues and humiliates Gunther cannot help but make her wonder how he possibly could have defeated her in the earlier contests. That wonder must then be compounded by Gunther's seeming sudden recovery of that earlier strength in the bridal chamber the following night, when unbeknownst to her it is Siegfried in his invisible coat who again bests her in a test of strength (666–680).

No less than with Kriemhild, albeit in a more elementally physical way, Brünhild's yearning is to be possessed by a great hero like Siegfried and, he being incomparable, by him and no other. Ten years after the weddings, Brünhild remains upset that Kriemhild, not she, became his bride. To be sure, the question she constantly asks herself is how Kriemhild can carry her head so high when she is married — supposedly — to her husband Gunther's vassal (724). Yet this is surely to avoid the more painful question, "why her and not me?"

This nagging question that leaves Brünhild no peace is, of course, what drives her to want to see if Siegfried will indeed answer a summons to visit them as their vassal. Perhaps her aim is simply to humiliate Kriemhild by having Siegfried fulfill the role of vassal; or perhaps she doubts the truth of the claim of his vassalage and wants to put it to the test. If she wonders how Kriemhild could have married a vassal, she has to wonder as well why she found herself so attracted to him. What is not in dispute, in any case, is that Siegfried is an incomparably great and handsome hero to whom all women feel powerfully attracted. The result of the invitation made at Brünhild's insistence is that she has to bear hearing Kriemhild declare precisely that: that her man is so magnificent that all of the lands represented at the festivities should belong to him (815). It is noteworthy that Kriemhild speaks not of what is, but of what ought to be in view of Siegfried's incomparability. The issue is Siegfried, the great and beautiful hero, not which or how many lands he rules. Here Brünhild has no case, because Kriemhild possesses Siegfried; moreover, Brünhild in her envy surely recognizes that Kriemhild was moved to her exclamation by unmitigated, passionate joy at the thought that Siegfried is hers. What Brünhild does not yet know is that Kriemhild mistakenly believes that Siegfried deflowered Brünhild, and may be thinking at the moment "he had you, but you don't have him; I do." That is in any case substantially the point that Kriemhild makes in subsequently denouncing Brünhild as Siegfried's concubine and showing the ring and girdle as supposed proof (839–840).

The erotic passion Siegfried inspires in women, these two beautiful queens in particular, and his own passion for Kriemhild, largely determine the course of the ensuing events. Had Brünhild not been so powerfully attracted to Siegfried, the seemingly well-founded insult hurled at her by Kriemhild might not have produced in her a willingness to lend an ear to Hagen's promise to make Siegfried pay for her disgrace (864). Were Kriemhild's passion for Siegfried not as great, she likewise might be less willing to accept Hagen's deceitful promise to protect him in battle and hence to divulge to Hagen the secret of Siegfried's physical vulnerability (897–898). Likewise, it is partly Siegfried's desire to continue as every bit the incomparable hero that he showed himself to be in winning Kriemhild that contributes to his boundless exuberance during the fateful hunting party. In departing for the hunt, he embraces her and kisses her tenderly and passionately (925); and his dying thoughts are chiefly of her, that she will now be without his protection and that she will grieve over his loss (994–996).

Kriemhild's thirst for revenge, to make Hagen pay with his life for murdering Siegfried, is born indeed of grief. Her grief at her loss is so great because her passion for Siegfried was so complete. At first, she does not want to remain with her relatives in Worms because she cannot bear the thought of ever having to see Hagen, her beloved husband's assassin (1077–1079). The decisive factor in her change of mind is her youngest brother Giselher's promise to help her overcome the loss of her husband (1080), suggesting that already at this point she has begun to recognize that revenge will be her only solace in her grief. Similarly, as she continues to grieve three and a half years later, she accepts her brothers' proposal to have the Nibelung treasure, the gift given to her as a dowry by Siegfried, brought to Worms (1116–1117), surely with the thought that great wealth can bring her the power she needs to achieve her aim of seeing Hagen slain for the murder of Siegfried. At least, that is precisely what she seems intent on doing once she has the treasure, as Hagen recognizes (1127–1128), whereupon he acts to prevent that by deceitfully arranging to have the treasure secretly submerged in the Rhine (1137).

As our narrator emphasizes, Kriemhild is left at this point (the end of the *Nibelungenlied*'s first part) with only her grief. New hope for revenge comes some thirteen years later with the proposal of marriage from Etzel, the king of the Huns. The immensity of Etzel's wealth and power offers Kriemhild the prospect of making Hagen pay with his life for having killed her beloved Siegfried (1259). The story in the *Nibelungenlied*'s second half concerns the lengths to which she is prepared to go to achieve that passionately desired result. Her passion for revenge is motivated by her passion for the incomparably handsome and powerful hero who was her husband. Her very last words, as she is about to behead Hagen with the sword he had taken from Siegfried, are of her love for her dead spouse, of how Hagen had caused her such bitter pain in her heart (2372). The story of Kriemhild's revenge amounts to a tribute to erotic love's omnipotence, to love's all-conquering power and the passions it is capable of engendering. In the last analysis, the *Nibelungenlied* is a tale not of heroism or revenge, but of erotic passion.

Hagen's heroism in the poem's second part consists in his defiant fight to the bitter end in the face of what he recognizes as the unstoppable force of Kriemhild's passion. He had indeed thrown down the gauntlet to Kriemhild by having Siegfried's bloodied corpse deposited at her doorstep (1003–1004). It is as though in doing so he had meant to challenge her to a battle of wits and determination, or at least to taunt her with her powerlessness to do anything about the assassination. Hagen's motivation in the murder may have been simply to ingratiate himself with his liege lord Gunther's wife, Brünhild, by avenging her for the insult hurled at her by Kriemhild. Certainly, Hagen for his own reasons wanted Siegfried out of the way as representing, in view of his superhuman strength and courage, a threat to the power of his liege lord and thus to himself. The deeper motivation, however, considering that next to Siegfried Hagen was held to be the greatest and most famous of heroes, was surely his wounded pride as only the second greatest warrior. Indeed, Hagen's depositing of Siegfried's corpse at Kriemhild's door may be intended to boast to her that with Siegfried gone there is no greater hero than he, Hagen. That boast, in turn, would represent a compensation to Hagen — who is singularly unattractive to women and in misogynous reaction seemingly unattracted by them — for his having failed to awaken in Kriemhild the sort of passion Siegfried did. If he cannot inspire passionate love in his liege lord's incomparably beautiful sister, inspiring passionate hate in her is the next best thing.

At the end of part one, Hagen has acted to prevent Kriemhild from seizing the one means at her disposal for taking revenge on him, he having had her Nibelung treasure deposited in the Rhine. When after thirteen years another opportunity presents itself to Kriemhild for gaining the power she needs in order to bring about the slaying of Hagen, the latter is of course quick to perceive the danger and tries unsuccessfully to block her acceptance of King Etzel's marriage proposal. Subsequently, a more imminent danger presents itself with the request from the Hunnish king, at Kriemhild's prodding, that the Burgundian kings pay a visit to him and their sister at his court. Hagen's honor as the Burgundians' vassal prevents him from declining to accompany them despite his acute awareness that he is Kriemhild's target. Where there is life there is hope; therefore Hagen can reckon with some chance that he might cheat the fate that Kriemhild plans for him. What he cannot allow himself to do, though, is to bring disgrace on his honor as the greatest of warriors, for being able to claim that status was surely the deeper reason for his assassination of Siegfried in the first place. His defiance of Kriemhild right up through his death at her hands is meant to display for her and all the world his unflinching strength and bravery, that while he is not the slain Siegfried's match in beauty and erotic appeal, still he is the greatest living warrior.

Hagen alone among the Burgundians and Huns understands the intensity of Kriemhild's passion for her slain hero. By getting Kriemhild to betray Siegfried's vulnerability, out of her passion to protect him, and then by assassinating him, Hagen has made himself the object of the only kind of passion he appears capable of engendering in a woman. The thousands of others who die as a result of Kriemhild's thirst for revenge are largely, as it were, innocent bystanders, or in today's military parlance "collateral damage."

The leaders and great warriors among the Hunnish and Burgundian forces in particular are bewildered that erotic passion can push a woman to such unbridled action. We as readers, however, know that the excesses of that passion are often the stuff of poetic literature, and in that light that the *Nibelungenlied* is a worthy successor to Homer's *Iliad*, in which the Trojan War is waged over the adulterous erotic passion of Paris and Helena, and to Virgil's *Aeneid*, with its famous depiction of Dido's erotic passion over Aeneas and her suicide when he leaves her.

While the *Nibelungenlied* focuses on Kriemhild's passion for her husband Siegfried, Wagner's *Ring des Nibelungen* concerns a woman's devotion to her father and the transferal of that devotion to a lover who is the father's grandson and hence her nephew. That is to say, erotic passion in Wagner's heroine, the valkyrie Brünnhilde, is no simple, straightforward matter as it is with Kriemhild in the medieval epic poem. By the same token, Wagner's opera trilogy with prelude depicts aspects of desire that had scarcely been portrayed with such boldness before.

The assumption is often that Wagner's operas are about philosophical questions — an admittedly justifiable conclusion in view of his manifest interest in philosophy and his own sometime indications that this was his poetic intent. A recent critic has maintained that it is the inherent philosophicalness of Wagner's operatic magnum opus that accounts for the resurgence of its popularity:

> The *Ring* is, it seems, more popular now than it has ever been. It is not that people go only to swoon, as we take it that they once did, but to see a work which, in its comprehensiveness, intensity and depth offers, more than any other in the history of an art-form not notable for sustained grappling with fundamental issues, an experience which can be indefinitely discussed and meditated on.[31]

The philosophical direction in early Wagner criticism, up to the turn of the century, was typically idealistic, that is platonic — albeit sometimes with a Christian cast to it. A French critic wrote that "the mind of the great artist was oriented toward eternal truth by that sentiment which, as we have seen, makes for the unity of his work ... : pity, devotion, disinterested love, and to use the word from the Gospel: Charity."[32] This viewpoint was echoed by another Francophone critic around the middle of this century: "[A]ll of his heroes ... are searching for the way to the true meaning of life."[33] Much other interpretive comment has been from quite specifically religious perspectives, such as:

> Die Darstellung des Werdens, des Schicksals, der Aufgabe und Bestimmung der göttlichen Monade, als der Menschenseele, die auf ihrem Wege durch die Welt der Erscheinungen ihre Erlösung sucht, ist der innere Gehalt jeder

[31] Michael Tanner, "Ideals and Sacrifices: Richard Wagner. *Der Ring des Nibelungen*. Bayreuth Festival," *Times Literary Supplement*, 23–31 August 1989, 921.

[32] Marcel Hébert, *Trois Moments de la Pensée de Richard Wagner: Tetralogie–Tristan et Iseult–Parsifal* (Paris: Fischbacher, 1894) 70.

[33] Marcel Doisy, *L'Œuvre de Richard Wagner: du Vaisseau fantôme à Parsifal* (Brussels: "La Boétie," 1945) 10.

> Religion und die Grundidee aller genialen Dichtungen, so auch die der Musikdramen Richard Wagners.[34]

Others have written about transcendent meaning in the operas: "Die wirklich großen Kunstwerke [wie die Wagners] sind unergründlich wie der Weltraum. Keine betrachtende Studie wird jemals auf ihren Grund stoßen. Hinter jedem Raume leuchten neue Räume."[35]

Existentialism, the dominant intellectual current of this century, has likewise affected Wagner criticism, especially in the post-World War II period. In the view of one critic, "Es muß ... der mannigfachen Verwandtschaften gedacht werden, die den Wagnerschen Anarchismus mit dem Existenzialismus des Jean Paul Sartre verbinden."[36] Marxism, too, sometimes in combination with existentialism, has provided the basis for Wagner criticism. Around the turn of the century George Bernard Shaw offered his famous interpretation of *The Ring of the Nibelung* as depicting capitalism and class struggle — a justifiable position in view of Wagner's original conception of the work. Shaw's interpretation was used as recently as Patrice Chéreau's centennial production at Bayreuth in 1976 and served, too, as the starting point for one of the most ambitious attempts at interpreting *the Ring*, that by Deryck Cooke.[37] For Cooke, the existentialist and marxist approaches are inseparable, reflecting a merger of the dominant post-World War II intellectual currents in Western and Eastern Europe, respectively.

Wagner has been viewed not only from marxist and existentialist perspectives but also from the standpoint of the third major intellectual current of our century, psychoanalytic theory. The chief example of this direction in Wagner criticism is the Jungian study of the *Ring* by Donington. For Donington,

> it is Jung's work that helps most in picking up the 'inexhaustible' contents of mythology, which may certainly include our personal repressions, but which just as certainly include a distilled essence of human experience from

[34] Walter Einbeck, *Der religiös-philosophische Gehalt in Richard Wagners Musikdramen* (Buenos Aires: Editorial "Schatzkammer"; Würzburg: Zettner, 1956) 12.

[35] Kurt Overhoff, *Die Musikdramen Richard Wagners. Eine thematisch-musikalische Interpretation* (Salzburg: Pustet, 1967) 10.

[36] Walter Keller, *Anarchismus im "Parsifal,"* Schriften der Schweizerischen Gesellschaft Richard Wagner-Museum Tribschen/Luzern 2 (Zurich: Michelsen, 1967) 12.

[37] Deryck Cooke, *I Saw the World End: A Study of Wagner's Ring* (London: Oxford University Press, 1979).

> untold generations before us: a truth of archetypes rather than a truth of persons.[38]

The Freudian direction in criticism on the *Ring*, in particular as practiced by Friedlander,[39] is closer to the presentation made here, as we shall see.

Some critics have chosen to focus on power instead of love as the main theme of the *Ring*. Cozzi saw Wotan's actions as standing for those of powerful people who do not live up to their bargains: "In Wotan the author reproduces all people with power."[40] Cooke concluded that "[t]he work presents, in symbolic terms, an entirely realistic diagnosis of the power-ridden world in which we live."[41] Gollancz found the *Ring* to be "packed with fascism."[42] Ritchie judged that

> "The Ring" is basically about the consequences following upon a man's renunciation of his "better self" to win power; of the collapse of a ruler's power after he betrays the central principle upon which his authority rests; and of the final eradication of the world's misery by the downfall of the established order.[43]

Such commentary ignores the fact that the action in the *Ring* revolves much more around love than power.

Other interpretations of the *Ring* view it as depicting or expressing an ideal. An early critic, Barthélemy, saw Wotan as representing "the Mind in search of the ideal, of eternity."[44] More recently, Cooke, while seeing the object of depiction as "a realistic representation of the power-dominated world of the past and present," found also "an idealistic prognostication of a possible future in which man's aggressive power-lust will gradually give way

[38] Robert Donington, *Wagner's 'Ring' and Its Symbols: The Music and the Myth* (1963; rpt. New York: St. Martin's, 1974) 33.

[39] Max Friedlander, "A Psychoanalytic Approach to Wagner's *Ring*," *Connotation: A Magazine of the Arts* (Fairleigh Dickinson University, Madison, New Jersey) 2 (Spring 1963): 25–53.

[40] Alfio Cozzi, "Wagner, l' 'Anello del Nibelungo' e I Wagneriani," *Cristallo: Rassenga di Varia Umanità* (Bolzano) 18.3 (1976): 45.

[41] Cooke 203.

[42] Victor Gollancz, *The Ring at Bayreuth: And Some Thoughts on Operatic Production* (New York: Dutton, 1966) 98.

[43] R. C. Ritchie, "Wagner's 'Ring': A Parable for All Time," *The Maynooth Review: A Journal of the Arts* 6 (May 1982): 22.

[44] Edmond Barthélemy and Louis-Pilate de Brinn' Gaubast, *Richard Wagner: La Tétralogie de l'Anneau du Nibelung* (Paris: Dentu, 1894) 217.

to mutual love and fellowship."[45] And McCreless has written of "Wotan's attempt to restore the natural order and redeem his guilt."[46]

Some critics, of course, have found the *Ring* to be about love, but rarely about erotic passion as such. Wagner's associate, von Wolzogen, early concluded that the *Ring*'s basic idea was "selbstlose Liebe" and therefore inwardly akin "derjenigen der christlichen Religion."[47] A more recent critic, Hall, judges "the 'love' theme" in the *Ring* to convey a message that "is, at least negatively, Christian, and it is but a short step from this to the positive Christianity of *Parsifal*."[48] Even the psychoanalytic critic Friedlander does not give erotic passion its due when he writes of Brünnhilde as being for Wotan simply "the best loved of children."[49]

G. B. Shaw did accord erotic desire a role, but one he would have rather done without: "[S]uch a love as that implied by Siegfried's first taste of fear ... is an experience which it is much better, like the vast majority of us, never to have passed through, than to allow it to play more than a recreational holiday part in our lives. It ... does not occupy more than two scenes of The Ring"[50] (Shaw is referring to Siegfried's awakening of Brünnhilde). A German literary contemporary of Wagner's, the novelist Theodor Fontane, meanwhile remarked — privately — on the prominence of "lust for gold and for love" in the *Ring*, commenting that Wagner "ist ganz Wotan, der Geld und Macht haben, aber auf 'Lübe' [= Liebe] nicht verzichten will und zu diesem Zwecke beständig mogelt."[51] Another critic wrote disapprovingly of Wotan — though not without humor — that

> even if his outbursts of grief were tragic instead of ridiculous and wearisome, we could hardly clothe with godlike dignity a character who pursues the female sex — divine, semi-divine, and purely human — with the persistency of a mythological Mormon, and has reared a numerous family, each member

[45] Cooke 274.

[46] Patrick McCreless, *Wagner's Siegfried: Its Drama, History, and Music*, Studies in Musicology 59 (Ann Arbor, MI: UMI Research Press, 1982) 2.

[47] Hans von Wolzogen, *Wagneriana. Gesammelte Aufsätze über R. Wagner's Werke vom Ring bis zum Gral. Eine Gedenkgabe für alte und neue Festspielgäste zum Jahre 1888* (Leipzig: Freund, 1888) 79.

[48] Robert A. Hall, "The Psychological Motivation of Wagner's 'Götterdämmerung,'" *The German Quarterly* 36 (1963): 256.

[49] Friedlander 31.

[50] George Bernard Shaw, *The Perfect Wagnerite: A Commentary on the Nibelung's Ring* (1898; rpt. of 4th ed., 1923: New York: Dover, 1967) 66–67.

[51] Theodor Fontane, *Schriften zur Literatur*, ed. Hans Heinrich Reuter (Berlin: Aufbau, 1960) 336: letter to Emilie Fontane of June 28, 1881.

of which would probably find considerable difficulty in identifying his or her mother.[52]

Whereas at the outset of the *Nibelungenlied* we are given a glimpse of Kriemhild's adolescent resistance to the thought of love and marriage, only to see shortly thereafter that on her spying Siegfried such resistance instantly vanishes, in the case of Wagner's Brünnhilde a whole opera, *Die Walküre*, is devoted to her passage from girlhood to womanhood, from devotion to her father to acceptance of the thought of marrying. When, in that opera, we first see Brünnhilde, she is still very much daddy's girl, siding with Wotan against his wife Fricka (II,1).[53] The bond between Wotan and Brünnhilde is the stronger because he sired her not with Fricka, but with a paramour. As his favored daughter, Brünnhilde is his confidante and companion. The turn to love and marriage in the nubile daughter's thoughts comes when her father, cowed by his wife's reproaches, withdraws his protection from the offspring of another of his paramours, the young warrior Siegmund. Wotan had raised Brünnhilde to be devoted to Siegmund and now orders her instead not to act to prevent his death (II,2).

Brünnhilde's reaction to the order is to appear before Siegmund and announce to him his impending death. She does so not to warn him however, but to comfort him with the prospect that in death he will be with her in Valhalla, where with the aid of his valkyrie daughters Wotan, as chief god, is collecting dead heroes for the defense of that magnificent fortress. What is going on with Brünnhilde seems to be the stage in which a girl conceives a "crush" on a man and sets about to test her charms on him. She is not out to seduce Siegmund, but does want to see how he will respond to her as a woman, as an object of erotic attraction. To her disappointment, Siegmund, who recognizes what she is about, does not take the bait (II,4).

Friedlander's interpretation of Brünnhilde's attraction to Siegmund is similar to that given here:

[52] Gustav Kobbe, *How to Understand Wagner's Ring of the Nibelung: The Story and Descriptive Analysis ... Together with a Sketch of Wagner's Life by N. Kilburn*, 7th ed. (London: Reeves, 1916) 36.

[53] References to Wagner's *Ring* are based on: Richard Wagner, *Das Rheingold: Vorabend zu dem Bühnenfestspiel "Der Ring des Nibelungen,"* ed. Wilhelm Zentner, Reclams Universal-Bibliothek 5641 (Stuttgart: Reclam, 1977); *Die Walküre: Erster Tag aus dem Bühnenfestspiel "Der Ring des Nibelungen,"* ed. Wilhelm Zentner, Reclams Universal-Bibliothek 5642 (Stuttgart: Reclam, 1981); *Siegfried: Zweiter Tag aus dem Bühnenfestspiel "Der Ring des Nibelungen,"* ed. Wilhelm Zentner, Reclams Universal-Bibliothek 5643 (Stuttgart: Reclam, 1981); *Götterdämmerung: Dritter Tag aus dem Bühnenfestspiel "Der Ring des Nibelungen,"* ed. Wilhelm Zentner, Reclams Universal-Bibliothek 5644 (Stuttgart: Reclam, 1982).

> Psychoanalysis reveals that the original tie in a girl's life is her attachment to her father. Later this love is transferred to another man.... [T]he conflict of the drama is born of Brünnhilde's first independent act; she finds an object of love who is not her father; it is his son, her half-brother Siegmund.[54]

Cooke, however, attributes the change in Brünnhilde to *caritas*, not *eros*: "[T]here can be no doubt that Wagner saw the metamorphosis of the cold, Wotan-dominated valkyrie into a warm, compassionate, and rebellious woman as a great step forward in humanity's quest for a world based on fellowship and love."[55]

Because of her "crush" on Siegmund, Brünnhilde does go against her father's orders and tries unsuccessfully to protect him (II,5). Although she attempts to persuade Wotan that she knew that at the bottom of his heart he really wanted her to act as she did, he recognizes that the daughter's rebellion was motivated by her awakening sexual desire (III,3). That is why the punishment he lays on her "fits the crime," as it were. Sexual desire is what made her disobey him, so he punishes her by declaring that the time has come for them to part ways and for her to take a husband. His difficulty in accepting her passage to womanhood is reflected in his decree that she shall surrender her virginity to the first man who comes along, as though in his mind if the daughter is no longer an innocent girl she is a slut, ready for intercourse with any man. Having uttered that decree to Brünnhilde in jealous anger, Wotan then quickly accedes, however, to the beloved daughter's flattering request that he arrange to see that her virginity shall be taken only by a man who is the equal of her dear father Wotan.

Because the erotic attraction that brings about Brünnhilde's passage from girlhood to womanhood was to a close male relative, her father's son by another woman, that passage remains incomplete. Moreover, her father had raised her to be devoted to that very offspring of his, so that in large measure she loves Wotan in Siegmund. Her first and only adolescent "crush" is one on her half-brother. Indeed, her failure to make the desired impression on Siegmund as his valkyrie does not end the matter. She rescues Siegmund's beloved Sieglinde in the correct belief that the latter is carrying the dead hero's son; and when she asks Wotan to see that the man who awakens her from virginal slumber will be a hero who is her father's equal, she has in mind, as we learn later, Siegmund's son. For this incestuous passion she has the example of Siegmund himself, whose beloved was his twin sister Sieglinde, the two of them sired by Wotan with a paramour called the wolf woman.

[54] Friedlander 32–33.

[55] Cooke 347.

Siegfried having not yet been born when Wotan "condemns" Brünnhilde to loss of her virginity, she must wait for him for the better part of a generation. When he does awaken her, she seems, despite her magical slumber, to have in the meantime become rather much an old maid (*Siegfried*, III,3). She is in any case aware of their generational difference. That awareness does not prevent her from reacting passionately to Siegfried's awakening of her, any more than it necessarily would in the case of a virgin sexually "awakened" only in middle age.

For his part, Siegfried is ready for, indeed emotionally in need of, a Brünnhilde. To begin with, he has reached late adolescence without having ever set eyes on a woman, though he does have an understanding of mating from watching birds and animals (I,1). More important, he has grown up without a mother, Sieglinde having died in giving birth to him. There having been no women around, he has not passed from boyhood to manhood in the sense of transferring devotion from his mother to a beloved. He yearns for both a mother and a lover. Brünnhilde fills the bill, being in a sense his self-appointed godmother and a passionate beauty as well. While Siegfried presumably is unaware that they are aunt and nephew, that her father is his grandfather, Brünnhilde knows this quite well and relates to Siegfried accordingly.

Rank emphasizes the incestuous element in Siegfried's passion for Brünnhilde.[56] Finch notes that the element of incestuous passion in Brünnhilde's love for Siegfried was Wagner's invention: "[D]ifferently from the sources, she tells him she has loved him since before he was even begotten. We know, of course, that, again differently from the sources, Brünnhilde must be Siegfried's aunt (even more incest?)."[57] Lindenberger refers to the themes of incest and adultery in the *Ring*, in the context of the literature and culture of Wagner's time, but does not discuss the erotic passion and conflicting emotions involved.[58]

Siegfried's subsequent infidelity in marrying Gutrune (*Götterdämmerung*) may be seen as owing to the ambiguous nature of his attraction to Brünnhilde, and of her passion for him. In her he found both a mother and a lover. In his powerful attraction to Gutrune he is no longer seeking a mother in the beloved, only a lover. For him with Gutrune it is erotic passion pure and simple.

[56] Otto Rank, *Das Inzest-Motiv in Dichtung und Sage: Grundzüge einer Psychologie des dichterischen Schaffens* (Leipzig and Vienna: Deuticke, 1912) 644–645.

[57] R. G. Finch, "The Icelandic and German Sources of Wagner's Ring of the Nibelung," *Leeds Studies in English*, n.s. 17 (1986): 15.

[58] Herbert Lindenberger, "Wagner's 'Ring' as a Nineteenth-Century Artifact," *Comparative Drama* 28 (1994): 285–310.

To be free to pursue Gutrune, he must forget all about Brünnhilde and his relationship to her. The intensity of his erotic desire demands as much. So hot is his passion, indeed, that he is ready, very much like his namesake in the *Nibelungenlied*, secretly to help Gutrune's brother Gunther subdue Brünnhilde in order that he may marry Gutrune (I,2). Whereas in the *Nibelungenlied*, however, it was a question of Siegfried's subduing of a virgin, Wagner's Siegfried is subduing a woman who was mother as well as lover to him. In effect, though he certainly is not conscious of it, Wagner's Siegfried is breaking away from the only mother he ever knew and procuring her for another man. To see it in a positive light, Siegfried is providing himself and Brünnhilde with spouses appropriate for breaking the chain of incestuous attractions fostered by Wotan among his offspring.

In the end, Siegfried's breaking away from the pattern of incestuous passions does not succeed. At least, his passion for Gutrune appears to wane almost from the wedding night. Within several days after the wedding, he is not only flirting with the Rhine Maidens but seems genuinely interested in intimate involvement with them (III,1). He in any case is more interested in hunting than in making love to Gutrune. Being Wotan's grandson, he may be expected to have inherited wandering eyes. Yet there is also reason to suspect that with Gutrune Siegfried has not broken the pattern of incestuous involvements after all, at least as regards his new wife herself. As we learn, she and her brother lived for a number of years together, evidently without much thought to providing themselves with spouses (I,1). To be sure, on first laying eyes on Siegfried, Gutrune is all fire and flame; but in the end, after Siegfried's death, we see the brother and sister again in one another's embrace (III,3). For his part, Siegfried out on the hunt shortly after the wedding comes to remember Brünnhilde, as though with the cooling of his passion for Gutrune thoughts and memories of his more maternal lover begin to arise in him again (III,2).

Friedlander's psychoanalytic interpretation is similar to that made here: "Let us try to understand the feelings of young Siegfried.... He has lived with a motherly wife and wants to leave her. Far away he finds a girl for whom he experiences mature sexual desire. Ardent and interested in his future fulfillment, he forgets his wife at once."[59] Friedlander comments, too, that Siegfried "likes the girls [i.e., the Rhine Maidens] and would willingly 'tame' one of them if he did not also care for Gutrune. This suggests a promiscuous character, a man who is not completely satisfied with his wife and who is ready to return to his first love" (here, Brünnhilde).[60]

[59] Friedlander 39.

[60] Friedlander 40.

Brünnhilde, of course, never does advance beyond incestuous passion. In Siegfried she loves the seed of Siegmund who was in turn the seed of Wotan. Indeed, when it comes time for her to bid farewell to her dead beloved, she does so with a return to her girlhood identity as one of Wotan's maiden valkyries. She mounts her steed Grane and forces him to leap into the flames of Siegfried's funeral pyre (III,3). Throughout, the horse has been associated in her mind and feelings with her maidenhood. The privilege and glory of her childhood and adolescence was to ride with her valkyrie sisters and most of all with her divine father, Wotan. That was the role she forfeited through her disobedience to Wotan's command regarding Siegmund, since that disobedience was punished by her being destined to take a lover. Grane remained with her during her long magical slumber, and it was toward him she looked at the moment of her surrendering herself to Siegfried, a gaze that betokened her farewell to maidenhood (*Siegfried*, III,3). When Siegfried then left her to go off in search of adventure, she made a gift to him of Grane, in the hope that her young beloved would not forget her and her surrender of her maidenhood to him (*Götterdämmerung*, Prelude). As once again the valkyrie now at the end, mounted on Grane, she seems to be re-enacting the surrender of her maidenhood to Siegfried, as a token of her undying passion.

Brünnhilde's throwing of herself upon Siegfried's funeral pyre, astride Grane as she had been as a virginal valkyrie, has still more direct meaning with regard to the incestuous nature of her erotic passion. We see that she understands that Wotan has been waiting for this moment to immolate himself in Valhalla, because she tells his raven that he may depart now to bring the welcome news to his master (III,3). Wotan is therefore not waiting to hear that Siegfried is dead, but rather that Brünnhilde's passion has brought her to join Siegfried in death. The news will provide Wotan the satisfaction that, while he could not become the object of her passion as a lover, her passion for his grandson, for his seed, was demonstrably so very intense and undying. Moreover, if he as her father could not enter into a union with her in life, he may do so — or see himself as now doing so — in death, by immolating himself at the moment she is doing the same. The foolishness of his incestuous passion is exposed by the fact that dying at the same moment and in the same way as the beloved daughter is not the same as going up in flames with her, the position of Siegfried in death that Wotan can only envy, not usurp. At the same time, though, Wotan's passion we know does not go unrequited really, because Brünnhilde's desire all along was for a man like her father. In Siegfried she largely loved Wotan.

Dettmering similarly concludes that Siegfried's death will be good news to Wotan, as the injured third party in a love triangle who is frustrated over having been barred from participation in the love between Brünnhilde and his grandson.[61] Also, Dettmering likewise sees the ravens' role as messengers to be one among many indications that the *Ring* represents a dream or fantasy on Wotan's part.

The meaning of the drama's ending has been much debated. Tonnelat sees it as representing the demise of an older generation of world rulers, to be replaced by a younger, more humane generation.[62] Andree's theosophist view is that the ending not only "symbolisiert das endgültige Ende der Götterherrschaft" but also points to "dem gesunden Fortschritt der Menschheitsentwicklung" fostered by "der durch das Leben bei der [Siegfried und Brünhilde] gelegte Keim" and their union.[63] Dieckmann writes of a "Tabula rasa für einen fundamentalen Neubeginn" that the opera's ending promises.[64]

Like Hagen in the *Nibelungenlied*, Wagner's Hagen is a cold fish when it comes to erotic passion. Wagner, however, in playing down the image of Hagen as the great warrior, depicts him as envious of Siegfried as the object of women's passion, an element that in the *Nibelungenlied* is only hinted at. The operatic Hagen was sired by the disgustingly ugly dwarf Alberich, who out of rage at his rejection as lover by the Rhine Maidens (*Rheingold*, Sc. 1) forswears love in exchange for the Rhinegold and the ring he orders fashioned from it. The apple proverbially does not fall far from the tree, so that Hagen's lust for power is a compensation for lack of attractiveness to women. While Wagner's Hagen is out to get Siegfried because he covets the ring made from the Rhinegold and the power it bestows, his means for achieving that end is to cause Siegfried to betray Brünnhilde's love so that she in turn, as the woman scorned, will betray to Hagen the secret of Siegfried's vulnerability (II,5). As we remember, Hagen in the *Nibelungenlied*, by contrast, used Kriemhild's concern for Siegfried's safety to get her to divulge the secret. The point remains in both cases, however, that Hagen takes advantage of the sort of passion that he does not or cannot arouse in a woman.

The object of depiction in the *Nibelungenlied* is ultimately intense erotic passion that knows no bounds, first especially Siegfried's for Kriemhild, then

[61] Peter Dettmering, *Dichtung und Psychoanalyse: Thomas Mann — Rainer Maria Rilke — Richard Wagner*, Sammlung Dialog 33 (Munich: Nymphenburg, 1969) 184.

[62] Ernest Tonnelat, *La Légende des Nibelungen en Allemagne aux XIXe siècle*, Publications de la Faculté des Lettres de l'Université de Strasbourg 119 (Paris: Les Belles Lettres, 1952) 67.

[63] Oskar Andree, *Richard Wagners "Ring des Nibelungen,"* Wege, Ziele, Geistgestaltungen 9 (Stuttgart: Mellinger, 1976) 105.

[64] Friedrich Dieckmann, "Zwei Grundfiguren im Werk Richard Wagners," *Merkur: Deutsche Zeitschrift für europäisches Denken* 34.6 (1980): 571–586; here 584.

particularly her undying passion for him that lives far beyond his grave. The *Nibelungenlied* in this sense continues the tradition of European literature's oldest classic epic, Homer's *Iliad*, in which Achilles' upset over the appropriation of his concubine Briseïs is so great that he is prepared to let the Greeks go down to defeat before Troy until his absence from the battle contributes to the death of his bosom friend Patroklos, moving him to return to battle out of a passion to avenge the friend's demise. Kriemhild's passion for Siegfried is similarly celebrated, and Brünnhilde's passion in Wagner's *Ring des Nibelungen* is of that selfsame intensity. Her attachment to Wotan is such that she has eyes only for young men who are his progeny. Thus, whereas Kriemhild's erotic passion was frustrated from without by the outrageous murder of her beloved husband, Brünnhilde's is subverted from within by her emotional tie to her father. Both Kriemhild and Brünnhilde perish as poetic celebrations of erotic passion's overwhelming power.

Brian Murdoch

Politics in the *Nibelungenlied*

The political business of a medieval king, if reduced to the essentials that will apply both to the barbarian Germanic kings on which the *Nibelungenlied* is partly based and also to rulers in the High Middle Ages or later, may be summed up under only a very few headings: to maintain order and stability within the land or society over which the king rules; to defend that country, society or economy against threats or incursions from others; and, where necessary or possible, to enlarge the territories or spheres of influence of that land or society by force, alliance or marriage, thus increasing its economic prosperity and its relative importance. Such a concentration on political essentials does, of course, ignore the religious dimension of the *rex Christianus*, the idealized medieval king portrayed in theocentric writings on the *via regia* by (clerical) medieval political theorists and compilers such as Bishop Jonas of Orleans, Smaragdus of St. Mihiel in Verdun, or Sedulius Scottus.[1] The religious dimension is highlighted in the influential *De XII abusivis saeculi* of the Irish pseudo-Cyprian,[2] but the king's tasks were still, as Alcuin made clear to Charlemagne,[3] to defend and judge, to be a warrior leader. Sedulius stressed the need for advisers to the king, and if the *stabilitas* insisted upon by Jonas of Orleans meant for him primarily the stability of a unified faith, it still carries a more generally pragmatic sense. There is a theoretical Christianity in the German *Nibelungenlied*, but it is not foregrounded, and provides little more than an underpinning for various key factors, such as marriage, and it can therefore be left out of consideration of the political structures in the work.

To note that studies of the politics of the *Nibelungenlied* have frequently been historical is capable of various interpretations: it may imply a specific linking of the poem with events contemporary to, or at no great remove

[1] R. W. and A. J. Carlyle, *A History of Medieval Political Theory in the West* (Edinburgh and London: Black, 1903); M. L. W. Laistner, *Thought and Letters in Western Europe AD 500 to 900*, revised ed. (London: Methuen, 1957) 315–321; J. M. Wallace-Hadrill, *The Barbarian West 400–1000*, 3rd ed. (London: Hutchinson, 1967).

[2] Roswitha Wisniewski, "Das Versagen des Königs. Zur Interpretation des Nibelungenliedes," *PBB* 95 (Sonderheft: *Festschrift Ingeborg Schröbler*) (1973): 184–186.

[3] J. M. Wallace-Hadrill, "The *via regia* of the Carolingian Age," in B. Smalley, ed., *Trends in Medieval Political Thought* (Oxford: Blackwell, 1965) 30.

from, the German version that we have;[4] or it may refer — as the early *Quellenforscher* established — to the relationship between historically documented events of Burgundian, Hunnish or Frankish history.[5] Early literary works may be used to provide evidence of political ideas, sometimes in spite of what the poet actually says — the presence of Thersites in the *Iliad*, for example, even though he is "cruelly caricatured and ruthlessly manhandled," has been cited as evidence for "the beginning of a democratic opposition."[6] In the *Nibelungenlied*, too, political interpretation and apparent authorial approbation may also seem to be at variance. The term historical, further, when applied to approaches to the *Nibelungenlied*, may be taken also in the literary sense, to imply the consideration of the presumed earlier stages of the German work, deduced from knowledge of other (principally Norse) texts. Elements from all these approaches may be used in establishing the political structure of the *Nibelungenlied*.

In one of the most perceptive studies of the politics of the *Nibelungenlied*, Siegfried Beyschlag (1952) distinguished between the poem as a recounting of events, and as a development of human psychologies.[7] The former aspect of the work provides the structural coherence for the whole, a structure common to the Middle High German poem and to related works such as the *Altkaviða* and *Waltharius*, as indeed to other Germanic heroic narratives.[8] Literary works may reflect, but do not necessarily record, historical events, however, and it is worth recapitulating briefly the discrete political events echoed in the Middle High German poem: the fall of the Burgundians, the decline of the empire of the Huns, and the political problems of the Merovingian Frankish rulers in the sixth and early seventh centuries. All are of political importance, and the key to each is political stability. Special attention may be paid to two historical persons: first, the figure who not only

[4] Siegfried Beyschlag, "Das Nibelungenlied als aktuelle Dichtung seiner Zeit," *GRM* 48 (1967): 225–231; Heinz Rupp, "Das Nibelungenlied — eine politische Dichtung," *WW* 35 (1985): 166–176; Norbert Voorwinden, "Die Markgrafen im Nibelungenlied: Gestalten des 10. Jahrhunderts?" in Fritz Peter Knapp, ed., *Nibelungenlied und Klage. Passauer Nibelungengespräche 1985* (Heidelberg: Winter, 1987) 21–42; Dieter Breuer and Jürgen Breuer, *Mit spaeher rede. Politische Geschichte im Nibelungenlied* (Munich: Fink, 1996).

[5] Andreas Heusler, *Nibelungensage und Nibelungenlied*, 3rd ed. (Dortmund: Ruhfus, 1929).

[6] T. B. L. Webster, *Political Interpretations in Greek Literature* (Manchester: Manchester University Press, 1948) 7.

[7] Siegfried Beyschlag, "Das Motiv der Macht bei Siegfrieds Tod," *GRM* 33 (1952): 95–108. Revised version in Karl Hauck, ed., *Zur germanisch-deutschen Heldensage* (Darmstadt: Wissenschaftliche Buchgesellschaft, 1965) 195–213.

[8] Brian Murdoch, *The Germanic Hero* (London: Hambledon, 1996).

links the fall of the Burgundians and the ultimate collapse of the Huns in historical terms, but who in his personal fate provides a bridge to the later events of Merovingian history, the Roman general Flavius Aëtius; and secondly the Visigothic princess Brunichildis, later queen of the Austrasian Franks, who, like the character in the poem who bears her name, was above all else a survivor.

Aëtius, the fifth-century Roman military leader of the Western Empire (and possible pretender for even higher office), used Hunnish auxiliaries to assist the Romans in the defeat of the Germanic kingdom of the Burgundians under Gundahari in 436, although Attila was not present on that occasion. This auxiliary force of Huns went on in 436–437 to destroy the Burgundians more or less completely, even though the original aim of Aëtius had merely been conquest. Attila was himself dealt a severe (though not in fact a mortal) blow by Aëtius and the Western Roman forces, who were this time aiding the Visigoths near Troyes in 451. The death of Attila and thereafter the rapid decline of his empire came about only in 453, however, immediately after his marriage to a Germanic princess (H)Ildiko. The link between his death and marriage seen by early historians is not provable. The Roman general is perhaps the least readily recognizable participant in the events that form the action of the *Nibelungenlied*. He remains, however, the outsider who caused the first problem to the Burgundian state, after which it was destroyed by the Huns. This sequence of events becomes a coherent construct, which assumes a narrative, and in political terms a potentially paradigmatic, quality. Two empires are shown, one defeated and then destroyed (the gap of one year between the fall of the Burgundians and their destruction is extended in the literary version), the other that of the Huns — eventually damaged so much as to decline, even if in the *Nibelungenlied*, the *Atlakviða* and the *Waltharius* that decline is shown as having been for radically different reasons each time. There is a reflection (which has both psychological and political relevance) in the *Nibelungenlied* also of the death of Aëtius, however, killed in 454 by the emperor Valentinian III. Evidence for the facts surrounding his death is somewhat confused, but John of Antioch relates — and we may concentrate upon those features with parallels in the German poem — the somewhat involved and essentially disjointed story that even Gibbon was hard pushed to present as a clear narrative without time-jumps.[9] Two elements are relevant: first, that a senator, Maximus, was jealous of Aëtius, either as a leader or for his closeness to Valentinian III, and as a result of this was able to accuse Aëtius of pretense to the purple, causing Valentinian to kill him with his own sword. Secondly that Valentinian, desiring the wife of Maximus,

[9] C. D. Gordon, *The Age of Attila* (Ann Arbor: University of Michigan Press, 1960) 50–52.

obtained a ring which had been taken from Maximus as a gambling debt and used it to entice Maximus's wife to the palace to seduce her. That Aëtius was aware of these events perhaps provoked the accusations by Maximus. Aëtius is, like Siegfried, a powerful figure, an outsider, but not a survivor, the victim of political and also of personal-sexual intrigue.

The plots surrounding the fate of Aëtius foreshadow some elements in the later historical source-material for the poem, the struggle for power amongst the Merovingian Franks in the latter part of the sixth century, as related by Gregory of Tours in his *History of the Franks* 4, 2–8.[10] Gregory opens his history with the general statement that he will write about the wars waged by kings against hostile people — a possible summary of the Middle High German poem — but the most important figure in late Merovingian history is arguably a queen. Brunichildis, daughter of Athanagild, king of the Visigoths in Spain, brought to her marriage with Sigibert, King of the Austrasian Franks, a considerable dowry in the form of treasure. Her sister Gailswintha, married to Sigibert's half-brother, Chilperic of Neustria, was strangled at the instigation of Chilperic's erstwhile concubine and later queen, the notorious Fredegonda. In the ensuing conflict between Sigibert and Chilperic, the initially victorious Sigibert (who had also helped another brother, Gunthram, in a war against the Saxons) was himself murdered on the orders of Fredegonda in 575. In spite of all this, Brunichildis outlived Fredegonda and ruled for many years with "diplomacy, boldness and (when necessary) assassination."[11]

It is not always helpful in interpretative terms to indicate a link between an historically attested character and one in a literary work, but Aëtius offers political analogues not only in his role in the destruction of the Burgundians and (eventually) the eclipse of the Huns, but also in his death in the context of a further power-struggle within a different political unit. Even given the (sexual) complexities of Valentinian's motives, the death of Aëtius as such is political. He is killed because he was, or was thought to be, a threat to the status quo. His accusation and murder find plenty of later historical and literary parallels beyond the *Nibelungenlied*. Nor is it difficult to find genuine cases of the removal of a real or perceived threat close to the crown.[12] Piers Gaveston in 1312, an outsider too close to the throne of Edward II of England, is a case in point, whilst in literature there are parallels in the

[10] Gregory of Tours, *Historia Francorum*, ed. W. Arndt and Bruno Kusch (rpt. Hanover: Monumenta Germaniae Historica, 1961). See also Lewis Thorpe, *The History of the Franks* (Harmondsworth: Penguin, 1974).

[11] Peter Lasko, *The Kingdom of the Franks* (London: Thames and Hudson, 1971).

[12] For early examples, see K. J. Leyser, *Rule and Conflict in Early Medieval Society* (London: Edward Arnold, 1979).

effective removal of Herzog Ernst by the Pfalzgraf Heinrich, or more famously the attempted removal of the much-favored newcomer Tristan by the Cornish barons.[13] If the death of Aëtius, killed by his sovereign, merges with the killing of Sigibert of Austrasia at the instigation of a concubine-turned-queen, it must be stressed that the historical events which may have provided inspiration for the *Nibelungenlied* are of value principally as analogues.

The theme of the *Nibelungenlied* is the fall of kingdoms and — far more importantly — the attempt by rulers to stop this happening. Politics, indeed, is to a great extent concerned even now with damage limitation. It is worth stressing at the outset, with Beyschlag (1952) and in spite of the interesting paper by Wisniewski (1973) mentioned earlier, that Gunther is not a *roi fainéant* (a term associated, by the way, with the late Merovingian kings), but a ruler whose acts are at least understandable in political terms. The role of an adviser (stressed by Sedulius as vital to medieval kingship) is filled by Hagen, the most variously interpreted character in the work,[14] and also the least easily associated with an historical figure. But whether he appears in literary form as a brother or as a vassal of the Burgundian king, his advice — whether the king takes it or not — is without exception politically justifiable and sound.

Traditionally there has been a focus in studies of the *Nibelungenlied* on the role of the individual hero, most notably Siegfried, or more recently on the treatment (rather than the function) of the women in the work.[15] Narrative layering is, however, a regular feature of medieval writing, and in the *Nibelungenlied* analysis of specific aspects, such as the political dimension, may require an artificial isolation of relevant elements which interact with other aspects of the work, such as those involving human emotions (love, jealousy, conflict). This layering process has caused interpretative problems in the establishing of irony in the work, for example,[16] or has led to comments such as the enigmatic footnote in A. T. Hatto's translation of the work to the effect that "there is always a touch of burlesque when Brunhild goes into action."[17]

[13] D. G. Mowatt, "Studies towards an Interpretation of the Nibelungenlied," *GLL* 14 (1960/61): 257–270, see 269.

[14] Olivier Gouchet, *Hagen von Tronje*, GAG 302 (Göppingen: Kümmerle, 1981).

[15] See Jerold C. Frakes, *Brides and Doom: Gender, Property, and Power in Medieval German Women's Epic* (Philadelphia: University of Pennsylvania Press, 1994).

[16] Hugh Sacker, "On Irony and Symbolism in the Nibelungenlied," *GLL* 14 (1960/61): 271–281.

[17] A. T. Hatto, trans., *The Nibelungenlied* (Harmondsworth: Penguin, 1965) 63.

The head of the Burgundian state, however, clearly merits special consideration, even if Gunther has been dismissed as a *dominus sine virtute*.[18] Focus on the state demands, too, the foregrounding of his chief adviser, Hagen, also dismissed, this time as an unscrupulous *Realpolitiker*.[19] Finally, consideration of the state demands proper consideration of Gunther's legitimate (and indeed surviving) queen, Brünhild, who is more literally dismissed from the story after the first part. However much the political standpoint of the *Klage* might differ from that dictated by a reading of the *Nibelungenlied* itself, its poet was nevertheless well aware of the importance of Brünhild. This essay invites a thoroughgoing reconsideration of Gunther, Hagen, and Brünhild in particular as the politically most significant figures, all defending as far as they can the Burgundian state against the intruder, with varying degrees of success in the process of damage limitation. Opinion has shifted since the nineteenth century away from the view of Siegfried (who never resembles the stoical and technically blameless hero Sigurd shown to us by Gripir in the Eddic prophecy poem *Gripisspa*)[20] as the ideally suited king, the *idoneus*, the strong contrast to the weak Gunther, although it is still voiced regularly enough.[21] In political terms, recent critics like Neil Thomas go even further than those who have been most dubious about Siegfried in the past, such as Mowatt. Siegfried is, indeed, a purely negative figure, an external threat to a stable society who is more subtly drawn than Beowulf's monsters and dragons, but who poses a threat, in essence, of the same nature. In spite of a celebrated paper by John Knight Bostock almost forty years ago,[22] it is questionable whether the *Nibelungenlied* actually *has* a message, in political terms at least, beyond that of showing the audience what can happen in a given set of circumstances. It is possible that the C-revision might, as Beyschlag suggests,[23] move towards a pragmatic indication of the avoidability of tragedy more fully expressed in *Kudrun*,[24] but the B-text simply presents a set of events, and it is entirely legitimate — indeed, it is

[18] Wisniewski (1973) 186.

[19] Hugo Bekker, *The Nibelungenlied: a Literary Analysis* (Toronto: University of Toronto Press, 1971) 135–148.

[20] See Murdoch 16–20.

[21] See Jan de Vries, *Heroic Song and Heroic Legend*, trans. B. J. Timmer (London: Oxford University Press); Wisniewski, "Das Versagen des Königs," and especially Carola L. Gottzmann, *Heldendichtung des 13. Jahrhunderts* (Frankfurt a. M.: Lang, 1987).

[22] J. K. Bostock, "The Message of the Nibelungenlied," *MLR* 55 (1960): 200–212.

[23] Beyschlag 213.

[24] Murdoch 147–175.

almost certainly part of the point of the work — to speculate on what might happen afterwards.

It is the state with which we are presented in the opening *âventiure*, a stable and ordered *Burgonden*, with a high king, a queen mother (whose importance should also not be underestimated, and who also survives the catastrophe), two younger brothers and a *comitatus* of allies as senior advisers, technically vassals, who function (and the term is specific in the cases of those named in strophes 10 and 11) as a ruling cabinet. There is also a royal princess, whose role in the story is (and this much her mother makes clear) to be marriage. At the end of the work, the rulers of the state of Burgundy to which we have been introduced have been destroyed, causing damage to another, even larger state, the empire of the Huns, in the process. The catastrophe comes about, however, not cataclysmically, but through a series of individual problems that erode by stages the stability presented in the initial picture, as the state is threatened first by a belligerent intruder, then by a Saxon army, then by the results of two uneasy alliances through marriage. Later still, the state comes under threat again, first from within (although steps are taken to limit the damage in that case), then from a new alliance by marriage. Where in the first part of the work marriages brought alliances to the dominant Burgundians, now a marriage between one of their family and the Huns leads rather to confrontation with the stronger power. An additional political development is presented in the role of a marcher lord,[25] who is allied to the Huns but who, precisely because he is a margrave, is quasi-independent, and linked both in sympathy and eventually in marriage with the Burgundians.

The first *Âventiure* contains, it is true, forebodings of disaster made clear through the stylistic technique of *Vorausdeutung* ("foreshadowing"), but they are small elements within a fully-drawn picture of an ordered and stable society.[26] In the medieval heroic epic, periods of stability are frequently passed over so briefly as to render them apparently insignificant. Beowulf rules for fifty years before there is a threat to his kingdom, and Hrothgar had ruled for a long time before the arrival of Grendel. Waltharius rules for thirty years after the end of the epic. Dancrat, too, has been an effective king, because he has clearly bequeathed a well-ordered kingdom to his sons. That these are in their turn served by other warriors, notably Hagen, Dancwart and others, including two margraves, Gere and Ekkehart, indicates the power

[25] Jochen Splett, *Rüdiger von Bechelaren. Studien zum zweiten Teil des Nibelungenliedes* (Heidelberg: Winter, 1968). See also Norbert Voorwinden, "Die Markgrafen im Nibelungenlied."

[26] See Walter Falk, *Das Nibelungenlied in seiner Epoche* (Heidelberg: Winter, 1974) 102–114.

and geographical extent of their influence. The roles of some of these men are given — *kamerære* and so on — which may be seen either as the actual roles in the small circle of a barbarian king, or as the symbolic roles (lord chamberlain, lord high steward) of later courts. The summary has a climactically placed impossibility-topos:

> Von des hoves krefte und von ir wîten kraft,
> von ir vil hôhen werdekeit und von ir ritterscaft
> der die herren pflâgen mit vröuden al ir leben,
> des enkunde iu ze wâre niemen gar ein ende geben.[27] (12)

The only potentially problematic element is Kriemhild, the king's sister, troubled by dreams and hence unhappy with her inevitable role of (political) marriage. Her falcon-dream of disaster — interpreted and dismissed by her mother, and known to no one else — leads her to decide to remain husbandless. Her mother is clear, however, that this is not an option, and the sole alternative — not even voiced here — would be a religious retreat.[28]

Thus far, the picture has been static. The first political *event* in the narrative is the arrival of Siegfried at this exemplary and stable court. Even though he has been quite specifically advised not to do so by his parents (who hear, indeed, only indirectly of his plan — strophe 50 — and are opposed to it from the first), he elects to go to Worms, ostensibly to woo Kriemhild, of whom he has heard praise. But it is a political decision in any case; Siegfried has reached an age when he is expected to marry; nevertheless, the warnings of his parents are directed against the military might of the Burgundians and against their powerful ally Hagen. Siegfried's father offers to call on *his* allies in support of Siegfried, who refuses this and sets out instead with a select band of warriors. Siegfried boasts quite unequivocally to his father that what he cannot obtain by peaceful means he will obtain by force: "swaz ich friwentlîche niht ab in erbit/daz mac sus erwerben mit ellen dâ mîn hant" (55,2–3). Nor is he dissuaded from his violent object by his father's implicit comment that diplomacy rather than force is necessary, and the real purpose of his expedition is clearly territorial: "ich trouwe an in ertwingen," he says, "beide liute unde lant" (55, 4). It is of interest, too, that the departure of Siegfried and his men from Xanten, even after all the pomp,

[27] Quotations from the *Nibelungenlied* are based on Karl Bartsch and Helmut de Boor, eds., *Das Nibelungenlied*, 21st revised ed. by Roswitha Wisniewski, Deutsche Klassiker des Mittelalters (Wiesbaden: Brockhaus, 1979).

[28] In this regard see Marianne Wynn, "Heroine without a Name. The Unnamed Girl in Hartmann's Story," in Volker Honemann, ed., *German Narrative Literature of the 12th and 13th Centuries. Studies Presented to Roy Wisbey* (Tübingen: Niemeyer, 1994) 245–259.

is accompanied by general sorrow, presented not as a *Vorausdeutung* based on authorial omniscience, but as reality.[29]

The arrival of Siegfried at Worms is also the first interpretatively difficult point in the work as a whole,[30] since it is characterized, as we have led to expect already, by a threat to usurp the throne. The problematic passage has been interpreted in various ways: as indicating that Siegfried is more suitable as a ruler than Gunther[31] or that Burgundian society was stagnant and ripe to be challenged, however stable.[32] A far more plausible reading, however, is that Gunther as a responsible ruler is faced with a problem — potential attack from an outside force, which he must take seriously and deal with in all speed.[33] He meets unwarranted aggression with diplomacy, and the net result is that, far from Siegfried taking over his lands and people, he comes to serve Gunther and the Burgundians, doing so, what is more, of his own volition.

The third *Âventiure* marks also the emergence of Hagen as the most important adviser to the king. Gunther wishes to know who these newcomers are and Hagen, who knows and recounts Siegfried's earlier exploits, tells him, drawing attention to several key elements: the possession by Siegfried of treasure, which implies political power; and the fact that he has won it by force, which implies that he is indeed a power to be reckoned with. Hagen correctly interprets the entrance of Siegfried as a potential threat, dangerous partly, at least, because Siegfried is youthfully impetuous, and it is he who advises diplomacy: "Wir suln den herren empfâhen deste baz,/daz wir iht verdienen des jungen recken haz" (101,1–2). This is endorsed by the king, who observes that Siegfried is *in strîtes vâr*, something borne out when Siegfried makes clear his intention: "ich wil an iu ertwingen, swaz ir muget hân:/lant unde bürge, daz sol mir werden undertân (110,3–4).

This is not empty bravado. Later, at Brünhild's court, Siegfried can call upon vast reserves of reinforcements, and Hagen is well aware of Siegfried's strength, visible or not. Indeed, Hagen refers to Alberich, from whom Siegfried will draw men later. Just as the historical Aëtius could and did come as an outsider to conquer the historical Gundahari by drawing on additional and perhaps unexpected forces, the literary Gunther is faced with a similar situation. Siegfried represents here the first of what Karl Heinz Ihlenburg

[29] See Breuer/Breuer 125f. on the father's advice.

[30] See Bostock 204; W. T. H. Jackson, *The Hero and the King* (New York: Columbia University Press, 1982) 37–40; Ursula Schulze, "Nibelungenlied und Kudrun," in Volker Mertens and Ulrich Müller, eds., *Epische Stoffe des Mittelalters* (Stuttgart: Kröner, 1984) 119–120; Breuer and Breuer 125-129.

[31] Gottzmann 24–27 and 63–65.

[32] Mowatt/Sacker 38 and 47.

[33] Beyschlag 207.

(95–97) has delineated with some clarity as a sequence of threats to Gunther's kingship,[34] and he can react in any of three ways: he may fight (the option proposed by Ortwin), he may capitulate and offer terms (which is what, in the eyes of some critics, he does);[35] or he may operate diplomatically to avert the danger and if possible turn it to his own advantage, which is precisely what happens. The leaders of the Germanic tribes in *Waltharius* are also faced at the opening of that poem with what they perceive as direct alternatives only: submission and payment of tribute to the Huns, or defeat by them, and in that work the leaders all agree — after discussion — to pay tribute.[36] The *Nibelungenlied* has a less formal but urgent debate amongst Gunther's counselors. Ortwin is inclined to physical resistance when openly provoked by Siegfried. Hagen, his uncle, takes longer to weigh up the situation, and certainly does not allow himself to be provoked in the same way. Hagen's silence, which is pointed up by the poet in strophe 119,3, is eloquent; it is the silence of deliberation. Hagen has, after all, advised Gunther to welcome this now unexpectedly belligerent guest, and in the event he has to give way to the Burgundian leadership, which, through Gernot, now forbids hostility. Even when Siegfried tries again to provoke Hagen, he has to hold back. He does, however, express his fears, and indeed, the entire political development of the poem can be traced from the — as yet only inchoate — concern of Hagen about this strong outsider: "uns mac wol wesen leit," he remarks, "daz er ie gereit/durch strîten her ze Rîne" (121,1–3). Certainty on the point will come later.

There is, however, no question of Gunther and the Burgundian rulers having backed down to Siegfried, nor has Gunther shown cowardice. It is hardly a weakness of a king to consult advisers,[37] and together they have faced out a challenge. Nor is it even necessary to see the incident in terms of the conflict between a Germanic warrior and a feudally legitimized king.[38] The situation is more generalized: a threat has been averted because each side realized the realities in the situation. It is significant that Siegfried at this point (123,4) thinks of Kriemhild, though, and the thought is not a romantic

[34] Karl Heinz Ihlenburg, *Das Nibelungenlied. Problem und Gehalt* (Berlin: Akademie-Verlag, 1969) 95–97.

[35] See Wisniewski 172.

[36] See Karl Strecker and Norbert Fickermann, eds., *Waltharius* in *Poetae Latini Medii Aevi* 6/1 (Hanover: Monumenta Germaniae Historica, rpt. Munich, 1978), and Brian Murdoch, *Walthari. A Verse Translation of the Medieval Latin Waltharius*, Scottish Papers in Germanic Studies 9 (Glasgow: Scottish Papers in Germanic Studies, 1989).

[37] Ihlenburg 96.

[38] As does Bernhard R. Martin, *Nibelungen-Metamorphosen* (Munich: iudicium, 1992) 88.

one. It is, rather, an alternative, which would lead not to possession, but at least to a closely integrated alliance. The essence of the diplomacy lies in Gernot's point that there is no benefit for anyone in belligerence, since there would be great losses on both sides were they to fight. This is the reason (and the reasonableness) that calls a halt to the battle between Hagen and *Waltharius* in the Latin poem; and although the scene in the *Nibelungenlied* may resemble superficially the initial parleying between Byrhtnoth and the Vikings at the start of the Anglo-Saxon *Battle of Maldon*,[39] there are important differences. The Viking spokesman argues that deaths can be avoided, but only if tribute is paid, and the Anglo-Saxon earl makes the valid decision to fight; and historical records tell us that his decision nearly paid off.[40] Siegfried emerges from his confrontation with nothing more than he would have been granted in any case. All that has happened is that he has given Hagen cause for some anxiety. Faced with this kind of challenge, the responsibility of the medieval ruler — like a modern politician — is to make an appropriate judgment, even if subsequent history may imply that the judgment was the wrong one. The Burgundian kings have in this case established a policy of diplomacy, and it is somewhat misleading to see it as appeasement,[41] the more so as that term has such specific connotations in a modern context.

Siegfried has accepted admission without gain, although both sides retain a now unspoken political agenda. Even if the question of a marriage-sealed alliance is not yet voiced, an orthodox political marriage could form a union between two clearly well-matched states, and could be advantageous to both. It is notable that Kriemhild (whom Siegfried has still not seen) remains a concept rather than a person for some time yet. The question of political marriage is, of course, a much debated one.[42] However, it is an historical fact that a daughter in aristocratic society in the sixth or the twelfth century was a marketable commodity and it is equally true that a woman in that position could, and in some circumstances might have to, exercise influence in her own right.[43] Even in the early Middle Ages, however, there was an awareness

[39] Donald Scragg, *The Battle of Maldon AD 991* (Oxford: Blackwell, 1991).

[40] Murdoch, *The Germanic Hero* 27.

[41] As does Neil Thomas, *Reading the Nibelungenlied* (Durham: University of Durham Press, 1995).

[42] On the varieties of medieval marriage, see Gunther Grimm, "Die Eheschließungen in der Kudrun," *ZfdPh* 90 (1971): 48–70.

[43] See Shulamith Shahar, *Die Frau im Mittelalter*, trans. Ruth Achlama (Königsstein im T.: Athenäum, 1981) 124–131; Barbara E. Crawford, "Marriage and the Status of Women in Norse Society," in Elizabeth Craik, ed., *Marriage and Property* (rpt. Aberdeen: University Press, 1991) 71–88; Christopher Brooke, *The Medieval Idea of*

that alliance by marriage was never straightforward, and that there is no pattern in such marriages is clear from the comparison of *Kudrun* with the *Nibelungenlied*, where the four political marriages in the text (Kriemhild to Siegfried and to Etzel, Gunther to Brünhild and Giselher to Rüdiger's daughter) and those mentioned or mooted (Kneading's bride, Blœdel) are quite different in effect.[44]

Before this stage of alliance is even reached, however, a new political situation presents itself to the Burgundian court, again one of threat from outside, this time from the Saxons and the Danes. Liudeger and Liudegast announce (just as had Siegfried, and with a similar argument about the sparing of lives) their intention of taking over the Burgundians' lands unless Gunther treats with them. After a brief and essentially romantic outburst in which Gernot invokes honor (150), Hagen assesses the situation, weighs up the strength of the enemy, and voices the rational difficulty of raising a sufficiently large force "in sô kurzen tagen" (151,3). The time-scale has been made clear already by the two would-be attackers. With this new threat to Burgundian stability, however, the situation is not quite the same, because the Burgundians now have a slightly touchy but powerful ally, and Hagen at once suggests using him. Gunther agrees, but needs to manipulate Siegfried with some skill. Since Siegfried, though a guest, is still outside the circle of close advisers, he can only protest his willingness to help Gunther without knowing what the matter is. After Gunther has commented that one should only speak of misfortunes to proven friends ("stæten vriwenden," 155,3), Siegfried gives Gunther a blanket promise of assistance, indeed, almost placing himself into the position of a vassal: "iu sol mit triuwen dienen immer Sîvrîdes hant," he declares (161,4). Siegfried at once assumes command over Gunther's men, including Hagen and Gernot, while Gunther remains at home, although the audience is reminded that he is still the provider of gold, the ring-giver (173,2). Siegfried fights strongly and it is his presence that causes the capitulation, after which he negotiates terms. The center of all this remains Gunther, however, and in spite of the temptation to over-interpret Siegfried's advice to the king to remain at home, there is no real justification for seeing his agreement as cowardice. Gunther is still in the ascendancy. In spite of Siegfried's wish to depart, he is twice persuaded to stay in Worms. The defeated Saxons return to their own lands, but Siegfried remains.

Marriage (Oxford: Oxford University Press, 1989).

[44] See Winder McConnell, "Marriage in the Nibelungenlied and Kudrun," in William C. McDonald, ed., *Spectrum Medii Aevi. Essays in Early German Literature in Honor of George Fenwick Jones*, GAG 362 (Göppingen: Kümmerle, 1983) 299–320.

The personal relationship between Kriemhild and Siegfried is developed in the work beside the next political theme. Gunther wishes to expand his territory by a political marriage, and the sixth chapter begins with this initiative. His choice is questioned by Siegfried, now clearly accepted as an adviser, parallel to Hagen, but although from other analogues with the work we know of a legend connection between Siegfried and Brünhild, within the context of this individual work there is no reason to take Hagen's comment that he seems knowledgeable about her (331,4) as anything but a generalized, if mildly hostile, comment. Brünhild's own recognition of Siegfried is no different from Hagen's or Liudeger's recognition of him.

The approach to Brünhild is made as a kind of raiding party, in the course of which it is Siegfried's own idea to pose as Gunther's vassal. The long catalogue of Siegfried's political errors of judgment is beginning to build up: his decision to go to Worms was made against strong advice; his arrival was ill-judged and required diplomatic handling; and his role in Island is equally ill-judged. Having voluntarily assumed the role of a vassal, he precisely acts as one, not only as the self-effacing (in this case quite literally invisible) assistant to the more important lord, but as the provider later of supporting forces.

The contest with Brünhild can be interpreted in political terms as a show of strength. The individual contest provides, of course, a great amount of foreground interest, but of equal significance is the fact that Brünhild can if she wishes carry out her threat to kill the Burgundian party. Seven hundred armed warriors stand ready to do so if necessary. Siegfried is of course instrumental in winning the contest, but the closest parallel in political terms is the battle with the Saxons, although the latter realized the identity of their adversary and Brünhild never does. Both might well take him to be Gunther's vassal. Even once Brünhild has admitted defeat, matters remain uneasy until Siegfried leaves to bring back reinforcements of a thousand men, identifying himself when he does so precisely by a further and again gratuitous show of strength in outwrestling the dwarf, Alberich. His men, though, are effectively placed at the assistance of Gunther.

It is difficult to exclude interpersonal considerations from a political reading, and Brünhild may well be attracted to Siegfried, seeing him as a more appropriate mate, though she has no reason to suspect any of the subterfuge. Nor, on the other hand, has she any real motive for insisting on Siegfried as an inferior: "vassal" and "ally," even "powerful ally" are closely related ideas[45] and there is a distinction between subordination and subju-

[45] Wallace-Hadrill 105–107.

gation.[46] Brünhild's ongoing resentment may be personal, but it may also reflect jealousy of her own position once she is established as queen in Worms. To see another clearly powerful and clearly dominant warrior, who is, moreover, closely related by marriage to the royal household, can only represent a threat to her own role. She must, furthermore, be well aware that Siegfried is a prince of Xanten.[47]

Siegfried has established himself as Gunther's strongest ally, but he proves to be by no means the most intelligent, continuing to demonstrate instead an unerring knack of doing precisely the wrong thing. The celebrated wedding-night substitution may certainly be read in a variety of ways — from farce to rape (Sacker, Frakes) — and there is a clearly mythic element in the loss of Brünhild's apparently superhuman strength with her virginity. After this point, however, Brünhild is less easily associated with some kind of Norse valkyrie than with the historical princess of the Visigoths who married into the Merovingian house. Brünhild's virginity, though, has political implications. There is no doubt on the parts of Gunther, Siegfried, and the audience on the events of the wedding-night. That Gunther needed the assistance of Siegfried at all reflects badly on the king, of course, but Siegfried's removal of the ring and girdle is yet another demonstration — pointed up by the poet in a *Vorausdeutung* (684,4) — of Siegfried's ineptitude. The display by Kriemhild later of the girdle and ring and her erroneous interpretation of how it was come by can only lead to doubts on the part of any of those unaware of the truth — which includes even Brünhild, perhaps — not only of any personal questions, but also potentially of the validity of the succession. Politically, it is imperative at this juncture that Siegfried, and the incorporation of doubt, be removed, to preserve visible stability, and it is from this point that Hagen comes to take a more dominant political role in situations which increasingly call for damage limitation.

What the Burgundians now have to face is not just a family quarrel, but a conflict just as political as the struggles in the Merovingian house chronicled by Gregory of Tours. In the poem, the quarrel between the women hinges on specific and legal terms, with Kriemhild picking up the technical word for vassal, *man,* but adding the equally specific role-word concubine, *kebse.*[48] Echoes of Merovingian history are clearly present, notably in Brünhild's celebrated answer, a question lent force by the author's immediate and quite specific designation of the speaker: "Wen hâstu hie verkebset? sprach dô des küniges wîp" (840,1). In view of what he now has to perceive

[46] Jan-Dirk Müller, "Das Nibelungenlied," in Horst Brunner, ed., *Interpretationen. Mittelhochdeutsche Romane und Heldenepen* (Stuttgart: Reclam, 1993) 158.

[47] Hermann Reichert, *Nibelungenlied und Nibelungensage* (Vienna: Böhlau, 1985) 70.

[48] See Reichert 71.

as a potential threat to the stability of Burgundian society as a whole, following Kriemhild's targeting of the queen of that state, Hagen's task is to remove Siegfried rapidly before further polarization can lead to armed conflict. The quarrel, after all, took place before all of Siegfried's men (833,4).

The removal of Siegfried and the renewed legitimization of Gunther's line necessitates the subterfuge first of the supposed (and eminently plausible) Saxon treaty-breaking to establish Siegfried's vulnerable point, and then the open murder during the hunting expedition. Siegfried is of course strong, but no man is invincible, and that Kriemhild betrays him is a weakness on her part, of which she is herself aware. Not, of course, that Siegfried's behavior at the last is anything but in character: his antics at the hunt are reprehensible and demonstrate again his eagerness for gratuitous and unnecessary displays of strength. Siegfried's death, too, has to be public, an overt punishment for his potentially having besmirched the Burgundian state. Hagen may be the spokesman, but there are plenty of others who wish to see Siegfried removed. Hagen's famous query "Suln wir gouche ziehen?" (867,1) is absolutely clear in its questioning of sexual (and therefore potentially legal) propriety, but more to the point is supported, in spite of protests from the king (and indeed, in spite of the disapproval of the poet in 876,1), by his inner council and by *genuoge* — many — of Gunther's men (871,4). Gunther has as little choice as Marke does over the removal of Tristan.

The political developments thereafter are complex, but the kingship of Gunther and the positions both of Ute as queen mother and Brünhild as queen now go unchallenged, and must be born in mind even if they are not in the foreground. A more immediate problem is posed by Kriemhild, who elects — perhaps surprisingly — to remain with the Burgundians. Clearly she is disinclined to stay where Hagen is, but first she is offered the assistance of Giselher, and then her blood-family is set against her family by marriage. The key to her decision is perhaps to be found in an at first glance reassuring statement by her father-in-law, Siegmund, that she can still rule in Xanten; but he adds, a little ominously, that no one will blame her for the fact that "we have lost Siegfried": "ir sult des niht engelten daz wir den helt verloren hân" (1086,4). The inclusivity or otherwise of that "wir" is never clear, but even so, she is in an impossible situation; Gernot has already made her vulnerability clear if she returns with Siegmund when he tells her "ez enlebet sô starker niemen erne müeze ligen tôt" (1082,2). Meanwhile, Siegfried's own men are concerned that they themselves will now come under attack (1089). Kriemhild remains at Worms, then, having guaranteed safe conduct home for Siegfried's kin, sends his and her son as a surety with them. He is, after all, Siegfried's heir. While it is true (and the historical case of Brunichildis makes the point) that a woman alone could indeed, as Siegmund promises in 1086, rule as strongly as before, it is appropriate to consider a relevant early medieval comment on marriage and alliance from the Anglo-Saxon *Beowulf*, a work that has recently been seen as a potential early analogue.[49]

On his return to the land of the Geats in the Anglo-Saxon poem, Beowulf relates the tale of Freawaru, Hrothgar's daughter. Freawaru is to be married to Ingeld, and this, Beowulf explains, is a move on the part of Hrothgar (who presumably has no son, else he would not have required the assistance of the eponymous hero against Grendel and his kin) to end feuds through this marriage. Beowulf is unconvinced and comments laconically but tellingly that:

Oft sældan hwær
æfter leodhryre lytle hwile
bongar bugeð, þeah seo bryd duge![50]

[After the fall of a prince, it is rare that the deadly spear is kept down for long, however dear the bride might have been.]

Beowulf goes on to envisage the sparking-off of a renewed blood feud by the sight of weapons that had once belonged to those killed, and his comment has a further resonance towards the end of the *Nibelungenlied* in connection both with Rüdiger's shield and Siegfried's sword. In the immediate context, however, the reference to the bride might well make Siegmund's reassurance that Siegfried's death will not be held against Kriemhild at least ominous.

Kriemhild decides that to stay is the lesser of two unpleasant options, although the parting from Siegmund is uneasy as the latter declares a complete severance with Burgundy (1092) and his men underscore in the following strophe precisely the point made by Beowulf. The highly significant *âventiure* ends, then, with a final flurry of somewhat hasty and again damage-limiting diplomacy. Just as when Siegfried made his over-bold entrance, Gernot and Giselher are again in the foreground on behalf of Gunther to calm matters and to ensure safe-conduct for Siegfried's men. But there is a weakening for the Burgundians in the loss of Siegmund as an ally.[51]

The final quatrain, though, focuses upon Brünhild's position and feelings: "Prünhilt diu schœne mit übermüete saz./swaz geweinte Kriemhilt, unmære was ir daz (1100,1–2). Both lines are significant. Indeed, she is now

[49] Roswitha Wisniewski, "Die Urform der Siegfriedsage im Beowulf?" in Waltraut Fritsch-Rößler, ed., *Uf der mâze pfat. Festschrift für Werner Hoffmann*, GAG 555 (Göppingen: Kümmerle, 1991) 55–69.

[50] F. Klaeber, ed., *Beowulf and the Fight at Finnsburg*, 3rd ed. (Boston: Heath, 1950) 76, vv. 2029–2031.

[51] See Beyschlag 210.

indisputably high queen, and although (as a *Vorausdeutung* makes clear) the day will come when Kriemhild causes her sorrow, Brünhild will never, in the poem, be removed from her position of power.

Kriemhild, having to make the best of her position, now ostensibly makes peace with the king, though she cannot forgive Hagen, nor indeed (1111–1112) herself for the death of Siegfried. Through the diplomacy of the two younger bothers once again (although the initial impetus had come, as the audience is aware, from Hagen), Siegfried's treasure, viewed as Kriemhild's bride-price, is brought to Worms. Fabulous as it is, however, the gold represents political power, and Kriemhild does indeed now begin to use it to buy support as a faction. This is at once clear to Hagen, who may or may not have harbored genuine thoughts of gaining some of the hoard directly. At all events, he recognizes the danger:

> ob si solde leben
> noch deheine wîle, daz si sô manigen man
> in ir dienst gewunne daz es in leide müez' ergân. (1128, 2b–4)

There is again a faintly ominous note in the comment about the length of Kriemhild's life; but instead of removing her — she is of royal blood, after all — Hagen seizes the hoard and sinks it in the Rhine. This is a pragmatic act perceived not just as absolutely necessary, but as immediately expedient. It is at this point that the German *Nibelungenlied* diverges perhaps most sharply from related texts such as the *Atlakviða*, where efforts are made specifically to keep the gold from the Huns.[52] Kriemhild is precisely where she was at the opening of the poem, without a position and dependent upon her brothers, albeit now with a sense of grievance. Moreover, Gunther now has a firmly-established queen. The situation is static once more; the only way in which things can change for Kriemhild is through marriage, and the impetus for this has to come from outside. Etzel, King of the Huns, now chooses to propose marriage, after the death of his wife Helche. A connection by marriage is sought, therefore, between the ruler of an empire which can command many powerful allies, and the now weakened Burgundian state, which has already lost one ally, Siegmund. The role of the marcher lord Rüdiger is of some interest here, and, as is indicated to the audience in his brief but important private conversation with Gotelind (1169–1170), the stability that would be brought to Etzel's lands by a new marriage and suitable alliance with a Germanic kingdom could only be of advantage to the marcher lords as well. Rüdiger, therefore, who knows both sides, has a great deal to gain from the potential alliance between a Germanic kingdom and the eastern empire. That

[52] Murdoch, *The Germanic Hero* 50–52.

the religious aspect of the matter — that Etzel is not a Christian — is never really viewed as a problem gives greater weight to the political importance of the negotiations.

The Burgundian ruling family is ready to agree to the proposed match, but Hagen advises against it, and this time does so alone, in contradistinction to his advice on the removal of Siegfried, when others supported him. This is the first time that Hagen's (sound) advice is overruled, and represents another significant turning point in the story. Hagen knows that such a marriage would provide Kriemhild with power. He is overruled only by the reasoning (used by more recent politicians, also with fatal results) that the Land of the Huns is a long way off and can be avoided. From now on he is forced to limit the damage for each new situation. The audience sees just after Hagen's objections (1210) how Rüdiger persuades Kriemhild to the match precisely by promising her armed support (1236, 1256–1257).

Each of the protagonists perceives the potential of the situation in political terms, then, but each perception is different; Hagen sees it as a potential disaster, while the Burgundians may either wish their sister well (as they protest), or they may wish to rid themselves of embarrassment whilst also forging an alliance with the powerful Hun empire. Rüdiger sees the marriage as making for stability on both sides, although he is Etzel's man. Kriemhild, finally, agrees only when the possibility of revenge is offered to her. When the marriage is celebrated, too, the audience is given an idea of the strength of Etzel in political terms as the rising dust indicates at the opening of *Âventiure* 22 the numbers of his warriors — the same image is used to terrify the Germanic tribes (including Burgundians) into submission at the opening of *Waltharius* (vv. 54f.).[53]

One of the most difficult political questions in the *Nibelungenlied* is precisely that in the *Atlakviða*, namely: what prompts the Burgundians to accept the invitation to visit the Huns? The Burgundian leaders had, after all, assured themselves that they would never do so. Of course, the situation as such is radically different from that in the Norse poem, in which Gudrun actually advises her brothers *against* coming, and they take action to prevent Atli from acquiring their gold. In the Middle High German poem, Kriemhild has established herself in the place of Etzel's former queen — this is frequently stressed — and she can now plot her revenge on Hagen, although this involves a break with Gunther which is clearly treacherous on her part, and is indicated as such by the poet in strophes 1395–1396. She has also to persuade them to come to her. The gold, too, is still an issue; if Hagen reveals its whereabouts, Kriemhild can theoretically regain it, even if she cannot regain Siegfried.

[53] Strecker 26; Murdoch, *Walthari* 47.

The treasure might still function in the literary sense as the *rógmálmi skatna*, the "treasure of strife" in the *Edda*,[54] but its political function differs between the Norse and German works. In the *Edda*, Gudrun adopts a subterfuge to prevent their coming; here Kriemhild adopts a different and less subtle one to insure that they *do*, asking the messengers to ensure that she is described as content with her lot, and urging that Hagen come to show them the way. The diplomacy of the German invitation scene is of some interest. The ambassadors make a point of addressing Ute, the matriarch of the clan 1451–56), who receives them courteously. They do not, however, present their compliments to the queen regnant: such a visit is mooted, but Volker (who is close to Hagen) prevents this and it never takes place:

> Der künic in erloubte (des was noch niht geschehen)
> ob si wolden gerne froun Prünhilde sehen.
> daz si für si solden mit sînem willen gân.
> daz understuont dô Volkêr; daz was ir liebe getân.
>
> "Jane ist mîn vrouwe Prünhilt nu niht sô wol gemuot
> daz ir si müget schouwen", sprach der ritter guot.
> "bîtet unz morgen, sô lât mans' iuch sehen."
> dô si sie wânden schouwen, dône kund es niht geschehen. (1485f.)

The passage is significant, and this is the last reference to Brünhild in the poem, with the single but vitally important exception of the resounding words of Hagen in strophe 1790, announcing himself as "Hagen who slew Siegfried in revenge for Kriemhild's insult to the beautiful Brünhild." Much is made of the point that Brünhild disappears from the action more or less completely after Siegfried's death.[55] But while she may disappear from the action, she survives what follows, and she has dedicated herself to the state of which she is now part,[56] but from which Kriemhild is now isolated. The poet of the *Klage* did not forget Brünhild, and neither should the reader.

The brothers, convinced by the display of friendship and Kriemhild's earlier reconciliation, and unaware of her treachery, wish to go to visit her. Hagen again advises against this, and this time he is again not alone, being supported by another counselor, Rumold.[57] Again the argument is based

[54] Ursula Dronke, ed. and trans., *Atlakviða* in *The Poetic Edda I. Heroic Poems* (Oxford: Clarendon, 1969) 8: v. 27.

[55] Theodore M. Andersson, *The Legend of Brynhild* (Ithaca: Cornell University Press, 1980); Marianne Wahl Armstrong, *Rolle und Charakter. Studien zur Menschendarstellung im Nibelungenlied*, GAG 221 (Göppingen: Kümmerle, 1979) 138 and 142.

[56] Thomas 37.

[57] Helmut de Boor, "Rumoldes rat," *ZfdA* 61 (1924): 1–11.

upon political stability, but it is not accepted by Gunther and the others, and this forces Hagen into a situation in which he must go with them. Potential cowardice on Hagen's part (a motif used in *Waltharius* as well) has already been hinted at (in 1462–1464) and the best that Hagen can do is to work within the terms now laid down for him, raising a large force of arms in the first instance. The approach is quite different from the *Atlakviða*, where there was no question of victory: here Hagen thinks they have to fight to win, even though he knows from the prophecy that they will not.

In political terms, the role of Rüdiger again comes to the fore. When the Burgundian army arrives at Bechelaren he even joins with them through the marriage of his daughter to Giselher. Rüdiger is clearly ensuring his position as far as possible *between* two great powers by marriage-alliance. During the visit, however, an event of significance occurs with the claiming by Hagen of a shield as a gift. Much attention has been paid to the reappearance of this motif in the 37th *Âventiure* and the implications of the later scene, in which Hagen receives a shield from Rüdiger in mid-fight,[58] but less has been paid to its first sounding here. Once again, the testimony of *Beowulf* is important. Beowulf comments in his discussion of the proposed marriage of Freawaru that in future the mere sight of a weapon might well remind warriors of older loyalties and conflicts. Here, the Margravine Gotelind is reminded of her kinsman Nuodung's death at the hands of Witege, companion of Dietrich, Etzel's principal ally. Nuodung's bride and lands, too, will later be promised to Blœdel, brother of Etzel. There are signals of conflict linking Rüdiger with the Burgundians and distancing him from Etzel.

Once Etzel's court is reached, the forces of diplomacy are pitched against those of revenge. Even so, there are tensions with, say Rüdiger, whose protestations over the loyalty of his wife's family (1815) sound a little overdone, and remind the audience of the undeveloped Nuodung-plot. The catastrophe comes, of course, in spite of the counsel of Dietrich, through the treachery of Kriemhild, who has deceived her husband and who now suborns (and effectively sacrifices) his brother Blœdel into striking the first blow in vengeance against Hagen. The promise of Nuodung's bride and the territorial rewards offered indicate Kriemhild's potential for putting at risk the treaties established by Etzel. Rüdiger does fight on Etzel's side, but his position is the most difficult and tragic of the work.

[58] See Peter Wapnewski, "Rüdigers Schild. Zur 37. Aventiure des Nibelungenliedes," *Euphorion* 54 (1960): 380–410, and in Heinz Rupp, ed., *Nibelungenlied und Kudrun*, Wege der Forschung 54 (Darmstadt: Wissenschaftliche Buchgesellschaft, 1976) 321–333 (cited); Mowatt and Sacker 138f.; Bekker 144; Ian R. Campbell, "Hagen's Shield Request — Das Nibelungenlied, 37th Aventiure," *GR* 71 (1996): 23–34.

What is crucial about the end of the poem, however, is that Hagen's methods of damage limitation are nearly successful. Unlike the final battle of the *Atlakviða*, in which the Burgundians are massively outnumbered, here the carnage is such that there are no real victors. Hagen is left alive almost to the last, and has the triumph of denying the treasure to the enemies of the Burgundians before he is killed. And at the last — as once again the poet of the *Klage* was very well aware — the state for which Hagen had fought survived in the hands of Brünhild, the queen who is, as we have seen, in his thoughts to the last.

In spite of readings which continue to see Siegfried as a hero, it is difficult in looking at the overall political development in the poem to view him even as ambiguous. Thomas correctly sees him as a dangerous subversive[59] and he is a constant cause of trouble, making minor and major errors at every turn, not a model but a warning. It would be easy to say that the Burgundians should have resisted him at the very start, but this is hindsight, and what has happened cannot be changed, although speculation about the future is always permissible, since the future is full of possibilities. The point of the *Nibelungenlied* is to demonstrate what can happen, and that political decisions — which have to be taken at specific points in time — may turn out to be politically advantageous ("right") or otherwise, judged by the events to which they lead.

If Siegfried behaves badly at almost every single point in the story, Hagen represents the counselor forced to cope as best he can at each point. His advice may be taken or ignored, however, and the ultimate responsibility rests with his masters; frequently he is overruled by them in the name of diplomacy. It is also difficult to condemn Gunther. He, too, must make decisions, and it is up to him to maintain the balance of stability without war as far as possible, which is still the *ultima ratio regum*. If there is a message to the poem, then it is the pragmatic presentation, objectively done, of the breakdown of diplomacy, even of a diplomacy supported by arms, in the face of irrational behavior (Siegfried) and superior political power (Etzel).

History moves onwards, and the *Klage* addressed the question of subsequent events, even though it did not take it very far. In terms of bare fact, one legitimate ruler of Burgundy — its queen — remains. Brünhild is the real political center of the work: she is the survivor. The *Klage* is quite clear on the importance of Brünhild, but is chiefly concerned to establish that Brünhild's son, the younger Gunther, is crowned, returning the state eventually to male legitimacy and indeed perhaps even to stability.[60] Brünhild

[59] Thomas 23–24.

[60] Winder McConnell, trans., *The Lament of the Nibelungen (Div Chlage)* (Columbia SC: Camden House, 1994) 176–179: vv. 3707–3764.

herself is remorseful, feeling that after the death of Kriemhild it is now her turn to suffer, while the people make the ultimate decision. They want a male heir legitimized: "vvir vvellen daz er chrone trage./daz vvir iht ane kvonech sin (4010f.). Frankish history offers an alternative reading of what happened afterwards. After the death of Fredegonda, the historical Brunichildis received at the Treaty of Andelot in 588 some of the lands given as a dowry, a *Morgengabe*, to her dead sister Gailswintha[61] and she annexed the rest after the death of Gunthram, her brother-in-law, ruling Orleans, Austrasia and indeed Burgundy, managing to outlive all her rivals and most of her relatives.[62] Her murder in 613 marked, according to Sir Charles Oman, the end of "the greatness of the house of the Merovings," and that Victorian historian summed up her career in the following terms:

> Considering that she was a woman and a foreigner, it is wonderful that Brunhildis continued for so long to sway the councils of Austrasia. Save her abilities and her force of character she had no advantages, yet she not only dominated in succession her husband, her son and her grandson, but held down the unruly counts and dukes, who were neither allied to her by blood nor constantly under her eye and influence.[63]

In the first part of the poem, and even, though she is largely off-stage, in the second, the literary Brünhild, too, is able to control warriors to greater effect, ultimately, than Kriemhild. She remains at its political center.

[61] Thorpe 505.

[62] Lasko 65.

[63] Charles Oman, *The Dark Ages*, 2nd ed. (London: Rivington, 1894) 175.

Werner Wunderlich

The Authorship of the *Nibelungenlied*

The concepts "author" and "authorship" and their significance

From the time of the Enlightenment in the eighteenth century, when the combination of an expanding market for literature and the emancipation of the bourgeoisie produced the free-lance writer, we associate with the term "author" the concept of a producer of texts who also disposes over their copyrights. The gender-determining syllable "-schaft" in the German word "Autorschaft" indicates a feminine noun that can be used to designate a collective class, the activity of writing (authoring), or the origins of the text, with respect to its particular quality or constitution. These origins may go back to a stage of orality, and then primarily to an anonymous collective group or an anonymous individual. However, anonymity may also pertain to the original author of a written text as well as to a later scribe or editor. To be sure, as a rule we are dealing in such instances with autonomous authors and those who came afterwards and continued the tradition were certainly also autonomous. The category "authorship" includes this complex when it is used in reference to an ascertainable or even merely suggested genesis of a work that has been written down, as well as in reference to the concrete author.

The concept "poet" underscores the aesthetic exclusivity of the creative occupation as well as the original artistic character of the individual's product as an autonomous art work. The term "writer" refers quite generally to the act of producing words and texts, which may be either fictional or non-fictional. In contrast, the term "author," as we understand it today, and without attaching any value judgment or hierarchy to it, is, first and foremost, a neutral idea referring to the creator of an oral or a written text, and includes the sense of copyright as it pertains to that text. At precisely this point, in fact, the medieval and the modern conceptions of an "author" coincide. The Latin *augere* (in the sense of *amplificare*, "to increase," "to cause to grow") is at the basis of *auctor*, a word which designates the person who initiates a text or who enhances it through substantive augmentation. Authenticity, and that means access to and imparting of, authentic truth, is something which the medieval *auctor* or "author" possesses, when he has at his disposal *auctoritas* in the sense of credibility and astuteness based on such authenticity. In the following, however, we wish to consider the concept of "author" removed from the above contemporary legal dimension as well as this medieval idea of "authority." Rather, we want to consider it in a neutral and comprehensive way, namely, in the sense of the creator of the work. "Authorship" will thus refer to the composer of the original text, in this case the individual who wrote down the *Nibelungenlied* in the form in which it has been passed on to us.

The extant manuscripts of the *Nibelungenlied* do not name the poet. He has disappeared into obscurity behind his work. As a result, not only the name of the author remains unknown, but also its origins. We do not know how it came into being. How did this epic emerge from a combination of myth and legend, history and literature? What are the circumstances of its composition, when was it written down, in other words, when was the oral epic transformed into a written narrative? Did the latter ever exist as an original work or were there, from the outset, various editions of one basic text? The nebulous situation surrounding the history of the manuscripts explains why preconceived notions, prejudices, presumptions, and assumptions have played a prominent role in the attempt to determine the work's authorship. Moreover, these have tended to be passed on in Nibelungen scholarship since the early nineteenth century, both as controversial views and, in the eyes of some, as ostensibly irrefutable facts.

In the wake of Kant and from the perspective of Subjectivism, the first scholars who concerned themselves with the *Nibelungenlied* were of the opinion that only personified, poetic imagination was capable of producing and reproducing epic images. It was believed that the artistic ability needed to produce a poetic work such as the *Nibelungenlied* could only have originated with a genius. The Romantics, however, transferred the idea of individual genius to the collective "schöpferischen Volksgeist" (Jacob Grimm), and, in keeping with their idea of *Volksdichtung*, subordinated the role of the individual author as an historical, empirical person to the concept of an original creative "community." Above all, they included anonymous literary works among the entire complex of a "poetischen Kultur" (Goethe). The *Nibelungenlied* was not exempted from this process. As a consequence, two different scholarly opinions emerged which, even beyond the nineteenth century, exerted a prime influence on the "search for the author," as well as the origins of the epic itself:

> [D]ie eine erkannte das rege, nie stillstehende wunder des volksmäszigen an, worin allein das epos geboren und getragen werden kann. die zweite hingegen sah in diesem gedicht die auch in manchen anderen werken des dreizehnten jahrhunderts blühende dichtkunst, wiewohl in einer bei allen

> gattungen seltensten vortrefflichkeit, und muste daher nach dem plan, der absicht und den namen des dichters fragen, von dem es herrührt.[1]

How one views the ideas of authorship and the author of the *Nibelungenlied* is intimately bound up with the various stages of the epic's evolution and its transmission throughout the ages. The present article seeks to examine the research that has concerned itself with the categories of author and authorship with respect to the aforementioned ideas regarding the genesis and transmitting of the *Nibelungenlied*.

Authority as authorship of manuscript transmission

"Uns ist in alten mæren wunders vil geseit" reads the famous first verse of the initial stanza of the *Nibelungenlied*, as it is recorded in manuscripts A and C.[2] The narrator informs us, from the perspective of one "within" the text itself, that he is relying on old reports. This reliance on hearsay as a "source" is a formulaic *topos* which can be traced to the lays and epics of the early Middle Ages which have been written down, for example, in the *Hildebrandslied* or *Beowulf*. It authenticates the oral tradition and, consequently underscores the veracity of the story that is to follow, one that is based on those old tales. Authorship is established on the basis of tradition. It cannot be determined with complete certainty whether the written narrative presents a later literary version of the oral forms of those old tales that were popular at the time, or whether it simply feigns the oral style that we associate with them and creates for posterity new versions and variations. Nevertheless, the aesthetic conception and the literary forms allow us to presume that the *Nibelungenlied*, transmitted in the form of a narrative epic, took oral tradition and molded it into a poetic idiom. This was an achievement, however, that was most likely undertaken by an individual, probably working in the service of a benefactor, when one considers the enormous expense of composing a medieval epic and having it written down in manuscript form. The *Klage* describes how it may have come into being. A *videlære* who was an eyewitness passes on the *mære* of the destruction of the Nibelungs to a *schrîber* who, commissioned by his lord, writes it down in Latin and also makes it available for various popular adaptations. Those *alten mæren* of the

[1] Jacob Grimm, review of Karl Lachmann, *Über die ursprüngliche Gestalt des Gedichts von der Nibelungen Noth*, Heidelbergische Jahrbücher der Litteratur 69 (Berlin: Mohr, 1816) 1089.

[2] Quotations from the *Nibelungenlied* are taken from Karl Bartsch and Helmut de Boor, eds., *Das Nibelungenlied*, 21st revised edition by Roswitha Wisniewski, Deutsche Klassiker des Mittelalters (Wiesbaden: Brockhaus, 1979) and are identified by verse and strophe. Here: 1,1.

first half-verse of *A and *C are archaic myths which include such things as the battle against the dragon and the death of the hero. There are also fairy-tale events such as the wooing mission and the acquisition of the hoard, and historical events such as the demise of the Burgundians in the fifth century and the wars of succession among the Merovingians in the sixth. They are sagas which have the tendency to link events that occurred at different times and occurrences that are independent of one another through standardized narrative patterns. By doing so, they not only interpret elementary patterns of human behavior and social relationships, but also preserve and pass on the memory of earlier times.

The manner in which the first stanza draws on the authority of sources almost reminds one of a postmodern concept of the idea of the author, as interpreted by Michel Foucault. In his opinion, it is questionable whether the author is to be considered as someone who has sovereign control over his text, since diverse discourses come together in his conversation. They were there long before he began to speak and by no means does he have complete control over them.[3] In fact, in the *Nibelungenlied*, the role of the narrator, in the guise of the author, is based on a tradition which predates the word of the latter. To some degree, this role may even be regarded as serving that tradition. The author pays heed to this tradition, which addresses its voice to him and relates, in a sovereign way, its story. This tradition represents an authority because, by medieval standards, it testifies to the truth of what has been told and what remains to be told. The role of the author is that of an intermediary in the service of an authority that is independent of him. Through his own work, he pays homage to that authority from the vantage point of distance, and accords it renewed recognition and respect through his words.[4] The author allows the subject matter that he has taken up to come into its own as a story, he transforms, develops, and expands it through a variety of images. Yet, authority is passed on to him through the fact that he gives life to the story and allows it to grow. He is the one who has the power to make relative, from a human perspective, an archaic conflict of values as evident in Rüdiger's gift of the shield. By so doing, he renders problematic norms and ideals in a manner that is both critical of, and pertinent to, the time in which he is writing. His authority as the one charged with transmitting the material, combined with the freedom of poetic expression, is shaped

[3] Michel Foucault, *Was ist ein Autor? Schriften zur Literatur* (Munich: Hanser, 1974) 7–31.

[4] Jean Starobinski, "Der Autor und die Autorität (Aus einem Notizbuch über die Beständigkeit und die Metamorphosen der Autorität)," in Felix Philipp Ingold and Werner Wunderlich, eds., *Der Autor im Dialog: Beiträge zu Autorität und Autorschaft* (St. Gall: UVK, 1995) 11–14.

into language and poetry through the ability of the author. They constitute the literary talents of the person or persons to whom we are indebted for the composition of *the Nibelungenlied.* We can detect a trace of the author's sense of creative consciousness in version *C, which delineates the narrative epic, in its final stanza, as a *liet,* thus explicitly reclaiming the quality of a traditional poetic convention for the current transmission in a modern form. The variations *A and *B, on the other hand, do not concern themselves with the matter of an aesthetic criterion, but simply designate the *mære* in the last half-verse as "der Nibelunge nôt," a reference to the content of the second part of the epic.

This tale, which has been resurrected from the past in a new narrative, is aimed at a specific public: "muget ir nu wunder hœren sagen" (1,4b). In this indirect way, the author includes the rhapsodist in the poetic endeavor; he is at center stage in the presentation of the lay. This realization of the form of presentation is simultaneously an indication that the epic exists in a more or less variable text which is dependent upon an oral recitation, regardless of whether or not the latter is based on the memory of the poet or a written text that he has at his disposal. When various singers are involved and the performance circumstances vary, we can assume that improvisation and variation took place, albeit against the backdrop of a narrative frame that remained consistent. There was no such thing as a firm, literal Nibelungen tradition, something which even the manuscripts demonstrate. In this respect, the singer involved in any given presentation to a certain degree played a role in the authorship of the Nibelung story.

With the epic singer as his medium, the author expressly addresses a group of listeners and presents his work to them. His role as intermediary, his style, and his composition are subjected to a form of value judgment. Here we see another form of authority, to which both the tradition and the author himself are subjected. The listener (or the reader) is transformed into a quasi co-author, who formulates the sense and significance of the story that is being presented, particularly when the latter has been passed down in a series of variants. Every time it is heard or read anew the question arises, what is the sense of the lay, and new interpretative aspects come to the fore. The reception of the epic in its written form gives rise to an experience of the text and its meaning that gradually stands in contrast to the ideal nature of oral tradition with its heroic way of viewing life that had been passed on unquestioningly. The orally confirmed truth of the *Nibelungenlied* gives way to the experience of the text and its meaning as heroic epic, and the latter is literature firmly anchored in written form with consistent attention paid to aesthetic criteria throughout. It is also now a work which sees the heroic world in a problematic light.

Even after the narrative tradition has been put down in written form, we still cannot maintain that an "authorial function" is discernible which can lay claim to having produced the one, unique text that can stand by itself. The various manuscripts demonstrate quite clearly the different ways in which scribes were inclined to record the narrative work. It is obvious that it was not seen as a unified and sacrosanct work. In his role as narrator in the introductory stanza of the epic, the Nibelungen author portrays himself as the "conveyer" of a text which had existed in terms of both its linguistic and spiritual substance prior to the point where he began to occupy himself with it and give it another shape. The material he uses for the narrative has its roots in historical events; narrative patterns brought together historical facts and data within the plot in such a way that past reality was increasingly fictionalized, particularly through the transformation to written form. It nonetheless continued to be presented as historical truth. Through the voice of the narrator, the Nibelungen author announces his participation in this narrative tradition and this is continued in an altered form. His own individuality recedes into the background behind this task. As was already the case with Virgil in his *Aeneid*, the Nibelungen author is merely a transmitter, an executor or guarantor of the material to be passed down, someone who provides it with new expression. He is not its originator, its creator. Consequently, his function lies in furthering the transmission process and in the possibilities he opens up for the readers' comprehension of the text.

This type of authorial consciousness does not manifest itself through the actual appearance of an author who would take responsibility for the narrated material, or what is sung by a bard, as though it were an autonomous work. The author is an anonymous individual who transmits and preserves tradition. As such, he identifies himself through the rhetorical formula of the introductory strophe. He makes himself conscious through aesthetic design — the form of the strophes and the narrative composition, as well as the idealistic and intellectual accentuation of his figures and their actions. For such a consciously poetic activity, there is no need for him to appear expressly in the form of a named individual. He sees himself as a link in a long chain of people who have always been there to tell the tale in the vernacular. He wishes to revitalize and hence to expand the oral style of divergent *alter mæren* by endowing them with literary attributes, without, however, giving up the claim of the authenticity of the heroic narrative. Nor does he seek to question the obligation of the genre "heroic epic" with respect to reflecting a supra-individual, narrative tradition and a collective, formulaic convention. For that reason he is not prepared to divulge his identity.

Virtually all of the vernacular heroic poetry extending into the thirteenth century has remained anonymous. This "law of the genre," so to speak, corresponds in some ways with a similar understanding of the author's role to be found in Latin writings of the early and high Middle Ages.[5] Biblical texts, for example, highlight the truth of prophecy, and depict the evangelist simply as a *scriptor*, someone who remains in the background as a personal intermediary. The idea of the author refers, in the first instance, to a quality which is quite literally ascribed to a manuscript and only secondarily to a person who composes texts full of *auctoritas* and who has, so to speak, embellished with the latter a tradition that was already in existence. In contrast to this, Konrad von Hirsau and Bernhard von Utrecht claim that the *poeta* is only the inventor, someone who replaces truth with falsehood and consequently composes *poema* without *auctoritas*. In terms of such an understanding of the role of the author — as a person who transmits the idea of a higher truth, namely history that has been handed down, as well as its genre — the Nibelungen poet just does not fit the bill.

In view of this process of transmission, we can dismiss Karl Lachmann's *Liedertheorie*. Lachmann had assumed that the *Nibelungenlied* had evolved from several individual lays.[6] He maintained that this could be recognized in the diverse textual strands, with *A, in his opinion, being the oldest and closest to the original. Based on his analysis of rhyme, Karl Bartsch considered *B and *C to be reworkings of a version that had originated about 1170–1180, with the latter itself dating back to a poem that had been written between ca. 1140 and 1150.[7] *A, he felt, belonged to a second version of the original and its manuscript could not be accorded independent status. In contrast, Wilhelm Braune developed a manuscript stemma which categorized *B as the version closest to the archetype, *A as a shortened edition of *B, and *C as a later, interpolated extension.[8] Helmut Brackert expressed his doubts that these texts could, in fact, be traced back at all to an archetype in the proximity of the original author.[9] He made a case for a basic text which had been revised numerous times under the influence of oral tradition. A diffuse tradition culminated in the narrative epic which today is to be found in eleven more or less complete and twenty-four fragmentary manuscripts dating from the thirteenth through the fifteenth century. These manuscripts

[5] See Jan-Dirk Müller, "Auctor — Actor — Author: Einige Anmerkungen zum Verständnis vom Autor in lateinischen Schriften des frühen und hohen Mittelalters," in Ingold/Wunderlich 17–31.

[6] Karl Lachmann, *Über die ursprüngliche Gestalt des Gedichts von der Nibelungen Noth* (Berlin: Dümmler, 1816).

[7] Karl Bartsch, *Untersuchungen ueber das Nibelungenlied* (Vienna: Braunmueller, 1865).

[8] Wilhelm Braune, *Die Handschriftenverhältnisse des Nibelungenliedes* (Halle a. S.: Niemeyer, 1900).

[9] Helmut Brackert, *Beiträge zur Handschriftenkritik des Nibelungenliedes*, Quellen und Forschungen 135 (Berlin: Schmidt, 1963).

offer a text which, with respect to length and unfolding of the plot, remains fairly constant, while quite diverse in vocabulary, phraseology, and number of strophes.

Andreas Heusler referred to the saga tradition to be found in the Icelandic *Poetic Edda*, dating from the middle of the thirteenth century, and suggested that the forerunners of the grand epic *Nibelungenlied* were a few, short, heroic epics composed by individual poets, similar to the *Ältere Not* (composed after 1160) that he had postulated. Indeed, on the basis of the Norwegian *Þiðreks saga af Bern*, written about 1250, we have some justification for assuming that both works are based on the same source. Joachim Heinzle has recently pointed to the fact that Hagen's killing of Etzel's son in the *Þiðreks saga af Bern* corresponds in terms of depiction and, to some degree, also in terms of diction, to the so-called *Heldenbuch-Prosa* of a Strassburg print dating from 1479. It also matches a Strassburg manuscript that was completed about the same time with respect to the following points: at Kriemhild's urging, her son provokes Hagen by giving him a slap in the face and is killed by him as a result, thus unleashing the conflict that Kriemhild had desired. The poet of the *Nibelungenlied* incorporates the motif of the son's murder; however, he does not depict it as a sacrifice, but rather as a blind motif, as the outbreak of hostilities is attributed to Dancwart's report of the Hunnish attack on the squires.

> Offenbar hat der Dichter des Nibelungenliedes diese Strophe aus der ihm bekannten Tradition stehen lassen, den Ausbruch der Kämpfe dann aber ganz anders motiviert, nach eigener Erfindung oder, wahrscheinlicher, auf der Grundlage einer anderen, konkurrierenden Tradition.[10]

Heinzle's allusion to another tradition could well involve a work which was used by the author of the *Nibelungenlied* as an earlier form of the extant manuscripts. The latter, as Heusler had already assumed in the case of his *Ältere Not*, could be quite a bit older than the *Nibelungenlied*.

If a conclusion is to be drawn from the controversial discussion that has raged for decades regarding the oral and written origins of the *Nibelungenlied*, as well as with regard to the original text, the following points can be asserted as "probable" with respect to the matter of its authorship: an individual poet transmitted both oral narrative and written tradition in "narrative [book] epic" which was subjected to various emendations by subsequent editors. The author does not name himself, in keeping with the traditions of the genre. We have in *A and *B the so-called *nôt*-version, and in *C the so-called *liet*-version, two revisions of an original text, for whose

[10] Joachim Heinzle, *Das Nibelungenlied: Eine Einführung*, Fischer Taschenbuch 11843 (Frankfurt a. M.: Fischer Taschenbuchverlag, 1994) 42.

existence there are indications in earlier Nordic Nibelungen tradition. Apart from the written transmission, there were, throughout all of the Middle Ages, continual influences on the entire complex of the Nibelungen tradition and its process of transformation up to the appearance of Emperor Maximilian's *Heldenbuch*. These influences have been based on the oral form of presentation as well as an oral narrative tradition that has continued to exist even into the present.

The personality of the author as an element of the text

The preceding section has made it quite clear that perceptions of the authorship of the *Nibelungenlied* are dependent upon the particular point of development or transmission of the epic. We now turn our attention to the author of the *Nibelungenlied*, inasmuch as we can identify him from the texts of manuscripts A, B, and C. The following observations are based on historical, geographical, and genealogical facts that have been imparted through the work. They allow some feasible conclusions to be drawn without, however, offering definitive proof. Language, aesthetic form, and the spiritual content of the work can also be used in order to gain a profile of its author within the historical and spiritual contours of the time.

Time of origin

There are some historical and literary clues as to the time the *Nibelungenlied* was conceived, but no certain, verifiable dates. The form of its strophes — four rhyming long verses, with a caesura in the middle, and with an extra stressed syllable in the second half of the fourth verse — can be found about the year 1150 in the lyrical *œuvre* of the Danubian *Minnesänger* Der von Kürenberg. This new form of presentation replaces the aesthetic forms characteristic of older tradition. The Nibelungen poet transferred the narrative patterns and linguistic formulae of the latter into the lyrical framework of the new strophic form. Purity in rhyme scheme, it might be mentioned, was not attained in Middle High German Literature until the early 1190s.

In Wolfram von Eschenbach's *Parzival* (420:26), Liddamus quotes the Burgundian kitchen master Rumolt, who warns his kings not to travel to the land of the Huns and who remains in Worms as Protector of the Burgundian empire. Scholars have assumed that Wolfram composed this passage about 1204–1205 and, at this time, must have been familiar with the *Nibelungenlied* in its book form, even if it cannot be determined which of the versions was available to him. For this reason, the date 1205 is considered the *terminus ante quem* of the epic. Regardless of how one views the chronological relationship of these two works to each other, they were composed about the same time. One of the criteria which is used in the attempt to establish a date of conception is the oldest piece of evidence testifying to the office of Court Kitchen Master, which can be found in a proclamation of Philipp of Swabia and which is dated July 25, 1205.[11] Philipp had already established this Imperial court office in 1202. It should be noted, however, that *magistri coquinae* had already existed before this time. Other facts are tapped to assist in the dating process, for example, the ordeal of the bier, which occurs as a literary motif already in Chrétien de Troyes' *Yvain* (ca. 1177), and Hartmann von Aue's *Iwein* (ca. 1203).[12] In the historical arena, there is the marriage of the Babenberg count Leopold VI to the Byzantine princess Theodora, performed by Bishop Wolfger of Passau in 1203, as well as the opulent celebrations which took pace in Vienna. It has been suggested that the author of the *Nibelungenlied* was an eyewitness and part of Wolfger's entourage, and that he used this event as a model for the wedding of Kriemhild and Etzel.[13] More recently, the year 1213 has been taken as the *terminus post quem* because of the parallels detected between the demise of the House of Andech in the years 1208–1213 and the plot of the *Nibelungenlied*.[14] Whether, however, an author really intended to depict the fate of this West Bavarian dynasty and their Hohenstaufen allies in the *Nibelungenlied* remains just as dubious as the claims that the epic is based on the downfall of a Westphalian royal family in the sixth century,[15] or on the destruction of the Bulgarians by the Bavarians in 631–632.[16] The evidence can always be interpreted in such a way so as to construct parallels or suggest connections between the *Nibelungenlied* and events in history, but these have no claim to historical veracity nor can they provide us with information regarding the anonymous author. One can concur with Joachim Heinzle[17]

[11] Heinz Thomas, "Die Staufer im Nibelungenlied," *ZfdPh* 109 (1990): 112.

[12] Lutz Mackensen, *Die Nibelungen: Sage, Geschichte, ihr Lied und sein Dichter* (Stuttgart: Hauswedell, 1984) 83f.

[13] Hermann Reichert, *Nibelungenlied und Nibelungensage*, Böhlau Studienbücher (Vienna and Cologne: Böhlau, 1985) 219.

[14] Luitfried Salvini-Plawen, "Zur Datierung des Nibelungenliedes: Bezüge zum Haus Andechs-Meranien," *Mitteilungen des Instituts für Österreichische Geschichtsforschung* 103.1–2 (1995): 42.

[15] Heinz Ritter-Schaumburg, *Die Nibelungen zogen nordwärts* (Munich: Herbig, 1981).

[16] Heinrich Kunstmann, *Vorläufige Untersuchungen über den bairischen Bulgarenmord von 631/632: Der Tatbestand — Nachklänge im Nibelungenlied*, Slavistische Beiträge 159 (Munich: Sagner, 1982).

[17] Heinzle 47.

that the *Nibelungenlied* was conceived in the years after 1190 and before 1205 and from this we can derive some idea of the span of the author's life.

Homeland

If we use language as a criterion, the author of the *Nibelungenlied* was a German domiciled in the southeastern region of the country. There are only a few traces of dialect in his rhymes which do not permit scholars to ascertain a more precise "homeland" than the Bavarian-Austrian region. Quite striking, however, are the accurate and detailed references to this area in the second part of the epic. They tend to be even more exact than the topographical and geographical allusions in the first part of the work. A number of places are named along the Danube, particularly between Donauwöhrt and Vienna, that can be identified without difficulty. This is all the more noteworthy as they do not play any important role in the plot. Above all, the town of Passau, at the confluence of the Danube, Inn, and Ilz, is described with great attention to detail.

The figure of Bishop Pilgrim is an integral part of the local tradition of Passau. With respect to the plot of the *Nibelungenlied*, this uncle of the Burgundian kings is actually quite insignificant. The *Klage* refers to him, however, as the one responsible for having had the fate of the Nibelungs committed to parchment. The actual, historical Bishop Pilgrim (971–991), under whose auspices the bishopric of Passau achieved supraregional significance, was a member of the Bavarian nobility, the Sigharding dynasty, among whose members one can detect numerous "Nibelungen names." It may also be possible to conclude that we are dealing here with a domestic transmission of the heroic epic as "adopted" or "assimilated" history. It is, however, no more than speculation to presume that Pilgrim might have brought the Nibelungen tale along to Passau, or that he could have had some anonymous scribe in his entourage undertake its Latin composition — as the *Klage* reports — either in the form of poetry or as a chronicle. It is just as speculative that he could then have had a cleric by the name of Konrad write it all down in order to associate his own name with a narrative tradition. If one assumes that there was such a thing as a story of the Nibelungs that was commissioned by Pilgrim, then, at least from the perspective of literary history, there is much to be said for the theory that there existed a Latin work from the Ottonian period. It is a fact that Pilgrim appears in the *Nibelungenlied*, and at a time when a Pilgrim cult was active in Passau. After the cathedral burned down, miracles are said to have occurred in the year 1181 at Pilgrim's grave. These caused many believers who generously supported the rebuilding of the church, to move into the bishopric see. The author of the *Nibelungenlied*, as one who was familiar with the situation in Passau, appears to allude to this veneration of Pilgrim.

Wolfger von Erla resided in Passau at the time the Middle High German epic is alleged to have been composed. He had assumed the office of Bishop in 1191, two hundred years after the death of Pilgrim, and occupied it until 1204, when he was appointed Patriarch of Aquileia, where he died in the year 1218. Wolfger was one of the staunchest allies of the Hohenstaufen emperors, an imperial diplomat, and a well-known supporter and benefactor of authors such as Walther von der Vogelweide and Thomasin von Zirklaere. It is thus completely feasible that he commissioned someone from his immediate circle in the bishopric court to undertake, among other things, the composition of the *Nibelungenlied*. Whether the author of the *Nibelungenlied* intended to honor him through the figure of Pilgrim is, however, complete speculation.

Manuscript C, which attempts to rationalize the plot in terms of courtly culture, is associated not with Passau, but rather with Lorsch, considered the home of the *Nibelungenlied*. In this manuscript, Siegfried is laid to rest in Lorsch. Under the assumption that *C originated at a later date, it has been conjectured that the Bavarian count Ludwig (to whom Friedrich II enfiefed the Rhineland Palatinate in 1214), in his capacity as patron of the Lorsch Abbey, entrusted the editing of the original version composed by the Passau poet to a Bavarian in his service, someone who had become familiar with Rhenish localities.[18] This assumption represents, of course, only one of a number of possibilities.

The poetic art

If we leave aside for a moment the suggestion to be found in the *Klage* that there was a Latin *Nibelungenlied*, the author of the epic was dealing first and foremost with the oral tradition inherent to a particular genre. This anonymous poet was not content, however, with simply transmitting the old *mæren* and preserving tradition. Within the entire narrative composition of the epic, his own aesthetic achievement is evident not in the conventionality of a traditional style associated with older epics, but rather in the courtly, poetic medium of rhyming couplets and the long verse. His literary creativity is to be found in the manner in which he accentuates aspects of the plot, such as dramatic dialogues, the moods of particular scenes, the way in which he lets the plot build to climaxes, the variations in perspective which essentially

[18] Norbert Voorwinden, "Lorsch im Nibelungenlied: Die Hs. C als Bearbeitung einer schriftlich fixierten mündlichen Dichtung," in *Stauferzeit: Geschichte, Literatur, Kunst* (Stuttgart: Klett-Cotta, 1978) 279–284.

make listeners into viewers, the monologues, the characterization of figures against the backdrop of the plot, and in the depiction of contemporary forms of chivalrous and courtly life. His individual intellectual achievement lies in the manner in which he endows the transmitted *mæren* with contemporary significance by illustrating the problematics of the concept of the heroic. He demonstrates how virtues and ideals such as loyalty and honor, set against the backdrop of a crisis in his own time in which the rule of the Hohenstaufen emperors was crumbling along with traditional norms and values (what Walther von der Vogelweide had complained about in his *Reichston*), no longer enjoyed the recognition and validity of former days.

Incongruities and inconsistencies in the narrative, such as: where is the slain ferryman? how is it that characters do not age? what is burning in Etzel's Great Hall? are not to be attributed to the incompetence of the author as a narrator. They are simply vestiges of the oral tradition and, as contradictions within the epic narrative, are of no significance whatsoever with respect to the way in which the plot moves inexorably towards its catastrophic conclusion.

It can be assumed that the unknown poet was familiar with the literary tradition. He not only knew the sagas dealing with Siegfried and Kriemhild, Brünhild, and the demise of the Burgundians, which he then allowed to unfold as a grand panorama in his epic. He was also quite clearly aware of Hagen's adventures as a youth, as they had been conveyed in the Latin *Walthari-Lied*, which was modeled after the epic tradition of Virgil. He knew about the conflicts of loyalty faced by vassals, such as the situation with Charlemagne's nephew, Roland, as recorded in the French *chanson de geste*, *Renaut de Montauban*.[19] It is only an assumption that the anonymous author may have had an archive or a library at his disposal in Passau. If we assume that we are dealing with someone who was attached to the court of Wolfger, then he could have been familiar with the verse poem about Attila which has obviously been lost and which is mentioned in the archive list (dating from ca. 1250) of Otto von Lonsdorf, Prince Bishop of Passau.[20] He may also have known the *poematii* which are mentioned by Wigoleus Hund von Sulzenmoos in the *Metropolis Salisburgensis* (1582). It is impossible to discern whether a Latin *Nibelungias* or other literary forerunners of the author of the epic actually lie hidden behind these non-extant works.[21]

[19] Friedrich Panzer, *Studien zum Nibelungenlied* (Frankfurt a. M.: Diesterweg, 1945) 42–72.

[20] Ernst Klebel, *Probleme der bayerischen Verfassungsgeschichte: Gesammelte Aufsätze*, Schriftenreihe zur bayerischen Landesgeschichte 57 (Munich: Beck, 1957) 90–99.

[21] Gustav Roethe, *Nibelungias und Waltharius*, Sitzungsberichte der preussischen Akademie der Wissenschaften zu Berlin, Phil.-hist. Klasse (Berlin: Preussische Akademie der Wissenschaften, 1909) 649–691.

Tenor of the work

We can be sure that neither the *Nibelungenlied* nor its author were "grundheidnisch," as Goethe maintained, undoubtedly in reaction to August Wilhelm Schlegel's view that the epic was "seinem innersten Geist nach Christlich."[22] It also does not do justice to the author of the *Nibelungenlied* to suggest that "der christliche Kultus" is "ohne den mindesten Einfluss," as Goethe remarked some years later.[23] It is not necessary to attribute to his epic any specific spiritual content, to say nothing of a pronounced Christian leaning. The pomp and circumstance surrounding the burial of Siegfried presents a graphic image of Kriemhild's sorrow; when the Burgundians go to church for the last time, it is as men who are doomed; Rüdiger's prayer is more akin to a sigh of resignation in a hopeless conflict of conscience. Church ceremonies and liturgies performed at masses, baptisms, or burials point to a solid knowledge of the usual spiritual rituals, similar to those which play a role within the context of chivalrous, courtly events, such as the knighting ceremony. However, in contrast to the *Klage*, which does present the events of the Nibelungen story from a Christian point of view, characters who are particularly devout or actions which underscore a certain piety are lacking in the *Nibelungenlied*.

It cannot be determined from the *Nibelungenlied* alone whether the author entertained marked "Hohenstaufen sentiments." Was he a poet with a pronounced critical stance towards the time in which he lived, who, under Philip of Swabia, warned his contemporaries that leadership which was not based on strength would collapse? It is impossible to say from reading the epic. The idealized image of the chivalrous world found in Arthurian romance or *Minnesang* is, in any event, countered by the author of the *Nibelungenlied* through the remorselessness of the ideal of loyalty and the suffering that emanates from unconditional heroism, which are presented as highly problematical norms and values.

Social standing

The class to which the *Nibelungenlied* poet belonged likewise cannot be established on the basis of definitive facts and arguments. Previously, scholars

[22] August Wilhelm von Schlegel, *Vorlesungen über schöne Literatur und Kunst, Teil III: Geschichte der romantischen Literatur*, Deutsche Litteraturdenkmale des 18. und 19. Jahrhunderts 19, ed. Jacob Minor (Heilbronn: Henninger, 1884) 124.

[23] Johann Wolfgang von Goethe, "Das Nibelungenlied übersetzt von Karl Simrock, 2 Theile, Berlin 1827," in *Goethe. Kunsttheoretische Schriften und Übersetzungen. Schriften zur Literatur I*, Goethe, Berliner Ausgabe 17 (Berlin: Aufbau-Verlag, 1970) 687.

had a somewhat romanticized image of a troubadour, who might even be identifiable with Volker, a wandering poet, a knight, even a townsman.[24] It is a most unlikely theory that the *Nibelungenlied* was the product of a "town author," or that it is permeated with the spirit of urban protest against an idealized, courtly (feudalized) world.[25] The most prominent view held today is that he was a *clericus*, which is not to suggest from the outset that he was a clergyman, but rather a person who had been educated by the clergy and who had attended a monastic or other ecclesiastical school. He was someone who could read and write and as such had been introduced to the basic traditions of a Latin education. If he is to be sought at the Passau court, then he could, in fact, have belonged to Wolfger's Chancellery, as a *notarius* or scribe, a diplomat, or an administrator. The suggestion that the author may have been a representative of a clerical protest against such courtly behavior and its moral consequences, which caused the old ethos to degenerate, is also nothing more than pure speculation.[26] Those interpretations which claim to have detected allusions to biblical stories and the psalms behind the numbers cited in the *Nibelungenlied*, which might then point to a clergyman as the author, are just as unconvincing.

The name and person of the historical author

Many of the works written in the vernacular in the Middle Ages, to which we are able to link the name of an author based on the manuscript tradition, were anonymous for many of the contemporary listeners and readers. The version performed before them or the manuscript they had at their disposal did not name an author. If the author of an epic wished to insure that his name lived on with his text, i.e., his "authority" over the latter, or his authorship of the latter, he had to name himself in either the prologue or the epilogue. These parts of the work were, however, often omitted in the manuscripts, not only because the authors wished to remain anonymous or lacked any strong claim to authorship, but also because the scribe and the person who commissioned the work had no interest in such matters.

[24] Werner Hoffmann, *Das Nibelungenlied*, 6th ed., Sammlung Metzler 7 (Stuttgart: Metzler, 1992) 91ff.

[25] Rolf Bräuer, *Literatursoziologie und epische Struktur der deutschen Spielmanns- und Heldendichtung*, Veröffentlichungen des Instituts für deutsche Sprache und Literatur 48 (Berlin: Akademie-Verlag, 1970) 24ff.

[26] C. Stephen Jaeger, "The Nibelungen Poet and the Clerical Rebellion against Courtesy," in William C. McDonald, ed., *Spectrum medii aevi: Essays in Early German Literature in Honor of George Fenwick Jones*, GAG 362 (Göppingen: Kümmerle, 1983) 177–205.

Consequently, the author might insure that he was remembered by weaving his name into the body of the work as an acrostichon. All the same, even in the case of exclusively anonymous texts, something was obviously known of the author. For example, we know from the literary excursus in ***Willehalm von Orlens*** by Rudolf von Ems that the author of the anonymous verse romance ***Flore und Blanscheflur*** was Konrad Fleck. References may also occur, however, to some authors to whom no specific work can be attributed, as is the case with Heinrich von Ofterdingen, cited by Herman der Damen. Vice versa, in the above-mentioned literary excursus by Rudolf von Ems, authors such as Bligger von Steinach are named, whose work, mentioned in the excursus, does not appear to have survived.

The matter of the uncertain source, which is typical for many cases of medieval authorship, has, since the re-discovery of the *Nibelungenlied*, time and again led to the question as to who the unknown, mysterious poet of this anonymous epic might have been. A long list of possible names has been suggested: Der von Kürenberg, Friedrich von Hausen, der Marner, Heinrich von Traunstein, Bligger von Steinach, Rudolf von Ems, Heinrich von Ofterdingen, Sighard von Lorsch, Wirnt von Gravenberg, Wolfram von Eschenbach, Walther von der Vogelweide, Konrad von der Vogelweide, Konrad von Würzburg, Konrad von Fussesbrunnen, Konrad von Göttweig, and Konrad von Russbach, among others. None of them, on the basis of the sources, can be shown with complete assurance to be the author of the epic *Nibelungenlied*. Neither the extant manuscripts, nor any other documents available to us, offer even the slightest bit of historical or biographical information regarding the name, social standing, birth, death, or events in the life of the anonymous author. Precisely this situation has repeatedly fired the imagination and fantasy of scholars and produced a plethora of hypotheses regarding the poet, for the most part highly questionable in nature. Besides, it is also extremely unlikely that any hypothetically conjured-up author of the *Nibelungenlied* would offer anything so new and earthshaking that could be of any use in our attempt to interpret and understand the epic. A critical appraisal of these hypotheses can be most worthwhile, however, both from the perspective of viewing the history of research, on the one hand, and for illustrating the changing opinions with respect to the concept of authorship, on the other.

The final verses of the *Klage* provide the only clue, albeit a literary one, to the identity of the author. The demise of the Nibelungs is based on a claim of veracity which is characteristic for heroic saga and heroic epic, namely, the reference to an eyewitness account. According to the information provided at the conclusion of the *Klage*, Bishop Pilgrim commissioned his scribe, Meister Konrad, to write down in Latin the history of the Nibelungs according to the eyewitness account of the Hunnish messenger, Swämmel.

The fact that the account attributed to him was supposedly composed in Latin lends an aura of serious historiography to the later vernacular dissemination of the story. Swämmel had witnessed the slaughter at Etzel's court as well as the subsequent departure of Dietrich of Verona and had described what he had seen to the Bishop of Passau. In the final analysis, however, it is not at all certain whether the reference is really to the *Nibelungenlied* or that the origins of the narrative epic itself are to be sought in this note regarding composition. It may well be that *auctoritas* is being feigned in order to lend credence to the origin of the entire tradition and to underscore the truth of the distress that has been expressed in the manner of a *topos*. As a result, the chronological order of composition with respect to the *Klage* and the *Nibelungenlied* is likewise not definitive. Moreover, it is impossible to determine from the allusion in the *Klage* whether the Nibelungen poet or even the later compiler was ever actually at the court of Passau.

If we assume that we are not simply dealing with a fictitious reference in the *Klage*, the above-named Meister Konrad could certainly only be considered the scribe and by no means the actual author of the *Nibelungenlied*. It would be imprudent to suggest that Pilgrim himself could be the poet, the individual who had composed, in German rhyming couplets, the oldest version of both the *Nibelungenlied* and the *Klage* in the last quarter of the tenth century for the Hungarian Count Géza in Gran, the father of Stephan I, and a friend of both the Christians and the Germans.[27] If one does, in fact, associate the reference in the *Klage* with Pilgrim's regency, then it is necessary to consider the existence of a Latin Nibelungen version in the form of either a chronicle or an epic, but not, as Adolf Holtzmann suggested, a German *Nibelungenlied* dating from the tenth century.[28] Scholars have tried to identify various "Konrads," not only at the court of Pilgrim, but also particularly at the court of Wolfger. In the Passau documents dating from Wolfger's time, there are several people mentioned by the name of Konrad. Dieter Kralik identified a *clericus*, as well as the chaplain Konrad von Russbach, with Meister Konrad of the *Klage*. Until 1208, the latter was in charge of a monastery and a schoolteacher, from 1216 to 1224 probably a scribe and notary in the service of a bishop, and subsequently active in the Chancellery of the Babenbergs.[29] There is no evidence that he, of all people, had anything to do with the *Nibelungenlied*. Uwe Meves has also shown, in

[27] Aloys Schröfl, *Der Urdichter des Liedes von der Nibelunge Nôt und die Lösung der Nibelungenfrage* (Munich: Hohenester, 1927).

[28] Adolf Holtzmann, *Untersuchungen über das Nibelungenlied* (Stuttgart: Krabbe, 1854) 125.

[29] Dieter Kralik, *Wer war der Dichter des Nibelungenliedes?* (Vienna: Österreichischer Bundesverlag für Unterricht, Wissenschaft und Kunst, 1954.)

minute detail, that identifying him with the "cuonrât" of the *Klage* is based on a faulty evaluation of the sources.[30]

Just as shaky is the attempt to connect the author with the Lower Austrian lyric poet Der von Kürenberg. He was the first, about 1150–1160, to use the two end-rhyming long-line couplets with three verses containing three stressed syllables and one final verse with four stressed syllables containing a slight stress at the conclusion of the strophe. Just the designation *Nibelungenstrophe* by scholars is, in itself, obviously laden with so much suggestive power that they have continually sought for complementary geographical and genealogical evidence to demonstrate that Der von Kürenberg was the author of the epic.[31]

It is also pure speculation to assume that Konrad von Fussesbrunnen (ca. 1165–1220) is the missing poet of the *Nibelungenlied*. Konrad is the author of the religious poem *Die Kindheit Jesu*, composed between 1195 and 1200, originally to be found at the conclusion of St. Gall Codex 857, which also contains version *B of the *Nibelungenlied*.[32] Walter Hansen considers it conceivable that Wolfger gave Konrad (who hailed from Fussesbrunnen which fell within the domain of Passau) the commission for the *Nibelungenlied* when he had completed his little epic on the marriage of Mary and Joseph and the miracles performed by the Christ child.[33] He finds this especially plausible because Konrad expresses in this work his regret that he had previously authored vernacular poetry. To be sure, this statement can no more be considered evidence than the allusion to the town of Traismauer on the Trais, where, in version *C, Kriemhild is reported to have spent four days before proceeding on to Etzel's court. Feuersbrunn is the old Fussesbrunnen, Konrad's home, and it is located in the vicinity of Traismauer. Hansen suggests that Konrad used something of a gimmick to introduce his home town into the work by transforming Traismauer into Zeiselmauer, a town that lies further to the east, and which is named in manuscripts A and B. This is certainly rather far-fetched.

[30] Uwe Meves, "Bischof Wolfger von Passau, sîn schrîber, meister Kuonrât und die Nibelungenlieferung," *Montfort* 32.3–4 (1980): 246–263.

[31] Franz Pfeiffer, "Der Dichter des Nibelungenliedes," in F. P., *Freie Forschung: Kleine Schriften zur Geschichte der deutschen Litteratur und Sprache* (Vienna: Tendler, 1867) 1–52 [first published in 1862]; see also Willy Krogmann, *Der Dichter des Nibelungenliedes*, Philologische Studien und Quellen 11 (Berlin: Schmidt, 1962).

[32] Peter Ochsenbein, "Entfremdete Blätter aus der St. Galler Nibelungenhandschrift," *Librarium* 31.1 (1988): 33–41; Michael Redeker, "Konrad von Heimesfurt und Konrad von Fussesbrunnen im Sangallensis 857," *ZfdA* 119 (1990): 170–175.

[33] Walter Hansen, *Die Spur des Sängers: Das Nibelungenlied und sein Dichter* (Bergisch Gladbach: Lübbe, 1987).

Zeiselmauer by Vienna was, in the eleventh century, the place where Bishop Altmann, who was subsequently canonized, spent his exile and where he also died. It was also, in fact, the town where the Bishop of Passau was accustomed to spending the night when on a journey. This is where that famous receipt was made out according to which "Waltherus cantorus de Vogelweide," who, in the company of Wolfger, was traveling back from Vienna and the wedding of Leopold VI, received five "solidi" from the Bishop's coffers for a fur coat. Considered along with Walther's claim that it was in Austria where he had learned "singen unde sagen" (L 32,14), these vague biographical allusions gave rise to the speculation that Walther could be the author of the *Nibelungenlied*,[34] and that he portrayed himself in the figure of Volker.[35] Apart from the lack of a solid basis in source materials, the differences in style between Walther's work and the *Nibelungenlied* make such an assumption quite improbable. One thesis is completely incorrect, namely, that a certain "Conrat meister Waltherus frater eius," who appears listed as a witness in the tax rolls of the Neumünster Monastery in Würzburg, was the brother of the lyric poet Walther von der Vogelweide and, as "Meister Konrad," was also an epic poet who composed version *C of the *Nibelungenlied*.[36]

Although they arrived at their conclusions independently, Peter Honegger, as well as Dieter and Jürgen Breuer, have recently claimed Bligger von Steinach as the Nibelungen poet.[37] Gottfried von Strassburg's catalogue of poets in *Tristan*,[38] as well as Rudolf von Ems's literary excursus in his *Alexander*[39] and in *Willehalm von Orlens*[40] mention Bligger von Steinach as

[34] George Fenwick Jones, "ze oesterrich lernt ich singen unde sagen (Walther 32,14)," *Leuvense Bijdragen* 58 (1969): 69–77.

[35] Walter Falk, "Wer war Volker?" in W. F., *Die Entdeckung der potentialgeschichtlichen Ordnung. Kleine Schriften 1956–1984* (Frankfurt a. M.: Lang, 1985) 177–201.

[36] Heinz F. Friedrichs, *Walther von der Vogelweide, der Mensch in Zeit und Umwelt: Stand — Familie — Heimat*, 2nd ed., Genealogie und Landesgeschichte 32 (Neustadt a. A.: Degener, 1979).

[37] Peter Honegger, "Bligger von Steinach als Verfasser und Rudolf von Montfort als Bearbeiter des Nibelungenliedes," in Werner Wunderlich and Ulrich Müller, eds., *Waz sider da geschach: American-German Studies on the Nibelungenlied. With Bibliography (1980–1990/91)*, GAG 564 (Göppingen: Kümmerle, 1992) 9–54; Dieter Breuer and Jürgen Breuer, *Mit spaeher rede: Politische Geschichte im Nibelungenlied* (Munich: Fink, 1995) 197–232.

[38] Günther Schweikle, ed., *Dichter über Dichter in mittelhochdeutscher Literatur*, Deutsche Texte 12 (Tübingen: Niemeyer, 1970) 7f.

[39] Schweikle 20.

[40] Schweikle 24.

the author of a "umbehanc." The medieval term for a tapestry is a metaphorical designation for the epic, which, just like a tapestry, intertwines its images artistically into a meaningful story. We do not have any details regarding this concrete work of Bligger, who is shown in one of the miniatures of the *Manesse Codex* dictating to a scribe. According to Honegger, it is not Bligger II of Steinach, whose father had erected a castle in what is now Neckarsteinach near Heidelberg, who appears as the lyric poet shown in the *Manesse Codex*, but rather Bligger III, who died in the year 1228, and who is also the author of an epic with the title "umbehanc." Based on his research into the documents, Honegger assumes that this Bligger III was with Wolfger in Passau and Aquileia between 1198 and 1209 and that he composed the *Nibelungenlied* between 1203 and 1209 which was then written down in the Alpine district in one of Wolfger's *scriptoria*. Gottfried and Rudolf are thus praising in Bligger III the author of the *Nibelungenlied*, for the reference intended by "umbehanc" can only be to this epic. Bligger III is thus seen as the author of the text as it has been passed on in version *A. He then expanded the text to form version *B, at the beginning of which Honegger, albeit through a rather arbitrary manipulation of the text and word order, maintains that he has discovered an author's mesostichon, i.e., an arrangement of the letters running from top to bottom in the middle of the verses which spell out Bligger's name. Further, Honegger believes to have identified in Rudolf von Ems, whom he calls Rudolf von Montfort, the editor of *C. Werner Hoffmann has demonstrated the fallacy of Honegger's theses.[41]

According to the latest hypothesis, advanced by Dieter and Jürgen Breuer, the Nibelungen poet is to be sought not at the court of the Bishop of Passau, but rather at that of the Bishop of Worms. In their study, they come to the conclusion that the author of the *Nibelungenlied* was a contemporary witness to the wars of succession between the Hohenstaufen emperors and the Guelfs and that he wished to depict imperial history in a stylized literary form as the *Nibelunge Not*. The purpose was to portray the splendor and the demise of the empire with the help of the old *mæren*. The Breuers point to the numerous occasions on which plot locations in the *Nibelungenlied* correspond with the actual territories ruled by the Court of Worms and the Court of Speyer, the area of Bavaria and Styria, as well as Friesland and Saxony, all of which point to an author who is well-versed in history. Since there is a document of Otto IV dating from the year 1210 which refers to Bligger von Steinach and Wolfger von Erla together as witnesses, the investigation has concentrated on the trail of the *Minnesänger* Bligger II of Steinach as the potential author, who, it is maintained, was

[41] Werner Hoffmann, "Bligger von Steinach als Dichter des Nibelungenliedes? Zu Peter Honeggers neuer These," *ZfdPh* 112 (1993): 434–441.

commissioned by Wolfger to write down the *Nibelungenlied.* Surviving documents do provide evidence of the following: the Bligger dynasty, which belonged to the nobility of the Empire, lived in the region of Worms from the time of the Carolingians on. The surname of the family in that region is "von Harfenberg," after the castle of the same name belonging to the earldom of the Rhenish Palatinate, which, in the year 1200, came into the possession of the Steinachs. The miniature of the *Manesse Codex* which is associated with Bligger depicts him under the coat of arms of the harp. Bligger's uncle, Konrad, was Bishop of Worms from 1150 to 1171. Genealogically, the family can be associated with Styria and Friesland. Documents from Worms and Lorsch from Bligger's time repeatedly turn up Nibelungen names and would explain Bligger's personal connections to the locations and the figures in the epic. In Bligger's brother, Konrad, who was the Dean of the Cathedral in Speyer, the Breuers presume they have identified that clerical commentator who, in the *Klage*, contemplates the demise of the Nibelungs from a Christian perspective. *In toto*, the Breuers consider the *Nibelungenlied* for this reason to be an example of domestic, aristocratic poetry. To what extent circular reasoning, incorrect assumptions, and allegorical misinterpretations are also characteristic of this theory regarding the author will have to be determined by future research.

In the search for the author, the adaptation of manuscript C, the so-called *liet*-version, has always been accorded special attention. *C does not appear to be based on the same tradition as *A and *B, but rather on an original manuscript on which the entire heritage is based. To be sure, one cannot prove that *C is a secondary version and that it does not contain the original text. Yet the striking peculiarities of *C suggest that an editor undertook a linguistic modernization of the textual base and interpreted the events from a moral point of view. Hagen is seen as the shabby cause of all evil, with Kriemhild as his victim and a loving and suffering woman, who is motivated by the Christian ideal of loyalty and, as such, declared free of all guilt.

Abbot Sigehart von Lorsch has repeatedly been suggested as the author of *C. Sigehart was a grandson of Uta von Calw, whose residence was situated not far from the convent of Lorsch. *C contains a reference to Ute's residing in a court near the Lorsch convent and, because of this, scholars saw a reason for connecting the *Nibelungenlied* with Sigehart. About the year 1150, he had supposedly combined the lay of Brünhild and the demise of the Nibelungs to form a Rhenish-Franconian poem, to which the *Nibelungenlied*, composed five decades later, could be traced.[42] It has also been suggested

[42] Julius R. Dieterich, *Der Dichter des Nibelungenliedes: Ein Versuch* (Darmstadt: Gesellschaft Hessischer Bücherfreunde, 1923).

that the clear familiarity with Middle Rhenish towns and localities lends credence to the theory that Sigehard was the author of version *C.[43]

It has even been postulated that a nun from the Benedictine Convent Niedernburg in Passau was the author of version *C of the *Nibelungenlied*. The theory suggests that this text is the earlier one and that it can be attributed to the nun because it is more favorably disposed towards women. Version *B, permeated with male chauvinism, was rewritten according to sexist criteria.[44] Aside from the lack of any historical evidence, the typical female elements that can, in fact, be pointed to, are hardly sufficient to allow us to draw the conclusion that the author was a woman. Furthermore, the enthusiasm with which the feminist perspective and Lösl-Wieland-Engelmann's position have been greeted in some quarters is no substitute for socio-historical proof and convincing arguments based on the evidence of literary history.[45]

The authorship of the *Nibelungenlied* has not been ascribed solely to authors whom we know by name, or to individuals whose existence can be verified through documentary evidence. One person, about whom we know nothing but who is, nonetheless, a character steeped in legend, appears to be "a man for all seasons": Heinrich von Ofterdingen. Both his name and his person were repeatedly the subject matter of poetry and research during the nineteenth century. The name itself is first recorded in the so-called *Fürstenlob* contained within the Middle High German epigrammatic poem *Der Wartburgkrieg* (1240–1260). Heinrich von Ofterdingen is the one who challenges the assembled poets and who accords the Babenberg count Leopold VI of Austria the highest praise. From that point on, this poet was clearly considered to be a real person. In 1287, Herman der Damen lists him among the deceased aphorists and *Minnesänger*.[46] The Jena and Kolmar *Liederhandschriften* refer to him as a composer of melodies, and the later vulgate version of *Laurin* cites him in the 1479 printed version of the *Heldenbuch* as an author or source. We cannot say definitively that an otherwise unknown author is, in fact, to be detected behind these allusions. There is also no solid information regarding the identification of Heinrich von Ofterdingen with individuals who are alluded to in documents and who

[43] Wolfgang Selzer, "Lorsch und das Nibelungenlied," *Laurissa jubilans: Festschrift zur 1200-Jahrfeier von Lorsch*, ed. Hans Degen and Wolfgang Selzer (Mainz: Gemeinde Lorsch, 1964).

[44] Berta Lösl-Wieland-Engelmann, "Verdanken wir das Nibelungenlied einer Niedernurger Nonne?" *Monatshefte* 72 (1980): 5–25.

[45] Jerold C. Frakes, *Brides and Doom. Gender, Property, and Power in Medieval German Women's Epic* (Philadelphia: University of Pennsylvania Press, 1994) 40–46.

[46] Schweikle 39.

had similar names. The patriotic need to ascribe to a great poet whose work had not survived a great work whose author was unknown led August Wilhelm von Schlegel to put together some *Vermuthungen über den wahren Dichter* of the *Nibelungenlied*. He unabashedly projected his romantic ideas on the matter of authorship onto Heinrich von Ofterdingen as the person responsible for completing the epic, "getreu nach den Kunden der grauen Vorzeit." Schlegel saw in him the popular poet, who had provided a true "Volksdichtung" with its final form.[47] Since then, the name and the figure of Heinrich von Ofterdingen have repeatedly "haunted" literature with the intention of providing the *Nibelungenlied* with its poet and infusing historical life into the imaginary Heinrich. This was most pointedly the case in the 1840 novel-like biography by the Linz official and dilettante philologist, Anton Ritter von Spaun, who also — for patriotic reasons — attempted to "vindicate" for Austria the Nibelungen-poet, Heinrich von Ofterdingen, along with his work.

Fictitious Poets

It was the famous Karoline Pichler, the individual at the heart of Vienna's most important literary salon, who first accepted Schlegel's assumption as fact. Her historical novel, *Friedrich der Streitbare* (1831), portrays Heinrich von Ofterdingen as an important secondary figure and it is here that one finds the genesis of the fiction of Meister Heinrich as a participant in the War of the Minstrels at the Wartburg, where he performs his *Nibelungenlied*. It would later crop up time and time again as a literary motif. Heinrich is the hapless lover who is not permitted to escort home the courtly Jutta von Raueneck until he has performed many heroic acts of chivalry. Some aspects of the figure can be attributed to the lyrical poetry of Walther von der Vogelweide and, just like the latter, Heinrich also receives his piece of land, awarded to him by his lord, the Austrian count Friedrich II, for loyal and courageous service.[48]

The writer Joseph Viktor von Scheffel also repeatedly concerned himself with the origins and authorship of the *Nibelungenlied*. In accordance with his own conception of himself as a literary figure, he regarded poetry as historical

[47] August Wilhelm Schlegel, *Ueber das Nibelungen-Lied*, Deutsches Museum 2 (Vienna: Camesinasche Buchhandlung, 1812).

[48] Fritz Peter Knapp, "Die altdeutsche Dichtung als Gegenstand literarhistorischer Forschung in Österreich von Jacob Grimms Wiener Aufenthalt (1814/15) bis zum Tode Franz Pfeiffers (1868)," in Herbert Zeman, ed., *Die Österreichische Literatur: Ihr Profil im 19. Jahrhundert (1830–1880)* (Graz: Akademische Druck- und Verlagsanstalt, 1982) 141–171. Here: 160–171: "Der Dichter des Nibelungenliedes als Gestalt historischer Romane."

revelation, in which was realized the ideal of a unity of one's life and work. He viewed his own literary occupation as a creative act with this aim in mind and he also projected this image of the author onto the figures in his historical novels. The latter he regarded as the realization of historical facts, on the same level as history texts themselves. In *Ekkehard* (1856), one of the most successful novels in German literary history, he took as his theme poetry as a form of creativity born of inner despair, an artistic act of self-liberation. In the Chronicle of the St. Gall Monastery, the *Casus sancti Galli*, compiled by Ekkehart IV (tenth century), can be found a vague reference to Ekkehart II's authorship of a *Vita Waltharius manufortis*, about which nothing further is known. With this as his basis, Scheffel has the title hero of his work compose the Latin *Walthari-Lied*, as a "Seitenstück zu den Nibelungen." By this means, the monk Ekkehard extracts himself from the ill-fated love he feels for the Swabian duchess Hadwig. Scheffel was pleased with the idea that the two most significant heroic epics had been created in the tenth century by two poets who shared kindred souls, and that they had been written down in their original Latin form. Thus by referring back to the *Klage* with its note on composition, he fabricates the idea in *Ekkehard*, that Ekkehard's friend, Meister Konrad, had simultaneously authored the Latin Nibelungen epic and received a steed as thanks from Bishop Pilgrim. Scheffel, a librarian in Donaueschingen who had access to manuscript C of the *Nibelungenlied* and the *Klage*,[49] was captivated by the thought of proving this literary fiction of the Nibelungen-poet from evidence to be found in the sources. Moreover, he wished to infuse it with a sense of real life, based on the text of the *Nibelungenlied* and the knowledge and experience he had gathered of the Danubian region between Passau and Vienna. Although only wishful thinking, Scheffel believed that a certain Meister Konrad had composed the Latin Nibelungen poem in the tenth century. It was then discovered by the poet of *Laurin*, Heinrich von Ofterdingen, who translated it into German, and, acting on a suggestion by Der von Kürenberg, remolded it using his metric strophe. Then, accompanied by Klingsor, he took it, as the *Nibelungenlied*, to the Wartburg, where he had lost the first competition, but where now, in the rematch of 1208, he would emerge triumphant with his performance of the epic. In the first singers' competition, Heinrich had lost against Walther von der Vogelweide, whom he had challenged, along with the rest of the poets present, on behalf of the young girl, Viola. This idea found its literary expression in diary entries, a few *Rollengedichte* by Meister Konrad, as well as in the drafts of two novels which were, however, never completed. Under the title *Viola argentea*, Scheffel had planned a novel

[49] Joseph Victor Scheffel, *Die Handschriften altdeutscher Dichtungen der Fürstlich Fürstenbergischen Hofbibliothek zu Donaueschingen* (Stuttgart: Metzler, 1859).

about the Wartburg to be presented to Grand Duke Karl Alexander von Sachsen-Weimar-Eisenach, whose central character was to be Heinrich von Ofterdingen. Nothing came of this plan, which was also the case with regard to his intention to create a monument to the poet of the Latin Nibelungen epic, namely, by writing a novel with Meister Konrad himself at the center. This project likewise did not get beyond some notes, drafts, excerpts from source materials, sketches, and a few songs and poetry cycles. Scheffel's ideal of a poet who overcomes his personal limitations in solitude, whose soul needs to experience nature and who requires history for inspiration, finds its literary expression in the fictitious life of Meister Konrad. Born in 945 in Alzey, later in the service of Bishop Pilgrim, Konrad flees from Passau to Bechelaren after the former city has been captured by the Bavarians and Bohemians. Here in Bechelaren he begins to weave legend and history, memory and experience, into a Nibelungen poem written in Latin hexameters. After Melk is overrun by the Hungarians, he accompanies Bishop Wolfgang to the mountainous isolation of the Mondsee district and concludes here the first part of his work. He then participates in military campaigns against the Hungarians and incorporates these events into the second part of his work. Having now become rather world-weary, he commits this second section to parchment in Melk, along with his memoirs. Konrad dedicates the entire work to his benefactor, Luitpald von Bechelaren, and buries the manuscript on a crag on the Danube where it is dug up again two hundred years later by Heinrich von Ofterdingen, who translates it into German and dedicates it to his benefactor, Leopold VI.[50]

A few years later, Adalbert Stifter used Heinrich von Ofterdingen as a character in his novel *Witiko* (1865–1867). In the latter, Heinrich and Der von Kürenberg both appear during the festival of Pentecost in Mainz in the year 1184 as minstrels performing the *Nibelungenlied.* It remains an open question as to whether they are also considered the authors of the epic. Karl Hans Strobl's festival play, *Die Nibelungen an der Donau* (1907), created for lay actors, includes Der von Kürenberg in the action as a relative of Rüdiger.[51] As a surviving eyewitness of the slaughter at Etzel's court, Kürenberg picks up Volker's fiddle (!), a symbolic gesture by which he assumes the poetic duty of recording the events that have transpired.

[50] Werner Wunderlich, "The invented Poet: Scheffel's Literary Imagination of the Nibelungenlied Author," *Poetica* 39/40 (1993): 247–258; see also Werner Wunderlich, "Wer war der Greis, den Worms solch Lied gelehrt? Der erfundene Dichter: Joseph Viktor von Scheffels Version vom Autor des Nibelungenliedes (Mit einem Textanhang)," *Euphorion* 89 (1995): 239–270.

[51] Karl Hans Strobl, *Die Nibelungen an der Donau: Ein Festspiel in vier Abteilungen* (Berlin: Fontane, 1907).

Fritz (Friedrich) Lienhard's drama *Heinrich von Ofterdingen* (1903)[52] has Bishop Pilgrim appear at the beginning of the thirteenth century as a collector and translator of Latin Nibelungen songs which were once destroyed by Ludwig the Pious. Because he considers his work to be imperfect, Pilgrim consigns it to the flames. Out of love for the young girl Mechthild, and at the urging of Klingsor, Heinrich devotes himself to this national theme and molds it into the German *Nibelungenlied.* With it, he emerges victorious in the singers' war against Wolfram von Eschenbach's *Parzival* and the dominant French literary fashion. Lienhard propagates Heinrich's work as a contrast to the Modernists, who are seen as decadent. He considers it as well a point of orientation arising from the transitional state that prevailed at the turn of the century and which was experienced as both a social and cultural crisis.

Albert Ritter's *Das Nibelungenjahr. Kulturroman aus der Zeit der Hohenstaufen* (1912)[53] contains a subplot which deals with the production of an ornate manuscript of the *Nibelungenlied* and its first public performance at Montfort in the presence of the Imperial couple by Rudolf von Ems. Ritter considers him to be the editor of what Scheffel already believed was the oldest version, namely, *C. Rudolf's performance of the work takes two days and is described with historical melodrama and an aura of overpowering kitsch: "So trat das gewaltige Heldenlied zum ersten Mal vor das Volk, dem es gehörte."[54] Rudolf von Ems also appears in the "romantisches Trauerspiel" written by the Hohenems native Richard Benzer.[55] In both a prologue and an epilogue he is portrayed as author, cleric, and singer of the *Nibelungenlied.* Rudolf performs the epic, which is constructed as a drama in ten sketches, before the guests of his benefactor, Graf Hugo von Montfort: "Nun schwelgt mein Dichterherz in stolzer Wonne,/Es euch zum erstenmale vorzulesen."[56]

Two other novels relate the story of the Nibelungs from the perspective of an invented chronicler, the reminiscing "I" of Meister Konrad: Karl Bleibtreu's *Der Nibelunge Not: eine Aventiure* (1884),[57] and Armin Ayren's

[52] Friedrich Lienhard, *Heinrich von Ofterdingen. Drama in fünf Aufzügen* (Stuttgart: Greiner & Pfeiffer, 1903).

[53] Albert Ritter, *Das Nibelungenjahr: Kulturroman aus der Zeit der Hohenstaufen* (Leipzig: Dietrich, 1912).

[54] Ritter 238.

[55] Richard Benzer, *Kriemhild. Romantisches Trauerspiel (nach dem Nibelungenliede) in zehn Bildern mit einem Vor- und Nachspiel (Hohenemser Heimatspiel)* (Hohenems: Eigenverlag der Marktgemeinde, 1951).

[56] Benzer 8.

[57] Karl Bleibtreu, *Der Nibelunge Not. Eine Aventiure* (Berlin: Auerbach, 1884).

Der Nibelungenroman (which first appeared in 1987 as though it had been written by a certain Meister Konrad).[58] Bleibtreu's work revolves around the figure of Konrad von Bechelaren, who shapes the fate of the Nibelungs, which he himself has experienced and suffered, into his epic of the *Nibelunge Not.* Finally, Ayren's novel gives new life to the idea that the Nibelungen poet may have been a von Kürenberg. His paperback edition of 1991 removes the anonymity of the work and integrates the fiction of the author into its title. Konrad von Kürenberg was a cleric at the court of the Bishop of Passau. He is the churchman whom Hagen threw into the Danube to test and fulfill the prophecy of the water sprites that the king's chaplain would be the only one to survive the expedition. At the end of his life, Konrad relates the story of the Nibelungs, in some parts paraphrasing the *Nibelungenlied*, as a reflection on the theme of power and leadership, revenge and forgiveness in a period of transition between heathendom and Christianity.

(Translated by Winder McConnell)

[58] Meister Konrad, *Nibelungenroman* (Bühl-Moos: Elster, 1987); Armin Ayren, *Meister Konrads Nibelungenroman*, dtv 11432 (Munich: dtv, 1991).

Index

Few works of the middle ages can boast the "staying power" of the "heroic" Nibelungenlied and few have generated more controversy both among scholars and the educated public. The Nibelung theme has been ubiquitous over the past 150 years in a wide spectrum of literary and as well as non-literary endeavors. It was used by Friedrich Hebbel as the basis for one of his best psychological dramas, by Wagner, along with the Old Norse analogues, for *Die Ring des Nibelungen*, and by the film maker Fritz Lang for his 1920s Expressionist masterpiece, *Die Nibelungen*. Its heroes provided suitable models for German troops who marched against Napoleon, while by the end of the Second World War, the Nibelung tradition had provided material for a speech by Göring, the name for Germany's western line of defense, and significantly, the cuff band designation of the last "division" formed in the elite Combat SS.

This *Companion to the Nibelungenlied* draws on the expertise of scholars from German, Britain, and the United States to offer the reader fresh perspectives on a wide variety of topics regarding the epic: the latest theories regarding manuscript tradition, authorship, conflict, combat, and politics, the Otherworld and its inhabitants, eroticism (in both the Nibelungenlied and Wagner's Ring), the reception both of the Nibelungenlied in the twentieth century and of its most intriguing protagonist, Kriemhild, key concepts used by the poet, the heroic, feudal, and courtly elements in the work, and an analysis of archetypal elements from the perspective of Jungian psychology.

Approximately 800 years have passed since the Nibelungenlied took on the literary form with which we have become familiar. Its popularity in the High Middle Ages, to which thirty-four extant manuscripts attest, has not been abated. The twelve essays contained in the Companion to the Nibelungenlied offer eloquent evidence of the continued vitality and relevance of this monumental work of art on the threshold of the third millennium.

WINDER MCCONNELL is Professor of German at the University of California, Davis.

. . . a collection of fine essays from many scholarly luminaries on a dozen topics. . . .
CHOICE

This book touches on most of the current problems of scholarship . . .
YEAR'S WORK IN MODERN LANGUAGE STUDIES